Mormon Studies

Mormon Studies
A Critical History

RONALD HELFRICH, JR.

McFarland & Company, Inc., Publishers
Jefferson, North Carolina

This book has undergone peer review.

ISBN (print) 978-1-4766-8261-7
ISBN (ebook) 978-1-4766-4511-7

LIBRARY OF CONGRESS AND BRITISH LIBRARY
CATALOGUING DATA ARE AVAILABLE

Library of Congress Control Number 2021058359

© 2022 Ronald Helfrich, Jr.. All rights reserved

No part of this book may be reproduced or transmitted in any form or by any means, electronic or mechanical, including photocopying or recording, or by any information storage and retrieval system, without permission in writing from the publisher.

Front cover image The angel Moroni delivering the plates of the Book of Mormon to Joseph Smith circa June 11 1886 (Library of Congress)

Printed in the United States of America

*McFarland & Company, Inc., Publishers
Box 611, Jefferson, North Carolina 28640
www.mcfarlandpub.com*

…mais je suis toujour la
pret a sortir de la coulisse
comme un Deus ex machina….
Cremieux/Halevy/Offenbach
Orphée aux Enfers

"The hardest thing in this world is to live in it."
—Buffy to Dawn in "The Gift"

Table of Contents

Acknowledgments ix
Introduction: When Intellectuals and Academics Do Mormonism 1

One. The Polemics and Apologetics of Mormon "Otherness" 21
Two. Intellectuals, Academics, and Mormon "Otherness" 36
Three. The "Old" Mormon Studies 51
Four. The "New" Mormon Studies 61
Five. Social Theory, Social Movements, and Mormon Origins 74
Six. Culture Theory and Mormon Origins 92
Seven. Mormon Studies and Its Discontents: The "New"
    Mormon Culture War 127

Conclusion: Whither Mormon Studies? 146
Chapter Notes 149
Bibliography 199
Index 227

Acknowledgments

Mormon Studies: A Critical History has been years in the making, probably far too many years in the making, I am afraid. I thus have a number of institutional, intellectual, and academic debts I need to acknowledge. The Department of Sociology at Brigham Young University in Provo provided financial support and a wonderful environment in which this "Gentile" could get to know Mormonism better during the year I spent at the Y. I have long thought that getting an ethnographic sense of a group one is studying, even when one is studying that group's past, is immensely helpful. I really enjoyed my time at the Y and found it to be a wonderful and stimulating intellectual environment, something all colleges and universities should be but often are not. The Department of History at the University at Albany and the Department of Sociology at the State University of New York College at Oneonta provided financial and moral support during the years I wrote this monograph. The staffs of the New York State Library, the New York State Archives, the New York Public Library, the Harold B. Lee Library at Brigham Young University, the Church Historical Library, the Indiana University Libraries, the Yale University Libraries, the University of Texas Libraries, and the Harvard University Libraries, helped me find books, journal articles, newspapers, and relevant primary documents, which proved essential to the research on which this monograph is based.

A number of scholars and intellectuals have helped me over the many years of my academic life understand social theory, culture, the sociology of knowledge, comparative history, history, religious history, and the history and sociology of American religion. Thomas Gieryn and Paul Lucas, both of Indiana University, Bloomington, and Eugene Halton of the University of Notre Dame, helped me understand and think about the sociology of knowledge, the history of American religion, and social theory. Gerald Zahavi, Richard Hamm, Robert Dykstra, Warren Roberts, Dan White, Gail Landsman, Walter Zenner, Peter Breiner, Kathy Trent, Susan Lewis, Mary Linnane, Edward Knoblauch, Mary Sullivan, Harriet Temps, M.J. Heisey, and Peter Eisenstadt helped me understand how to think about history, how to do history, and how to do the history of American religion. The late Brigham Card, Canadian Mormon historian and sociologist *extraordinaire*, helped me understand Mormonism and social theoretical approaches to Mormonism. John Clark and Lynn England listened attentively to my thoughts on Mormonism and social theory and helped me pull them together. Marie Cornwall, Carol Cornwall Madsen, Lawrence Young, Carol Ward, James B. Duke, John Clark, Tim Heaton, and Cardell Jacobsen helped introduce me to Mormon history and Mormon sociology. Alan Avens, my favorite Yoderian Latter Day Saint, kept this "Gentile" in Zion intellectually and morally alive and helped me to better understand the ins and outs of Mormon theology and doctrine. Bonita Weddle, my best friend and comrade in all things history, social theory, *Inspector Morse, Lewis, Buffy, Father Ted, Broadchurch, Life on Mars, Due South, Slings and Arrows, Schitt's Creek, Bron/Broen*, and *Forbrydelsen*, listened to me ramble on about Mormonism, social theory, and culture, and read and edited the manuscript helping me clarify my arguments and keeping me from silly errors in the process. Dré Person and all at McFarland, including the two anonymous readers who read and commented on the manuscript, helped turn my manuscript into a book and it is all the better for it.

Last but not least I need to thank books. Books provided me with the best education an inquiring mind could ever want. I owe debts of gratitude to Karl Marx, Emile Durkheim, Antonio Gramsci, the Frankfurt School, Georg Lukacs, Peter Berger, Thomas Luckmann, Clifford Geertz, Keith Thomas, Raymond Williams, Christopher Hill, Eric Hobsbawm, Robert Wiebe, Jackson Lears, Michel Foucault, Victor Turner, Jean Baudrillard, Alan Tractenberg, Aileen Kelly, Sheila Fitzpatrick, Jan Shipps, R.I. Moore, and most of all to Max Weber. All of these intellectuals and scholars have made me think extensively about theory, method, culture, knowledge, and how we do history, ethnology, ethnography, and sociology. All of them have deeply influenced the writing of this monograph.

You can probably see from this list of influences that I am old school. And I must admit, dear reader, that I have never really been a dedicated follower of intellectual fashion and I have never been particularly impressed by the linear and progressivist notions of knowledge or history that still seem to underlie so many of the theoretical approaches in the humanities and the social sciences. However, I am all right with that.

One last thing: The inadequacies of this monograph, and I am sure there are many, are, of course, mine and mine alone.

Albany, New York, 2021

Introduction
When Intellectuals and Academics Do Mormonism

Mormon Studies: A Critical History is primarily a critical cultural history of Mormon, LDS, Latter-day Saint (the Mormon Church headquartered in Utah), or Latter Day Saint (the Mormon Church headquartered in Missouri) Studies from its beginnings in the early nineteenth century to the end of the twentieth century and the beginning of the new millennium.

Chapter One explores the history of anti–Mormon and pro–Mormon apologetics (our views are true) and polemics (your views are false). Chapter Two explores the history of religious studies, sociological typological, and qualitative and quantitative approaches to religion and to Mormon Studies. Chapter Three explores the history of what in retrospect might be called the "old" Mormon Studies. Chapter Four explores the history of what many call the "new" Mormon Studies. Chapter Five explores economic and political approaches to Mormon origins. Chapter Six explores cultural approaches to Mormon origins and attempts to put Mormonism in its broader cultural contexts. Chapter Seven explores the history of tensions between Mormon apologists and polemicists, including those tensions between Mormon leaders in Salt Lake City and Mormon apologists and polemicists in Provo, and the practitioners of the old and the New Mormon Studies.

Although this book is primarily and fundamentally a history of Mormon Studies from its beginnings in the nineteenth century to the end of the twentieth century, it also has relevance to those working in a host of other social science and humanistic fields and to those whose work focuses on a number of social science and humanistic subdisciplines. It, for instance, says something, if somewhat indirectly, about the history of history and the social and humanistic sciences, and the history, more specifically, of the academic disciplines of history, sociology, cultural anthropology, religious studies, and psychology.

My historical tale about nineteenth- and twentieth-century Mormon Studies is also a tale of the transition from the non-professional and amateur analysis of Mormonism to the scholarly and professionalized social scientific and humanities analysis of Mormonism, although the former remains an important part of Mormon Studies even today. This transition, of course, also occurred in the academic disciplines of sociology and cultural and social anthropology in the late nineteenth and early twentieth centuries and thus this book is a small scale or microcosmic example of broader trends happening in the social sciences and humanities during those years.

History and the other social and humanistic sciences are, of course, both cultural and institutional-bureaucratic phenomena. As cultural or meaning systems, history, the social sciences, and the humanities, can be traced back to the Ancient Near East and the ancient Greeks, as several commentators and the introductions to general history and social science textbooks rarely fail to point out. One can, for instance, make a case that certain books of the Tanakh, such as the "Book of Kings," and the writings of Herodotus and Thucydides, are "histories" in some way, shape, or form. One can make a case that the philosophical speculations of ancient Greek intellectuals and philosophers on the nature of society, culture, literature, and human beings gave birth not only to philosophy but also to sociology, anthropology, geography, political science, and psychology as well.

However, it is difficult if not impossible, to argue that the institutional or organizational beginnings of history, the social sciences, and the humanities lie in these speculations and observations. As disciplines or as bureaucratic phenomena they have much more recent origins. Throughout the late nineteenth and early twentieth century, history, the social sciences and the humanities, not to mention state bureaucracies and quasi guilds such as law and medicine, were professionalizing in industrializing and industrialized societies, in modern societies, in other words, all around the globe. In the United States universities adopted the Prussian and German higher education model and professional graduate schools arose at places such as Clark University, Johns Hopkins University, and the University of Chicago. Departments of English, history, political science, geography, sociology, anthropology, and psychology eventually became part of these new "modern" academic institutions.

Where Clark, Hopkins, and Chicago led, others followed. Soon colleges and universities across the United States adopted the Prussian and German model and instituted graduate schools, including Harvard and Yale, which had entered the nineteenth century as basically somewhat provincial Oxbridge style theology schools. The Ph.D. was established as the top professional degree in these educational bureaucracies. As disciplines developed at universities around the country, professional organizations were formed, and professional standards were adopted. Professional journals and academic tomes soon followed.

Professionalization in the academy gave rise to academic cultures that were both distinctive yet similar. In history, for instance, it became a rite of passage for graduate students to pass through primary source research as the discipline professionalized. In cultural anthropology and sociology, at least initially, the central rite of passage was fieldwork, the latter particularly in "exotic" cultures, the former generally in modern cities such as Chicago and in rural modernizing core nation communities in places such as Quebec.

In the 1930s, the social sciences, once imbued with the progressive ideal of advocacy and reform, became centers of clinical research and statistical analysis. As a result, it became a rite of passage for advanced psychology, sociology, political science, and to a lesser degree, cultural anthropology students, to be socialized into the ideology of positivism with its mania for numbers and typologies. Positivism and statistics, in the process, began to dominate the social sciences. The Holy Grail for all these disciplines was now "objectivity." This positivist turn, as some have called it, also began to increasingly impact more qualitatively inclined academics. Thanks to academic socialization qualitative social scientists and historians increasingly adopted social, cultural, psychological, biological "deep structure" approaches to human action and human history. Regardless of whether they adopted more quantitative approaches or qualitative approaches both factions or fractions came to see themselves as trained "experts" who, thanks to this "expertise," could uniquely and singularly discern and unearth the "real" stuff of human existence and the real causal forces at work in human societies and cultures.

Throughout the entire professionalization process those who earned a degree from a recognized academic institution were distinguished from the amateurs and armchair social scientists who had once dominated intellectual culture thanks to their newly acquired expertise, by completing a series of rites of passage, including writing a thesis or a dissertation, resulting in an earned degree, particularly a doctoral degree. "Amateurs" were increasingly read out of the academic professions. As academia professionalized and eventually proliferated, academic historians and social scientists would, as we will see, come to dominate the historical and social scientific subculture and counterculture of Mormon Studies.[1]

Mormon Studies: A Critical History also has relevance for those interested in cultural studies since, again if indirectly and by extension, this book is an exploration of Mormon, and by extension American and Western academic, culture. As numerous commentators have noted the term "culture" has a knotty and complicated history. Culture is part intellectual construct and part social fact in the Durkheimian sense. Although social facts are, at least in part, socially and culturally constructed, their constructedness does not make them any less "real" or any less capable of impacting human behavior. Culture in the form of ideology, for instance, clearly impacts human behavior as anyone living in the era of Trump knows. Culture also, as I mentioned, has a history, a history embedded within a number of discourses (ethnocentric, racist, positivist, modernist, relativist, scientific, positivist, postmodernist, economic, and political). Culture is dynamic. Culture varies within and across time and space. Culture is expressed in symbols, rituals, intellectual activity, material culture, institutional forms, and stories. This book provides an indirect case history of the construction, structure, and dynamics of one American intellectual subculture or counterculture, intellectual Mormon culture.[2]

Additionally, this book has relevance to those interested in the sociology of knowledge in its broadest sense. It will be one of the contentions of this book, admittedly hardly a novel one, that the cultural stories intellectuals and academic historians and social scientists tell us about Mormonism are ideological, and that the stories academic historians and social scientists tell reveal something about their own academic culture and their own broader contexts.

Some, intellectuals and academics, as we will see, "read" Mormonism as the product of economic change wrought by the Erie Canal in the Burned-Over District of western New York State and upper north-eastern Ohio in the early nineteenth century. Others read Mormonism as an authoritarian reaction to Jacksonian democracy. Still others read it as the product of an American biblical culture. Still others read it as the invention of one of the nineteenth-century's greatest flimflam men. Still others read Mormonism as the product of Joseph Smith's creative imagination. Finally, some, including most of those who became Mormons in the early nineteenth century and most of those who are believing Mormons today, read Mormonism as the intervention of God in human history.

The fact is that theory and methodology, oftentimes uninterrogated theory and methodology as in the discipline of history, underlie all historical "work." In fact, social and human science analyses are all characterized by a dialectical relationship between empirical evidence (exegesis), theory and interpretation (hermeneutics, ideology), and advocacy (homiletics), even when that theory, those interpretations, and those social ethical assumptions are not fully conscious to the observer and researcher. It is this dialectical relationship between theory and practice that has led, as we will see, to so many controversies in the past (not to mention in the present) in the historical and social scientific subculture and counterculture of Mormon Studies.[3]

With professionalization historians of all theoretical and methodological stripes have typically emphasized the importance of primary documents as the foundation for any understanding of human history. Historians like to think that they take these primary documents seriously and that the history they write is founded on and grounded in a close reading of primary source material, but are they? When one actually looks at primary source materials relating to early Mormonism it is clear that notions, common notions among intellectuals and academics such as the hypothesis that Mormonism arose in the Burned-Over District of upstate New York as a result of economic changes brought about by the construction of the Erie Canal or that Mormonism arose as a hierarchical and anti-democratic response to the democratization of the United States during the Jackson administration, are second order or, to use the language of cultural anthropology, etic statements. One does not find in the primary documents of early Mormonism statements such as "I became a Mormon because it helped me to deal with economic changes wrought by the Erie Canal," or "I became a Mormon because I was upset with the democratization brought about by the Jackson administration." Instead, one finds, time after time in the journals of early Mormons, statements of faith, faith that Joseph Smith was a prophet, faith in the truth of Smith's message, and faith that the Book of Mormon and the revelations Smith was receiving came from God. In the language of cultural anthropology, these are all emic or first order statements.

The second order, or etic, readings of Mormonism of intellectuals and academics, on the other hand, are notions that arose in specific social and cultural contexts particularly in the modern and postmodern core nation world, namely the rise of modern capitalism, particularly corporate capitalism, the rise of the modern state in all its bureaucratic and cultural forms, the rise of and dominance of means-end "rational" bureaucracies, and the advent of new forms of culture, particularly secular forms of culture, including nineteenth-century social theory, and new cultural industries, such as the growing universities and colleges and the academic culture that developed and percolated in it particularly in the twentieth century. These were all things, of course, that many intellectuals and academics generally noticed were going on around them at the time. The difference between these etic or outsider approaches and emic or insider approaches, have given rise, as we will see, to a culture war within Mormon culture. Etic approaches to Mormonism have tended to emphasize the role "secular" forces played and play in the rise of Mormonism and those who make use of them tend to dismiss emic primary documents that emphasize faith.

Emic approaches, on the other hand, tend to accept the tales of the faithful or assume, when they take a more secular form, that belief or faith impacted and impacts human action in history.

Given all this, it needs to be pointed out that so much of history is vanity history, a kind of academic identity boosterism, something I try to avoid in this book. Most of those who study and teach Jewish Studies, for instance, are Jewish. Most of those who do Anabaptist Studies are Anabaptists. Most of these scholars who do American history are Americans and for some of these the only valid form of history is a history that is a boosterist, one that celebrates the supposed "exceptionalism" of United States history. Most of those who study the working class depict it in celebratory hues and consciously or unconsciously see it as the engine leading humanity toward a more glorious and radiant future. Most of those who engage in Mormon Studies are Mormon. As we will see, battles over Mormon history—history is central to Mormon ideologies of restoration—have given rise to an intellectual and academic culture war particularly in the Mormon culture region of Utah, southern Idaho, northern Arizona, the area around Cardston, Alberta, and even more particularly in that buckle of the Mormon belt, Brigham Young University.

Finally, this book has relevance to those interested in social theory. *Mormon Studies: A Critical History* explores and critiques a host of economic, political, geographic, demographic, and cultural frames that social scientists and those in the humanities have utilized in order to try to explain the rise of Mormonism and, by extension, to other social movements. This book argues, again not uniquely, that although economic, political, geographic, and demographic factors play important roles in the rise of social movements it is culture that plays a critical and crucial role in giving rise to identities in social movements, identities which provided (and provide) a sense of community and common purpose to social movements such as Mormonism.

At its heart, this book attempts to critically interrogate the various interpretive perspectives or frames intellectuals and academic social science and humanities commentators have viewed the Mormon social movement through, validly in my opinion. My approach can perhaps best be characterized as, in the language of the academic fad of the moment, a hybrid. It is part historical analysis, part textual analysis, part intellectual history, and part history of and excursion into social theory. My primary source materials are the texts that intellectual and academic humanities and social scientist analysts have produced on Mormonism. This book is thus an example of textual analysis. My approach is to take seriously what scholars have written and continue to write about Mormonism.

This book, then, is an attempt at a historically situated exploration of historically constituted and constructed interpretations of the emergence of a religious oriented social movement in nineteenth-century America. It is not an apologetic and polemic and should not be taken as a contribution to Mormon or Christian apologetics and polemics. It simply tries to explore apologetics, polemics, and historical and social and humanistic science analysis in an empirical way.[4]

Given that this book focuses on the history of Mormon Studies, it seems appropriate and helpful to end this introduction with a very brief and a very selective sketch of the history of Mormonism. However, before we do that, we need to put Mormonism in the nineteenth-century American context in which it arose.

Mormonism arose in what has come to be called by twentieth-century historians the Burned-Over District of western New York and upper north-eastern Ohio in the early part of the nineteenth century. The America in which Mormonism arose was settled and unsettled, rural and urban, agrarian and capitalist, democratic and republican, and rich and poor. Its population was growing. Many young people were migrating in the hope of finding better land and greater economic security. Agrarian and capitalist economies were changing while the transportation revolution that would turn New York City into the economic, financial, and shipping capital of the United States (and a global economic, financial, and transportation center) and communities such as Buffalo, Rochester, and Utica into mercantile centers, was, thanks to the building of the Erie Canal by New York state, impacting America's economy, politics, and culture.[5]

Political parties made their first appearance in American life during the Jacksonian era. Whigs opposed Jacksonians and favored some degree of government intervention. Jacksonian Democrats claimed they were bringing greater "democracy" to American politics. In reality both political parties, despite their democratic rhetoric, were dominated by America's wealthy elite and, more specifically, by different factions or fractions of America's elite. Beyond the mainstream parties several third parties arose during the era that focused on such issues as freemasonry, working people's rights, nativism, slavery, and reforming corrupt urban political machines such as Tammany Hall in New York City. While these "third parties" had some success none of them, in the end, would replace America's two major parties in importance and influence.

Beyond politics Jacksonian America saw Protestant nationalist religious revival, a communication revolution, the rise of the working class, value conflicts, the rise of an ideology of egalitarianism, slavery, fights over banks, racism, "Indian hatred," the brutal removal of Eastern First Peoples across the Mississippi to the west, increasing immigration, the rise and spread of a national identity, nativism, reformism, utopian communalism, abolitionism, sabbatarianism, temperance movements, the cult of true womanhood, the feminization of religion, the masculinization of religion, and religious revival.[6]

The revivals of the Jacksonian era, which are particularly important for understanding the rise of Mormonism, were part of a broader revival process that stretched back to the seventeenth century and beyond. In Colonial America during the late seventeenth and early eighteenth centuries, Northampton in Colonial Massachusetts experienced revivals in 1679, 1683, 1696, 1712, and 1718. In the seventeenth and eighteenth centuries pietistic revivals swept through various ethnic religious communities—Dutch and German speakers, Scandinavians, Scots, and Scots-Irish members of Reformed, Presbyterian, and Lutheran Churches—in the Middle Colonies where pietist leaders such as Theodorus Jacobus Freylinghausen, Bernardus Freeman, Philip Otterbein, Martin Boehm, and Gilbert Tenant, expressed, in what some claim was a kind of proto-democratic language, suspicion of theological scholasticism, ecclesiastical structures, and formal liturgy, and emphasized self-examination as a prelude to conversion, an experiential piety, ecumenicity, and exacting standards of morality.

In the late 1730s and 1740s George Whitfield, an itinerant evangelist, Calvinist, and friend of the pietistic John Wesley, preached emotional and dramatic sermons emphasizing human depravity, free grace to all, "soul searchings," the new birth, and spiritual piety, up and down Colonial America's Atlantic Seaboard "bringing" many from all denominations and ideological persuasions "to Christ." In Virginia and North Carolina, Calvinist Baptists with their emphasis on biblically based ritual, emotional worship, the immediate teachings of the spirit, offers of salvation to all, personal and collective austerity, and the egalitarian community of all the Saints, grew and began to challenge the established Anglican Church. In Nova Scotia, and in the Canadian Maritimes, revivalism gave birth to a New Light "radical evangelicalism" that was democratic and populist in spirit and placed an emphasis on individual relationships with Christ, restoring, according to its adherents, the primitive church of the apostles and human freedom. These radical revivalists, in turn, influenced the even more radical antinomian sects of New England.[7]

Nineteenth-century "awakenings" set revival fires alight in many regions of the new nation. In Kentucky and Tennessee between 1795 and 1810, the Presbyterian and Methodist churches sometimes adapted to and adopted the rhetoric and style of the camp meeting revival and experienced significant growth as a result. Alexander Campbell, one of the charismatic leaders of one of the new "restored" churches of the Kentucky and Tennessee "awakenings," claimed that his "Christian" or "Christianite Movement" was the restored New Testament Church and called upon all Christians to join his ecumenical movement. In the deeper South, Methodist and Baptist circuit riders planted churches where there were none. These two denominations eventually came to dominate the region and continue to play major roles in the religious life of the old South, including Texas, even today.[8]

Between 1810 and 1825, some of New England's best and brightest debated the merits of revival activity just as they had done earlier during the Colonial American revivals. Some thought that revivals brought conversion. Others, including many church leaders, thought it brought nothing but emotional "excess." Those sympathetic to revivalism tended to move from more Calvinist or deterministic theologies or doctrines to more arminian or free will theologies or doctrines.[9]

In the Burned-Over District of western New York State and upper north-eastern Ohio between the 1820s and the 1840s, arminian evangelicalism, utopian communes, reformers, and "new religious movements" were the order of the day. The "mainstream" Christian revivalist Charles Finney spread his arminian gospel of God's moral government, the need for repentance, the possibility of perfectibility, and the benevolent role Christians could play in bringing about the kingdom of God on earth across New York and Ohio.[10]

On the more "marginal," or outsider, part of the of the "mainstream" Christian spectrum, the apocalyptically oriented Baptist William Miller engaged in an exhaustive empirical textual study of the Bible and predicted that the world would come to an end sometime between 21 March 1843 and 21 March 1844. When 21 March passed without incident, he revised his calculations and gave 18 April 1844 as the date when Christ would come again. When that date too passed without the second coming, Miller's disciple Samuel Snow, predicted that Jesus would come again on 22 October 1844. When Snow's date likewise passed without Christ's second coming, thousands of believers experienced what has come to be called the "Great Disappointment." In the late nineteenth and twentieth centuries those who remained convinced Millerites after the disappointments of 1843 and 1844, formed themselves into the Seventh Day Adventists and the Jehovah's Witnesses[11]

Finally, there were what some historians call the "radical" groups of the Burned-Over District, religious oriented social movements such as the Shakers, the Oneida Community, the Spiritualists, and the Mormons. Shakerism, influenced by the French Prophets and the Quakers, arose in England in the eighteenth century. Its leader, Mother Ann Lee, and eight of her followers immigrated to the New World in 1774 settling in Watervliet near the capital of New York state, Albany. Before the Shaker migration to America, Shaker prophet "Mother" Ann Lee had a vision or a revelation in which she was shown that human misery was the result of the lust inherent in sexual intercourse. To avoid this sin of lust and to separate themselves from a fallen world, Shakers built perfectionist or holiness communes in the New World. Soon Shaker communities stretched from New York and New England to Ohio, Kentucky, and Indiana. In 1830 there were 2316 Shakers. By 1840 there were 3608. By 1860 there were 3409. During these years over fifty percent of Shakers were women.[12]

Another of the "radical" Burned-Over District marginal religious groups was the child of its founder and theologian-patriarch, the Dartmouth, Andover and Yale educated John Humphrey Noyes. After what he referred to as an extensive study of the Bible, Noyes concluded that there had been two resurrections and judgments, the first one in 70 CE, and the second in his own time. Believing that the Book of Acts revealed that inner perfection was possible and influenced by the communal practices of the Shakers and Brook Farm, a transcendentalist commune in Massachusetts, Noyes founded a community in Putney, Vermont, in which Christians could, he believed, perfect themselves or make themselves holy. Tensions over the group's novel sexual practices eventually led the community of thirty-five to forty-five members, including many children, to migrate to Oneida, New York, in order to rebuild their community. To populate this perfect community Noyes carefully chose those individuals he would draw out of what he regarded as a fallen individualistic oriented world into a community of "love" in which all things were in common. Only those who had achieved "holiness" were allowed to become members of the community. In this community of love members shared sex (which they called "free love"; later analysts have called it complex marriage), work ("association in labor"), and meals, as they strove to achieve the "fulness" of the godly life in "immortality." At its height in 1878 Oneida numbered 306 members. The Oneida experiment would last until the demise of complex marriage in 1879 and the community itself two years later.[13]

Spiritualism arose in 1848 when Margaret and Kate Fox claimed to hear rapping sounds in their father's farmhouse in Hydesville, Wayne County, New York. They believed these spirit rappings were an attempt by the spirit dead to communicate with the living. Margaret and Kate, along with their sister Leah Fox Fish, established the major feature of the new Spiritualist faith, the séance. The séance was a gathering in which interested parties asked questions of the dead to a medium, a figure with the ability to communicate with the spirits of the dead while in a trance. Though Rochester was the initial center of the new Spiritualist movement, Spiritualism grew throughout the 1840s and spread across the nation. New Orleans, Chicago, and Cincinnati became centers of Spiritualism in the middle of the nineteenth century. By 1849, California had active Spiritualist circles. By 1851 there were one hundred and fifty Spiritualist circles operating in New York State alone. By 1854 at least ten Spiritualist publications were circulating to the faithful and the interested. The movement collapsed in the 1850s as skeptics exposed frauds perpetrated by Spiritualist mediums.[14]

Finally, there is the social and cultural movement that is the subject of this book, Mormonism. For the faithful the beginnings of Mormonism can be traced to a spring day in 1820 when a fifteen year old went into the woods near his home in Palmyra, New York, and, according to Mormon tradition, asked God which of the existing churches was the true one. According to Smith, each religious group he came into contact with, claimed to be God's true and only Church.[15] Smith reasoned that not all of these "sects" could be equally true since they preached different and inconsistent doctrines. So, he decided to ask God which specific church was the true one. To Smith's amazement, God and Christ, at least in one variant of the tale he later told, answered his query. None of the existing churches, he was told by the voices, were the one and only True Church of Christ. Such a church, they told Smith, did not, in fact, exist.[16]

It would be through Joseph Smith, so the faith history tale goes, that God restored the "one true Church" Smith sought. Smith, Mormonism's first prophet, seer, and revelator, was given a book of sacred scripture by the angel Moroni. Over the next several years Smith translated what he called the Book of Mormon, which told a tale about remnants of a "lost tribe of Israel" who had immigrated from the Old world to the New in the sixth-century BCE and published it in 1830.[17]

The year of 1830 was also the year that Smith officially incorporated the Church of Christ, as he called it. In the same year the new Church got a boost when a group of Campbellite Christians in Kirtland, Ohio, converted to Smith's new church when Smith and his followers moved westward. This mass conversion more than doubled the size of the Church and Mormons now begin to "gather for a little season"[18] to this small town in north-eastern Ohio. In Kirtland, Smith received revelations from God, revelations that would eventually be published as the Book of Commandments in 1833 and later the Doctrine and Covenants in 1835, and there the "Saints" built their first temple. Temples ever since have been central to Mormon material culture and symbology.[19]

With the move to Kirtland "the gathering" became a central part of Mormon symbology. In 1831 Smith received a revelation that revealed that the "center place" to which the Saints were to "gather" was at a place near the Missouri River. In 1831 Independence, Missouri, was "appointed and consecrated" by God for the "gathering of Saints." As a result, Saints began to "gather" in the "new Jerusalem" buying as much land as they could.

Divine communication between God and Smith continued as "revelations" were received laying out church organization and church doctrine.[20]

During the Kirtland and Missouri period between 1830 and 1840, Mormons engaged in proselytization with some success and newly converted Saints continued to "gather" to Kirtland and the counties around Independence, Missouri. However, Mormon economic and political communalism, doctrinal novelties, and dealings with non–Mormons, some of which perceived as shady, led to conflict between the growing Latter-day Saint communities in Kirtland and Independence and their non–Mormon or "Gentile" neighbors. This continuing tension between Mormons and Gentiles provided an important context for so much of early Latter-day Saint history and structure some of its dynamics.[21] Eventually the violence become so fierce that it would drive the Saints from Kirtland[22] and Independence.[23]

After the Saints fled persecution in Missouri and Ohio, they "gathered" to Nauvoo on the banks of the Mississippi River in western Illinois, where they established what was for all intents and purposes their own autonomous kingdom.[24] Proselytization continued as the Twelve Apostles, one of the governing bodies of the Church, were called to do missionary work in North America, Europe, the Middle East, the Antipodes, and Polynesia. Between 1830 and 1844, the year Smith was murdered by vigilantes in Illinois, his restored church grew. In 1836 there were roughly three thousand Latter-day Saints in Kirtland. In 1837 approximately ten thousand Saints "gathered" at Far West, Missouri. By 1845, according to Illinois census takers, there were 11,057 residents in Nauvoo, most of them Mormons. Immigrant converts from Britain boosted the population of Nauvoo to around 15,000 later that year.[25]

It was in Nauvoo that the most distinctive Mormon doctrines and practices were introduced. Smith received revelations concerning the doctrine of baptism for the dead, the Relief Society, new temple rituals, the doctrine of plural marriage, and the doctrine of eternal progression, and proclaimed a doctrine of deity that was non–Trinitarian, polytheistic, materialistic, and evolutionary.[26] Smith also announced that he would run for President of the United States, crowned himself King of the city, and established the Council of Fifty to govern the kingdom that would arise, Smith prophesied, in the wake of an apocalypse that was expected soon.[27]

It was also in Nauvoo that Mormon ideology and symbology really took form. The doctrine of deity Smith developed there was particularly important and impacted a number of aspects of Mormon ideology and symbology. At the heart of Mormon ideology and symbology was the doctrine of "eternal progression." Eternal progression, the "plan of salvation," is, it seems to me, the key or central symbol of Mormon ideology and symbology. Every aspect of Mormon doctrine and practice was linked to it and through it to other important symbols in Mormon culture, including "the Principle" of plural marriage. Eternal progression is, simply put, the life cycle that all human beings (or at least Mormons) go through either partially or fully. Eternal progression consists of pre-existence, earthly existence, death, resurrection, judgment, and finally immortality in one of three degrees of nearness to God, the "Celestial," "Terrestrial," or "Telestial" kingdoms. "Gathering to Zion" and practicing "the Principle" were simply two important life cycle choices "worthy Saints" made along the path to the "Celestial Kingdom." In Smith's conceptualization the more wives one had the more children one could have and hence the more power one had, at least potentially. Plural marriage thus accelerated eternal progression, the path to godhood. It fulfilled the promise of numerous offspring made by God to Abraham (Genesis: 12:1–4) and reunited family members around the Patriarch-God in the afterlife. Smith believed that in the afterlife the whole process began anew as the Patriarch-God and his wife or wives (Mothers in Heaven or Heavenly Mothers) gave birth to spirit children. These spirit children, in turn, cycled through life stages from pre-fleshly existence to godhood and worshipped as God the one who had made them flesh or given them life.[28] To eternally progress from human to god, one needed to follow the doctrines and precepts set out in the "revelations" given to the Church and take the advice of prophetic church authorities.[29]

These novel doctrines exacerbated tensions between Mormons and "Gentiles" or non–Mormons, and increased conflicts within the Mormon community. Antagonism between Mormons and Gentiles and within the community of Saints itself, reached a fever point in June of 1844 when a Mormon mob led by Smith, destroyed the printing press of the *Nauvoo Expositor*, a newspaper published by a group of Mormon dissidents, who called Smith a false prophet, in part, because of what they saw as his proclamation of a false revelation urging the practice of "the Principle." In the wake of the destruction of the printing press, Smith and his brother Hyrum were arrested and jailed in Carthage, Illinois. On 27 June 1844 the prophet and his brother were lynched by a mob of vigilantes.[30]

Max Weber noted how critical the death of a leader is to the life cycle of a religious oriented social movement and that whether or not the social movement is able to institutionalize leadership is critical to the survival of a religious oriented social movement. Left without a leader the majority of Saints reorganized under the leadership of the Quorum of the Twelve Apostles and its President Brigham Young. After completing the Temple in Nauvoo and performing "sealing rituals," these Mormon Israelites, who called themselves the Camp of Israel, began their exodus to the American

West in 1846 in search of a sanctuary from persecution. They reached the nominally Mexican controlled Great Salt Lake City in Utah in 1847. "This is the place" Brigham Young is reputed to have said when he saw the valley below, and soon the Saints began to build the Mormon Kingdom of Deseret in that "place."

In the Mormon Kingdom proselytization continued apace as more and more "consent Saints," more and more converts to Mormonism, gathered to this stake of Zion, this sanctuary in the heart of the Great Basin Desert.[31] They came by boat, by wagon train, by handcart, and eventually by rail.

Although Mormon leaders hoped that the Mormon exodus westward would end tensions between Mormon and Gentiles, it did not. In 1850, after the United States' victory in the Mexican War, Utah became a part of the United States and was granted territorial status. Mormons tried to obtain statehood for their theocratic kingdom but the church's political and economic control of the territory ("Zionism") and the official announcement of the practice of polygamy in 1852 made for difficult relations between the church, the United States government, and critics of polygamy.

For critics of Mormonism polygamy was one of the "twin relics of barbarism" along with slavery.[32] Federal attempts to end Mormon Zionism and the Mormon practice of polygamy and to establish its control of Utah Territory led to the Utah War of 1857. While the war did not end Mormon dominance of the territory or the practice of polygamy, the United States did finally, and with some difficulty, manage to establish its political hegemony in Utah.[33]

In the wake of the Utah War anti-polygamy groups and individuals began to lobby the American Congress for an end to polygamy and urge the federal government to take action against the recalcitrant Saints. These efforts resulted in the passage of a federal law, the Anti-Bigamy Act, which made plural marriage illegal in 1862. Mid-nineteenth-century Mormons, on the other hand, defended polygamy on the grounds that it would tame male sexuality and that it would put an end to the need for male extra-marital affairs and in the process end the heinous practice of prostitution, another major concern of nineteenth-century reformers and particularly nineteenth-century female reformers. Polygamy would, Mormon polemicists argued, produce both healthier relationships and healthier offspring. The Mormon faithful also argued that it was God's will that the "practice" of "celestial marriage" be restored. The fact that so many "worthy" Saints were practicing what their religion preached and, in many cases, defended a practice they did not engage in themselves, clearly shows how important plural marriage and, by extension, Mormon ideology, was in the lives of individual Saints. In the end nearly nine hundred and seventy Mormon men, including Apostle and Utah territory delegate to the

United States Congress George Q. Cannon and Apostle Rudger Clawson, and a few female Saints were convicted of unlawful cohabitation by the United States government. Most were held in the Utah Territorial Prison.[34]

Polygamy was not the only thing anti-Mormons attacked as I noted earlier. Anti-Mormon polemicists also pointed to the evils of the Mormon political and economic domination of the Utah territory. They asserted that Mormons practiced a form of political, economic, and cultural tribalism. In doing so they spoke in a paranoiac language about a Mormon totalitarianism that brainwashed the minds of its adherents. They asserted that Mormons were conspiring to take over the America.[35]

During the Civil War federal action against "the Principle" and Mormon theocracy, declined.[36] However, after the war continued lobbying by anti-polygamy groups led to a tougher anti-polygamy measure in 1874, the Poland Act. This act extended federal jurisdiction over criminal and civil cases, such as "bigamy," which had heretofore been prosecuted in courts controlled by Mormons.

The Saints decided to test the Poland Act. George Reynolds, a polygamist, was chosen by the Church to be the guinea pig in this test case. After Reynolds was convicted of violating the anti-polygamy laws passed by the Congress, the case was appealed to the Supreme Court. While Church lawyers argued for freedom of religion, the court decided on 6 January 1879 that America's anti-bigamy laws were constitutional. The Court concluded that polygamy was a threat to national health that, if unchecked, would undermine the nuclear family structure on which, or so the justices claimed, a "civilized" and "healthy" nation such as the United States was built.[37]

Although the second Mormon prophet Brigham Young died in 1877 plural marriage did not. John Taylor, who succeeded Young, continued to preach the necessity of practicing "the Principle" even while hiding on the polygamy underground from anti-polygamy hunters. In 1882 Congress passed another anti-polygamy act, the Edmunds Act. The Edmunds Act allowed federal marshals to arrest and imprison polygamous "cohabitors." Once again, this act failed to end "the Principle" so in 1887 Congress passed the Edmunds-Tucker Act. The Edmunds-Tucker act disincorporated the Church, dissolved the Perpetual Emigration Fund, which helped fund the Mormon "gathering to Zion," abolished female suffrage in the territory—women had been given the vote in Utah territory in 1870, in large part, to increase the pro-polygamy vote—and began proceedings to strip the Church of all its property, save that used for worship services. Still the practice of "the Principle" continued.[38]

In 1887 Mormon prophet and president John Taylor died. He was succeeded by Wilford Woodruff. Woodruff, a polygamist himself, finally bowed to federal pressure on 24 September 1890 and issued a "manifesto" stressing that the Church no longer sanctioned the doctrine of plural marriage.[39] The Church also put an end to the "gathering to Zion," undermining and ending, in the process, the Mormon Zionist theocracy in Utah territory. At the same time the Church disbanded its political party. The Church now began to urge its members to join, they hoped in equal numbers, the Democratic and Republican parties, thus nudging the Church in the direction of the American political mainstream. These actions ended the overt period of Mormon civil disobedience.[40]

While some prominent Gentiles believed that the manifesto did indeed end polygamy, many "anti–Mormons" did not. And they were right. As many scholars have noted over the years, the manifesto of 1890 was somewhat ambiguous. It is worded very differently from previous revelations. Additionally, thanks to historical scholarship since the 1960s, there is ample evidence to indicate that despite the public anti-polygamy rhetoric, the practice and "solemnization" of "the Principle" continued after 1890. Plural marriages continued to be "consecrated" in the Mormon culture region and in Latter-day Saint colonies in Mexico and Canada for quite some time afterwards.[41]

In the wake of the 1890 Manifesto, Mormonism began to change. The Church was now involved in a very difficult balancing act, for at the same time that it was continuing the sanctification of plural marriages it was simultaneously denying publicly that it was doing so. The Church tried to maintain "the Principle" at the same time that it tried to integrate and ingratiate itself into and to the mainstream of American culture and society. This dual strategy worked for a while. However, the rub came when Mormons tried to move into national American political life and political institutions.[42]

With the apparent demise of Mormon theocracy and polygamy, Utah was finally granted statehood in 1896. In 1904 Senator Elect Reed Smoot was appointed Senator from Utah. However, when he tried to take his seat in the United States Senate anti-polygamy groups opposed seating Smoot and generated so much pressure that between 1904 and 1907 the senate held hearings on Mormonism and Mormon practices and whether to seat Smoot.[43]

Central to these hearings was the issue of polygamy. Anti-polygamy groups demanded that Smoot not be seated because they were convinced that Mormons were still practicing plural marriage. In answer to the anti-polygamy opposition, Joseph F. Smith, Mormonism's fourth prophet, seer, and revelator, issued what later came to be called a "second manifesto."

In this second manifesto of 1904, Smith denied that the Church was actively solemnizing plural marriages though it was secretly doing just that.[44]

Smoot was finally seated in the senate, but the polygamy controversy did not go away. In a 1907 General Conference speech, Joseph F. Smith again denied that Mormons were engaged in plural marriage. In 1910 the First Presidency issued a letter directing stake presidents to search out and punish those who engaged in "the Principle."[45]

In 1931 Church president, prophet, and revelator Heber J. Grant devised a new approach to the polygamy question, he urged that the Church avoid the issue entirely.[46] As Martha Bradley noted, this sidestepping of the issue of polygamy was, in large part, a response to the growing sectarian Fundamentalist movement afoot in the Mormon culture region. By the 1930s, a movement that had previously been individualistically oriented and unorganized had begun to coalesce into specific groups that were actively proselytizing and decrying the fact that the Church had given up "the Principle."[47]

Despite the anti-polygamy campaigns of the Church's enemies between the 1850s and early 1900s and the transformation of the Church, Church growth was not hurt significantly largely because Saints continued to gather to Zion from overseas despite the demise of official Mormon Zionist ideology and symbology. In 1850 Church membership stood at fifty thousand. By 1870 it was one hundred and ten thousand. By 1890 it grew to two hundred and five thousand while in 1900 it stood at two hundred and sixty-eight thousand.

The end of the "gathering to Zion" and the establishment of a missionary system in which young people went on missions across the globe has had, from the Church's point of view, its pluses. By 1960 Church membership had reached 1.6 million. By 2010 the Church had a worldwide population of over thirteen million and Mormonism was no longer a regional American religion. By 2020 there were almost seventeen million Latter-day Saints around the world.[48]

As Max Weber noted, the dramatic growth of an organization inevitably and invariably compelled routinization. Between the 1960s and 1970s the Mormon bureaucracy was rationalized and made more efficient and effective. However, "Correlation," as this routinization was officially called within the Church, has come with a price. The campaign against polygamists was expanded to encompass dissident intellectuals and political "extremists."[49] Women's groups (such as the Relief Society) lost their autonomy as they were brought fully under the control of an increasingly aged male hierarchy. And, of course, the internationalization of the Church brought with it its own set of problems as a peculiarly American institution that sanctified the geography of the United States as well as its Constitution, tried to adapt to new global realities and new global consumers.[50]

Part of this adaptation process involved the adoption of a revised symbol system necessitated by the decline of Mormon Zionism and Mormon polygamy, although neither have completely disappeared from Mormon symbology and rhetoric. They remain central aspects of the Mormon symbol or meaning system though in adapted form. However, both have declined in importance as Mormonism has moved, theologically and culturally, closer to Christian evangelicalism and fundamentalism.[51]

In the post-manifesto period, the Church no longer urged Saints to move to the Mormon culture region though many still come of their own volition if only to attend Brigham Young University, a ritual life cycle act that is important to and for many of the faithful. Mormons now build stakes of Zion wherever there are enough Saints to constitute a "stake." Increases in the number of "stakes" are seen as evidence that the tent of Zion is growing ever larger and that a new world is just around that bend or over that hill. Temples have been constructed throughout the world from Washington, D.C., United States of America, to Hamilton, New Zealand, and to Freiburg, Germany. Today, few "mainstream" Latter-day Saints speak of Independence, Missouri, as Zion. The hope of one day gathering to Zion and building its temple and its broad avenues may still exist in the hearts and minds of some Mormon leaders and some Mormon intellectuals, and especially in its sectarian groups, but it is no longer as central to Mormon lives as it once was.

The impact the decline of the "gathering" has had on Mormonism and to Mormon culture and ideological life can be readily seen through the lens of Mormon demography. Between 1849 and 1930 one hundred and thee thousand plus mostly European Saints gathered to Zion.[52] In 1930 one out of every two Mormons lived in Utah (an additional thirty percent lived in the American West). By 1960 only ten percent lived in Utah (forty percent in the American West). Ideology and ideological change have had, in other words, geographic consequences in Mormon society and culture.[53]

Nor is polygamy as important as it once was. Fundamentalists and a few (secretive) members of the Church practice "the Principle." However, if they are caught excommunication is likely since the Church hierarchy and most Church members are now staunchly opposed to its practice. Brigham Young University students have even been subject to expulsion simply for talking to the proponents of Mormon fundamentalism in recent years.[54]

This transformation of Mormon symbology can also be seen in the changing rhetoric of Mormon General Conference discourses.[55] Gordon and Gary Shepherd's content analysis of General Conference speeches before and after 1890 shows a decline of emphasis on plural marriage, the

Kingdom of God (a measure of Mormon apocalypticism), and persecution (a measure of Mormon distinctiveness) over the years and an increasing emphasis on family, the "Word of Wisdom," and "Jesus" over the same years.[56]

For religious studies scholar Jan Shipps the demise of Mormon theocracy and plural marriage is *the* critical moment in Mormon history. For non–Mormon anthropologist and archaeologist Mark Leone Mormon radicalism was replaced by Mormon conservatism in the wake of the decline of Mormon polygamy and theocracy. Mormon historian of Mormonism D. Michael Quinn has likened the demise of Mormon theocracy and polygamy to Western political, economic, and cultural imperialism of the semi-peripheral and peripheral world, where the conquered adopted the economic system, political system, and, if only perhaps somewhat, the culture of the conqueror. As several scholars have noted, Mormons and Mormonism became in the period after the issuance of the manifesto, more American than Americans, and more Victorian than the Victorians.[57]

The most radical changes that impacted Mormons in the years after the issuance of the manifesto had to do with their integration into the American political and economic life. Mormon integration into the American economy meant that putting communal United Orders into practice, which was important during the presidency of Brigham Young, became difficult if not impossible. Mormon integration into American economic and political culture meant that building the Mormon Zion was, under the circumstances, next to impossible.[58]

However, these symbolic changes were not the sea changes that Shipps and Quinn suggest. As Leone noted, Mormons remain distinctive and "eternal progressions" remains, as I mentioned earlier, the central, key, or dominant symbol of contemporary Mormonism, while fundamentalists and some Mormon intellectuals keep "the gathering" and "the Principle" alive in theory if not in practice.[59]

ONE

The Polemics and Apologetics of Mormon "Otherness"

Introduction

In the beginning Mormonism was viewed by the faithful as God's one true and only church restored to earth through the medium and the message of the Mormon Prophet Joseph Smith. For "mainstream" critics of Mormonism, on the other hand, Mormonism was hardly the one true brand of Christianity. Instead, Protestant polemicists believed that their denomination, whichever denomination they happened to be a member of, was God's true church. For many American Protestants, Mormonism was a confidence scheme, an "unorthodox" form of Christianity, an instance of "blasphemy," and even a "heresy." For many nineteenth-century and early twentieth-century Protestants Mormonism was, like Roman Catholicism, "tyrannical" and hence a danger to "democratic" America. As we will see, this dichotomy of Mormonism as the one true faith and, as its sometimes evil doppelganger other, a false unorthodox heresy, would have a very long shelf life. It was also a cultural discourse grounded in an even longer history of apologetics and polemics and its cultural scripts.

It is not difficult to understand both reactions to Mormonism. When humans construct communities, they tend to perceive their communities in positive hues. And when humans construct communities, particularly communities built on notions of metaphysical truth and that have distinct cultural or ideological and social boundaries and a strong sense of superiority or ethnocentrism, they tend to see those who are not members of their ingroup as an outgroup that lacks something relative to their own community of truth. When a community explicitly or implicitly challenges another community's monopoly on truth, an ideological culture war that can be hazardous to human health, can result.[1]

The Christian construction of orthodoxy and unorthodoxy and of "otherness" has a long history. Europe was, of course, the place where theocratic Christianity, with its categorization of Christianity as true or orthodox and other faiths as false or unorthodox heresies, first took hold. There was, for example, an anti-Jewish Christian variant of this manichean binary with its accompanying prejudices, discriminations, pogroms, and mass murders. There was a Christian anti-heresy variety which resulted in the mass murder of Anabaptists and others for their supposed heresy. There was a Christian anti-Muslim form with its antagonistic attitudes toward and crusades against a new rival religion or meaning system that spread out of the Middle East after the seventh century, Islam.[2]

When many European Christians migrated to the settler societies of the new worlds, one of the things they brought with them were their manichean and binary notions of orthodox and heresy. For instance, laws against members of the Religious Society of Friends or Quakers were passed in the Protestant and Puritan theocratic colony of Massachusetts and Quakers were imprisoned, inquisited for witchcraft, flogged, or, as in the case of four Quakers, killed when they showed up in Massachusetts colony to preach their gospel.[3]

In the new American nation, notions of orthodoxy and heresy were, in the freer relative to Europe religious marketplace of the United States, adapted when they eventually intersected with modern notions of nationhood and national identity. In the nineteenth century, religion, nationhood, and national identity, specifically White Anglo Saxon and Protestant religion and national identity, interacted with notions of orthodoxy and heresy to produce anti-Catholic, anti-Mason, anti-Shaker, anti-Oneidan, and anti-Mormon social movements. All of these movements gave rise to conspiracy theories grounded in an ideologically constructed fiction in which each of these outsider groups were "tyrannical," one of the central profane symbols of American civic culture in the wake of the Revolutionary War. As a result, campaigns against each of these social movements, campaigns that were sometimes violent and occasionally deadly for those they were aimed against, resulted.

For instance, anti-Catholic crowds in several American cities burned monasteries and a significant body of anti-Catholic literature was produced that accused Catholics of all sorts of sexual and other assorted perversions. For many White Protestant Anglo-Saxon Americans, Roman Catholicism was anti-democratic and authoritarian if not totalitarian, and America's Roman Catholics were thought to be involved in a covert campaign to overthrow America's nascent "democracy."[4]

Shakers were accused of being an authoritarian and anti-democratic group that deceptively lured the naïve into a dangerous and unhealthy faith. Mary Dyer, the leading eighteenth-century critic of Shakerism and herself a former Shaker, claimed that Shaker society was a slave society and that Shaker leaders used physical violence to maintain Shaker discipline. She accused Shaker leaders of hypocrisy by leading lives of luxury, drunkenness, and sexual vice. She claimed Shakers were utilizing electricity and mesmerism to break the will of potential converts in order to bring them into the fold. Dyer placed Ann Lee in a long line of religious imposters from the serpent in the Garden of Eden to Simon Magus and to Muhammad. Shaker critics filed lawsuits against Shakers and occasionally engaged in physical violence against them. Many commentators, in fact, have attributed Shaker leader "Mother" Ann Lee's early death to the beatings and stonings she suffered and endured at the hands of anti–Shaker vigilante mobs throughout her life.[5]

Throughout its existence the Oneida Community, founded by John Humphrey Noyes, was accused of un–American behavior and harassed by polemicists. In Putney, Vermont, where the Oneida movement began in 1841, Noyes and his followers faced protests and potential arrest for "adultery." Before he could be arrested in 1848, Noyes fled to New York where he and his Putney followers settled on one hundred and sixty acres of land in Oneida and built a commune. In Oneida, the group continued to face harassment from their broader and, to a lesser extent, their immediate community. The Oneida community's marriage to all sexual practices were the target of an obscenity bill Congregationalist and anti-vice reformer and crusader Anthony Comstock persuaded the New York State Legislature to enact. They were also the target of an 1873 obscenity bill Comstock convinced the federal government to pass, which, among other things, forbade the dissemination of literature dealing with birth control, something widely practiced at Oneida and something which the group evangelized about through their newspapers and books, many of which passed through the postal service. Oneida was also the target of Professor John Mears of Hamilton College who wrote and preached against the systematic "concubinage" taking place in the community's Mansion House, which he classed with what was for him "evil and uncivilised polygamy." Eventually, Methodists, Baptists, and Congregationalists joined Mears adding their voices to his calls for an end to Oneida "debaucheries."[6]

It is worth noting that the transformation of former members of a new religious group from true believer to true believing enemy, claims that members of certain religious groups were in thralldom to or brainwashed by a religious group and its charismatic leader, the contention that leaders of new religious movement were manipulative swindlers, the assertion that new religious groups engaged in "deviant" sexual practices, the inaccurate representation of new religious groups, and reformer lobbying of the powers that be to do something about unorthodox or heretical groups, would reappear again and again in "mainstream" responses to new religious movements. The anti-cult movements that propagated such claims and the journalists who listened to them and told their sensationalistic tales to a mass audience via the mass media, have played a major role in verbal and physical attacks on new religious movements ever since.[7]

"Anti-Mormon" Polemics and Apologetics

Many nineteenth-century Americans believed that Mormonism and Mormons were, unorthodox, other, heretical, and "alien."[8] Mormons, of course, did not see themselves as "other," as "unorthodox," or as "heretical." They believed that their Church, as Church revelations proclaimed, was the only true and living church upon the face of the earth.[9] However, for many Christian ministers, journalists, and intellectuals, Mormonism was both unorthodox and heretical and it was certainly, they believed, not God's one and only true church.

Literature doctrinally and dogmatically critical of Mormonism began to appear just a few years after the incorporation of the Church of Christ in 1830. In 1834 Eber D. Howe, the publisher of the *Telegraph* (Painesville, Ohio), published *Mormonism Unvailed, or a Faithful Account of that Singular Imposition and Delusion*. In *Mormonism Unvailed*, Howe described the Mormon prophet Joseph Smith as one of the "vilest wretch[es] on earth," dismissed the Book of Mormon as a "fabrication" aimed at the "lowest ... passions," and claimed that it could not have been written by an illiterate such as Joseph Smith. According to Howe. the author of the Book of Mormon was really Sidney Rigdon, a former Campbellite minister who had converted to Mormonism and who had become a prominent figure in the Church in Kirtland, Ohio, after he converted to Mormonism from Campbellitism. Howe suggested that Rigdon had based the Book of Mormon on a romance by Solomon Spaulding entitled "Manuscript Found," a claim that would, as we will see, have a long history in "anti–Mormon" polemics.[10]

In the early or primitive period of Mormon history dissidents also played an important role in the formation and diffusion of an "anti–Mormon" discourse. Included within *Mormonism Unvailed* were nine affidavits collected by Doctor Philastus Hurlbut,[11] an excommunicated Saint, who, during travels in New York State, collected the affidavits and later published them in the *Ohio Review* (Ravenna). In these affidavits several individuals who knew Joseph Smith when he lived in New York, swore that he had been involved in money digging. Money digging, of course, would become a major theme in "anti–Mormon" polemics.[12]

Where Howe and Hurlbut led others followed. Howe's *Mormonism Unvailed* and the Hurlbut letters included within it, were immensely important in their time and remain influential even today. Both provided the template for "anti–Mormonism" as a subgenre of a Christian polemical literature that goes back to the beginnings of Christian polemics in the first century of the Common Era.

Anti-Mormon writers who came after Howe generally repeated the claims about Mormonism and Smith made in *Mormonism Unvailed* and sometimes added their own accusations into the mix. Methodist minister and abolitionist La Roy Sunderland, for instance, claimed, like Howe, that Mormonism was a false and blasphemous religion, and that the Book of Mormon was based on the Spaulding manuscript.[13] John Bennett's *History of the Saints; or an Expose of Joe Smith and Mormonism*, a tract by another excommunicated and dissident "Saint," borrowed the money digging and Spaulding claims from Howe and Hurlbut and added a charge of "spiritual wifery" or polygamy into its polemical mix.[14] Episcopalian minister John A. Clark's *Gleanings by the Way* repeated the Spaulding charge maintaining that if Rigdon was not the one who got hold of and copied Spaulding's "Manuscript Found," it must have been Joseph Smith. Clark's book also contained an interview with Smith's New York collaborator, scribe, and financial supporter Martin Harris.[15]

Although most nineteenth- and twentieth-century anti–Mormon writers were indebted to the polemics of Howe and Hurlbut others added new wrinkles to the anti–Mormon faith over the years. Non-Mormon Origen Bachelor's *Mormonism Exposed Internally and Externally*, for example, pointed out errors in style, reasoning, and historical fact in the Book of Mormon. Arranging his book in categories such as "Barbarisms," "Improbablilities," "Abusurdities," and "Contradictions in Fact," Bachelor, mimicking the style of Thomas Paine's iconoclastic and rationalist *Age of Reason*, argued that the language of the Book of Mormon was New England colloquial, denied that the "Mormon Bible" was consistent with the Christian Bible, claimed that the Book of Mormon was a ridiculous imposture, and maintained that Smith was a "liar."[16] Episcopalian minister Henry Caswall's *The Prophet of the Nineteenth-Century; or, The Rise, Progress, and Present State of the Mormons* claimed that Smith was a "low juggler" lacking education and character who interpreted "...Scriptures according to his own fancies leading ... his followers into the lowest abyss of mental degradation."[17] Pomeroy Tucker, who knew Smith, Harris, and Oliver Cowdery, a prominent early Mormon leader who had read proofs of the Book of Mormon, claimed in his *Origin, Rise, and Progress of Mormonism: Biography of Its Founders and History of Its Church*, that Smith was a vagabond given to telling tall tells and drinking whiskey.[18] John Gunnison's *The Mormons; or, Latter-day Saints in the Valley of the Great Salt Lake City* argued that it was Joseph Smith not ancient Americans who wrote the Book of Mormon.[19]

In the mid- to late nineteenth century with the Mormons ensconced in their kingdom in the valleys of Utah practicing polygamy and into the twentieth, accusations about the supposed dark side of Mormonism increased exponentially. In his *Roughing It* Mark Twain asserted that Young was a monarch and that Mormons had massacred a wagon train of non-Mormons at the Mountain Meadows (both of which are accurate claims). At the same time, taking a more normative approach, Twain argued that the Book of Mormon was a cure for sleeplessness (a pun on the Book of Mormon book of Ether).[20] Arthur Conan Doyle's 1888 Sherlock Holmes novella *A Study in Scarlet* depicted Mormon Utah as a land where residents were terrorized by Mormon leaders and those critical of the Church mysteriously disappeared.[21] In his *Mormonism Unveiled* (1877) ex-Mormon John D. Lee accused Brigham Young of ordering the Mountain Meadows Massacre and accused Young and Mormon leaders of using assassins known as the "destroying angels," against its enemies.[22] Ex-Mormon "Wild" Bill Hickman confessed to being one of these "destroying angels" and to carrying out murders on the orders of Brigham Young.[23] Bruce Kinney's *Mormonism: The Islam of America* (1912) asserted that the Book of Mormon was based on a second Spaulding manuscript. He went on to accuse Mormon leaders of financial impropriety, of "blood atonement," of engaging in secret ceremonies, which, if divulged, required "horrible penalties," of moral perversity as a result of their practice of polygamy, of polytheism, of interfering in political life, and of hypocrisy. Finally, he accused Mormon fathers of killing those of their children who tried to escape the "thralldom" of Mormonism (brainwashing has a long pedigree in Christian and later secular anti-new religious movement polemics).[24] Kinney's book also added an orientalist motif to the anti-Mormon subgenre by making explicit, in its title, that Mormonism was the new Islam, a false exotic religion (yet another accusation often made by "orthodox" critics of new Christian religious movements) that engaged in polygamy and other forms of sexual licentiousness. Kinney, self-described "evangelical" Christian and "Patriotic Christian" citizen of the "American Republic," regarded Mormonism, like Islam, as a false religion, Smith, like Muhammad as a false prophet, and the Book of Mormon, like the *Koran*, as a false scripture. Presumably he expected his readers to make the same "logical" doctrinal jumps he did.[25]

Claims that Joseph Smith was an illiterate money digger and sexual deviant, and that the Book of Mormon was written by Smith or based on another manuscript, have continued to find traction with twentieth and twenty-first-century "critics" of Mormonism. From the 1960s into the new millennium the ex-Mormon converts to evangelicalism, Jerald and Sandra Tanner, long tried to convert Mormons from what they regarded as their "false" faith to what they regarded as the "true" faith of evangelical

Christianity. Somewhat ironically, they tried to do this via historical and rational means. Throughout these years the Tanner's published works critical of Mormonism from the nineteenth and early twentieth centuries, published important and embarrassing primary source documents relating to Latter-day Saint history, and published their own criticisms of Mormonism through their Utah Light House Ministry (formerly Modern Microfilms) in Salt Lake City.[26]

The Tanner's publications ranged across the entire array of Mormon "criticism" from claims that Smith was a treasure hunter, to assertions that Mormon temple ceremonies were borrowed from Freemasonry, to a list of changes that have been made by the Church to the Book of Mormon and the Mormon Temple ceremony, to an exploration of changes made to Mormon doctrine over the years, and to claims that Smith plagiarized the Bible when he wrote the Book of Mormon. Where the Tanner's differed from their nineteenth-century forebears was that while they engaged in polemics and evangelical apologetics, they also did extensive work in Mormon unpublished primary documents, published documents secreted away in the LDS archives (a Mormon culture region version of Soviet *samizdat*), which raised questions about Smith and his hermeneutics, and grounded much of their work in an analysis of primary source material. The Tanner's work, in other words, was one-part polemics and apologetics and one part descriptive and historical analysis.[27]

Probably the most controversial of late twentieth-century anti–Mormons was Ed Decker. Decker, an excommunicated Mormon, convert to evangelicalism, and director of Saints Alive, a self-proclaimed anti-cult organization, made two films documenting the supposed "evils" of Mormonism, "The God Makers" (1982) and "The God Makers II" (1993). Both films drew on the nineteenth-century anti–Mormonism but added a mid- to late- twentieth-century twist to the polemical mix. In "The God Makers" and "The God Makers II" Decker accused Mormonism of being non–Christian, of changing its Scriptures, of manipulating its own Scriptures, of being a cult, and of practicing occultism and Satanism. He also alleged that Mormonism was destroying families, sexually abusing women, abusing children, undermining the mental health of individual Mormons by holding members to unobtainable ideals, exploiting its members, engaging in political intrigue, and of controlling and manipulating the media. He charged that Mormonism was a potentially dangerous mega-business and financial giant that had the potential for undermining American democracy. Finally, Decker and company resurrected accusations that Smith was involved in treasure digging. "The God Makers II" closes with accusations that Gordon B. Hinckley, the man who was Church president and prophet at the time, and other Church leaders were engaging in acts of sexual immorality, including bisexuality (a somewhat updated spin on the old claims of sexual deviance that have been a part of Christian polemical discourse aimed at the other at least since the nineteenth century).[28]

Another important subgenre of anti–Mormon polemics has been that associated with the muckraking tradition. Drawing on the same Progressive Era journalistic playbook that exposed the practices of Standard Oil and governmental corruption, Frank Q. Cannon, disaffected son of Mormon leader, First Counselor, and former Utah senator George Q. Cannon, and Harvey J. O'Higgins, published a series of exposes on Mormonism between 1910 and 1911 in *Everybody's* magazine, one of the prominent muckraking publications of the era. These articles later served as the basis for Cannon and O'Higgins's book *Under the Prophet in Utah*.[29]

Despite its sociological emphasis the work of Cannon and O'Higgins with its emphasis on uncovering anti-democratic conspiracies and its emphasis on advocacy and reform, shares a great deal with early anti–Mormon literature. *Prophet* tells the tale of "the great American despotism," Mormonism, and its great American "despot," the Mormon "Czar" or prophet, who lives like "the Grand Turk openly with his five wives" in Salt Lake City. Cannon and O'Higgins condemned Mormon leaders for promising to give up the practice of polygamy in 1890 in order to gain statehood for Utah but reneging on that promise after winning statehood.[30]

A more recent entry in the Mormon muckraking tradition is *The Mormon Corporate Empire* by Mormon born anthropologist John Heinerman, who was interviewed for "The God Makers II," and Gentile academic sociologist Anson Shupe. Heinerman and Shupe accuse Mormon leaders of building an anti-democratic and anti-pluralistic theocracy. They investigate Latter-day Saint investments and explore Mormon influence in politics and the military all of which they see in largely negative hues.[31]

Attacks on Mormons, such as the works we have been exploring, were not only literary and verbal, by the way. When Mormonism arose in early nineteenth-century New York and when Mormons gathered first in Ohio, then in Missouri, then in Illinois, and finally, by the mid-nineteenth century in Utah, they were condemned by many Americans for group think, for voting as a political block, for communalism, for self-righteousness, and for "deviant" sexual practices. Members and leaders of the Mormon community were attacked, beaten, and tarred and feathered by vigilante mobs all across the American Midwest. Lilburn W. Boggs, the governor of Illinois, went so far as to issue an order for the extermination of Mormons in 1838. The assassination of Joseph Smith by an angry mob in Carthage, Illinois, on 27 June 1844 did not end attacks on Mormons. As noted in the introduction to this book, even after the Saints immigrated to the valleys of what became Utah, they were hounded by opponents and by the

American government because of their practice of polygamy and as a result of their mixing of Church and state.[32]

Mormon Polemics and Apologetics

Mormon polemics and apologetics developed, in large part, in this normative and polemical anti–Mormon context, and was a response by faithful Mormon intellectuals to the normative "anti–Mormonism" of Howe and Cannon and their many heirs.[33]

At first, Mormon intellectuals largely ignored their critics and concentrated instead on chronicling their own history. Now and again, Mormon intellectuals did respond to the claims of polemical critics of Mormonism to correct, so they claimed, the historical record, or to argue for the superiority of restored Mormon Christianity over other brands of Christianity and other religions. In 1834 and 1835, "Second Elder" Oliver Cowdery, Smith's chief assistant, for instance, wrote a series of letters to W.W. Phelps, an early Mormon leader and publisher, about Church History.[34] Letter 4 discussed the translation of the Book of Mormon while letter 8 explored how the Book of Mormon came into Smith's possession. Cowdery answered those making claims about the negative character of the Smith family in letter 8 referring to them as "honest, virtuous, and liberal to all."[35]

Mormon apostle Parley P. Pratt's pamphlet *Mormonism Unveiled: Zion's Watchman Unmasked and Its Editor Mr. L.R. Sunderland Exposed, Truth Vindicated, the Devil Mad, and Priestcraft in Danger!* delineated what Pratt considers to be Sunderland's errors and misrepresentations of the Church and responded to his "mistakes" point by point. Pratt challenges Sunderland's contention that the Book of Mormon was based on Spaulding's "Manuscript Found" and in a kind of turnabout is fair play strategy, refers to Hurlbut, whose letters Sunderland made use of, as, a man of "notorious character."[36]

Joseph Smith's letter to John Wentworth, in which Smith discussed his "first vision," his "translation" of the Book of Mormon, the Missouri War, and which laid out the "Articles of Faith" of the Church, was a response to charges that Mormonism was blasphemous and unorthodox. In many respects, the "Articles" are pretty much your standard "mainline" nineteenth-century garden variety Protestantism and differed little from the statements of faith of mainline American Protestant Churches. In the Wentworth letter Smith asserts that Mormons believe in God the Eternal Father, his son Jesus Christ, and the Holy Ghost, the fall and original sin, the atonement of Christ, the centrality of faith, repentance and baptism, the organization of the primitive church, the Bible as the Word of God, and obedience to authority. Where the "Articles" do differ from nineteenth-century mainline American Protestantism is in their emphasis on the literal gathering of Israel to the American "new Jerusalem," and the Book of Mormon as the "Word of God."[37]

Just as anti–Mormon polemics did not end with the nineteenth-century Mormon polemics and apologetics did not end with the nineteenth century. As the Church bureaucratized and professionalized and Utah modernized and expanded in the twentieth century, Mormon polemics and apologetics finally, so to speak, came of age.[38] In 1946, Hugh Nibley, who took his doctorate from University of California in Berkeley and who taught at Brigham Young University from 1946 until 1994, published a rejoinder to Fawn Brodie's famous psychobiography of Joseph Smith, *No Man Knows My History*, entitled *No Ma'am, That's Not History*. *No Ma'am* marked a turning point in the history of Mormon apologetics and polemics in that it adopted, at least in part, the descriptive language of academia to help make its apologetic and polemical points. Nibley challenged Brodie's book on methodological, source use, and theoretical grounds. However, he did it in a sometimes normative dismissive and patronizing language, referring, for example, to Brodie as "the lady" four times, a reflection, one might argue, of Nibley's Mormon patriarchalism and paternalism.[39]

Nibley's more intellectual and academic apologetics and polemics, including his style and method, would become standard operating practice for many Mormon apologists and polemicists in his wake and remains at the heart of Mormon apologetics and polemics even today. In the late twentieth and early twenty-first centuries Nibley-style Mormon apologetics and polemics were institutionalized with the founding of the Foundation for Ancient Research and Mormon Studies (FARMS) and the Foundation for Apologetic Information and Research (FAIR). FARMS, dedicated to "faithful scholarship" on the Ancient Near East and the ancient background of the Book of Mormon and the Book of Abraham, was founded by Mormon attorney John Welch in 1979 as an independent research organization in Los Angeles. In 1980, when Welch joined the faculty of the Brigham Young University Law School, FARMS moved with him to a location near the Mormon owned and run campus in Provo, Utah. In 1984. it teamed up with the Church owned Desert Books to publish the collected works of Hugh Nibley. The following year it began to publish books by its members and fellow travelers, those who were not members of FARMS but who shared its members belief in the ancient origins of the Book of Mormon, on ancient history, and on the Book of Mormon. In 1997, Church prophet Gordon D. Hinckley invited FARMS to become part of BYU. In 2006 it became a sub-unit of BYU's Neal A. Maxwell Institute of Religious Scholarship.[40]

Another Mormon polemical and apologetic Mormon institution, one bred for the brave new postmodernist digital age, FAIR, was founded in 1997 by Mormon "defenders of the faith" to, as its website says, "defend the Church against" its online "detractors."[41]

Both, FARMS, through its website, its journal the *FARMS Review*, (formerly the *Review of Books on the Book of Mormon*), and conference presentations, and FAIR, through its website and its annual conference, which FARMS members attend and present papers at, carry on the work of nineteenth-century Mormon apologists and polemicists and Nibley. Both offer faith historical critiques of all stripes of evangelical, conservative Christian, and secular "anti–Mormonism" and seek to rebut claims that the Book of Mormon has human origins, and that Joseph Smith was a very fallible flim flam man.

Just as Christians have battled and continued to battle heretical outsiders and insiders, so do the faithful of FARMS. Although some FARMS essays and books are aimed at outsiders, others are aimed at the "snares of disaffected insiders," and their readings, in particular, of the Book of Mormon and Mormon origins. FARMS members and fellow travelers have long argued that the Book of Mormon was both a sacred and an ancient text. Over the years, they claimed to have found evidence of the ancient origins of the Book of Mormon in its chiasms, literary structures of symmetric order or pattern, parables, references to coronation ceremonies, geographic references, Egyptianisms, Hebraisms, and references to ancient Yucatan.[42]

Not all Mormons have followed FARMS's lead. Some "insiders" were and are critical of the ancient origins of the *Book of Mormon* hypothesis of FARMS members and fellow travelers. With the help of LDS businessman George Smith and his Smith Research Associates and the Smith-Pettit Foundation of Salt Lake City, insider outsider critics of increasingly countered FARMS's claims that Mormonism and the Book of Mormon were the products of the ancient world.[43] Smith's Salt Lake City based Signature Books published and continues to publish works taking a "new" approach to the *Book of Mormon*, most prominently among them the two manifestos of the "new" Book of Mormon Studies, Brent Metcalfe's edited collection *New Approaches to the Book of Mormon* and Metcalfe and Dan Vogel's edited collection *American Apocrypha*.[44]

A diversity of views underlay "insider outsider" new criticism of the Book of Mormon. Some, such as Blake Ostler, argued that there was a divine core to the "Mormon Bible." Others, such as Vogel and Metcalfe, argued that the *Book of Mormon* was a nineteenth-century work of fiction that reflected its nineteenth-century environment. Taking a more secular and historical approach and borrowing heavily from higher biblical criticism, the same higher biblical criticism that helped give birth to the

American fundamentalist and modernist culture wars of the 1920s along with fundamentalism and evangelicalism, insider outsider critics such as Vogel argued that the Book of Mormon was influenced by Indian origins, by anti-Masonic and by anti-Universalist ideologies from the fifteenth through nineteenth centuries, that, as in the case of Edward Ashment, the Egyptian and Hebrew elements FARMS members and their fellow travelers saw in the *Book of Mormon* simply were not there, and, as in the case of Deanne Metheny, that there were no Nephites and Lamanites who lived in the Yucatan peninsula of present-day Mexico. FARMS's critics, in other words, used the latest in academic discourse in their cold intellectual polemical and apologetic war against FARMS.[45]

FARMS, of course, responded to these insider outsider challenges. Some of their responses proved controversial. FARMS reviewers such as Daniel Peterson and George Mitton, impacted as they were by the legacy of Nibley, sometimes wrote in a dismissive and patronizing way when reviewing work by both "outsider" and "insider outsider" critics of Mormonism, often linking, as did many of their Mormon polemical predecessors, the two in the process.

Brigham Young University professor of ancient and mediaeval Near Eastern history and FARMS contributor William Hamblin's 1994 critique of an essay by Brent Metcalfe took this dismissive and patronizing discourse, or so some thought, to new levels. Hamblin's essay contained an *ad hominem* acrostic in its first several paragraphs, "METCALFE IS BUTTHEAD." When Metcalfe discovered the acrostic and informed a FARMS editor of its existence the editor stopped the print run of the journal and the offending essay was revised before the journal reappeared in a new incarnation. Despite all this, most of the original acrostic remained and putting the pieces of the acrostic puzzle together proved to be relatively easy for those on the other side of the twentieth-century Mormon culture war battlements. Associated Press reporter Vern Anderson disseminated news of the acrostic throughout the Mormon culture region and beyond. FARMS contributor and BYU political science professor and FARMS member Louis Midgley responded to the controversy claiming that the acrostic was none too subtle critique of critics of Mormonism's claims that chiasms in the *Book of Mormon* were accidental. Midgley also charged that critics of FARMS were not taking FARMS work seriously enough. Midgley may have believed that critics of Mormonism were far too readily dismissive of FARMS members and fellow travelers work, though the criticisms of FARMS's argument that the *Book of Mormon* was an ancient document in Metcalfe's edited collection *New Approaches to the Book of Mormon* and Metcalfe and Vogel's edited collection *American Apocrypha* suggests otherwise.[46]

One. The Polemics and Apologetics of Mormon "Otherness" 33

Mormon insider outsiders were not the only ones lobbing criticism at FARMS members and their fellow travelers. Some non–Mormons were paying very close attention to the work of FARMS. The 1990s and early 2000s saw a new type of Christian and Mormon apologetics and polemics emerge that did what those at FARMS had long advocated. They took FARMS scholarship on the Book of Mormon and Early Christianity seriously. Evangelical theologians Carl Mosser and Paul Owen, for instance, decried the lack of evangelical engagement with FARMS's scholarship in their paper "Mormon Apologetic Scholarship and Evangelical Neglect" and called for evangelical Biblical Scholars, historians of early Christianity, and theologians, to engage Mormon apologetics and polemics in a "scholarly" manner. The evangelical collection *The New Mormon Challenge*, edited by theologians Francis J. Beckwith, Carl Mosser, and Paul Owen, contains scholarly essays attempting to do just that.[47]

This new evangelical apologetics and polemics did not simply try to engage Mormon apologetics and polemics on their own turf, they also entered into a dialogue with Mormon apologists and polemicists. Whether Mormonism was Christian or not was one of the focal points of this largely genial debate. In 1997, evangelical Craig L. Blomberg and Mormon Stephen E. Robinson debated this question in their book *How Wide the Divide? A Mormon and an Evangelical in Conversation*. Blomberg here and in his essay in the Beckwith, Musser, and Owen collection, "Is Mormonism Christian?" answered no. Robinson here and in his book *Are Mormons Christian?* answered yes. While disagreement between the two was hardly unexpected, the way it was conducted was, at least for some, surprising. They did it in largely respectful fashion. In the wake of this debate FARMS members and fellow travelers rarely fail to note just how seriously Beckwith, Musser, Owen, and their fellow travelers took them and their claims.[48]

Although chronologically outside the scope of this book, "Anti–Mormon" and Mormon polemics and apologetics has continued into the new millennium. In the 2000s, for instance, Mormon intellectual and University of Richmond academic Terryl Givens and the American arm of the venerable Oxford University Press, has taken Mormon polemics and apologetics in the direction of the increasingly postmodernist diverse and multicultural theological mainstream. Givens's two books on the *Book of Mormon* published by Oxford, *By the Hand of Mormon: The American Scripture that Launched a New World Religion* and *The Book of Mormon: A Very Short Introduction*, are grounded on the apologetic and polemical bedrock of the archaeological, historical, and textual work of Nibley and several members of FARMs and their fellow travelers. In these books Givens argued that the *Book of Mormon* was what Joseph Smith, other early

Mormons, and Mormon apologists and polemicists said it was, an ancient scripture.[49]

Conclusion: Polemics and Apologetics and Their Discontents

Polemics and apologetics of all types and varieties are generally grounded in universalist, binary, and manichean (good versus evil) notions of absolute truth and absolute falsity. Polemicists and apologists assume that their meaning system, their religion, is true, whether that true variety of religion is some form of Protestant Christianity or Mormonism, and that the meaning systems or religions of the other, whoever that other happens to be, are false. For the Apostle Paul, for example, his brand of Christianity was true while the Judaism of his time was false and his brand of Christianity was true while other varieties of primitive Christianity, such as the very Jewish brand of Christianity of that of Jesus's brother James and Jesus's apostles, was false.

There is, of course, an irony at the heart of apologetics and polemics of all types, whether cultural, religious, political, or economic. Conservative Christian critics of Mormonism, such as the Tanner's, for instance, who draw on naturalistic or materialistic arguments to condemn Mormonism by pointing out, for example, inconsistencies in the Book of Mormon, changes in Mormon doctrine, Smith's involvement in treasure hunting, and so on, take a naturalistic approach and draw on empirical evidence in order to "prove" metaphysical, theological, or doctrinal, truth and falsity. The irony is that if they took a similar naturalistic and empirical approach to their own faith, in the Tanner's case evangelical Christianity, with its literalist and ahistorical conception of the Bible, its historical and ideological variability, its less than perfect past and present, it too would likely be found wanting on the basis of these same criteria. Additionally, if we wanted to play strictly on the theological and doctrinal level, the criticisms that the LDS had changed its scriptures and its doctrines are simply irrelevant since Mormonism asserts the metaphysical reality of continuing revelation, a belief that revelation is dynamic and that it continued after the first century of the common era and is an inherent aspect of historical Mormonism. Evangelical Christians, in other words, despite their turn toward secular historical and social scientific approaches to Mormonism—aspects of modernity with its de-magicification, demystification, or secularization which created a hybrid sacred and secular culture among evangelicals—are judging Mormonism on the basis, in the final analysis, of their own ideological, theological, or doctrinal perspective, one that asserts that revelation ended with Jesus and the New Testament.

Another phenomenon often closely associated with polemics is that of cultural defamation. Polemicists, historically speaking, have often accused those whom they are polemicizing against of being unorthodox, heretical, alien, conspiratorial, cultish, brainwashers, deviant, particularly sexually deviant, and so on. Sometimes, such accusations have been condemned. Sandra Tanner and her husband Jerald, for instance, charged that Ed Decker's "The God Makers II" contained several errors and factual inaccuracies while Rhonda Abrams, the Central Pacific director of the Jewish Anti-Defamation League in San Francisco in 1984, charged Decker and Company with defaming Mormonism.[50] Generally speaking, such condemnations, particularly within the metaphysical truth claiming group, are simply accepted as factual and actual and confused and conflated with empirical reality.

It is, of course, impossible to empirically prove, verify, or falsify the accuracy of the theological and doctrinal issues which are at the heart of polemics and apologetics, particularly polemics and apologetics associated with monotheistic religions, political parties, or economic ideologies, for instance, that maintain that they and they alone are true and that other religions, political parties, or economic approaches, are inherently false. It is to this issue of cultural "otherness" and academic and scholarly attempts to escape the prison house of notions of "otherness" grounded in manichean binaries of true and false religion and orthodox versus unorthodox religions and the stigmas attached to the latter, that I now want to turn.

Two

Intellectuals, Academics, and Mormon "Otherness"

Introduction

In Chapter One we explored "anti-Mormon" and Mormon apologetics and polemics. However, at least since the expansion of academia in the twentieth century and the diffusion of modern scientific ways of seeing with their emphasis on classification and objectivity, apologists and polemicists have not been the only ones to wonder whether Mormonism was "Christian" or not, or "heretical" or not. Intellectuals and academics, those who generally did not see or perceive themselves as apologists and polemicists, have also waded into the normative debate about how to classify Mormonism and Mormons and how to understand Mormonism's founding prophet, Joseph Smith.

Christianity, Mormonism, and Academics

Over the years intellectuals and academics have answered the question of whether Mormonism is "Christian" in a variety of ways. Some argued that Mormonism was indeed a variety of Christianity. For example, pioneer historian of American Christianity and American reform movements and evangelical Presbyterian Robert Baird, who once claimed, in a language that was more ideological or normative than descriptive that Mormonism was "the grossest of all the delusions that Satanic malignity or human ambition ever sought to propagate," divided American Christians into evangelical and non-evangelical categories. The former category, argued Baird, contained those churches that were "true" varieties of Christianity, while the latter, consisted of varieties of Christianity such as Mormonism, Roman Catholicism, Swedenborgianism, Unitarianism, and others, which were, according to Baird, false varieties

Two. Intellectuals, Academics, and Mormon "Otherness"

of Christianity.[1] Influential non–Mormon sociologist, social ethicist, and Reformed Christian H. Richard Niebuhr saw Mormonism, more descriptively, as a denomination that arose out of the radical wing of the Christian frontier movement in the United States.[2] Mormon historian Klaus Hansen saw Mormonism as a type of kingdom or theocratic Christianity.[3] Gentile historian and evangelical Mark Noll saw Mormons as American Christian "outsiders" along with Millerites, Roman Catholics, Oneida Perfectionists, African American Protestants, and some Immigrant Protestants such as Huguenots and Palatines.[4]

Other intellectuals and academics have equivocated on the question of whether Mormonism was and is "Christian," arguing that Mormonism both is and is not a variety of Christianity. For example, Gentile historian and religious studies scholar Jan Shipps, who took her Ph.D. at the University of Colorado in Boulder and who taught in the History and Religious Studies departments at Indiana University-Purdue University Indianapolis, distinguished between historical, apologetic/polemical, and theological approaches, and empirical and normative approaches to the question of whether Mormonism is Christian or not. For Shipps, Mormonism was historically and more descriptively speaking, to Christianity what Christianity was to Judaism. Both, she argued, were new religious movements and as such bore both similarities to and differences from their religious forebears.[5] Non-Mormon sociologist Rodney Stark agreed with Shipps categorizing Mormonism as a "new world faith."[6] Fawn Brodie, in her biography of Joseph Smith, made an argument similar to that of Stark. She categorized Mormonism as a new religious movement.[7]

Other intellectuals and academics have answered the question of whether Mormonism is Christian with an unqualified no. For example, Catholic sociologist Thomas O'Dea, maintained that Mormonism was a new religion in the making.[8] Gentile historian Mario DePillis called Mormonism a new religion.[9] For Gentile historian John Brooke, Mormonism was a product of the extreme occult and hermetic fringe of the sixteenth-century Radical Reformation, a fringe that mixed Christian restorationist motifs with alchemical hermeticism, although, as Brooke admits, he cannot provide any empirical proof for his claim.[10] For non–Mormon religious studies scholar Catherine Albanese, Mormonism was an American sectarian religion whose novel doctrines made it distinct from Christianity.[11] For the Yale University cultural and literary Gentile critic Harold Bloom, Mormonism was the prototypical American religion. Mormonism, just like its major rival for dominance of the American religious scene for much of the twentieth century, the Southern Baptist Convention, and its other rivals in the American religious marketplace, among them Seventh Day Adventists and Jehovah's Witnesses (both the children of

Adventism), reflected, in its doctrines, a prototypically American emphasis on individualism.

For Bloom, Mormonism was a form of gnosticism with an American twist. Mormonism, in its theology, he argued, held that a part of the individual, namely human intelligence, preceded the divine. Somewhat like Frederick Jackson Turner before him, Bloom argued that Mormonism, like other prototypically "American religions" he explored in his book, universalized or generalized the American tradition of rugged individualism. This tradition, argued Bloom, may have originated in European intellectual culture, but it was actualized, in the frontier environment of nineteenth-century Western America. Bloom concluded that Mormon theology was the product of the interaction or intersection of Joseph Smith's extraordinary creativity and theological imagination with the cultural stuff of Smith's environment. It was Smith's creative prophetic imagination that distinguished the American religion Smith created from other forms of Christianity.[12]

Although intellectuals and academics differed on their answer to the question of whether Mormonism was "Christian," intellectuals such as Baird, Noll, Shipps, Bloom, Albanese, and Brooke did agree on one thing. They concurred that regardless of whether Mormonism was "Christian" or not, it was an "outsider" or "marginal" religion.[13] It would be through these two frames, outsiderness or otherness and marginality, that many psychologists, historians, and sociologists would view or perceive Mormonism.

Psychobiography, Psychology, and Mormonism

Although some social scientists asked the question of whether Mormonism was a form of Christianity, a query that seems more a theological or dogmatic issue than an empirical or historical one, others explored whether Mormonism was "the product of the psychological abnormalities of its founder and prophet, Joseph Smith." They saw Mormonism, in other words, as psychologically "other."

Historian and dissident Mormon Fawn Brodie, who received a master's from the University of Chicago and who taught at the University of California, Los Angeles, pioneered this approach in her psychobiography of Joseph Smith, *No Man Knows My History*, published in its first edition in 1945. In *No Knows My History* Brodie argued that Smith began his religious career as a manipulative megalomaniac but gradually he became convinced that he truly was a prophet communing with the divine. Over time, she asserted, Smith was increasingly unable to distinguish fantasy from reality. Brodie also claimed that Smith's sexual excesses which eventually gave rise to Mormon polygamy, underlay many of his actions, and played a central role in his eventual downfall.[14]

Brodie has not been the only academic to see Mormonism and Smith in rather negative psychological, psychiatric, and medical hues. A host of other Non-Mormon historians followed in Brodie's footsteps. For instance, historian Alice Felt Tyler saw the Mormon prophet as a con man. Historian Louis Kern interpreted the Mormon practice of "the Principle" of polygamy as Smith's personal response to the familial and sexual ambiguities of the early nineteenth century. Historian Charles Sellers portrayed Smith as a fraud and a trickster and speculated that Latter-day Saint theology, with its patriarchalism, was the product of a kind of "male panic" caused by economic dislocations in family structure brought about by the transformations wrought by the Erie Canal in upstate New York. Historian Lawrence Foster wondered whether Smith might have been a manic-depressive.[15]

Typologizing Mormonism

Trying to determine whether Mormonism was a variety of Christianity or whether it was the product of a diseased mind or flimflammery were not the only approaches twentieth-century social scientists took to Mormonism particularly in the post–World War II period. A number of sociologists of religion reacted to apologetic and polemical debates over "true" versus "false" Christianity, "orthodox" versus "heretical" Christianity, and approaches to social and cultural movements that saw religion as the product of psychopathology or sociopathology. Academic sociologists of religion expended a great deal of time and effort trying to construct an "objective" or "value-free" approach to religiously oriented social and cultural movements such as Mormonism.[16]

Historically speaking, the sociological attempt to construct a value free sociology of religion goes back to one of the totem figures of the discipline of sociology itself, Max Weber. Weber, in the sections of his *Economy and Society* dealing with the sociology of religion, used the term "sect" to denote a group that accepted only religiously qualified individuals into its membership.[17] Drawing on and expanding Weber's sociology of religion, German Protestant theologian and social ethicist Ernst Troeltsch distinguished between "sect," "church," and "mysticism." Troeltsch defined "church" as a conservative institution accommodated to the world and which was part of the social order, "sect" as an exclusive group that was in tension with the social order and that aspired to perfection and direct fellowship among its members, and "mysticism" as a radical movement uninterested in engaging the world and characterized by spontaneity, iconoclasm, and idealism.[18]

German Reformed theologian, historian, and social ethicist H. Richard Niebuhr added "denomination" into the smorgasbord of religious group typology mix, defining it as an institution which had accommodated to the world and which was powerful enough to dominate its social order context if it so chose.[19] Finally, sociologist Howard Becker, who taught for years at the University of Wisconsin in Madison, added the term "cult" to the typological mix. Becker defined "cult" as a loose association of persons characterized by a private and eclectic religiosity.[20]

However, as is so often the case in academia, increasing definitional specificity combined with a measure of "objectivity" was hardly the end of the debate about what "church," "sect," and "cult" meant. In fact, despite the good intentions behind the attempts to achieve definitional specificity and "objectivity," both seem to have exacerbated the very problems the typologisation of religious oriented social groups sought to quiet. Additionally, the cult explosion in the 1960s and 1970s and the cult moral panic that followed in the 1970s and 1980s, led to further debate among sociologists of religion as to just what "church," "denomination," "sect," and "cult," and, in particular the term "cult," meant.

The most influential recent attempt to bring clarity to what "church," "denomination," "sect," and "cult," meant has been that of the prolific Gentile sociologists Rodney Stark and William Sims Bainbridge. Writing in the 1970s and 1980s Stark, who taught sociology for years at the University of Washington and who taught most recently at Baylor University in Waco, Texas, and trained Bainbridge, argued that "churches" were organizations that dominated society (e.g., Lutheranism in mediaeval Sweden), "denominations" were organizations which accommodated to society (e.g., Methodism in the United States), "sects" were schisms within "churches" or "denominations" that attempted to purify the movements out of which they emerged and hoped to restore to their "original" form (e.g., Conservative Mennonites in the United States), and "cults" were either new religious movements (e.g., Mormonism in the United States) or transplanted religious groups or movements (e.g., American forms of Hinduism and Buddhism) that were, to some extent, in tense relationship with the broader social, cultural, and religious environments of their new milieus. Stark and Bainbridge went on to delineate three types of "cults": "audience cults," which were diffuse and little organized (e.g., "New Age Movements" such as astrology), "client cults," which were largely therapeutic and magical (e.g., est), and "cult movements," which consisted of full-fledged organizations that were evangelical or missionary oriented in nature (e.g., the Unification Church and Mormonism).[21]

Stark and Bainbridge's attempt to end debate over the meaning of "church," "denomination," "sect," and "cult," was, at least for a time, remarkably successful. However, as times changed so did the "church," "denomination," "sect," and "cult" typology. In an attempt to update the typology for a postmodernist text-centered age, Jan Shipps, writing in a postmodernist era, offered a narrative or story centered conception of all four. For Shipps, a "church" was an institution that assumed direct responsibility for a traditional story, keeping it alive and transmitting it from generation to generation through ritual and liturgy. A "denomination," she asserted, was a subset of a "church." It was, she wrote, an institution that told its own stories but recognized that other "denominations" told their own different stories. A "sect," Shipps defined, as a group with a charismatic leader that found itself in disagreement the leaders of a "church" or a "denomination" and its ritual, liturgy, and tradition. A "cult," she maintained, was a group with a charismatic leader that challenged the stories of churches or denominations.[22]

Of course, not every scholar of religion, has been enamored of the "church," "denomination," "sect," and "cult," typology. For instance, Gentile religious studies scholar Linda Woodhead, who teaches sociology at Lancaster University, offered an alternative typology of Christian social and cultural movements. Woodhead argued that several different broader forms of Christianity with varying conceptions of authority arose and, over the course of Christian history, took institutional form. Woodhead delineated three types or forms of Christianity: Church Christianity, Biblical Christianity, and Mystical Christianity. Church Christianity, she argued, which developed after the fourth century CE and included the Roman Catholicism and Eastern Orthodoxy traditions, attributed the highest authority on earth to the church, its rituals, traditions, priests, and sacraments. Biblical Christianity, which arose during the Reformation and included the Lutheran, Presbyterian, Congregational, and Anglican communions, attributed the highest authority on earth to the Bible. Mystical Christianity, which arose in its Christian form in the second century CE, included Christian monastic communities, Meister Eckhart, the Munster Anabaptists, the Schwenkfelders, Pietists, and the Quakers, attributed the highest authority on earth to the mystical union with God or Christ.

The Book of Numbers

There was and is, of course, another way religion in general and Mormonism in particular could, or so some intellectuals and academics believed, be made "objective" and "scientific." They could be studied as "insider" or "outsider" forms of religion and turned into objects of quantitative statistical analysis. Statistical analysis, with its means, medians, and modes, became increasingly important in sociology in the 1930s and became dominant in the discipline by the 1950s. Quantitative approaches to the stuff of society and the stuff of religious groups have remained, ever since, at the heart of postgraduate training in sociology and in the practice of sociology.

As sociology in general was becoming more "scientific," so was the quantitative analysis of religion. The 1930s saw the founding of research departments within religious denominations and the growth of social science departments not only in secular colleges and universities but also in religious colleges and universities. Religious bodies, not surprisingly, initially played a central role in the rise of professional sociological organizations with an interest in the study of religion. For instance, the American Catholic Sociological Society (CSA), later the Association for the Sociology of Religion (ASR), was founded in 1938 by scholars affiliated with Catholic institutions of higher learning in the United States. The Society for the Scientific Study of Religion (SSSR) was established in 1949. The Religious Research Fellowship, later the Religious Research Association (RRA), which was founded in 1951, had ties to the American Protestant Federal Council of Churches. The RRA's membership was initially made up of scholars employed by the research divisions of America's "mainstream" denominations.

The sociological subdiscipline of the sociology of religion also grew dramatically from the 1960s onward. Between 1960 and 1962 the membership of the SSSR grew from 200 to 800. By 1973, when the SSSR became an international organization, its membership was 1,468. This growth eventually led to the founding of the Section on Religion within the American Sociological Association, the national organization of and for American sociologists, in 1994.[23]

The 1940s, 1950s, and 1960s also saw the rise and growth of professional sociology of religion journals. The CSA's *American Catholic Sociological Review* later renamed *Sociological Analysis*, and *Sociology of Religion*, were founded in 1940. The RRA's *Review of Religious Research* was established in 1959. The SSSR's *Journal for the Scientific Study of Religion* was first published in 1961. Over time, the last two academic and professional journals became important venues not only for the dissemination of quantitative work on religious groups in general but also for quantitative oriented studies of Mormonism.

Despite the religious origins of the CSA and the RRA, members of both organizations were almost more scientific in orientation than their secular counterparts in the sociology of religion. Most were trained in quantitative research methods and most did their graduate work at the leading research universities in the United States. Virtually all of them sanctified scientific research methods and virtually all of them were obsessed with obtaining unbiased results from their study of religion.

The professionalization and expansion of the social scientific study of religion arose out of some of the same forces that were impacting post–World War II Western and American intellectual culture in general and academic culture at large: professionalization, the rise and growth of the "cult" of the expert, the expansion of universities and university positions particularly after World War II, increases in the number of young people matriculating at universities and pursuing graduate degrees, and the rising prestige of science. The social scientific study of Mormonism arose, initially in less bureaucratic form, out of the same forces that were sweeping across America and the core nation Western world, and in American and Western higher education.[24] One of, if not the key figure in the rise of the social scientific study of Mormonism, was Harold T. Christensen. Christensen, who received the very first master's degree in sociology awarded by the Latter-day Saint owned Brigham Young University (BYU, the Y) in 1937, received a Ph.D. in rural sociology at the University of Wisconsin in Madison in 1941. Throughout his long academic career at Purdue University, Christensen published a number of articles on the sociology of religion and on the sociology of Mormonism. In the 1930s, while a student and faculty member at BYU and a student at Wisconsin, Christensen, began to collect data on Mormonism. He eventually published his findings on Mormon marriage and fertility rates in one the most prestigious journals in the American sociological community, the *American Journal of Sociology*.[25]

By the 1950s, more and more sociologists and cultural anthropologists, many of them Mormons themselves, began focusing on the study of Mormonism. Throughout the 1950s, Mormon sociologist Glenn Vernon, who received his Ph.D. at Washington State University in 1953 and who taught courses in Mormon Studies at the University of Utah (the U) beginning in 1972, published a number of articles that included samples of Mormons. In the 1950s, noted non–Mormon cultural anthropologist Clyde Kluckhohn, a faculty member in Harvard's famous or infamous, depending on your point of view, interdisciplinary Department of Social Relations, led a group of social scientists to rural New Mexico to study the values of the five cultures in the region around the Mormon village of Ramah. The book that emerged from this ethnographic research, Evon Vogt and Ethel Albert's *The People of Rimrock*, explored Mormon, Zuni, Texas, homesteader, and Spanish American cultures, in and around Rimrock, the fictitious name Kluckhohn and his colleagues, following a social scientific tradition that went back at least to Robert and Helen Lynd's 1929 study of Middletown, the fictitious name the Lynd's gave to Muncie, Indiana. In the area around Ramah, Kluckhohn and his colleagues found that despite the similarities of geography and climate there were significant differences in the ways of life in each of the five cultures they studied. In the decades that followed this assertion of Mormon cultural distinctiveness in the Rimrock study, would become a hallmark and the bedrock of much subsequent Mormon social science.[26]

One of the researchers on the Rimrock Five Cultures project, the Harvard trained Catholic sociologist, Thomas O'Dea, continued to focus on social institutions and values in his 1957 book *The Mormons*. Writing at a time in which secularism had become a hot topic within the discipline of sociology and within the subdiscipline of the sociology of religion, O'Dea argued that social strains or contradictions set in motion by secularism and its impact on Mormon life, and, in particular, on Mormon intellectual culture, were causing strains or tensions within late 1950s Mormon culture including Mormon intellectual culture. The process of secularization, he argued, increased contradictions within Mormon culture, contradictions between rationality versus charisma, authority and obedience versus democracy and individualism, consent versus coercion, plural marriage and change of doctrine versus cultural stability, family ideals versus equality of women, progress versus agrarianism, political conservatism versus social idealism, patriotism versus particularism, and belief versus environment.[27]

It was in the 1960s, and particularly in the 1970s, that the social scientific study of religion in general and Mormonism in particular really began to take off. Beginning in the 1960s an increasing number of Mormons undertook graduate work in sociology and, to a lesser extent, cultural anthropology, all across the United States and Canada. In a sign of the times, the 1970s saw the founding of what would become the central professional organization for the social scientific study of Mormonism, the Society for the Sociological Study of Mormon Life (SSSML). The SSSML emerged, informally at first, out of the meetings of those interested in Mormon Studies at the Pacific Sociological Association (PSA). In 1978, at a meeting of the American Sociological Association (ASA) in San Francisco, University of Utah sociologist Glenn Vernon and others interested in Mormon Studies established the organization that would eventually become the SSSML and provisional officers of the organization were selected. In 1979, the constitution of the SSSML was adopted at the meeting of the Pacific Sociological Association in Anaheim, California. Since 1989 the SSSML has met during the annual meeting of the Society for the Sociological Study of Religion (SSSR) and the Religious Research Association (RRA). In 1995, the SSSML changed its name to the Mormon Social Science Association (MSSA).[28]

Thanks, in part, to the professionalization of Mormon Studies and the increasing numbers of Mormons taking doctorates in sociology, the

Department of Sociology at Brigham Young University became home to a number of statistically sophisticated sociologists studying various aspects of contemporary Mormon life. BYU's quantitative sociologists studied a number of social aspects of Mormon life and found numerous social and demographic variations between Mormons and non–Mormons. For example, Harold Christensen's work on adolescent sexual behavior in Utah, Indiana, and Denmark, led him to conclude that the much lower rates of premarital sex among Mormons were the product of the LDS cultural emphasis on chastity before marriage. Mormon sociologist Tim Heaton, who received his Ph.D. from the University of Wisconsin in Madison, working alone or sometimes in tandem, found, in research carried out in the 1980s, 1990s, and 2000s, that Mormons continued to exhibit more conservative sexual behaviors prior to marriage than the average American, divorce less than the average American, were more pro-marriage than Americans in general, had families which were larger than the American national average, and were characterized by a gender division of labor that was more patriarchal than that of the average American. Heaton's research also revealed differences within the Mormon community between Mormons married in temples and Mormons married outside of temples, and between Mormons living in the North American Mormon culture region of Utah, southern Idaho, and parts of Arizona, and parts of Alberta, where Church influence is strongest, compared to Mormons residing outside of the Mormon culture region. Heaton and his colleagues found that within the Mormon community divorce rates were lower and family size rates were higher for those married in temples than for Mormons not married in temples and that Mormon religiosity and marriage rates were higher for Mormons living in Utah than outside of Utah.[29] Mormon sociologist Stan Albrecht found a positive relationship between education and Mormon religiosity that contrasted with American national patterns where higher levels of education generally resulted in decreased religiosity.[30] Both Heaton and Albrecht argued that these variations could be attributed to the differences between Mormon culture and non–Mormon culture.[31]

Social Scientific Approaches to Mormonism and their Discontents

Chapter One explored how Christian conceptions of "otherness" structured perceptions of Mormonism and Mormons. Chapter Two has explored how academics, under the impact of the scientific revolution and its mania for classification, tried, after the 1930s and particularly in the post–World War II period, to escape the prison house of apologetics, polemics, and

Mormon "otherness" in which many nineteenth-century and even some twentieth-century critics of Mormonism were trapped. But did these new approaches allow intellectuals and academics interested in religion and in Mormonism to escape from the iron cage of apologetics and polemics?

Etic or outsider attempts to define what is "Christian" and what is not, inevitably wade into theological and apologetic and polemical waters. My own position on this issue is that any reasonable and dispassionate approach to what constitutes Christianity must get beyond the cultural and ideological, must get beyond the notion that Christianity can be grounded in any particular "orthodox" theological or doctrinal formulation. I would argue that Christianity can only be defined on the basis of emic or insider criteria. In this formulation, Christianity is what self-proclaimed Christians say it is. In this formulation Mormonism is a form of Christianity since most Mormons view themselves as Christians. I would, by the way, take the same approach to defining any other social or ideological movement.

Thanks to their inherent distinction between "normal" and "abnormal" forms of religion, the psychological and psychobiographical approaches to the life and work of Joseph Smith are also deeply problematic. In the end, Brodie's, Tyler's, Kern's, and Sellers's portraits of Smith seem more caricature and stereotype than flesh and blood historical analysis. In the final analysis, they seem less grounded in empirical evidence than in nineteenth-century anti–Mormon polemics and apologetics. Foster, in fact, essentially admitted to this when he noted that his claim that Smith may have been a manic-depressive is, empirically speaking, tenuous. What little documentary evidence he found to back up this conclusion comes, as Foster admits, primarily from anti–Mormon texts. Given the ideological nature of these texts, which are in some respects akin to Soviet portrayals of dissidents in the 1950s and after, such a conclusion is more than tenuous.

By assuming that Mormon religious experiences were patently ludicrous and that the Mormon Prophet was a neurotic, a calculating fraud and swindler, or a manic-depressive, Brodie, Tyler, Kern, and Sellers are unable to approach Joseph Smith and Mormon origins with even a measure of dispassionate sympathy, empathy, and neutrality. As a result, they fail to grasp the deeply held cultural motivations of those early Mormons who believed that Smith was God's prophet and that he was receiving revelations. Additionally, even if we assume that the country "bumpkins" who became Mormons were hoodwinked by a master swindler and his partners in crime, one still needs to describe how this massive con game worked and how it ultimately succeeded. Far too often, those who make such claims do not and probably cannot do so.

There have been, of course, and there are alternatives to the "normal" versus "abnormal" psychological approaches to religious origins. For example, Robert Anderson's approach to the history of early Mormonism, with its developmental emphasis and its contention that one can discern in the Book of Mormon the various egos and alter egos that Smith knowingly and unknowingly wrote into it, would, on the surface, seem resistant to many of the criticisms leveled at other psychological and psychohistorical approaches to Mormonism since it avoids the discourse of sociopathology that too often characterizes scholarly attempts to deconstruct Mormon mass psychology. However, Anderson's analysis raises the same questions that more problematic psychohistories raise, namely that of the use of sources. The only evidence Anderson offers in support of his thesis, and the psychological assumptions that underlie it, is the very text he claimed was the product of Smith's mind, the Book of Mormon. As a result, one invariably wonders whether the reconstructed mind of Joseph Smith is more Anderson than Joseph Smith. Beyond the problem of sources Anderson's approach also raises the issue of the role broader societal, cultural, and historical forces and contexts play in the construction of individual minds. Mormonism, after all, was a social and cultural movement and the Book of Mormon may reveal more about the social and cultural context in which it took form more than it does about the inner life and psychological projections of Joseph Smith.[32]

The attempt to typologize Mormonism has been and is no more successful at escaping the iron cage of apologetics and polemics. Several intellectuals and academics have noted and continue to note that the very concepts of "church," "denomination," "sect," and "cult," are inherently ambiguous and fluid. To take one example, Mormonism, as Stark and Bainbridge recognize, is a "church" in the Mormon culture region because it dominates the social and cultural landscape of that region, a "denomination" in Missouri, where the Reorganized Church of Jesus Christ of Latter Day Saints (now the Community of Christ) formed and institutionalized, a "cult" in the minds of many nineteenth-century and contemporary mainstream American Christians, and a "sect" when we are speaking of the many American fundamentalist Mormon groups trying to restore what they see as the original pure Mormonism of "the Principle" in the Mormon culture region and beyond. In his *Religious History of the American People*, noted Gentile religious historian Sydney Ahlstrom was so confused by Mormonism that he admitted that he thought the Mormon faith could rightly be labeled a people, a nation, a subculture, a denomination, a church, a sect, a mystery cult, and a new religion, all at the same time.[33]

Although Woodhead's typology seems to get us beyond these problems—it is sensitive to history, to variations within Christian culture without privileging any, and to relationships between varieties of Christianity and worldly powers—it does not entirely escape the prison house of normative conceptualization since many readers will simply assume that one variety of Christianity is superior to the others. Nor does Woodhead's typology solve the problem of Mormonism. Is Mormonism a variety of Church Christianity? Is it a variety of Biblical Christianity? Is it a variety of Mystical Christianity? Is it a variety of Christianity at all? Is it all, some, or most of these at the same time? Finally, there is the issue of how historically and sociologically generalizable Woodhead's typology is beyond Christianity[34]

Other social scientists have argued that the "church," "denomination," "sect," and "cult," typology is problematic in and of itself because it is ahistorical. For instance, sociologist James Beckford, argued that the "church," "denomination," "sect," and "cult," typology has turned religion into something singularly different from other similar organizational forms. Beckford instead urged analysts to view religion as just another organizational type and analyze it as such.[35] Sociologist Roy Wallis asserted that cults should be viewed in historical terms when he suggested that all "cults" were and are proto religions. All religions, he claimed, originated as cults. Over time they routinized and bureaucratized, becoming, in the process, churches (Roman and Orthodox Christianity in Europe), denominations (Methodists), or established sects (the Mennonite Church). Wallis went on to distinguish three types of new religious movements: world affirming, world rejecting, and world accommodating.[36]

It is also worth noting that the "church," "denomination," "sect," and "cult," typology remains undergirded, to a great extent, by the very notions of "orthodox" and "unorthodox" sociologists hoped to escape. Whether sociologists intended this or not the categories of "church" and "denomination," contains groups that most see as "orthodox" or "mainstream," while the categories of "sect" and, in particular "cult" remain categories that most see as "unorthodox" or "marginal." Sociological typologies, in other words, have not, even at their best, entirely escaped the iron cage of ideological categorization.

It is, of course, possible to delineate "mainstream" and "marginal" religions statistically as quantitative sociologists of religion and Mormonism have tried to do. It is possible, in other words, to construct a notion of normal (means, modes, medians) and deviant (outliers) from statistical data on the basis of the numbers alone. There are, for example, more Methodists than Anabaptists, so the former is, by definition, more mainstream than the latter. However, the problem of Mormonism still remains. Mormonism may have started small, but Mormons now outnumber Methodists. Have Mormons, one has to ask, moved from "marginal" status to "mainstream" status or from "cult" to "denomination" status over the last one hundred years or so simply because of demographic growth? Not everyone would want to dismiss cultural variations so easily. Additionally, we must recognize that when we approach religious movements quantitatively, we are universalizing or fetishizing numbers and thereby eliding the fact that regardless of the numbers "mainstream" and "marginal" are social and cultural constructs. We must thus explore the social and cultural construction of both the notion of "mainstream" and that of the "marginal" over time and across space. A social and cultural constructionist approach such as this, of course, inevitably and invariably raises the same questions that a critique of structural functionalist approaches to new religious movements raises, namely, how do we construct our conceptions of what is "normal" and what is not?

In the final analysis notions of "mainstream" and "marginal" are both historically and contemporarily, not only about numbers but also often about power. "Mainstream" religions have often been tied to and provided the ideological justifications for the political and economic powers that be. Statistical notions of mainstream and marginal thus often do not escape the world of power politics, a world that is just as constructed as any other aspect of human life. All of this should make us reflect on the social and cultural construction of intellectual and academic categorizations and ask whether it would perhaps be better to eliminate the "mainstream" versus "marginal" approach entirely and simply look at social and groups such as Mormonism and study them just as we would any other social and cultural movements and groups.[37]

Finally, questions about the validity of the conclusions of much of Mormon quantitative analysis, that Mormons were culturally distinctive from other religious groups and from most Americans on a number of different indicators, can and have been raised. Even quantitatively oriented Mormon sociologists have been questioning the conclusions of their predecessors and even themselves. For instance, Tim Heaton increasingly urged quantitatively oriented Mormon sociologists to compare Mormons to similar groups with similarly committed members. Given this admission, one cannot help but wonder whether the supposed Mormon quantitative distinctiveness would look so exceptional when compared with data on similarly committed Christian groups with ethnic like identities such as the Anabaptists (Amish, Mennonites, Church of the Brethren, River Brethren), who likewise emphasize large families, chastity, marriage, not divorcing, and church attendance as godly. One cannot help but wonder whether ideologies of Mormon distinctiveness are impacting Mormon quantitative analyses.[38]

Conclusion: The Iron Cage of Classification?

If definitional, psychological-medical, typological, and quantitative approaches did not enable intellectuals and academics to move beyond normative responses to controversial religious movements entirely, can the social sciences reach the "objective" nirvana that was, for the most part, their goal from the late nineteenth century and beyond? In the remaining chapters of this book, I want to explore whether historical and social theoretical approaches to social and cultural movements and social groups that emphasize economic, political, demographic, geographic, and cultural causal factors can do what definitional, psychological-medical, typological, and quantitative theories of religion could not and cannot, namely, help us escape from the iron cage of apologetics and polemics?

Three

The "Old" Mormon Studies

Introduction

As we saw in Chapter One, the polemics and apologetics associated with Mormonism is as old as Mormonism itself. For critics of Mormonism, the history of the Church is a tale of fraud, chicanery, confidence men, human gullibility, and strange visions. Polemicists critical of Mormonism believed and maintained that Mormon origins, in particular the origins of the Book of Mormon and the claim that the Church was receiving continuous revelations from God, were, at the heart of this fraud. For faithful Mormons, on the other hand, the story of the Latter-day Saints was and is the story of God acting in history. For them, Church history was the epic tale of how God chose an uneducated young man as his prophet in order to restore his one true Church to an earth that was desperately in need of it.

As we saw in Chapter Two, one approach to Mormonism has been a typological approach that views Mormonism through the lens of Christian and social science categories of "usness" and "themness," an approach somewhat similar to, but at the same time somewhat different from, the polemical and apologetic approach to Mormonism. Despite the rise of ostensibly "objective" and "scientific" typological approaches to religion and religious groups, intellectuals and academics have not entirely, if at all, succeeded in escaping from the prison house of ideologically grounded perceptions or readings of Mormonism because these approaches encased Mormonism, to a large extent, in what might be called a Petri dish of "otherness."

In this and in the several chapters that follow I want to focus on what might, in retrospect, be called the "old" Mormon history studies and on the "new" Mormon history studies. Both the old Mormon history and the new ran somewhat parallel to the apologetic and polemical approach and the various typological approaches that dominated much sociological thinking about religion and religious oriented groups.

The Old Mormon Faith History

The earliest examples of what might be called the old Mormon faith history writing by faithful Mormons was more akin to the historical chronicles of Ancient Israel contained in the historically oriented books of the Tanakh (for example, the books of "Kings" and "Chronicles"), than to the polemics and apologetics and amateur history writing characteristic of nineteenth-century America. This was intentional. Mormons saw themselves as the new Israel.[1] History, so God told his believing restored Church through periodic revelations, was important to him. The Saints believed that God, in "revelations" received by Mormon prophet Joseph Smith, told the faithful that "a record" should be "kept" of the restoration of his Church.[2] So, when God commanded that his Church establish the Office of Church Historian and Recorder in 1830,[3] John Whitmer was "called" or appointed first Church Historian in 1831.[4]

Latter-day Saint newspapers served as a medium for the dissemination of the message Mormon chroniclers wanted to tell the faithful about the history of what might be called, in retrospect, primitive Mormonism, the era from the birth of the Church to the death of Joseph Smith. *The Latter-Day Saints Messenger and Advocate*, for example, published Second Elder Oliver Cowdery's eight letters on church history between 1834 and 1835. In them Cowdery discussed various aspects of early Mormon history including the visitation of the Angel Moroni to the Mormon prophet, the revivals that impacted Joseph Smith, the history, particularly the religious history, of the Smith family, and the coming forth of the Book of Mormon.[5]

In 1840 Church Apostle Orson Pratt published his historically oriented *Interesting Account of Several Remarkable Visions, And of the Late Discovery of Ancient American Records*. Pratt's "interesting account" focused on the discovery of the "gold plates" that became the Book of Mormon, the translation of the Book of Mormon, and the formal organization the Church of Jesus Christ of Latter-day Saints.[6]

In 1838, while in the Liberty County, Missouri, jail, Joseph Smith[7] appointed a travelling committee to gather materials related to Church history. In 1839 Smith, and his clerk, James Mulholland, began the "Joseph Smith History" while in Commerce, Illinois (later Nauvoo). Over the next six years twenty-four scribes gathered materials for the "History." At the time of Smith's death in 1841, the "History" had reached 5 August 1838.

According to Howard Coray, one of those who served as Smith's clerk and who helped compile the "Joseph Smith History," the "History" consisted of various materials that were collected and put in chronological order. These materials were then combined with other materials and amplified with even more materials collected from other sources. This material, in turn, was then transposed into Smith's voice even after Smith's death in Carthage, Illinois.[8]

The "Joseph Smith History" was first published in installments in the LDS newspaper *Times and Seasons* between 1842 and 1844. During the Mormon trek to the West, publication of the "History" was disrupted. It was not until the 1850s, once Mormons had settled in their Great Basin Kingdom in what would eventually become the state of Utah, that the publication of the "History" resumed, this time in installments in the Church owned newspaper *The Deseret News* and, in the LDS British newspaper the *Latter-Day Saints Millennial Star*.[9]

In the late nineteenth-century George Q. Cannon, a member of the First Presidency, was authorized by Mormon leaders to prepare the "Joseph Smith History" for publication in book form. When Cannon died, B.H. Roberts, a member of the Quorum of the Seventies, a body second only to the Twelve Apostles in power and authority, took over editorial duties on the "History." Working on the project between 1902 and 1912 Roberts made "corrections" to the manuscript of the "History," deleted items from it, and made emendations to it. The first volume of the *History of the Church of Jesus Christ of Latter-day Saints* was published in 1902. The last volume, volume seven, was published in 1932.[10]

The year of 1922 saw the publication of Joseph Fielding Smith's one-volume *Essentials in Church History*. Smith served as Church Historian from 1921 to 1970 (and later briefly as the tenth president of the Church) and his *Essentials* therefore had the unofficial imprimatur of Church leaders. *Essentials* took a less critical and more faith historical approach to Church history and emphasized the role that God had played in the history of the Church from its beginnings to the 1920s. Since its publication, *Essentials* has been so popular with Mormon readers that it went through some twenty-eight reissues alone during the middle decades of the twentieth century. It is still widely available, particularly in the Mormon culture region, and is still widely read by Church members even today.[11]

Early Approaches to Mormon History

Early Mormon writing on Church history was, by and large, and not surprisingly, partisan and grounded in the apologetic belief that the church Joseph Smith founded was the church God restored. As a result, Church history was, for most Mormons, sacred since the history of God's Church was also the history of God's actions within that history. As a result, many early Mormon histories are, in many ways, an inverse mirror image of the equally doctrinally and theologically grounded "anti–Mormon" literature we explored in Chapter One and a mirror image of many of the nineteenth and early twentieth-century denominational histories written by believing Methodists, Presbyterians, Mennonites, and other denominational historians in the early and middle parts of the twentieth century. The difference, of course, was that what was sacred for Mormons was profane for its polemical critics and what was profane for Mormons was sacred to its polemical critics.

There has been and there continues to be, a much less apologetic and polemical approach to Mormonism. This historical approach to Mormonism, like the polemical and apologetic approach to Mormonism, is as old as Mormonism itself. For non–Mormon Ralph Waldo Emerson, the famous American essayist, philosopher, and Transcendentalist, Mormonism was an "after clap of Puritanism," a form of revived Puritanism. For non–Mormon Alexander Campbell, the founder of the Restorationist group that eventually became the Disciples of Christ and the Churches of Christ, Mormonism was a response to nineteenth-century religious and theological pluralism. The Book of Mormon, claimed Campbell, was written by Mormon prophet Joseph Smith to provide authoritative answers to every theological dispute current in early nineteenth-century America including infant baptism, regeneration, repentance, and the fall of man.[12] To non–Mormon British journalist and poet Charles Mackay, author of the still popular *Memoir of Extraordinarily Popular Delusions and the Madness of Crowds* (1841), Mormonism was, like Roman Catholicism and Anglicanism, a brand of theocratic Christianity.[13] For non–Mormon amateur historian H.H. Bancroft, Mormonism was a product of its American and Atlantic contexts.

Establishing, to some extent, the shape of more professional histories to come, the prolific Bancroft, who wrote histories on a number of American states over the course of his life, utilized LDS Church records along with government documents to write what he called a "fact-based" history of Utah. A quarter of Bancroft's history of the territory and state was devoted to the history of Mormonism and it, somewhat novelly, treated the Saints in a relatively favorable light. Critics at the time and ever since have suggested that Bancroft's favorable treatment of Mormonism was the price he paid for access to Church records. The fact that Bancroft allowed Church Authorities to read the finished product before publication added fuel to the critical fire that Bancroft had sacrificed objectivity on the altar of primary source material.[14] Bancroft's work in general and particularly his assertions that Mormonism was a product of its American and Atlantic environments and that history should be grounded in primary source materials, would, nevertheless, become central components of historical analysis in general and the study of Mormonism in particular in the twentieth century.

In the early twentieth century, a different kind of Mormon Studies began to emerge within the Mormon intellectual community. Church Authority B.H. Roberts would be at the vanguard of this history writing revolution within Mormon intellectual culture. Between July 1909 and July 1915 Roberts published a series of forty-two articles on Church history in *Americana* magazine under the collective title "The History of the Mormon Church." Roberts's articles were a response to a number of articles published in the *American Historical Magazine*, as *Americana* was previously called, that claimed that the Book of Mormon was an adaptation by Mormon leader Sidney Rigdon of Solomon Spaulding's unpublished romance about a group of Romans who, while sailing to England, were blown off course and ended up landing on the eastern coast of North America in the fourth century CE. In the Church centenary year of 1930, Church leaders authorized publication of Roberts's expansion of these essays. When published, this six-volume work, titled the *Comprehensive History of the Church*, became the first somewhat "official" history of the Church.

The *Comprehensive History of the Church* chronicled, sometimes for the first time and in detail, incidents from Mormon history from its origins to the early twentieth century. It was grounded in primary source material and it explored a number of controversial episodes in Mormon history, including, for the first time in a semi-official publication of the Church, the infamous Mountain Meadows Massacre in 1857, a series of attacks by the Saints on the Baker–Fancher emigrant wagon train at Mountain Meadows in southern Utah that ended with the death of all of the members of the wagon trains save for around seventeen children under the age of seven in 1857.[15] Arguably, Roberts's *Comprehensive History* marks the beginning of a more critical approach to Mormon history and to Mormon Studies within Mormonism and within official Mormon culture.

While one can find polemical elements in the writings of Emerson, Campbell, McKay, Bancroft, and Roberts, they, nevertheless, strove, somewhat successfully, to offer, dispassionate and descriptive analyses and interpretations of various aspects of Mormon history, particularly when compared to the polemical works that came before them. Beginning in the early and middle twentieth-century attempts at a dispassionate and descriptive analysis of Mormon history would become even more common.

The Rise of Academic Mormon Studies

More than anything else it was the advent of professional history programs and organizations in the late nineteenth and early twentieth centuries and the expansion of higher education and the expansion of history programs within academia, that transformed intellectual culture in general and Mormon Studies in particular throughout the United States and throughout the Western world. Many historians and social scientists, Mormon and non-Mormon, have not been content to take a polemical approach aimed at combating Mormonism or an apologetic approach that asserted that those who became Mormons did so because they believed Smith was the prophet of God's restoration and that the Book of Mormon was proof that God had intervened in human history. Drawing on a host of theoretical perspectives that have their origins in mid-nineteenth-century Europe, American intellectuals and academics, particularly in the early twentieth century, have attributed the rise of Mormonism instead to a variety of what Mormon faith-oriented historians would call "secular" forces, specifically economic forces, political forces, demographic forces, geographic forces, and cultural forces. They attributed the dynamics of history, in other words, to deep structural forces that required that historians look and dig beneath the surface, in a kind of intellectual and scholarly archaeology of human life and action, in order to ascertain the real underlying causal forces that were driving human history.

The rise of new academic disciplines and the transformation of the academic world, would, slowly but surely, impact Mormon Studies as well. Throughout the early and middle twentieth century, at a time when the economic, political, and cultural isolation of Mormons and Utah was decreasing and Mormondom was being increasingly impacted by the same economic, political, cultural, and demographic forces that were impacting America and the Western world at large, a "professional" Mormon Studies began to emerge, if, initially, in fits and starts.[16]

In the early part of the twentieth century, a more scholarly and dispassionate version of Mormon Studies appeared. Richard Ely was among the first of these professional scholars of Mormonism. Ely followed a path many American academics took in the late nineteenth and early twentieth centuries. He took a higher degree in Germany. Ely was an Episcopalian, a social gospel advocate, a progressive, and a prominent figure in the development of the American Economic Association, the professional organization of America's academic economists. He studied with Gustav Schmoller at the University of Heidelberg, the same university at which Robert Park, co-founder, along with Ernest Burgess of the influential Chicago School of Sociology, studied. Schmoller, an important figure in the German historical school of economics, emphasized the need for a historical understanding of economics. In his 1903 "Economic Aspects of Mormonism," Ely tried to provide an historical understanding of Mormon economics. His article, which was published in the popular *Harper's* magazine, looked at Mormon irrigation practices, Mormon communalism, and the Mormon command economy across time. The essay simultaneously reflected the advocacy aspects of American and global Progressivism in that it praised Mormon irrigation practices, Mormon communalism, and the Mormon command economy, seeing them all as models for a Progressive economics and Progressive economic development.[17]

Another student of Mormon Studies who followed an arc that many young American academics followed in the late nineteenth and early twentieth century was Mormon Ephraim Edward Ericksen. Ericksen received his degree from one of America's new German-influenced graduate schools in the 1920s, the University of Chicago. Ericksen's 1922 dissertation, "The Psychological and Ethical Aspects of Mormonism," was influenced by functionalist theory, with its claim that societies tended toward equilibrium, and the work of several University of Chicago professors including the social interactionist pragmatism of sociologist, social psychologist, and philosopher George Herbert Mead, the pragmatic philosophy of Edward Scribner Ames, and the human behavior centered sociology of Robert Park. In his dissertation Eriksen argued that Mormonism was a functional response to the crises of the early nineteenth century, including the Mormon-Gentile conflicts of 1830–1844, Mormon interaction with the harsh environment of their Great Basin Kingdom from 1850 to 1900, and the impact of modernity on the Saints.

Ericksen's dissertation focused not only on Mormonism but also on Joseph Smith. For Ericksen it was not only Mormonism that was a functional product of nineteenth-century tensions, environmental adaptation, and social change; the Mormon prophet too, he argued, was "highly sensitive" to the impulses of his religious flock and, as a result of this sympathy and empathy, became their creator, their Mormon prophet, the individual who helped them adapt to the changing realities of nineteenth-century Western America.[18] Like Ely's work, Ericksen's more objective approach to Mormonism was also grounded in normative values and ideology. For Ericksen, the Mormonism of his time was in the process of being transformed from a "socialistic" to an "individualistic" religion and he was pessimistic about what this meant not only for the Mormonism of his time, but also for the Mormonism of the future.

Another important figure in the early years of the Old Mormon Studies, was Mormon Lowry Nelson. In the 1920s Nelson received his Ph.D. from the University of Wisconsin, one of the centers of American Progressivism thanks to its integration of scientific analysis and political advocacy and reform. Early on in his career Nelson spent most of his professional life working on the advocacy side of the progressivist ledger. From 1919 to 1937 he worked to promote scientific agriculture as an agriculture agent, a field agriculturalist, an editor, an employee of the BYU Extension Division, dean of BYU's College of Applied Science, and director of the Utah Agriculture Experiment station. During the Great Depression he worked for the New Deal Relief Administration serving as regional advisor to the Federal Emergency Relief Administration and director of the Resettlement Administration. Like many other Progressives, Nelson also had an academic side. Throughout the 1920s he wrote a series of articles on the Mormon village claiming that Mormon villages retained the more traditional European village form that promoted homogeneity, unity, and sociability rather than individualism. He contended that the Mormon village was "a social construction" that made Mormon religious devotion and group solidarity a concrete reality and allowed for the successful Latter-day Saint colonization of the Great Basin Desert. In 1937, as a result of developing tensions between himself and LDS leaders, Nelson left Utah behind and took up a position in the Sociology Department at the University of Minnesota.[19]

Still another important figure in the rise of the old Mormon history was Sociologist Nels Anderson. Like Ericksen, Anderson studied at what was then the leading center of American sociology, the Sociology Department of the University of Chicago. Like his Gentile mentors Robert Park and Ernest Burgess, Anderson engaged in ethnography. Ethnography had not yet come between sociology and social and cultural anthropology and become a central rite of passage of these two anthropological subdisciplines. Anderson's first fieldwork experiences were with American hobos. At some point during his ethnographic journeys among the hobos of Utah, Anderson converted to Mormonism.[20] His second book, *Desert Saints*, published in 1944 by the University of Chicago Press, married ethnographic fieldwork on Enterprise and St. George, Utah, to historical research on Mormon colonization. *Desert Saints* told the historical tale of Mormon pioneering from the settlement of Utah in the 1850s to the proclamation of the manifesto ending Mormon polygamy in 1890.[21] Like so many other Progressives, Anderson's academic and work life reflected the mixture of objectivity and advocacy that was so much a part of academic life and political culture in early twentieth-century America. He worked as a public servant in welfare agencies, for the United Nations after World War II, and in academe, taking up a position in the Sociology Department at the University of New Brunswick in 1965.

Several other historians and historically oriented social scientists also made contributions to the analysis of Mormonism in the early and middle years of the twentieth century. Like their apologetic and polemical forebears of the nineteenth century, many of these other practitioners of the Old Mormon Studies tended to focus on the Book of Mormon and on Mormon polygamy, though in a much less polemical and apologetic way than most of their predecessors. In his 1902 book on Mormon founder Joseph Smith, non-Mormon I. Woodbridge Riley, who earned his doctorate at Yale and. taught philosophy at Vassar College, argued that Mormon founder Joseph Smith had unconsciously taken the Hebrew origins of American Indians hypothesis and clothed it in a Protestant garb. In 1917, Episcopalian psychologist and official investigator of the American Society for Psychic Research Walter F. Prince, argued that the Book of Mormon revealed Smith's unconscious debt to New York's anti–Masonic movement. In 1920, historian and Mormon Franklin D. Daines published a work on Mormon millenarianism, exclusivism, and separatism, decrying their decline in Mormonism. In 1917, economist Hamilton Gardner published a study on Mormon cooperation and communalism. In 1924, Joseph Geddes completed a dissertation on Mormon United Order communalism. In 1932, Mormon Feramorz Fox completed a dissertation on the Mormon land system and Mormon communalism at Northwestern University. In 1935, Arden Beal Olsen published a dissertation on the cooperative Mormon mercantile system in Utah. In 1929, William McNiff completed a dissertation on the rise of cultural institutions in early Utah. In 1954, Mormon and sociologist Kimball Young published his seminal book on Mormon polygamy. In 1956, Mormons Austin and Alta Fife published their landmark book on Mormon folklore.[22] In 1945, ex–Mormon historian Fawn Brodie published her ground-breaking biography of the Mormon prophet Joseph Smith.[23]

Non-academic historians and archaeologists also made contributions to the Old Mormon Studies in the 1950s. Lapsed Mormon Dale Morgan explored the Indian superintendency of Mormon Prophet Brigham Young, Mormon literature, the history of Salt Lake City, and the early history of Mormonism.[24] Mormon Juanita Brooks wrote on polygamy and one of the most controversial moments in nineteenth-century Mormon history, the Mountain Meadows Massacre.[25] In 1952, Mormon Thomas Stuart Ferguson founded the Middle American Archaeological foundation, later the New World Archaeology Foundation (NWAF), to raise funds for archaeological digs in what he thought were the Book of Mormon lands of Central America. The NWAF, in which a number of professional archaeologists were involved, did field work and conducted excavations in southern Mexico beginning in 1952, received funding from the Church beginning in 1953, and became part of BYU in 1961.[26]

Conclusion: Polemics, Apologetics, and the Professionalization of Mormon Studies

What all of the Old Mormon Studies analysts shared was, at least in part, a "naturalistic" approach to Mormon Studies and a devotion to the deep structural theoretical perspectives that were coming to dominate history and the social sciences in the early twentieth century. Instead of repeating the faith pronouncements of primary documents and writing "faith promoting" tracts, Ely, Ericksen, Nelson, Anderson, and others, looked to economic, psychological, and cultural and ideological forces underlying Mormon behavior just as Gentile historians and social scientists in general were turning to economics, psychology, politics, geography, and culture for explanations for human behavior.

However, there was also a polemical and apologetic side to much of the work of those engaged in the Old Mormon Studies. Ely promoted what he believed were viable Progressive irrigation programs. Ericksen praised "socialistic" practices. Nelson promoted New Deal agricultural programs. Ferguson turned to naturalistic archaeology to "prove" the historicity of the Book of Mormon just as many Christian professional archaeologists were turning to archaeology in the 1920s and after to "prove" the supposed historicity of the Bible. The Old Mormon Studies historians, in other words, had only partially escaped the prison house of polemics and apologetics.

Between 1928 and 1950 the Old Mormon Studies really began to take shape and form in academia and beyond it. Between those years two hundred theses on Mormonism were written and fifty dissertations on Mormonism were produced. A number of publications and publishers also began to play important and central roles in disseminating the work of Old Mormon Studies scholars. In 1928, the *Utah Historical Quarterly* was founded and has published, since its founding, numerous articles on Mormon related topics. Between 1928 and 1950, seventy-five articles on the Saints were published and books on Mormon topics began to appear from the presses of national and university publishers such as Holt, Knopf, and the Indiana University Press. Mormon Studies, in other words, was beginning to take on an institutional life.[27]

Since the late 1950s Mormon Studies has taken on an even more of an institutional and professional life with the advent of the New Mormon Studies. It is to the history of this New Mormon Studies that I now want to turn.

Four

The "New" Mormon Studies

Introduction

The 1950s through the 1980s was a tumultuous period in the United States and in Mormon dominated Utah. It was an era characterized by the latest great power struggle, this one between the United States and the USSR. It was an era that saw the myth of American consensus give way to battles over racism, civil rights, segregation and desegregation, the Vietnam War, and Watergate. It was an era characterized by changing American demographics thanks to the baby boom generation and increasingly diverse and mostly non–European immigration into the U.S. after 1965. It was an age, thanks to all of the above and more, of culture wars.

One of the culture wars of the era centered on history and was fought between those who preferred their history nationalist and celebratory and those who preferred it warts and all. Within the academic discipline of history itself the post-war period saw the older White Anglo-Saxon Protestant and predominantly male consensus history that dominated so much of history writing in the United States challenged by a younger and more diverse group of scholars who practiced a conflict history that decried the selective cultural amnesia of consensus historians, particularly their amnesia about such traditionally American "outsiders" as Blacks, Hispanics, women, workers, and, even Mormons, a history that was too often ethnocentric, and from younger scholars engaged in the practice of the newest historiographic fads, the new social history and the new cultural history, both of which became prominent approaches in the history profession in the late 1960s and afterwards. Historians, impacted by Einsteinian and Kuhnian "relativism" and the approaches to history of the French Annales School, increasingly took up the quest for a long-range history and a short-range history, along with a quest for totality that sought to move beyond the selective great men, the selective great events, and the Western Civilization orientation that dominated parochial nationalist histories. These changes in history paralleled the development of macro, meso, and micro approaches in sociology and the American anthropological quest for totality institutionalized in the discipline's division into biological, social, cultural, and linguistic fractions or domains.

Utah was not immune from the economic, political, cultural, and demographic revolutions sweeping across the nation or its American culture wars, as we will see in Chapter Seven. Mid-twentieth-century Utah saw the state become even less isolated. It saw the University of Utah and Brigham Young University develop into important research universities with graduate programs in, for example, history, sociology, psychology, and anthropology. It saw increasing numbers of Mormons, some of them working on Mormon topics, receive advance degrees from major universities in Utah and across the United States. It saw increasing numbers of Gentiles begin to work in and in some cases even specialize in Mormon Studies. The growth and transformation of Mormon Studies was so great during this period that non–Mormon historian Moses Rischin called the revolution against what he called Mormon "cultural isolation" and intellectual isolation "'the new' Mormon history."[1]

Despite Rischin's rhetoric, one can question just how "revolutionary" the New Mormon Studies was relative to the "old." The practitioners of the New Mormon Studies, Mormon insiders, Mormon insider outsiders, Mormon outsider insiders, Gentile insider-outsiders and Gentile outsiders, remained wedded, as did historians and social scientists at large, to a host of theoretical perspectives that largely had their origins in nineteenth-century Europe including economic theories, economic deprivation theories, economic relative deprivation theories, social mobilization theories, various Marxist economic theories, political theories, geographic theories, demographic theories, cultural theories, cultural hermeneutic theories, cultural phenomenological theories, and scientific positivism. Mormon and Gentile scholars and scholars to be, and even some gifted amateurs, were socialized into these nineteenth-century theoretical perspectives during their academic sojourns in American universities or thanks to their reading of Mormon history. What was different were the numbers of insiders and outsiders of various stripes and configurations doing research in and publishing on Mormon Studies compared to the relatively few practitioners engaged in the Old Mormon Studies. If this quantitative change in the numbers of those engaged in the study of Mormonism is revolutionary, then there was indeed a "revolution" in Mormon Studies in the wake of World War II.

The Rise and Expansion of the New Mormon Studies

There were several pivotal figures in this New Mormon Studies "revolution." Among the earliest were S. George Ellsworth and Eugene E.

Campbell. Mormon S. George Ellsworth received his doctorate from the University of California in Berkeley in 1950, writing his dissertation on Mormon missions in the United States and Canada between 1830 and 1860. After graduation Ellsworth took a teaching position at Utah State Agricultural College (now Utah State University) in Logan where he began training students in the intricacies of Mormon Studies and historical and social scientific approaches to religious movements and groups.[2] Mormon Eugene E. Campbell took his master's degree at the University of Utah and his doctorate at the University of Southern California, where he completed a dissertation on Mormons in California in 1952. He initially took up a teaching position at the LDS Institute of Religion in Logan before moving to the Department of History at BYU, where he too began training students in Mormon Studies and "modern" approaches to religious groups.[3]

While Ellsworth and Campbell were important proto figures in the development of the New Mormon Studies and may be seen as bridges between the Old Mormon Studies and the new, the father, as consensus has it, of the New Mormon Studies was Leonard Arrington. The Idaho born and Mormon Arrington took a doctorate in economics at the University of North Carolina in Chapel Hill in 1952. Influenced by the regionalist movement, a perspective that was prominent at the University of North Carolina when Arrington studied there, a perspective which saw the United States as a patchwork of different regions, and by Richard Ely, who emphasized as we learned earlier economic history, Arrington explored, in his dissertation "Mormon Economic Policies and Their Implementation on the Western Frontier, 1847–1900," the Latter-day Saint settlement of the Mormon culture region with its homogeneity, egalitarianism, and unity, and explored Mormon centralized economic planning.[4]

Between the late 1940s and the 1990s Arrington would play, as he later wrote, the role of a historical entrepreneur to a host of budding Mormon Studies scholars. In 1946, Arrington took a position in the Economics Department at the Utah State Agricultural College in Logan. In 1958, the prestigious Harvard University Press published his dissertation, *Great Basin Kingdom: An Economic History of the Latter-day Saints, 1930–1900*. This book, which Mormon and historian Richard Poll called the most significant and important book published on Mormonism and Utah history in the last century, the first of twenty books Arrington would publish, went on to win the Award of Merit from the American Association of State and Local History and the Best First Book award from the Pacific Branch of the American Historical Association, both indicators of the increasing mainstreaming of Mormon Studies in the academy in the late 1950s and early 1960s.[5] Between 1972 and 1982 Arrington served as Church Historian in the Church History Office. From 1972 to 1987 he was Lemuel H. Redd, Jr.,

Professor of Western American History at Brigham Young University. Over these years Arrington mentored a host of students who would go on to be important practitioners of the New Mormon Studies in the late twentieth century including Dean Jessee, D. Michael Quinn, Richard Jensen, William Hartley, Maureen Ursenbach Beecher, Jill Mulvay Derr, Ronald Walker, and Carol Cornwall Madsen.[6] Writing and teaching were not the only things Arrington did to kick start the New Mormon Studies "revolution." He also played a major role in the professionalization and institutionalization of the field. In 1965, he helped found the Mormon History Association (MHA) at the American Historical Association meeting in San Francisco, California.[7]

Where the MHA led other organizations soon followed as the New Mormon Studies really began to take off and take institutional form. The year of 1972 saw the founding of the Charles Redd Center for Western Studies at BYU. The Redd Center collected oral histories on Mormon polygamy and Mormon ethnicity and published collections on these and other aspects of Mormon and Western history. The founding of the Reorganized Church of Jesus Christ of Latter Day Saints (RLDS) variant of the MHA, the John Whitmer Historical Association, and the founding of the Mormon Historical Demographic Project at the University of Utah took place in 1973. In 1975, the Religious Studies Center at BYU was established. The Religious Studies Center undertook research on and published materials on LDS history and social life. The year of 1976 saw the founding of the Society for the Sociological Study of Mormon Life, later the Mormon Social Science Association. Even LDS Church officials got in on the New Mormon Studies act. In 1976, they established the Demographic Research Institute at BYU (later the Center for Studies of the Family and the Family Studies Center), which, at its founding, did evaluation research on LDS visitor centers and LDS media. In the 1980s the Demographic Research Institute began to undertake analysis of LDS member demographics, conversion, and inactivity. In 1978, the Women's Research Institute at BYU was founded, which lasted until 2010.[8] The early 2000s saw Mormon Studies programs or chairs established at Claremont Graduate School in southern California, Utah State University, the University of Virginia, the University of Southern California, the University of Utah, the University of Wyoming, and the Graduate Theological Union in the San Francisco area.

With the increasing professionalization of Mormon Studies came increasing numbers of professional Mormon Studies oriented journals. The year of 1959 saw the debut of a more scholarly and academic *BYU Studies*. In 1966, *Dialogue: A Journal of Mormon Thought* was born. Founded by two young LDS scholars, Eugene England and G. Wesley Johnson, both students at Stanford University at the time. *Dialogue* billed itself as an "independent national quarterly established to express Mormon culture and examine the relevance of religion to secular life." In 1974, the MHA initiated publication of the *Journal of Mormon History*. The same year saw the first publication of *Exponent II*. *Exponent II*, which took its name from the LDS semi-official *Women's Exponent*, which began publication in 1872 and published articles in favor of women's suffrage and plural marriage. *Exponent II* was founded by several Mormon women including Claudia Lauper Bushman, wife of noted historian Richard Bushman, and now well-known historian Laurel Thatcher Ulrich, and devoted itself to the exploration of Mormon women's history. The year of 1977 saw the appearance of *Sunstone*, a magazine published by the Sunstone Education Foundation whose motto was "faith seeking understanding," a magazine that has proven to be quite controversial in the years since as we will see in Chapter Seven. In 1981, the journal of the John Whitmer Association, the *John Whitmer Historical Association Journal* debuted.[9]

It was not only journals specializing in the New Mormon Studies that were being published. A growing number of academic and trade presses began publishing books on Mormon Studies in the 1970s as well. Prominent amongst these were the University of Utah Press, the Brigham Young University Press, the Utah State University Press, the University of Illinois Press, Signature Books, Oxford University Press, Greg Kofford Books, and, on the more Church friendly side, the Church owned Deseret Books, and Bookcraft, which was acquired by Deseret in 1999. By 2011, the University of Illinois Press alone had published or republished almost fifty books in Mormon Studies.

The growing maturity of the New Mormon Studies can also be seen in the rise of Mormon archives and archives holding important Mormon materials among them the Church Archives in Salt Lake City, the J. Willard Marriott Library at the University of Utah, the Harold B. Lee Library at BYU, the Utah State University Libraries and the Beinecke Rare Book and Manuscript Library at Yale University. Increasingly, the practitioners of the New Mormon Studies availed themselves of these archives and often published their findings in articles, often in professional peer reviewed history and social scientific journals, and in book form.

In retrospect the work of the practitioners of the New Mormon Studies reads like a microcosm of what was going on in academic history and the social sciences in the United States and across the core Western world at large. The era from the 1960s to the end of the twentieth century saw studies of a variety of topics related to or focusing on Mormonism. It saw studies of Mormon geography including studies of the Mormon culture region, Mormon colonization, and the globalization of Mormonism. It saw studies of Mormon politics including studies of the Mormon hierarchy, the Mormon attempt to make Utah a state, the Mormon domination of Utah, and tensions between Mormondom and the United States. It saw studies of Mormon demographics including Mormon historical demographics and Mormon social demographics. It saw studies of Mormon economics including studies of Mormon communalism. It saw studies of Mormon culture including studies of Mormon perceptions of and use of the Bible, of Mormon doctrine, of Mormon ritual, of Mormonism and the magic world view, of Mormon millennialism, and of the Mormon concept of the Kingdom of God. It saw the appearance of books and articles on the general history of the LDS and RLDS and on specific aspects of Mormon history such as Mormon origins and on post-manifesto Mormonism, on Mormon polygamy, on Mormon identity and ethnicity, and on Mormon women. The 1960s to the new millennium, in other words, saw the study, in the post–World War II language or discourse of broader mainstream Western history and social science, of virtually everything under the Mormon sun.[10]

The New Mormon Studies and Polygamy

As we will see in the next chapter, these young Turks of the New Mormon Studies have probably had their greatest impact on our understanding of Mormon origins. It is in the history of Mormon origins that one can really see the impact of nineteenth and twentieth-century theoretical perspectives on the conceptualization and practice of the New Mormon Studies. However, Mormon origins were not the only area of Mormon Studies that the practitioners of New Mormon Studies "re-wrote." They also "revised" the history of that most controversial aspect of Mormonism in the mid- and late nineteenth century, the practice of "the Principle," the practice of Mormon polygamy.

Studies of Mormon polygamy by the practitioners of the so-called New Mormon Studies are a reflection in miniature of what was going on in "secular" universities after the 1930s and particularly after World War II. Students of Mormon polygamy explored "the Principle" of Mormon polygamy from a variety of different angles. Some, such as Lawrence Foster, explored opposition to polygamy within the Mormon community.[11] Some, such as Eugene and Bruce Campbell, examined the rates of divorce among Mormon polygamous families.[12] Some, such as Julie Roy Jeffrey, Joan Iverson, Maureen Ursenbach Beecher, and Julie Dunfey, debated whether polygamy liberated Mormon women helping them create a sense of sisterhood in the process or whether "the Principle" was the ultimate example of a patriarchal marriage system.[13] Some, such as J.E. Hullett, examined the role males played in the institution of polygamy.[14] Some, such as Jessie Embry, explored the tensions between Mormon polygamous wives.[15] However, the topics that dominated scholarly writing on Mormon polygamy by the practitioners of the New Mormon Studies were explorations of its origins and how extensively "the Principle" was practiced by Mormons during the pre-manifesto era of the Church.

The exploration of the origins of Mormon polygamy and how many of the Mormon faithful practiced "the Principle" are particularly difficult histories to write. We do not know precisely when and where Mormon polygamy began. This lack of clarity has, of course, been grist for the academic mill. However, a strong scholarly consensus exists that plural marriage was introduced and practiced in Nauvoo in the 1840s. It is clear from historical evidence that the revelation on plural marriage was introduced in "the City beautiful" and that plural marriages were being "solemnized" in the Nauvoo Temple after its construction.[16]

There is controversy as to whether Mormon polygamy was being practiced before the Nauvoo period. Mormon and historian Daniel Bachman suggested that the doctrine of restoring "the Principle" goes back to Mormon Kirtland in the 1830s. However, evidence for this contention is largely circumstantial. Bachman noted that during this period Joseph Smith was engaged in the study and "revision" of the Bible and that during his "translation" of "restored" sections of the Old and New Testaments, the prophet encountered the polygamic practice of Hebrew Patriarchs such as Abraham and Jacob and tried to make doctrinal sense of it. Other circumstantial clues that polygamy may have begun in Kirtland includes evidence that the prophet may have taken a second wife, Fanny Alger, statements that indicate that Smith was convinced plural marriage would be restored to the church one day, and the issuance by the Church, in the midst of accusations that it was practicing polygamy, of a statement reiterating Mormon support of monogamy. All of these suggest, claimed Bachman, that polygamy was in the air if not in the flesh in that small Ohio town.[17]

The secretive nature of polygamy in Kirtland and Nauvoo, combined with the almost frenetic pace of early Mormon history, has not made it easy for scholars to study the practice of "the Principle" between 1831 and 1852. A great deal of scholarly attention has focused on the external and internal opposition to "celestial marriage."[18] Several scholars have noted the strong but inconsistent opposition of Emma Smith, the first wife of the prophet, to "the Principle."[19]

Analysts of Kirtland and Nauvoo polygamy also noted that "the Principle" was put into practice only in the lives of Smith and his most intimate and powerful associates.[20] In this context, a great deal of scholarly attention has focused on the number of wives the prophet had. Fawn Brodie enumerated forty-eight[21] while Stanley Ivins counted sixty.[22] However, as Foster noted any enumeration of Smith's wives is fraught with difficulties. First, given the secrecy of the practice of "the Principle," the evidence itself is not easy to come by. Moreover, lists of the wives that Smith had often fail to distinguish between those with whom Joseph lived and had sexual relationships and those with whom he did not share sexual relationships and were sealed to him "for eternity."[23]

However, there is one thing upon which most scholars agree, and that is the theological rationale for the practice of polygamy. Smith, by the Nauvoo period, believed that humans progressed from a material spirit existence, to a "fleshly tabernacle," and back to a material spiritual existence in which, if one followed the doctrines and precepts set out in the revelations given to the Church, one could achieve godhood. Plural marriage was central to this "eternal progression" because families were held to be eternal "beyond the veil." In this ideology the more wives a man had, the more children, and hence the more power he had. Plural marriage accelerated "eternal progression" or the process toward godhood. It also fulfilled the promise of numerous descendants God made to Abraham (Genesis 12:1–3) and reunited family members around their Patriarch-God in the afterlife. Smith believed that in the afterlife the whole process began anew as the Patriarch-God and his wives (Mothers in Heaven) gave birth to spirit children. These spirit children, in turn, cycled through the stages from pre-fleshly material existence to godhood and worshipped as God the one who had given them life.[24]

As we have seen, the Mormon practice of polygamy was quite controversial in the nineteenth and early twentieth centuries. Many Gentiles attacked "the Principle" as heretical and barbaric. This latter, by the way, points up the prominence of notions of unilinear evolution and ideological notions of civilizational superiority and inferiority that undergirded so much intellectual thought in the nineteenth and early twentieth centuries.[25] On the other hand, many Mormons defended "the Principle" as a commandment from God and as having healthy consequences for its practitioners.

As I noted earlier, approaches to Mormon polygamy, like Mormon historiography itself, transformed from normative apologetic defenses of "the Principle" and polemical attacks on it to more "scientific" and descriptive ones particularly in the mid- and late twentieth century. As academia professionalized so did Mormon Studies as academics, most of them Mormons, began to take a more "scientific" interest in the practice of Mormon polygamy. Among the first to approach polygamy descriptively were University of Wisconsin trained sociologist James E. Hulett and University of Chicago trained sociologists Nels Anderson and Kimball Young, all of whom looked at polygamy through the lens of the sociology of community.[26]

While Anderson, who had converted to Mormonism, had done some analysis of the numbers of Mormons engaged in polygamy in St. George, Utah, it was Mormon Stanley Ivins who took the statistical analysis that was all the rage in academia in the 1930s through the 1950s, to new heights in his analysis of Mormon polygamy. Ivins, a professor of animal husbandry, utilized a sketchbook of Mormon families by Frank Esshom and histories and biographies from Emery and San Pete counties, Utah, and found that fifteen to twenty percent of Mormons were practicing "the Principle." However, Ivins noted that these rates rose and fell depending upon particular circumstances. Increases in the practice of "the Principle" occurred in 1855–57, the years of the Mormon Reformation which saw a revival in Mormonism, 1869, 1882, and 1884–85, when Mormonism was under attack from outside. Polygamy rates declined in 1852, 1858, 1881, and 1890, all periods when outsider attacks on Mormonism subsided. For Ivins, then, polygamy was most prominent when Mormonism was under attack by outsiders. It was, in other words, a kind of identity marker for the faithful."[27]

Ivins set the scholarly standard for estimates of Utah polygamy in the mid- to late nineteenth century. Scholars, such as Julie Roy Jeffrey uncritically accepted Ivins's fifteen percent to twenty percent estimate of the practice of "the Principle."[28] Others, among them Eugene and Bruce Campbell,[29] refined Ivins's rate to eighteen percent. Still others, including Leonard Arrington and Davis Bitton, rejected Ivins's rate as too high without reanalyzing Ivins's data. Arrington and Bitton argued that the polygamy rate was around five percent for Mormon men and twelve percent for Mormon women.[30] However, they did qualify this assertion by suggesting that plural marriage probably varied across nineteenth-century Mormon time and across Mormon space.[31]

Just as Arrington had kick-started the New Mormon Studies in general, he, and Davis Bitton, were instrumental in stimulating New Mormon Studies of polygamy when they claimed that Mormon polygamy rates probably varied both historically and regionally.[32] In the wake of Arrington and Bitton's intuition that polygamy rates varied both historically and regionally, a host of new Mormon historians and social scientists began to reanalyze earlier data on polygamy or probe heretofore untapped contemporary sources related to plural marriage in order to ascertain the incidence of the practice of polygamy in the Mormon culture region. This new historical and social scientific scholarship was aided and abetted by recent methodological developments in the social sciences and in history that had become dominant in the universities where these scholars trained in the 1950s and 1960s. Mormons and sociologists James Smith and Phillip Kunz undertook the first of these new social scientific analyses of polygamy. Using census data and the same Essholm genealogical summaries that Ivins had exploited, Smith and Kunz estimated the polygamy rate was 8.8 percent.[33]

However, Smith and Kunz's study really did not add much to what was already "known" about Mormon polygamy. They simply applied more sophisticated statistical tests to data that had been previously exploited by earlier scholars such as Ivins. Other studies would apply the same sophisticated statistical techniques to the study of plural marriage, and they would apply these methods to data that had not been exploited by previous scholars. What these new studies found is that virtually everyone had previously underestimated the incidence of plural marriage. Mormon Lowell "Ben" Bennion, professor of geography at Humboldt State University, and Larry Logue, professor of history and political science at Mississippi College, pioneered in these new analyses of Mormon polygamy. Bennion, utilizing the manuscript census and Latter-day Saint family group sheets submitted to the Church Genealogical Department, found significant regional variation in the practice of "the Principle" in 1880s Utah. In the St. George region, he claimed, thirty percent were practicing "the Principle." In Orderville seventy-five percent were living it. Rates in other parts of Utah ranged from 30.4 percent in Kanab to 21.8 percent in Davis County. Interestingly, Bennion found that variation existed even within regions themselves. In Davis County, for instance, Bennion found that rates of polygamy ranged from five percent to thirty-two percent.[34]

Larry Logue focused his study of Mormon polygamy on the area around St. George, Utah. Utilizing 1880 census data, Latter-day Saint family group sheets, and the 1870 settler's list, Logue found general male plural marriage incidence rates of thirty percent in 1870 and thirty-three percent in 1880. Like Bennion, Logue also found variation in incidence rates within the St. George area.[35]

Where Bennion and Logue led others soon followed. Using census data from 1860, LDS Ancestral File data, and Latter-day Saint Family Histories and biographies, Mormons and social scientists Marie Cornwall, Camelia Courtright, and Laga Van Beek focused on the incidence of polygamy among Mormon women in three wards in the Salt Lake City Valley. They found plural marriage rates of forty-three percent in the 13th Ward, thirty-three percent on the 20th Ward, and fifty-eight percent in the Mill Creek Ward. In their essay on the Sugar House Ward in Salt Lake City, historians Jan Shipps and Mormons Cheryl May and Dean May found a polygamy rate of twenty-eight percent in 1870.[36]

The New Mormon Studies and the Study of Mormon Women

Another area of Mormon Studies that saw a major re-evaluation of the history and culture of Mormonism and which proved as controversial as that of Mormon origins and Mormon polygamy was the new

Mormon study of Mormon women. The civil rights and youth movements of the late 1950s, 1960s, and 1970s and the second wave feminist movement of the late 1950s, 1960s, 1970s, and 1980s began to have an immense impact on the humanities, including history, and the social sciences in the 1960s. Thanks in part to increasing numbers of women who received Ph.D.'s in history, sociology, cultural anthropology, and psychology from the 1960s onward, the books and articles on the role of women in history and the place of women in society and culture exploded.[37]

In the 1970s these developments began to be felt in the New Mormon Studies as well. The seemingly omnipresent Leonard Arrington once again, played an important role in propelling an interest in Mormon women's history through his own publications on Mormon women and his hiring of budding scholars of Mormon women's history including Maureen Ursenbach Beecher, Jill Mulvey Derr, and Carol Cornwall Madsen, while he was Church Historian.[38] *Exponent II*, *Dialogue*, the *Journal of Mormon History*, the University of Illinois Press, and Signature Books, among others, provided venues for publications on Mormon women's history. Articles and books began to appear on topics as diverse as women in the Latter-day Saint community, Mormon women's work, individual Mormon women, the institutional role women played and play within the Church of Jesus Christ of Latter-day Saints, the Relief Society, the leading organization for women in Mormonism, the relationship between gender and power and authority within the Mormon Church and the Mormon community in general, Mormon women and politics, and, of course, Mormon women and Mormon polygamy.[39]

As with the study of the incidence of polygamy among Mormons between 1852 and 1890 the study of Mormon women and Mormon polygamy has generated a significant degree of controversy within both the New Mormon Studies and within the halls of Mormon male power in Salt Lake City and Provo. One of the central academic debates surrounding women and Mormon polygamy has, not surprisingly, given how important the issues of equality and sisterhood were within the second wave feminist movement, revolved around the question of whether "the Principle" liberated women, allowing them to create a "female world of love and ritual," or represented the ultimate instantiation of a patriarchal marriage system. Non-Mormon historians Julie Roy Jeffrey, Lawrence Foster, and Joan Iverson argued that polygamy gave those women engaged in it a degree of autonomy, independence, and real power they did not have in monogamous relationships. They argued that women engaged in polygamy were allowed to do jobs that had previously been closed to them. Polygamous women assisted in the support of their families. "Sister" wives helped each other in good times and in bad creating a sense of sisterhood among themselves, they argued. Joan Iverson argued that "the Principle" offered a limited critique of the romantic love that imprisoned women within the Victorian cult of domesticity. Mormon and historian Maureen Ursenbach asserted that "the Principle" helped give rise to and sustained a female elite that paralleled the male elite of the Latter-day Saint Church and dominated Utah women's organizations. Several commentators attributed the passage of an 1870 law allowing women to vote in the territory of Utah to female activism that had, at least in part, roots in Mormon plural marriage and support for plural marriage.[40]

However, other scholars have given little credence to the notion that polygamy liberated Mormon women. Instead, they saw polygamy as a strongly patriarchal institution. Mormon B. Carmon Hardy, who taught history at California State University in Fullerton, for instance, argued that plural marriage was a device by which husbands and fathers tried to maintain male dominance in nineteenth-century America. Women were regarded as inferior to men and as the property of the "Patriarchs" they wed. Julie Dunfey, who took a master's degree in history from Stanford and who went on to act as consultant to and later as co-producer of several of Ken Bruns's documentaries, asserted that Mormon polygamy was a repressive sexual ideology and created a culture of loneliness and emotional distance in the women who practiced it. It was, she wrote, a "trial" for the women who lived it. Several scholars have noted that the extension of the franchise to women in territorial Utah was a male Mormon strategy to maintain male Mormon power in Utah Territory.[41]

A few scholars have taken a middle ground. J.E. Hullett, for instance, argued that although polygamous women could own property, vote, control their own children, and command their own home affairs, they were still financially and spiritually dependent upon their husbands.[42]

The impact of the second wave of the women's movement was not limited to the study of Mormon polygamy. The historical analysis of the Relief Society, the Church organization that was, for most of Latter-day Saint history, the dominant female organization in the Church, proved an enticing subject of interest for many of the new Mormon historians of Mormon women. Their scholarship proved to be particularly controversial within Mormon intellectual circles and Mormon culture. It was the late Mormon and later cultural Mormon (someone who remains culturally Mormon but who is no longer a member of the Church or who attends church regularly but who still believes in aspects of the faith), and historian D. Michael Quinn's claim about the Relief Society and priesthood that would, in particular, ignite this controversy. For Quinn, Mormon prophet Joseph Smith set apart the Relief Society to, in addition to its calling to aid the poor, as a female priesthood organization. Quinn asserts that for the Mormon prophet the "sisters" of the Relief Society came into possession of the "[p]rivileges, blessings, and gifts" of the "Priesthood" once Smith called his wife Emma to organize the Relief Society.[43]

On the other hand, Mormon historians Jill Mulvay Derr, Janeth Cannon, and Maureen Ursenbach Beecher argued, in their semi-official history of the Relief Society, that the "Relief Society," while autonomous, was meant to operate under the direction of the male "Melchizedek Priesthood." Although Derr, Cannon, and Beecher conceded that certain "callings" in the Relief Society paralleled those of the male priesthood structure, they argued that these callings were not as broad as those of the priesthood organization nor as central to the power structure of the broader Church. They also noted that it should not be forgotten that it was a male, Joseph Smith, who organized the Relief Society and specified how it should be organized. It was Smith, they noted, who "laid hands" upon its female leader, his wife Emma Smith, transferring power and authority to her through him. It was, in other words, through Smith's charismatic and patriarchal power and authority that Emma gained her position of power in the "Relief Society" and her power and authority to "lay on hands."[44]

Conclusion: The Professionalization of Mormon Studies

If nothing else, the late twentieth century analyses of mid- to late nineteenth century Mormon polygamy and Mormon women show just how much social science methodologies had impacted the New Mormon Studies. Mormon Studies had, one might say, come of academic age and there seemed to be little difference between the methodologies and theoretical perspectives and approaches and practices of Mormon academics and their non–Mormon counterparts. Just how much Mormon Studies had changed can perhaps best be seen in the numbers of scholarly works produced. As a 2000 study showed, since 1945 1700 individuals have written theses or dissertations focused on Mormon Studies. Approximately 450 of these were Ph.D. dissertations. From World War II to 1960, as many historical works on Mormonism were produced as in the previous half-century. Between 1960 and 1969, some 1100 titles were published in Mormon Studies. The number of published titles in Mormon Studies rose to about 2100 between 1970 and 1977 and rose to around 2700 between 1980 and 1989. In 1991 and 1992 alone some 1200 titles were published in Mormon Studies.[45] Mormon Studies, it seemed, really had come a long way.

FIVE

Social Theory, Social Movements and Mormon Origins

Theoretical Approaches to Social Movements and Social Groups

The intellectual and academic study of social groups and social movements—Mormonism is, of course, a social and cultural group and began its life as a social and cultural movement—is not new. Social scientific and historical approaches to social movements were stimulated by and grounded in the assumption that humans could understand and describe the immense economic, political, cultural, geographic, and demographic changes of the nineteenth- and twentieth-centuries, including the rise of capitalism, increasing urbanization, the advent of new accounting methods, colonialism, imperialism, professionalization, the scientific revolution, the cultural, the technological, and other changes going on around them.

One of the central concerns, if not the central concern, of much nineteenth- and twentieth-century social theory, was, of course, the rise of capitalism or the transition, in some places around the globe—the core nations—from a traditional world dominated by agriculture to a modern world dominated by industry and manufacturing. Founding father of sociology Karl Marx emphasized economic factors in the transition from feudalism to capitalism. Founding father of sociology Max Weber argued that the modern form of capitalism with its cult of efficiency, its bureaucracies, its professionals, its experts, and its managers, and its culture of meritocracy, was the product a host of economic, political, and cultural factors including Calvinism, with which, he argued, modern capitalism had an elective affinity. Founding father of sociology Émile Durkheim saw the rise of capitalism in the transition from small communities dominated by face-to-face relationships to larger communities dominated by large-scale industrial forces and the industrial division of labor. Philologist and student of social change Ferdinand Tönnies saw the transition from traditional to modern in the transition from *gemeinschaft* to *gesellschaft*, in the transition, in other words, from community to society.[1]

Over time, "materialist" explanations emphasizing economics, politics, geography, demography, and culture as causal factors, triumphed over traditional religiously oriented approaches, at least in most colleges and universities, and in segments of intellectual culture in the core nation world. It was not long before academics and intellectuals began applying these "materialist" approaches to social movements.

Social scientists and historians have long been interested in the rise, nature, characteristics, and dynamics of social groups. Professional historians, sociologists, anthropologists, social psychologists, and political scientists of every theoretical stripe, have, at least since the late nineteenth century, offered a variety of explanations, most of which stem in some shape, way, or form, from the materialist social theories of the mid- to late nineteenth century, for the rise, expansion, institutionalization, and, in some cases, demise of social movements. These social scientific explanations for the rise of social groups have ranged from deprivation theory to relative deprivation theory and from status anxiety theory to resource mobilization theory, and beyond.

Economic explanations have been particularly prominent and popular approaches to social movements. One of the pioneers of social movement analysis was James Mooney, an ethnographer with the Bureau of American Ethnography. During his fieldwork among the First Peoples in the American Great Plains in the late nineteenth century, Mooney observed and studied the now famous Ghost Dance religion, a millennial movement that prophesied that the white man would, at some point, disappear from the American landscape as a result of some supernatural force, leaving behind wealth and material goods that would allow native First Peoples to revive their traditional cultures. For Mooney the Ghost Dance revival was the product of inequality and wealth differences between First Peoples and European Americans. For Mooney, in other words, it was economic deprivation that gave rise to the millennial Ghost Dance movement.[2]

In the wake of Mooney's monograph deprivation theory became a prominent part of the sociological and social anthropological landscape in the United States and Western Europe. In the 1950s social anthropologist Peter Worsley attributed the millenarianism of the Melanesian cargo cults to economic deprivation in the same way Mooney attributed First People's apocalypticism to economic deprivation. In the 1960s historian Norman Cohn, taking a deprivation theory meets functionalist approach, argued that Northern and Central European Middle Age millenarian movements (and, by extension, modern-day counterparts such as twentieth-century revolutionary movements such as communism) were a response to economic deprivation and were a means to eliminate or at least diminish the social anxieties of the powerless.[3]

Deprivation theory was not the only economic explanation for social movements prominent among intellectuals and academics of the nineteenth and twentieth century. Marxist theorists who emphasized societal and cultural conflict, maintained that many social movements were the product of the transition from feudalism to capitalism. Marxist historian George Rudé, for instance, saw the French Revolution as the product of economic changes in eighteenth-century France and Europe that resulted, eventually, in the political triumph of the increasingly economically dominant and powerful bourgeoisie over the feudal aristocracy and monarchy.[4]

Historians Paul Johnson, Mary Ryan, Carroll Smith-Rosenberg, and Charles Sellers, all influenced by Marxist social movement theory, saw American Christian evangelicalism and, in the case of Smith-Rosenberg and Sellers, radical religious movements such as Shakerism and Mormonism, as the products of economic changes set in motion by the building of the Erie Canal in upstate New York in the early nineteenth century.[5] For Johnson, Ryan, and Smith-Rosenberg, religion, particularly evangelical religion, provided the cultural or ideological rationalization and justification that made these economic changes possible, homologous with, and palatable to, the emerging middle class in upstate New York.[6]

Social mobility theorist and historian Richard Hofstadter mixed class analysis with social psychology to produce an explanation for, or so he thought, the rise and spread of American Populism in mid-nineteenth to mid-twentieth-century America. According to Hofstadter, American Populism was the product of falling social status. Those whose status was falling, he claimed, grew anxious over their falling positions in the hierarchies of the time and organized to try to stop it from happening.[7]

Not every academic and intellectual has emphasized the role of economics in the rise of social movements. Historian David G. Hackett saw religious change in upstate New York, where Mormonism originated, as the product of the transformation of America from a European organic community to an individualistic one.[8] Historian Richard Brown saw religious change in America as the product of the transition from traditional society to modern society.[9] Historian Rowland Berthoff saw religious change in Colonial and Early National America as the product of value disorientation brought about by social mobility.[10] Social mobilization theorists and sociologists John McCarthy and Meyer Zald asserted that social movements were led and guided by rational strategizers who were able to logically determine what would be the most rational use of available political and economic resources in order to mobilize those not mobilized. For McCarthy and Zald, social movements were and are organized hierarchical movements that mirror the organizational and bureaucratic structure of modern "advanced" societies.[11]

Social Movement Theory and Mormon Origins

Theories centering on deprivation, relative deprivation, economic change, status anxiety, political change, urbanization, modernization, social mobilization, and cultural approaches to social movements have long been popular, consciously or unconsciously, with post World War II academics and intellectuals trying to understand the dynamics of social and cultural movements. Not surprisingly they have also been popular with post-war academics and intellectuals seeking to understand the reason or reasons for the rise of Mormonism.

Social scientists and historians attributed the rise of Mormonism explicitly or implicitly to a variety of sources. Jan Shipps, Mark Noll, and Jon Butler saw Mormonism as a cult or a new religious movement. Kenneth Winn and Mario DePillis saw Mormonism as the product of the tensions that resulted from the rise of Jacksonian democracy. Whitney Cross asserted that Mormonism was the product of the transformation of America from a frontier nation to a nation of settled communities. Carroll Smith-Rosenberg argued that demographic factors and economic factors gave rise to Mormonism. Mavin Hill saw Mormonism as the product of modernization. Michael Barkun saw Mormonism as a reaction to modernity. Hill, Gordon Wood and Mario DePillis saw Mormonism as the product of social dislocation and/or migration. Hill, Lawrence Foster, DePillis, and Wood attributed the rise of Mormonism to the overthrow of monarchical hierarchies and tensions resulting from religious pluralism. Louis Kern, Fawn Brodie, Alice Felt Tyler, Lawrence Foster, Robert Anderson attributed the rise of Mormonism to Joseph Smith's psyche. Newell Bringhurst attributed Mormonism's rise to status anxiety. For John Brooke, Mormonism was the product of occult culture. For Jon Butler, Mormonism was a mixture of Christianity and the occult. Marianne Perciaccante ascribed Mormon origins to an anti-formalist revolt against formalism or religious routinization and bureaucratization in upstate New York. Nathan Hatch and Newell Bringhurst saw Mormonism as the product of poverty. Ralph Waldo Emerson, David Brion Davis, Rowland Berthoff, Rex Cooper, and Donald Meinig saw Mormonism as Puritanism reborn. Leonard Arrington saw Mormonism as a hybrid of Puritanism and democracy. Cushing Strout saw it as a Hebraic form of Puritanism. Harold Bloom maintained that Mormonism was the product of American individualism. Foster saw it as the product of the subversion of the patriarchal order. Foster, Shipps, Hill, Richard Hughes, C. Leonard Allen, and Timothy Smith saw Mormonism as the product of a prevalent biblical culture in America. Although this list of causal factors for the rise of Mormonism seems, at first glance, rather long, these causal factors can, in the final analysis, be boiled down to five ideal causal types: the economic, the political, the geographic, the demographic, and the cultural.[12]

Economic, Political and Geographic Approaches to Mormon Origins

It would particularly be in the post–World War II period that social theories which originated in the mid- to late nineteenth century would increasingly be applied to Mormonism both by non–Mormon and by Mormon social scientists and historians. During and after World War II the United States and Mormon dominated Utah experienced great economic, political, cultural, and demographic changes. Both experienced, for instance, increased industrialization, a growth in federal and state bureaucracies, and a massive expansion of higher education. Utah experienced a decrease in its economic, political, and cultural isolation from broader currents of American society and culture, a change represented in microcosm by the founding of Geneva Steel in Utah Valley in 1944. As for Mormonism, it experienced spectacular growth and became an international religion rather than a regional one in the wake of World War II.

Academic interest in Mormonism, both within and outside the Mormon community, began to take off in the 1950s. In 1950 the non–Mormon historian Whitney Cross in his now famous book on revivalism in upstate New York and north-eastern Ohio, *The Burned-Over District*, argued that "ultraist" movements, like the Mormons, were the product of an America transforming from a frontier society to a commercial society. For Cross, Mormonism was the product of a non-revivalist civilizing impulse rather than the chaos of the frontier. In making this argument Cross was, of course, taking a swipe at one of the giants of twentieth-century American history, Frederick Jackson Turner, who argued that American democracy and American social movements were the products of the unique American frontier.[13]

Gentile historian Charles Sellers, influenced by Marxism and functionalism, suggested that the economic changes brought about by the construction of the Erie Canal gave rise to Mormonism and that these, in turn, created the Mormon psyche. For Sellers Mormonism's appeal was not cultural or theological but social. Those dislocated by the economic chaos brought about by the building of the Erie Canal, argued Sellers, found comfort in Mormonism's communal organization. This, in turn, eventually brought those experiencing social psychological dysfunction as a result of economic change into a new state of equilibrium.[14]

Sellers was not the first or the last intellectual and academic to emphasize the important role the Erie Canal played in stimulating economic changes and giving rise to social movements such as Mormonism in the Burned-Over District. However, those who followed him have been less willing to reduce political and cultural changes purely to economic factors. Borrowing from deprivation and status anxiety theory, non–Mormon historian Nathan Hatch interpreted Mormonism as a revolt of the poor against the increasing commercialization of expanding America. Emphasizing what he saw as a populist strain in Mormonism, a strain, that for him, was readily apparent in the Book of Mormon, Hatch pointed to numerous condemnations of the rich, the proud, and the learned (clergy prominently among these last) in it as evidence supporting his argument that Mormonism was, at least in part, a reaction to economic inequality in early America.[15]

Mormon and BYU historian Marvin Hill also stressed the importance of the economic changes taking place in upstate New York for understanding the rise of Mormonism. Hill argued that technological innovations, the growth of cheap transportation, industrialization, social mobility, migration, and the coming of mass political parties to the region, were important factors leading to the rise of Mormonism. These phenomena, he claimed, fractured the communities of the Burned-Over District, transforming closely knit religious communities into more loosely knit urban and more secular cities. Hill claimed that those who experienced these changes and became Mormons sought refuge in authoritarian and authoritative religious ideology to counter the uncertainties wrought by these changes; others sought refuge in experientially authoritative religious forms such as evangelicalism.[16]

Political explanations for Mormon origins have also been popular. Historian Kenneth Winn, who was a student of Rowland Berthoff, regarded Mormonism as a product of the political divisions that characterized Jacksonian America. Emphasizing Mormon communalism, Winn asserted that Mormonism was an attempt to restore a co-operative community of virtue in the face of social changes taking place in the Burned-Over District. According to Winn, Mormonism arose in opposition to growing inequality in Jacksonian America and to increasing religious anarchy in the new republic.[17]

In another political interpretation, Mormon historian Newell Bringhurst placed Mormonism in the context of the reform movements that were so prominent in Jacksonian Era America. For Bringhurst, the Mormon emphasis on political reform was a product of status anxiety, specifically a product of the downward social mobility of the Smith family. Reflections of Smith's status anxiety, Bringhurst maintained, can be found in the Book of Mormon with its many condemnations or the rich, the learned, and the proud, in early Mormon involvement in anti-slavery and temperance movements, in Smith's attempt to reform the place of women in American society and the American family structure in the Mormon community of Nauvoo Illinois, in the anti-vagrancy, anti-brothel, and anti-profanity legislation instituted in Mormon Nauvoo, in the Mormon attempt to build the communal united order, in the reform platform of Smith's presidential campaign of 1844, and in the health reform impulse evident in the revelation now known as the "Word of Wisdom."[18]

Finally, Gentile political scientist Michael Barkun saw Mormonism as the end product of a variety of interconnected factors. For Barkun, Mormonism was fundamentally a reaction against modernity with its rationalized industrialization, professionalization, urbanization, and rational bureaucratization. These social and economic forces, Barkun argued, caused stresses among the largely rural inhabitants of the Burned-Over District. That most of these individuals were of Yankee or New England backgrounds "modified these stresses and produced a special receptivity to millennial or evangelical, and utopian or separatist movements in the era." Inhabitants coped with the stresses, Barkun argued, in two broad ways. Those with a religious orientation drew on biblical interpretive frames that emphasized millennialism. Those who reacted to the stresses in more utopian ways also drew on biblical interpretive frames but did so in a more secular and flexible way than the millennialists.[19]

Social Movement Theory and the Problem of Mormon Origins

As this chapter has made clear, historians and social scientists have often looked to and utilized social theories that arose in the mid- to late nineteenth and twentieth centuries to help unlock, understand, and comprehend the origins of religiously oriented social and cultural movements such as Mormonism. Some, as I noted, found the key to unlocking the mysteries in theories of deprivation, relative deprivation, and cultural revitalization. Others found the key to understanding them in status anxiety theories. Still others found the answer as to why Mormonism arose in economic, social control, psychological, or cultural perspectives. But do these perspectives and approaches really help us understand social and cultural movements such as Mormonism?[20]

There are, I think, fundamental and perhaps even insoluble problems with many, if not all of these approaches to social movements in general and to the Mormon social movement in particular. Generally speaking, deprivation theories suggest that some economic want, not enough food to satisfy survival needs or a lack of wealth, for instance, is the base or ground from which social movements spring. Relative deprivation theories tie economic deprivation to cultural interaction, to the differences in wealth that characterize such interactions, and finally to collective sociopathology.[21] For example, non–Mormon historian Nathan Hatch, who applies deprivation theory to Mormon origins, argued that social groups such as the Mormons, Methodists, Campbellites, and Adventists, all of whom were influenced by the questioning of traditional authority explicit and implicit in the American Revolution, were democratic revolts of the poor. Just as many relative deprivation theorists and Marxist conflict theorists found poverty and marginality at the heart of apocalyptic or millennial movements, Hatch found condemnations of the rich, the wealthy, and the educated at the heart of Mormonism and in the Book of Mormon with its apocalyptic condemnations of the rich, the wealthy, and the educated.[22]

There is no doubt that Joseph Smith and the Smith family were, to some extent, "marginal" and that Smith grew up in a poor and "marginal" family.[23] There is no doubt that Smith believed the second coming was close. However, apocalypticism is not simply, or is not always simply, the product of poverty and marginality. Elites such as Joachim of Fiore, James I, Oliver Cromwell, Thomas Hobbes, Sir Henry Vane the Younger, Isaac Newton, and John Milton, were millennialists.[24] Additionally, forces other than deprivation and marginality may have been equally if not more responsible for the condemnations of the rich in the Book of Mormon. They could just as easily be the product of a Biblical culture that emphasized Old Testament prophetic texts such as the books of Amos, Hosea, and Isaiah, all of which condemn the rich and the wealthy in no uncertain terms for their breaking of Israel's covenant with God.

Demographic studies of early Mormons also problematize the arguments that the Mormon social movement was the product of poverty. Mormon historians Mark Grandstaff and Milton Backman found that fifty percent of LDS converts in Kirtland, Ohio, were "poor," around twenty-nine percent were of "moderate" wealth, and twenty-one percent were "affluent," making early Mormonism hardly a movement of the poor. In fact, Grandstaff and Backman found that the percentage of wealthy people who converted to Mormonism was greater than the percentage of affluent individuals in the general population at the time. Converts to Mormonism included farmers (fifty-eight percent), millers (eight percent), shoemakers (one percent), teachers, hatters, tanners, carpenters, lawyers, clerks, doctors, merchants, and ministers. Mormon historian Steven C. Harper's study of those who converted to Mormonism between 1831 and 1833 in Erie County, Pennsylvania, found that Mormon converts were representative of the overall pattern of property ownership in the county. Given this data, one can raise questions about the notion that Mormonism was a movement of the poor and whether Mormon apocalypticism was an epiphenomenon or product of Mormon poverty.[25]

This story, by the way, is similar for other "marginal" and "radical" groups in the Burned-Over District and New England. David Rowe, drawing on letters sent to William Miller, who predicted that Jesus would come again in the 1840s, by some of his followers, found 21 farmers, 7 merchants, 2 industrialists, 4 professionals, 16 craft producers, 3 laborers, 1 clerk, 52 ministers (33 of whom were Baptist minister/farmers), and 9 wives among early apocalyptic Adventists. Sociologist Henri Desroche found that most converts to apocalyptic Shakerism in 1800, including several New Light ministers, those who embraced the American revivals of the nineteenth century, brought significant property with them, while in the 1860s Shaker converts included farmers, tailors, schoolteachers, merchants, and craft producers. According to Robert Sutton early converts to the Oneida Community, a community that saw itself as an instantiation of a new millennial order, included farmers, a printer, a trap maker, a machinery manufacturer, an architect, a bookkeeper, a shoemaker, a lawyer, a doctor, and a former Methodist minister. They were, as one contemporary described them, "men of good character," substantial means, and substantial power.[26]

As for "mainstream" evangelicals, they were, or so scholarly consensus would have it, middle class. However, the evidence for such an assertion is not quite so conclusive as commentators have sometimes made it out to be. Beyond the Burned-Over District a number of analysts have found that most Methodists came from the poorer classes with a smattering of the "better classes" among them, while historian John Wigger found that most early Methodist itinerants and preachers hailed from artisan and petty merchant backgrounds. According to historian Dee Andrews, Methodists were the most diverse geographically, ethnically, class wise, status wise, and rural versus urban wise, of any religious group in Revolutionary era America.[27]

In the end, then, deprivation and relative deprivation theories do not explain the reasons for the rise of Mormonism or new social groups of a religious character in the Burned-Over District of upstate New York and north-eastern Ohio. Nor, in general, do they explain why some of the "anxious" poor revolt while others do not nor why some of those who are not "poor" revolt.[28]

Status anxiety theories do not do any better in explaining the rise of new social groups and social movements in the American Northeast like Mormonism. One of the most popular status anxiety informed explanations among historians and social scientists has been the social control thesis. For example, political scientist Clifford Griffin argued that the revivalism of the Second Great Awakening, which flowered into a host of benevolent associations, was an attempt by New England elites to reassert their political and moral authority which had been challenged by democratic and egalitarian impulses unleashed by early nineteenth-century Jacksonian democracy. Griffin claimed that New England elites reacted to Jacksonian democracy by claiming that the America of "godliness," "order," "safety," and "quiet" they had known, had been replaced by an America of "godlessness," "disorder," and "crime" with the rise of the Jacksonians to power. In order to return America to the "godly," "orderly," "safe," and "quiet" nation it once was, these elites established associations whose goal it was, was to turn individual members of the "dangerous classes," for example, frontier settlers, immigrants, and workers, into "civilized" and "godly" individuals who knew their place in "civilized" American society and culture.[29]

Griffin's thesis *may* explain the actions of a New England elite that *may* have had an interest in maintaining the status quo and who were associated with Congregationalism and Presbyterianism. However, it does not explain why the groups that grew the most as a result of the early nineteenth-century revivals, including in New England, were the Methodists and Baptists. These were the very groups that were not part of the American religious elite, that were most opposed to the idea of an elite educated paid ministry, and that were the most democratic, at least rhetorically.[30]

Other status anxiety theorists have offered perhaps more nuanced explorations and explanations for the rise of new nineteenth-century social movements. As did Griffin, sociologist Joseph Gusfield saw the anxiety surrounding status decline as the key to understanding one early nineteenth-century social movement, the temperance movement. However, unlike Griffin, Gusfield distinguished between the status anxiety associated with the temperance social movement of New England elites attempting to regain their traditional place in the American status hierarchy and that of the temperance social movement associated with a middle class that was coming to dominate American political, economic, religious, and cultural life during that era and who wanted to show that they too were "civilized."

In Gusfield's view, the New England elites who led the first stage of the American temperance movement, which flourished from the 1820s through the 1830s, wanted to recapture the religious, social, and political dominance they had lost when middle class Jacksonian Democrats took control of America. The temperance societies of the New England elite did not offer ways for the "common man" to reform himself. They offered him instead a means by which he could model his life around what the elites thought constituted a "good" and "civilized" life. By offering themselves as a model for the "common man" and by offering their expertise as to how the "common man" could achieve the ideal of how Americans should act, these New England elites sought to regain the power and influence they felt they had lost.

On the other hand, the second stage of the temperance movement from the 1840s through the 1860s, claimed Gusfield, was populated with and run by members of the rising middle class who wanted to reform themselves so that they could achieve the good life the American dream promised. They believed alcohol and alcoholism was keeping them from achieving this good life. They therefore founded anti-alcohol organizations to combat its negative effects.[31]

As we saw earlier, status anxiety perspectives have been applied to Mormonism. For example, Whitney Cross, suggested that Joseph Smith's family was characterized by rising status after they migrated to New York. Newell Bringhurst saw Mormonism as a product, along with religious pluralism, of status anxieties.[32]

Status anxieties theories can be reductionist, viewing psychological anxiety as the result of some single factor, whether economic, political, or cultural, or they can be multifactorial, asserting that anxiety is a product of a combination of economic, political, and cultural sources or forces. Mormon historian Newell Bringhurst, for instance, emphasized Mormon political status anxieties and concentrates on Mormon political reform efforts.

In general, status anxiety theories may explain one or several social psychological aspects of anxiety, but they do not explain why some of those experiencing status anxiety resist or rebel against their falling status while others do not. Nor do they explain the mechanisms which allow some groups to mobilize for resistance and/or rebellion while others are not able to. And finally, they do not explain the cultural components of social groups. Even if we assume that people are "anxious" about their statuses, status anxiety theories do not explain either the impetus for the rise of social groups nor the cultural form these social groups take.[33]

A variation on the deprivation and social anxiety theses is the marginality thesis. According to historian Norman Cohn apocalyptically oriented groups of the middle ages were made up of marginal types. A number of scholars have applied Cohn's social marginality thesis to groups beyond mediaeval northern Europe. For instance, some have claimed that seventeenth-century Quakerism and nineteenth-century Shakerism, Mormonism, the Oneida Community, and Adventism, all drew marginal men and women into its ranks.[34]

"Marginal" groups and individuals, including some sixteenth-century Anabaptists, some seventeenth-century Quakers, and many nineteenth-century Shakers, Mormons, Oneidans, and Adventists, were apocalyptic. However, they also grappled with the less than eschatological questions of what the structure of the true Church should be, what doctrines the true Church should have, and what role the Bible and continuing revelation should play in the one true Church. So too did religious groups that quickly became "mainstream" after the Protestant Reformation, including Lutherans and Calvinists, along with a host of intellectuals connected to "mainstream" Protestantism and Roman Catholicism. However, "mainstream" Christian groups that experienced bureaucratization and routinization, are no longer obsessed with the second coming but did and do continue to regard it as a central component of Christian doctrine. Additionally, as I noted earlier, the Shakers, the Mormons, and the Oneidans were not made up solely of the marginal. These facts problematize Cohn's linkage of apocalypticism and marginality.[35]

One can and some have seen revival movements as the products of their ability to mobilize resources. Sociologists John McCarthy and Mayer Zald's resource mobilization theory, for instance, hypothesizes that the success of a social group or its leader in raising money, attracting supporters, and making important alliances, particularly with those in positions of power, authority, and influence, determines the success or failure of a social movement. The more money a group raises the more converts a group makes, and the more alliances the group makes with the powers that be, the more successful a social movement will be.

However, as with relative deprivation theory, the resource mobilization perspective is problematic. It has no explanatory power when it comes to single acts of resistance or "unorganized" group resistance or rebellion; social mobilization theorists usually regard the latter as instances of unorganized mob action. Moreover, given its emphasis on organizations and bureaucracies, social mobilization theory tends to focus on movements in large-scale societies and thus seems to turn every social movement into a "rational" organization or a bureaucratic lobbying group typical of twentieth-century modernity. Given the social mobilization emphasis on organization and its singular notion of rationality, one cannot help but wonder how relevant this theory is to understanding social and resistance movements across time and space, particularly in areas where bureaucracies are minimal and where, as is usually the case, rationalities are multiple. As presently constituted, resource mobilization theories raise questions about whether non-bureaucratic movements are social movements, whether there is only one type of "rationality" or whether "rationality" is grounded in various logics, and whether the social movements they analyze are only one form of possible social movement.[36]

However, these problems do not mean, that social mobilization theory is without its pluses. We can, if we broaden our conception of the resources mobilized, explore the social, economic, and political networks Mormon prophet Joseph Smith, for instance, drew on to mobilize resources in his battle with those who were persecuting Mormons. Smith did try to establish ties to political and other important leaders in Ohio, Illinois, and Washington, D.C., in order to alleviate the persecution Mormons were suffering.

If we broaden the resource mobilization theory even further, it is possible and helpful to explore the cultural resources on which Joseph Smith drew, among them restorationism, Biblicism, apocalypticism, dispensationalism, primitivism, perfectionism, romanticism, Jewish Christianity, and historic Christian debates over baptism, marriage, family structure, and church structure, to manufacture Mormonism and, in the process, Mormons. Smith clearly drew on previously existing cultural resources, cultural scripts, or cultural templates, though not necessarily immobilized ones, to manufacture a new movement that was compelling to some men and women who found a home and perhaps a haven in the Mormon faith. Clearly those who converted to the Latter-day Saint faith were drawn to Mormonism, at least in part, by the cultural resources Smith mobilized, particularly that of continuing revelation.[37]

Another problematic social movement theoretical perspective is the frontier hypothesis of Frederick Jackson Turner. As historian Whitney Cross pointed out, the Jacksonian era Burned-Over District was marked by good soil productivity, relatively equal sex ratios, and decent population size, hardly what one would expect to find on the frontier. Nor was the Burned-Over District a frontier in the institutional sense. Cross, historian Curtis Johnson, and historian Marianne Perciaccante have pointed out, that formal institutions were already present in the supposed "wilds" of the New York "frontier" even before Mormonism arose.[38]

Even if we accept the notion that the Burned-Over District was a "frontier" and that Shakerism's communalism and celibacy, Oneida's communalism and marriage in common, and Mormonism's communalism and theocratism, were biblically filtered reactions to the democratizing tendencies of the frontier, some of the ideologies and practices some analysts often point to as being products of this frontier were not manufactured on the "frontier." Shakerism, for instance, brought many of its ideologies with it when its adherents migrated to the New World from England. John Humphrey Noyes's ideas developed in the non-frontier community of Putney, Vermont, and at Dartmouth, Andover and Yale colleges. Beyond the three "radical" religious movements of the Burned-Over District, Methodists and Baptists brought many of their ideologies, practices, and institutions with them from the Netherlands and Great Britain when they settled in frontier regions in the South. The early Baptists arose in the years surrounding the English Civil War and were the product of English Separatism and Anabaptism. Methodism, initially a movement to purify the Anglican Church of its supposed doctrinal inaccuracies and accretions, was the product of Continental European Pietism. Arminian or free will doctrines and theologies existed in Continental Europe and Britain long before they appeared on the American continent. In fact, the Arminianism and antinomianism that most analysts see as characteristic of frontier religious groups are actually as old as Paul's letters to the Corinthians (circa 50 CE), and infused the fourteenth-century Brethren of the Free Spirit, Martin Luther (1483–1546), sixteenth-century Anabaptists, and the sixteenth- and seventeenth-century theologies of Jacobus Arminius (Jakob Harmensen, 1560–1609), George Fox (1624–1691), English and Dutch Baptists like John Smyth (1570–1612) and Thomas Helwys (1550–1615), and Anne Hutchinson (1591–1643).[39]

Leaving the frontier behind and focusing on other economic theories of social movement origins, the assertion that the Erie Canal profoundly impacted the Burned-Over District is certainly true. But can this perspective explain the rise and culture of social and cultural movements as different as the Mormons, the Shakers, and the Oneida Community in the Burned-Over District?

Perhaps the most influential economics centered argument about revivalism is the social control thesis of historian Paul Johnson. For Johnson, Charles Finney's revival efforts in Rochester, New York, in the wake of the construction of the Erie Canal and the rise of a mercantile oriented capitalism in upstate New York during the Second Great Awakening, represented a successful attempt by the new American merchant middle class to impose a new capitalist discipline on themselves and on their workers.[40]

In a variation on Johnson's perspective, historian Charles Sellers argued that economic changes in the Burned-Over District gave birth to a culture war between "antinomians" who emphasized localism and were committed to non-commercial agrarian values such as egalitarianism and patriarchalism, and "arminians," those committed to capitalist enterprise and the values associated with it: individualism, discipline, and efficiency. "Antinomians" tended to be Jacksonians and included revival-oriented religious groups such as the Baptists and Methodists, while arminians tended to be Whigs and included religious groups such as the Unitarians, Congregationalists, and New Light Presbyterians. For Sellers, it was the rise of capitalism in the Burned-Over District in the wake of the construction of the Erie Canal that brought about a sense of familial victimization among some in the region. Mormonism, to take one instance, was, Sellers asserted, an antinomian reaction against rising capitalism and its impact upon family structure and family life in the Burned-Over District. Its appeal was not its theology but its familial communalism.[41]

Sociologist George Thomas takes a somewhat similar view arguing that the entrepreneurship and small capitalist enterprise that transformed Jacksonian America, bred revivalism and later republicanism and temperance. The Calvinism that had dominated American religion prior to the market revolution was no longer compatible with the new world of American market capitalism. However, revivalist Christianity with its radical Arminianism, its hint of antinomianism, its rational means ends rationality, its perfectionism, its millennialism, and its individualism, was. Revivalist Christianity, Thomas asserted, made America and Americans, particularly middle-class America and Americans.[42]

There are several problems with the perspectives of Paul Johnson, Sellers, and Thomas. For instance, Charles Finney was not uncritically pro-capitalist. During the Panic of 1837 he called debt "a sin" and concluded that "the whole credit system, if not absolutely sinful, is nevertheless so highly dangerous that no Christian should embark on it." This is hardly an unambiguous ideology for a new capitalist middle class. Additionally, even if we accept that Johnson's thesis does apply to middle class evangelicals it does not explain the rise of more radical groups like the Mormons in the Burned-Over District.

There is a similar problem with the approaches of Sellers and Thomas that extends beyond Sellers' unconventional definition of "antinomian" and "arminian." Numerous studies have shown that, in many cases, Sellers' traditionalist antinomians and Thomas's revivalist arminians were actually staunch defenders of the market revolution. The Methodists, who Sellers and Thomas saw as archetypal antinomians and arminians respectively, were, thanks to their doctrines of individualism, self-discipline, and self-improvement, in some instances, able to harmonize their faiths with the changes while remaining critical of laissez faire capitalism. Some Methodists did this, at least in part, through their attempts to reform, humanize, and Christianize capitalism in ways they found fully consistent with their faith.[43]

Historian Carroll Smith-Rosenberg's argument that economic change was at the heart of what was going on in the Burned-Over District is more general in orientation and more nuanced than Johnson's and Thomas's and less psychologically based. Smith-Rosenberg asserted that there were two broad social movements that resulted from economic change in the Burned-Over District: a middle class movement characterized by evangelicalism, merchant males, middle class husbands who worked outside the home, and women who took care of the home and the children (the cult of domesticity), and a radical movement populated by the young, mobile,

Five. Social Theory, Social Movements and Mormon Origins 89

relatively "poor" people who were more experimental in their gender and marriage forms and who, as a result, stood outside the cult of male capitalist merchants and female homemakers and moral mediators.[44]

However, Smith-Rosenberg's distinction between "mainstream" social movements and "radical" social movements in the Burned-Over District, while helpful, still does not provide us with an understanding of the mechanisms that created or manufactured the different religious groups that arose in the region. Nor does it help us understand the mechanisms that created the different "mainstream" and "radical" religious groups in the first place.

Historian Robert Wiebe attempted to square these two circles. He tied the rise of Mormonism to identity formation. He argued that ethnic identity is tied to population explosions and migration. Mormons were forever migrating during the early years of the faith and this pattern of migration created strong and expansive notions of kinship that helped Mormons and others alleviate the problems and dangers associated with migration. Mormons, he claimed, created a collective identity characterized by a theocratic Zionism that envisioned a Mormon state in sacred space.[45]

However, Wiebe's emphasis on ethnic forms of identity is, I think, too narrow. Instead, we need to broaden our focus in order to explore how identity in general is constructed. Shakers migrated to the New World and much of their culture, their identity, and their ideology, came with them. Like Mormons, Shakers were geographically, culturally and ideologically marginal. Like Mormons, Shakers created broad and extensive kinship networks (fictive kin) that tied the brothers and sisters of the community together. Like early Mormon culture, Shaker culture was both imperiled and strengthened by the harassment and persecution cultural marginality brought. In sum, it was not migration that created Mormon and Shaker identity. It was a common culture built around a shared ideology. The persecution that resulted because of this ideology of marginality and separatism allowed Shakers to collectively migrate from the Old World to the New and Mormons collectively to migrate from New York to Ohio, from Missouri to Illinois, and eventually from Illinois to the Great Basin Desert.[46]

Mormons and Shakers did draw converts from among those moving into the Burned-Over District, the Old Northwest, Kentucky, and Tennessee. However, both attempted to acculturate and socialize these new converts into a culture and an identity that was already, in large measure, in place. The Oneida Community, on the other hand, originated in Vermont and originally drew its converts from the area near Putney. It moved to the Burned-Over District only after persecution and the threats and the reality of prosecution drove it from New England and brought with it an identity that already existed. Nor were those who joined the community in New York migratory.[47]

Given that the majority of early Mormon converts were, as Grandstaff and Backman argued, "poor," while those who joined the Oneida community were largely middle class, one could argue that class or status was the crucial independent variable here. However, as we saw earlier in this chapter, Mormon and Shaker converts did not only come from the ranks of the poor. A significant number of those who became Mormons were poor but many who became Shakers came from the middle class and from higher status groups. Then there is the problem of the "bourgeois" Adventists, Adventism drew converts from all walks of life. In sum, converts to these groups, in sum, came from a variety of class backgrounds.[48]

One perspective that gets around the problems of economic or class reductionism is that of historian Curtis Johnson. Johnson argued that it is not economic change or class that was central to what was going on in the Burned-Over District, but it was whether a church was formalist or anti-formalist. Like Smith-Rosenberg, Johnson argued that the churches of the upper and upper middle classes and those of the lower upper and lower classes were different. Formalist churches, such as the Congregationalist, Presbyterian, Low Church Anglican, and some Reformed denominations, made up of mostly of upper middle-class members, were characterized by formal or ordered worship forms, and an educated clergy, and were the mainstay of the voluntary societies that would attempt to reform nineteenth-century America. In contrast, antiformalist denominations, such as the early Methodists, Restorationists, and Baptists, drew their members from the middle and lower classes, and were characterized by emotional worship forms, a charismatic or called clergy, plain living, and a suspiciousness of voluntary societies.

However, Curtis Johnson's assertion that formalist groups were the bedrock of the voluntary societies that became commonplace in Jacksonian America and that anti-formalist groups were opposed to them, is not, as nuanced as it needs to be. As Richard Carwardine noted, the early anti-formalist Methodist Church contained members who had both positive and negative assessments of voluntary societies. Nor is his approach easily applicable to Mormonism or Shakerism, which were, like early Methodism, characterized simultaneously by both formalist and anti-formalist elements such as a hierarchical notion of the priesthood and a sometimes very emotional form of worship.[49]

Other analysts have stressed the role social dislocation brought about by social and especially economic changes, played in "manufacturing" religious oriented social movements in the Burned-Over District. For example, historian Rowland Berthoff, argued that those who sought conversion through revivals were the first generation or two to experience the revolutionary economic changes and dislocations of the social order and sought a return to the communal experience of the revivals. However, even if this is true, this perspective does not help us understand why some of these isolated rural or urban folk became Mormons and others became Adventists or Shakers. Cultural and identity differences remain largely and unfortunately unexplained and unexamined in this and many of the other theoretical perspectives in this chapter.[50]

Although all of these perspectives on social movements get us somewhere, they only get us so far. Clearly there were similarities and differences between "bourgeois" social movements such as the evangelicals, Adventists, and Campbellites, and "radical" social movements such as the Mormons, the Shakers, and the Oneida Community. They were all the children of Christianity after all. But the question remains as to whether these cultural differences and the identities and communities they created were the products of geographical mobility and class and status variations brought about by economic change, as Smith-Rosenberg asserts, or whether they were products of some other factor or combination of factors.

Conclusion: From Social to Cultural Approaches to Mormon Origins

Chapter Five has focused particularly on the economic and political approaches to Mormon origins that scholars of social movements and practitioners of the New Mormon Studies have turned to in order to understand the origins of Mormonism as a social movement. However, economic, political, and to a lesser extent geographic and demographic approaches have not been the only approaches to Mormon origins. In Chapter Six I will explore the cultural approaches some scholars have utilized in their attempts to unlock the secrets of Mormon origins in the Burned-Over District, and to the cultural scripts on which the Mormon prophet Joseph Smith drew when he created or manufactured Mormonism.

Six

Culture Theory and Mormon Origins

Introduction

In Chapter Five I focused on and explored the economic and political approaches that have dominated the New Mormon Studies and some of the theoretical problems associated with them. In Chapter Six I want to explore the cultural approaches that practitioners of the New Mormon Studies and others have applied to the study of Mormon origins. Additionally, I will argue for a cultural approach to Mormon origins that places Mormon origins in their broader American, Christian, and Atlantic cultural contexts, and is, at the same time, sensitive to the broader economic, political, demographic, and geographic contexts in which Mormonism took shape. In so doing, I want to try to move Mormon Studies beyond the apologetic, polemical, ideological, and exceptionalist discourses that have tended to dominate Mormon Studies since the advent of Mormon Studies.

Multifactorial Approaches to Social and Cultural Movements

All of the approaches that we have looked at in the previous chapters raise a host of questions. If, for instance, evangelicalism, Mormonism, Adventism, and the Oneida Community were caused by the same social force or combination of social forces, whether economic, political, demographic, or social psychological, why do each of these groups have somewhat different cultures? If radical movements were populated by the poor, why are they characterized by somewhat different cultural forms? If social movements arise as a response to deprivation, relative deprivation, or status anxiety, why is it that only some people respond to deprivation and anxiety by joining social movements and others do not? Why is it that some movements successfully mobilize resources while others do not? And beyond this, given the dynamic nature of the economy, politics, social settings, geography, and culture, why is it that movements arise and thrive only at certain times? Can one hypothesize the existence of a kind of social version of punctuated equilibrium?[1]

It seems to me that multifactorial approaches do offer more "sensible" answers to these questions than do single factor causal approaches, but only if they are truly multifactorial and only if they are truly dynamic and historical. The problem is that so many of the perspectives that claim to be multifactorial are in fact reductionist theories in disguise. Paul Johnson, Nancy Ryan, and Carroll Smith-Rosenberg, for instance, do explore the role culture played in the rise of social movements like Mormonism in the Burned-Over District. However, in the final analysis, all three see culture as the direct or indirect product or epiphenomenon of economic changes and as ultimately reducible to economic causal factors.

Broader demographic, geographic, economic, political, and institutional contexts surrounded and undoubtedly impacted both old and new "religious" movements in the Burned-Over District. For instance, the evidence shows that Mormons came from specific class or status and gender backgrounds, that Mormonism did arise in specific geographical contexts, that Mormons migrated into the ever expanding and contracting frontier, that Mormons did have to make a living within an economic environment in transition from agrarian to mercantile forms, that Mormonism took shape in a political culture experiencing the impact of democratization and reactions to greater democratization, and that Mormonism emerged and grew in areas within specific institutional and non-institutional frameworks. However, these facts do not come close to telling the whole story of Mormonism. In my opinion, any analysis worth its salt has to address the issue of why Mormons and other social and cultural groups, religiously oriented or not, in the Burned-Over District and beyond, were impacted by the same demographic, geographic, economic, political, and institutional forces, yet gave rise to both culturally similar *and* culturally different social movements. In the final analysis it is these cultural differences that allow us to get at the heart of the question as to why some seekers became Mormons while others joined the Shaker community, the Oneida Community, the Adventist Church, evangelical groups, and the "Christian" or Campbellite Church. Understanding cultural variation in the religiously oriented groups that arose in the Burned-Over District allows us to understand the differences that marked off each of these similar yet distinct social movements.

The only way we can truly begin to understand why some individuals became Mormons and others did not is through attentiveness to the culture of each of the groups that arose in the Burned-Over District. We need, in other words, to pay attention to the historical pedigrees of these cultural movements and to the ways cultural scripts framed group responses to broader economic, political, institutional, and cultural factors. Religious systems, after all, are interpretive systems that give meaning to the world around their adherents and to the events that occur in that world as they impact believers.[2]

In the remainder of this chapter, I want to try to get at the cultural scripts or cultural templates on which Joseph Smith drew. These cultural scripts are both similar to and different from, in both content and assemblage, those cultural scripts on which other early American religious social and cultural movements drew and manipulated. I want to move beyond the economic, political, geographic, and demographic approaches to the social and cultural movements I examined in Chapter Five in order to try to understand the forces that manufactured one nineteenth-century religious movement, Mormonism, and created a community, the Church of Jesus Christ of Latter-day Saints. I want to explore, in other words, the cultural elements on which the charismatic Mormon prophet Joseph Smith drew and how he and his followers put them together to create Mormonism and create Mormons.

Cultural Approaches to Mormon Origins

Some analysts have argued that culture underlay religious change in early nineteenth-century America. For instance, non–Mormon historian Dickson Bruce argued that it was the nineteenth-century revivals, with their liminal rites of passage, that transformed American religion in the American South by creating a greater sense of community and a shared identity in a world becoming increasingly individualistic.[3] For non–Mormon historian Daniel Walker Howe religious change in early nineteenth-century America was the product of a Protestant quest for identity.[4]

Some of those who have focused on political approaches to Mormon origins have also seen culture as central to the rise of Mormonism in the Burned-Over District. Michael Barkun whose work we discussed in Chapter Five, and other scholars who have taken political approaches to Latter-day Saint origins, pointed to the role cultural factors played in rise of Mormonism and other new religious movements in early nineteenth-century America.

So have a number of other analysts of early Mormonism. Nazarene historian Timothy Smith, for instance, places Mormonism firmly in the revival tradition of early nineteenth-century America. Smith noted that

Six. Culture Theory and Mormon Origins

Methodists, Baptists, "Christians," Presbyterians, and Mormons were involved in intense debates over issues such as freewill, original sin, universal redemption, moral perfection, the nature and nearness of the millennium, and the recovery of apostolic Christianity. For answers to these questions each turned to the Bible. The factor that differentiated Mormons from the other seeker groups of the era was the Mormon belief in "continuing revelation." Mormonism claimed to have been given several new scriptures that offered authoritative answers to a number of the questions that troubled so many early nineteenth-century religious "seekers." In other words, Smith asserted, Mormons turned not only to the Bible but also to the Book of Mormon and the Doctrine and Covenants, a collection of revelations the Mormons received from the divine, for answers to the questions about Christian doctrine that troubled so many in the era.[5]

Gentile historian Lawrence Foster also explored the role Biblicism, the focus on the Bible, played in Mormon culture, but from a broader theoretical perspective than that of Barkun. Foster argued that the biblical metaphors through which Mormons saw the world of economic change, religious pluralism, geographical expansion, the dissolution of kinship bonds, and the decline of the patriarchal household, all contributed to the rise of Mormonism. Focusing on plural marriage, he asserted, that the "restoration" of plural marriage among Mormons was a biblically filtered response to the confusion caused by economic changes in the Burned-Over District. Additionally, Foster argued, the restoration of polygamic practice by the Mormons in the American Midwest, and its continuation in what would become Utah, was a product of the relative freedom and the inequalities of the American frontier.[6]

Several scholars have emphasized the restoration and primitivist aspect of early Mormon culture. In an unpublished University of Chicago doctoral dissertation Mormon and historian Marvin Hill situated Mormonism in revivalist and primitivist contexts. He argued that Mormonism attempted to restore or recover the Christianity of the apostolic period. In the sectarian strife of the early nineteenth century where competing "sects" all claimed to be the one true brand of Christianity, Mormonism, Hill asserted, arose as a revolt against American religious pluralism by claiming that it alone had authoritative new revelations. This claim, Hill argued, attracted converts to the faith and became the foundation for Mormon missionary zeal.[7]

Gentile historian Mario DePillis likewise emphasized the role religious pluralism played in the rise of Mormonism. For DePillis, it was the frontier and its competing religious groups, each claiming to be the one true faith, that is central to the rise of Mormonism. Mormonism's success in the frontier regions of Ohio and Missouri was strongly related to its claims that it alone had proper godly authority. DePillis linked Mormon stabilization and growth to the widely held beliefs in the Mormon community that Mormonism alone had the true apostolic priesthood, that it was only they who were experiencing the true gifts of the spirit, that only its adherents had restored true apostolic authority to the earth, and, most importantly, that it was only they who were receiving revelations from the divine. These factors provided the authoritative bases or foundations from which Mormonism made its claim to being God's one and only true Church.[8]

This emphasis on Christian restoration, the belief that one could recreate the church of Jesus's apostles, as a lens through which to view the rise of Mormonism and other contemporary revival groups, has probably received its fullest exploration in the essays of historian of American Protestantism Richard Hughes. Like Hill, Hughes, a member of the Disciples of Christ, saw Mormonism as a response to the religious and theological diversity of the American milieu. Like Hill, Hughes contended that the Church of Jesus Christ of Latter-day Saints grounded its claims to be the one true Church on its insistence that it and it alone, represented the restoration of true primitive or apostolic Christianity. However, Hughes goes further and explores the particulars of Mormon primitivism in relationship to other restorationist groups such as the Puritans and the "Christians" or Campbellites. For Hughes, Mormon primitivism was romantic rather than rational in form. The Campbellites, on the other hand, tied their restoration claims to a Scottish Enlightenment methodology in which rationality and logic were applied to the New Testament text allowing one to discern from the biblical text the "true" form of apostolic Christianity. The Mormon claim to be the only true form of Christianity, a claim that transcended time and space, rested instead on the claim that Joseph Smith had received direct revelations from Christ that set out the form and structure the true Apostolic church was to take and that Mormons alone received such gifts of the spirit through visions and dreams. What distinguished Mormons from "Christians," claimed Hughes, was that Mormonism went beyond the biblical text asserting instead that true apostolic authority resided not on or in biblical texts, but instead in charismatic experiences between Mormons, and particularly Joseph Smith, and God and Christ.[9]

Gentile historian and religious studies scholar Jan Shipps also explored this restorationist aspect of early Mormonism. Like Smith, Foster, Hill, and Hughes, Shipps grounded Mormon restorationism in American biblical culture. Shipps argued that Mormon restorationist ideology was different from other primitivist groups such as the Campbellites. Mormons saw themselves as literally fulfilling biblical and Book of Mormon prophecies. The Saints believed that the restoration of primitive Christianity could take place only when communication between the divine and the human were restored. Mormons believed that they were that restoration, a restoration, they believed, that had been prophesied in scripture and a restoration reflected in the presence of the gifts of the spirit and continuing revelation within the primitive Mormon community.[10]

Some have argued that Mormonism was the product of one particular form of American Christian culture, Puritanism. Gentile historian David Brion Davis, who offered a geographical and cultural argument to account for Mormon origins, argued that the Yankee or New England background of Mormonism's founders was and is of crucial importance for understanding how Mormons countered the religious confusion and economic turbulence of the nineteenth century. It was Mormon belief in a close personal God, their providential history, their theocratic ideology, their stress on the importance of a calling, and their Calvinist or determinist leanings, the belief that God and God alone determined whether one was saved or not, that point up the cultural links between Mormonism and Puritanism.[11]

Likewise, Gentile historical and cultural geographer Donald Meinig and Mormon anthropologist Rex Cooper emphasized the New England backgrounds of early Mormon members and leaders. Meinig argued that Puritanism provided the theocratic and authoritarian culture that would become central to Mormonism. However, Meinig does not reduce Mormonism to its Puritan background. Taking an interactionist perspective, he asserted that it was the interaction between culture and the environment, between Mormon culture and the harsh Great Basin Desert environment in which it settled after its exodus from Nauvoo, that created or manufactured a Mormonism that was culturally distinctive from Puritanism.[12]

Another approach emphasizing cultural factors in the rise of Mormonism, although in a somewhat different fashion, is that of non–Mormon sociologist Marianne Perciaccante. Countering, as did Whitney Cross, assertions that the frontier was the major factor in Mormonism's appeal, Perciaccante noted that evidence from Jefferson County, New York, which had already undergone the transformation from an agrarian economy to a commercial one by the time Mormonism arose, suggested that Mormonism's success was theological and doctrinal. Utilizing church records to find out who was converting to Mormonism and why, Perciaccante found the key to understanding the rise and success of Mormonism was its rhetoric emphasizing that Mormonism and Mormonism alone had an unmediated relationship with God.

Perciaccante emphasized that Mormon claims of direct relationship with the divine occurred at a time when groups such as the Methodists, which had formerly been anti-formalist in structure and emphasized a personal relationship with God, were becoming more formalized and more bureaucratized, both in institutional terms and in terms of how they conceptualized a believer's relationships with God. As this transformation was occurring in Jefferson County Mormons appeared preaching their gospel of continuing revelation and capitalized on the disenchantment of some Methodists with the processes of formalization going on in their increasingly formalized and bureaucratized religious community. As a result, many in Jefferson County converted to Mormonism.[13]

Gentile historian R. Laurence Moore also took a cultural approach to Mormon origins. In his chapter on Mormonism in *Religious Outsiders and the Making of Americans*, he argued that Mormon theology, especially that which characterized Mormonism's Kirtland, Ohio, period in the early and mid–1830s, became enmeshed in a kind of dialectical relationship with the rhetoric of anti–Mormon groups in the areas around Kirtland. In Moore's view, Mormon theological novelties played a major role in constructing a Mormon identity in opposition to its Gentile combatants. These doctrinal novelties then played a central role in the increasing vehemence of anti–Mormon attacks on the Church itself. In a seemingly endless and sometimes deadly dialectical dance, the Mormons developed singular doctrines that gave rise to anti–Mormon attacks. These attacks, in turn, led Smith to propagate even more peculiar doctrines, such as that of the plurality of gods and that of plural marriage in Nauvoo, which, in turn, led to even more aggressive attacks on the Saints. This dialectical dance, Moore suggested, eventually led to the assassination of Joseph Smith in Illinois. The importance of this dialectical dance of new doctrine, aggression toward the "Saints," newer LDS doctrines and more aggression toward Mormons, lies in the role this process played in the continuing structuration of Mormon identity. For Moore, it was culture, in the form of theology and doctrine and negative reactions to it, that made Latter-day Saints.[14]

Social and Cultural Tensions and Mormon Origins

As Moore notes, one thing that can give us insight into primitive Mormon culture is non–Mormon responses to Mormonism and to Mormons in the 1830s. For example, inhabitants living in Kirtland before the arrival of the Mormons regarded the Saints, when they arrived in significant numbers, as intruders. Kirtland's inhabitants were disturbed by what they regarded as the transformation of their township's political culture from a Whig stronghold into a Democratic one thanks to the influx of Latter-day Saints. By 1837, this transformation was such that Mormons controlled all the major town political offices in Kirtland except for that of constable.[15]

Kirtland's Gentiles also believed that Mormons threatened the economic security of the community. Many felt that the influx of Mormons into Kirtland increased poverty in the area. Landholders believed that the Saints were responsible for driving down land prices, which had previously risen due to inflation, population increases, and the rising value of land in neighboring communities. Non-Mormon residents also believed that the failure of the Kirtland Savings Bank, a Mormon owned and run quasi-bank, was partly responsible for the decline in land values in Kirtland.[16]

Mormon communalism was another source of tension between Mormons and Gentiles in Kirtland. In 1831, Mormon leaders established an economic organization, the "Law of Consecration and Stewardship," also known as the "Order of Enoch" or the "United Order," which was communitarian in nature, and which was limited exclusively to members of the Church. Non-Mormons interpreted this institution as a sign of both Mormon economic and cultural and ideological exclusiveness and as proof that Mormons were enthralled or brainwashed by their false prophet. Finally, rumors that Mormons, or at the least Mormon leaders, were practicing "free love" and plural marriage, fueled tensions between Mormons and Gentiles.[17]

Gentile concern over Mormon communalism and sexual practices and the attention the non–Mormon sensationalist press reports of the era gave to them, suggests that cultural differences were as much if not more responsible for the tensions between Mormons and their Gentile neighbors than political and economic disputes in Kirtland. Rumors that Mormons were practicing "free love" and polygamy circulated through non–Mormon circles in Kirtland and beyond highlighting the extent to which "unorthodox" Mormon beliefs unsettled Gentiles. So do Gentile attacks on Mormons and Mormon leaders including Smith, who were beaten, tarred and feathered, and verbally attacked by their Gentile neighbors. Accusation and rumor eventually gave rise to the polemical literature against Mormonism we explored in Chapter One, whose mission it was to "expose" Smith and the "unorthodox" faith he created. Anti-Mormons hoped that their tracts, pamphlets, and books might keep potential converts from joining what they saw as a dangerous "unorthodox" faith.[18]

Political, economic, and cultural tensions between Mormons and their non–Mormon neighbors did not end in Ohio. They followed the Saints to Missouri where Mormons migrated in order to build Zion in 1831. In Jackson County, Missouri, vandalism of LDS property in 1832 quickly turned to violence in 1833 forcing some Saints to flee to nearby Clay County. By 1836, many Clay County Gentiles likewise turned against the Saints and began attacking members of the Church. In order to quell the violence, Missouri lawmakers established Caldwell and Davies counties as Mormon counties. However, this did not solve the "Mormon problem" in the state. Several Mormon and non–Mormons were killed in a number of skirmishes in the region, including one at Haun's Mill, which the Saints came to refer to as a massacre, where seventeen Latter-day Saints were killed during a Mormon and Gentile battle there. These skirmishes eventually led Missouri Governor Lilburn Boggs to issue his now infamous order that Mormons should either be driven out of Missouri or exterminated. Under great pressure and threat, the Mormons were forced to flee Missouri and to give up their plans to build the temple of Zion in Independence, a site they considered to be of the same sacred importance to God's chosen people in America as Jerusalem was to God's chosen people in the old-world Zion.[19]

In Missouri the same economic, political and cultural tensions found in Ohio were further complicated by other political and cultural ones, specifically the Mormon position on slavery and its notion that America's First Peoples or Native Americans were the Jews of the new world. Missouri's Gentiles, most of whom were migrants from the pro-slavery hill country regions of Kentucky and Tennessee and most of whom were Democrats, believed that the Saints taught that once black people became members of the Church, they could no longer be slaves. They also believed that Latter-day Saints were inciting slaves to revolt. In addition, Gentiles saw Latter-day Saints as allies of the First Peoples. They believed that the special place First Peoples held in the Book of Mormon and in Mormon ideological discourse, namely as Jews who had fled the Old World for the New, was dangerous to the political status quo in Missouri.

Hoping to put an end to persecution and mob actions, Mormons fled Ohio and Missouri for Illinois. Receiving a charter from the state of Illinois, something both Illinois Democrats and the Whig Abraham Lincoln were in favor of, the Saints settled in a town that they renamed Nauvoo, the city beautiful. In Nauvoo, tension within the community and persecution by outsiders invariably followed thanks to what non–Mormons saw as the novel and questionable practices of the Saints. The practice of polygamy, though secret and limited to leading members of the church, had become more widely known both inside and outside of the Mormon community by this time, dividing not only Mormon and Gentile but Saint and Saint. In 1844 an article critical of the practice of polygamy by Mormon leaders and of Mormon leaders themselves appeared in the newspaper the Nauvoo *Expositor*, a newspaper published by a small but vocal group of Mormon dissidents. In response Joseph Smith led a mob that destroyed the printing press of the newspaper. Smith and his brother Hyrum were arrested for the destruction of the *Expositor's* printing press, though political, economic, and other cultural tensions were also behind the arrest. On 27 June 1844 the prophet and his brother Hyrum were murdered by a mob while being held in the Carthage, Illinois, jail. Reorganizing under the leadership of Brigham Young, the Saints once again tried to escape persecution. This time they left the United States entirely and settled in the Great Basin Desert, which was then part of Mexico.[20]

Gnosticism, Hermeticism and Mormon Origins

This exploration of Mormon and non–Mormon cultural tensions points up the important role culture played in a series of culture wars that characterized relations between Mormons and Gentiles and that characterized Jacksonian America. The role culture played in Mormon-Gentile tensions has led a number of analysts to focus on and explore the diverse ways culture impacted the rise of Mormonism and other movements in the Burned-Over District. However, not all of these cultural approaches are helpful in delineating the cultural scripts or cultural templates on which Smith drew to create both Mormonism and Mormons.

For instance, Gentile literary critic and historian Harold Bloom asserted, in *The American Religion*, that Mormonism was a brand of individualistic American gnosticism. The fundamental problem with Bloom's argument is that one never grasps from Bloom's book that Mormons instituted communal practices, established cooperative institutions, constructed their communities according to a plan laid down by Joseph Smith, and almost always followed the counsel of their leaders. All of these actions were sources of tension between Mormons and their neighbors, and all of them raise questions about Bloom's contention that Mormonism was a form of American hyper individualism. Bloom's overemphasis on individualism and his resulting under emphasis on the Mormon communitarian impulse makes his approach of limited, if any, help in understanding the rise of Mormonism and the making of Mormons.[21]

Another less than helpful approach to Mormon origins and Mormon identity construction is that of John Brooke. Where Mormonism was for Bloom a form of gnosticism, Brooke saw Mormonism as heir to the European hermetic tradition. For Brooke, Mormons were hermetic perfectionists who preached the co-equality of spirit and matter, the covenant of celestial marriage (plural marriage), and the ultimate goal of humankind as the achievement of godhood (the "Plan of Salvation" or "eternal progression"), all important doctrines, or so he claimed, both within the hermetic tradition and in primitive Mormonism.

Brooke argued that Smith's money digging, along with his primitivism or restorationism, his attempt to go back to and to restore the primitive apostolic church, and his dispensationalism, his belief that the restoration of the primitive apostolic church ignited a new age, places Mormonism within the hermetic tradition. He also asserted that certain Mormon practices, such as the Kirtland Safety Society Bank debacle, were hermetic in origin. The Kirtland Safety Bank debacle was, he argued, an instance of counterfeiting and hence hermetic alchemy since Smith and other elite Mormons were trying turn paper into gold. He asserted that Mormonism's secret temple rituals were hermetic in origin because they were secret and required special and secretive knowledge in order to perform them.[22]

But is there a direct relationship or even an indirect link between European hermeticism and Mormonism? For instance, polygyny, one of the cultural scripts Brooke argued Smith consciously or unconsciously borrowed from hermeticism, was practiced by "radical" eschatological or end-time oriented Anabaptists, Anabaptists who thought Jesus's second coming that would transform the world was imminent, in sixteenth-century Munster, an independent city in North Rhine-Westphalia. While many Radical Reformation and Anabaptist scholars interpreted Munster polygyny as the product of a demographic imbalance between men and women, others, more correctly in my opinion, saw it and see it and Munster Zionism in general, with its patriarchalism, millennialism or apocalypticism, and notions of Davidic lineages, as a sectarian attempt by Munster's Anabaptists to restore the apostolic biblical practices and emphases of the early church.[23]

Just as the introduction of polygyny in Munster was the product of Biblicism so was the Mormon restoration of polygamy in Kirtland and Nauvoo. Smith came to the conclusion that plural marriage had to be practiced by God's people while he was engaged in his revision or, as it is sometimes called, his "translation" of the Bible in the early 1830s. As Charlotte Haven, a non–Mormon living in Mormon Nauvoo at the time wrote in a letter, there was much discussion amongst the Saints about Tanakh or Old Testament polygamic practices. Additionally, the pamphlet *The Peace Maker*, written by church member Udney Hay Jacob in 1842, justified polygamy by referencing Scripture. Mormon polygamic theory and practice thus has its roots in the reading and interpretation of the Bible rather than in the hermetic tradition.[24]

Plural marriage was not the only thing on Joseph Smith's mind at the time he was "revising" the Bible. He was also concerned with other issues surrounding marriage. For instance, section 74 of the Doctrine and Covenants (1832) deals with the question of whether Mormons could marry non–Mormons. In this revelation Smith queries God about whether interfaith marriages are proper. In reply, God makes reference to St. Paul's counsel on the subject in I Corinthians. Smith was clearly turning to the Bible rather than to the hermetic oral tradition for answers to doctrinal questions that troubled him.

Nor were the magical and occult activities of Joseph Smith, his family, and many of the early members of the church, which Brooke made much of and claimed as proof of Smith's hermeticism, evidence of Mormonism's direct or indirect relationship to the hermetic tradition. Both "popular" and "high" magic occult cultures were present in Early National America. To take just one example, the belief that buried treasure might lie in "Indian" mounds was common in Jacksonian America and was grounded in contemporary oral and written romances of First Peoples origins and tales of finding lost treasure. However, there is no evidence that this oral tradition or these romances were direct or indirect descendants of a hermetic tradition. Unless and until additional evidence is found that substantiates links between the sixteenth-century hermetic tradition and nineteenth-century Mormonism, the most likely place that Smith picked up his folk magic beliefs was from the world of nineteenth-century American occult and romantic popular culture.[25]

The Christian Cultural Contexts of Mormon Origins

Although Brooke may have been mistaken when he asserted that the historic cultural roots of Mormonism lie in hermeticism, he was almost certainly accurate when he claimed that Mormonism's cultural roots lie in its European and, I would add, its Mediterranean roots. Mormons, Shakers, and the Oneida Community shared biblical, apocalyptic or millennial, perfectionist, dispensationalist, and restorationist or primitivist cultural scripts or cultural templates that were central to each of these faiths in their own ways. While Brooke traces these cultural scripts to the Radical Reformation and to the hermetic tradition, they are actually older than both. They are biblical, they are grounded in a reading of the Bible, and they are, as such, as old as parts of the Jewish and Christian Bibles themselves.[26]

First-century CE Jewish sectarian groups, including the Jewish sect that ultimately became the Christian sect, were apocalyptic. They expected Jesus to come again and they expected Jesus's second coming to transform the world into a kind of second Eden or paradise. The Jewish sectarianism of Jesus, for instance, as best as we can ascertain given the problematic nature of the evidence, and that of the Apostle Paul, were apocalyptic. Joachim of Fiore's (1132–1202) eleventh-century speculations about the future were apocalyptic as were seventeenth-century primitive Quakerism and Puritanism, with its emphasis on building a utopian "cittie set upon a hill" in the New World. Nineteenth-century primitive Mormonism was also apocalyptic. Mormons believed that the world they lived in was about to end and be transformed into a paradise and that Mormonism would play a central role in the end times and in the Edenic world that was expected to emerge after the second coming.[27]

Christian perfectionism, the belief that Christians could become perfect and holy in their everyday lives like Christ, likewise has a long historical genealogy. For example, Roman Catholic and Orthodox Christian monasticism were and are perfectionist, grounded as they are in the notion that it is possible to live a holy and perfect Christian life on earth in isolated monastic communities. In the sixteenth and seventeenth centuries, many Anabaptists, spiritualists, and Quakers attempted to bring this Christian perfectionism or holiness ideology out of the monastic cloister and into the world. In "On Free Will" Anabaptist Balthasar Hubmaier (1480–1528) argued that humans, after their "'new birth,' were free to both do good and be good." Anabaptist Menno Simmons (1496–1561) maintained that the divine nature of the soul lost in the fall was restored upon repentance and could be maintained by leading a good life. Perfectionism also informed numerous eighteenth- and nineteenth-century Christian religious leaders and movements. Methodist founder John Wesley (1703–1791) and revivalist Charles Finney (1792–1875) believed that sanctification could be manifest in Christian lives and linked perfectionist notions to reform efforts. The nineteenth-century Shakers and the Oneida Community linked perfectionism and millennialism, the second coming, believing that they were instantiations of the "Kingdom of God" on earth. Shakers believed that their second "Christ," "Mother" Ann Lee, helped women overcome the subservience that had been their lot since "the fall," helped believers triumph over the apostasy that had given the anti–Christ temporary ascendancy in the world between the coming of the first Christ and the coming of the second, and that Lee's instantiation of Christian celibacy in her life and its subsequent embodiment in the lives of other Shakers, could and would lead to perfection in this life and eternal life in the next. Oneidans believed that disease and death could be conquered through sexual control and that the "holiness" or perfection resulting from sexual control and a communal lifestyle sanctified their all things in common community. Mormons believed they were building a community of saints, sacralizing, in the process, the space in which Saints were called by God to reside ("Zion") and the life cycle ("eternal progression") Saints were urged to follow, a life cycle that allowed each Saint the possibility of becoming as gods.[28]

The dispensationalist story is no different. Dispensationalism is inherent in Christian notions that Christianity, through Jesus, had brought about a new period of human and divine history. Shakers believed that different ages and the people living in varying degrees of perfection in those ages, were characterized by varying sexual practices of varying degrees of perfection. Shakers believed that they represented supreme perfection because celibacy was, in their ideology, the most perfect form of these sexual practices of the ages. Mormons believed that their restored church could only come into existence in the "fulness of time" in the United States, in the land of liberty and freedom they sacralized. They believed that Joseph Smith was the prophet of this new age or dispensation thanks to his restoration of the one true apostolic church that had disappeared with the rise of "orthodox" Christianity in the mediaeval West.[29]

A related cultural script, one which was heavily debated not only in nineteenth-century American Christianity and culture but also in the Christianity of the Middle Ages and the Reformation, was Christian restorationism or primitivism, the notion that the only true brand of Christianity was that of the apostles and that the only true Christian church was an apostolic church. As a number of commentators have noted, religious tensions surrounding the issue of which church was the one true Church were quite prevalent in Jacksonian America. Many "seekers" saw a contradiction between the Christian pluralism of Jacksonian America, in which each church claimed to be God's only true church, and the notion that there was only one true and orthodox Christian church, a notion that goes back at least to the debates over what constituted "orthodox" Christianity in the fourth-century Roman Empire.

The establishment of "orthodox" Christianity at Nicaea did not, as is evident particularly in retrospect, put an end the search for the one true Christian Church. In the wake of the Protestant Reformation many sixteenth-century Anabaptists, seventeenth-century Quakers, Puritans, John Wesley (1703–1791), the eighteenth and nineteenth-century Scots Robert and John Haldane, late eighteenth- and early nineteenth-century American "Christians," Republican Methodist Church founder James O'Kelly (1757–1826), former Baptist Abner Jones (1772–1841), ex–Presbyterian Barton Stone (1772–1844), ex–Presbyterian Scottish father and son Thomas and Alexander Campbell (1763–1854 and 1788–1866), and many others, sought the true form of the one true primitive apostolic church and formed churches that they claimed instantiated it.[30] So did Shakers, the Oneida Community, Millerites, Methodists, and Baptists, all of whom claimed that they represented the restored the primitive church.[31] Significant numbers of converts to Shakerism, the Oneida Community, and to Adventism, believed they had found the one true apostolic community and church.[32]

As I noted in Chapter One, the Mormon prophet Joseph Smith was much vexed by the issue of which of the many churches, if any, of Jacksonian America, was God's one true Church. Many who became Mormons were, like Smith, searching or seeking for God's one true Church. Mark Grandstaff and Milton Backman found that Kirtland Saints had switched religion on a number of occasions before they became Mormons. Additionally, a number of early Mormon journals and diaries reveal that their authors, churched or unchurched, were searching for the one true Church until they found it in the Church of Jesus Christ of Latter-day Saints. For instance, early Mormon leader Sidney Rigdon saw in the Book of Mormon, authoritative proof of the truth of Mormonism and the prophethood of Joseph Smith. Solomon Chamberlain became a Saint after talks with Mormon missionaries convinced him that Mormonism embodied his dream that a church would arise with proper apostolic authority. Brigham Young, who would lead the Church after the assassination of Smith, was convinced of the truth of Mormonism after reading the Book of Mormon. He had previously searched for the one true Church amongst Anglican, Freewill Baptist, Reformed Methodist, and Quaker churches. Primitive Mormon apologist and polemicist Parley Pratt became a Saint after he was convinced that ancient apostolic authority had been restored with the advent of the Mormon Church. Wilford Woodruff, who, like Young, would later lead the Mormons, became a Saint because he believed "the Church of Christ [was] coming out of the wilderness."[33]

Other Mormon converts wrote of how they left their old churches, Methodist, Baptist, Presbyterian, Campbellite, or Universalist, for Mormonism when they heard Smith preach or heard about him from convinced and very convincing Mormon missionaries. Some of them had visions that they interpreted as evidence that the Mormon Church was God's Church. Others saw the miracles Mormons performed, the tongues they spoke in, and their ability to interpret tongues, all things also prominent in the New Testament as well, as evidence of the truth of Mormonism. According to Grandstaff and Backman fully one-third of Kirtland's Mormons came from restorationist churches, churches that maintained that they were the true church, before converting to Mormonism. All of this suggests that these "seekers" found something in Mormonism they did not find in the restorationist churches they previously joined. What they found, or so they believed, was God's one and only true Church.

According to Grandstaff and Backman, Mormon converts in Kirtland gave Smith's apostolic authority (forty-seven percent), the Book of Mormon (twenty-nine percent), and spiritual manifestations (fourteen percent), all of which were interrelated and all of which were seen in the context of restorationist ideologies, as their reasons for converting to Mormonism. It was, it seems, Smith's prophetic status and the continuing revelations and spiritual manifestations associated with this status, including dreams, visions, revelations, and the Book of Mormon, that drew converts to Mormonism.[34]

Particularly after the Reformation the issue of which church was God's one and only true church was intimately and inherently tied to the question of authority and who or what had the authority to restore God's one true Church to the world. Both Haldane's emphasized the Bible as the basis of churchly authority. O'Kelly, opposed to what he saw as inequality in the Methodist Church, emphasized congregational autonomy and the equality of clergy and laity as the foundation of true Christian authority. Jones asserted that the Bible was the sole source of authority and emphasized the need for Christian unity. Jones polemicized for an anti-elitist believer's church grounded in the New Testament and its "perfect law of freedom." Stone, one of the founders of the "Christian Movement," emphasized the authority of the Bible and believer's baptism by immersion. Alexander Campbell, another of the founders of the "Christian Movement," influenced by Francis Bacon, John Locke, and the Scottish Enlightenment, believed that the New Testament provided everything one needed to know about the pure ancient church provided one applied the correct method in unlocking it. Campbell, not surprisingly, asserted that his "Christian" Church, the church he restored on the basis of his empirical biblical research, was the one true apostolic church.

Other Christians looked for apostolic authority beyond the Bible. After all the apostle Paul claimed to have had a vision of the risen Jesus on the road to Damascus and asserted that this personal experience of a risen Jesus was the basis of his apostolic authority.[35] The twelfth-century Calabrian Catholic Joachim of Fiore (ca. 1135–1202) claimed he had prophetic visions. The sixteenth-century Christian reformer Martin Luther was regarded by some as a *reformator*, a holy man or prophet sent by God to institute change. Sixteenth-century "radical" Central European Anabaptist Thomas Muntzer believed he received revelations via dreams and visions. Many of the followers of seventeenth-century English Quaker leader George Fox believed he received utterances from the divine. Eighteenth-century Swedish scientist and mystic Immanuel Swedenborg claimed to receive revelations from God and claimed that he had the ability to speak with the angels that populated his dreams. According to Swedenborg, an angel commanded him to take up a pen so that God could dictate the meaning of the Bible to him. Shakers claimed that "Mother" Ann Lee received revelations from the divine. A compendium of these, *The Testimonies of the Life, Character, Revelations, and Doctrines of Mother Ann Lee...*, came to be regarded as scriptural within the Shaker community. The Ephrata Community of colonial America believed that their leader, Conrad Beissel (1691–1768), had received divine revelations. Late eighteenth-century American Methodist itinerant Freeborn Garritson claimed to have a dream vision in which an angel in a white robe appeared to him and offered him instruction in the nature of religious truth. Late eighteenth-century agrarian evangelical Nathan Barlow claimed to have been carried by Christ to heaven and hell. The nineteenth-century American Spiritualist Andrew Jackson Davis was known as the "Poughkeepsie Seer." Nineteenth-century Canadian Children of Light leader David Willson claimed to have had divine visions.[36]

Somewhat like Saint Paul, the Mormon prophet Joseph Smith claimed apostolic authority on the basis of his receiving continuing revelations from God and his ordination by God and Jesus. Smith claimed apostolic authority for the Mormon priesthood, the institution at the heart of the Mormon power and authority structure, on the basis that it was literally restored to his church by John the Baptist and three of Jesus' apostles.

According to Mormon ideology, the Mormon priesthood structure, which arose between 1829 and 1835, consisted of two restored priesthood forms from the biblical past, the Aaronic and Melchizedek Priesthoods, that were restored through the medium of the prophet Joseph Smith. The Aaronic priesthood, which governed the temporal affairs of the church and whose members were usually regarded as descendants of the "sons of [the Tanakh patriarch] Aaron," was restored in 1829 when John the Baptist appeared and laid hands-on Smith and his second in command, Oliver Cowdery, forgiving them of their sins in the process. The Melchizedek Priesthood, a priesthood organization whose genealogy went, according to Smith, back to the priest who blessed the Hebrew Patriarch Abraham in the Book of Genesis, was restored in 1830 when Peter, James, and John laid their hands on Smith and Cowdery, making them, in the process, Melchizedek high priests. According to primitive Mormon ideology, these three apostles of Christ gave Smith and Cowdery the authority to confer the Holy Ghost upon believers once they were baptized and ordained into the Melchizedek Priesthood, the body governing the spiritual affairs of the Church. All "legitimate" power in the Mormon Church stems, in Mormon ideology, from ordination to the Mormon priesthood.

Each Latter-day Saint man—Mormonism was, as was its era, patriarchal—was "called" to serve in priesthood offices with specific duties and specific powers in the early Church. A trinity of "callings" characterized both the Aaronic and Melchizedek priesthoods. The Aaronic Priesthood consisted of "priests," "deacons," and "teachers" while the Melchizedek Priesthood consisted of "elders," "seventies," and "high priests." In primitive Mormonism church "elders" were empowered to baptize, administer the sacrament or communion, bestow the Holy Ghost, ordain other priesthood offices, bless children, and take the lead in meetings. "Priests" had the same duties save for bestowing the Holy Ghost, blessing children, and ordaining elders. "Teachers" and "deacons" assisted the "priests" and watched over the Church to ensure that it was strong. They differed from "priests" in that they lacked any powers of ordination. Although "priests" could ordain "priests," "teachers," and "deacons," only "elders" could issue a license authorizing "each ordained person to perform the duty associated with his calling."[37]

The Book of Mormon, American Culture and Nationalist Epics

The Book of Mormon is one of the products of Mormon revelation on which many analysts have focused in order to gain insight into the broader contexts of Mormon origins. Some analysts of early Mormonism have argued that Joseph Smith "borrowed" his "tale" of Jewish clans in America from other popular romances of his time. For example, Alexander Campbell argued that Smith, with the aid of former Campbellite and communalist Sidney Rigdon, took the outline of the Book of Mormon from a manuscript written by Solomon Spaulding masquerading as a lost ancient text. Spaulding's manuscript tells the tale of a group of Romans, who, while sailing to England in the fourth century, were blown off course and landed instead on the shores of North America. It then details the experiences these Romans had among the Native American tribes of the North America.[38]

Others, like Quorum of the Seventies member B.H. Roberts, argued that the Book of Mormon was based on Ethan Smith's *View of the Hebrews*. Ethan Smith's book, first published in Poultney, Vermont, in 1823 and later revised by Smith in 1825, is a romantic history that postulates that America's First Peoples were the descendants of the Lost Ten Tribes of Israel. In his posthumously published book on the parallels between the *View of the Hebrews* and the Book of Mormon, Roberts noted a total of 26 parallels between the Book of Mormon and Ethan Smith's romance.

The question, of course, is whether these parallels "prove" borrowing or whether they are simply evidence of a shared cultural milieu. Dan Vogel pointed out that the theory of Indian origins that underlies both Ethan Smith's book and the Book of Mormon has a long genealogy; for instance, it was prevalent in seventeenth-century England. Whitney Cross noted that Smith drew on local Burned-Over District folklore and its romantic tales of a fabulous and wealthy pre–First Peoples culture. D. Michael Quinn pointed out how widespread popular magical practices were in early America. While it is possible that Smith knew of the *View of the Hebrews* and could have borrowed from it, it is equally possible, if not more likely, that whatever parallels exist between the Book of Mormon and the *View of the Hebrews* are reflective of the common culture milieu and the common cultural pedigree of the two rather than an instance of direct borrowing.[39]

Part of this common culture, of course, was America's religious and biblical culture. Some commentators have noted that much of the Book of Mormon is grounded in the same narrative structure of Joseph Smith's first vision with its tales of angelic visitation, darkness versus light, testimony of the true gospel, apostasy, apostolic condemnation, and restoration. This narrative arc of the book, with its repeating (and repetitious) tale of apostasy and restoration, constitutes a substantial portion of the tales in Smith's "sacred book" of the New World Jews. Others have pointed out that significant parts of the Book of Mormon are made up of quotes or paraphrases from the Tanakh or Old Testament Book of Isaiah. Others have noted that the Book of Mormon reflects its nineteenth-century Jackson Era environment in its ideologies of America as a Promised Land (1 Nephi 13:12–15, 2 Nephi 1:2 and 10:19), its complaints about the wickedness of the existing churches (4 Nephi 1:24–27), its nineteenth-century notions of freedom and liberty, particularly freedom and liberty from tyranny (Alma 43:30, 48, 46:18, 35 ff., Ether 9:25, 3 Nephi 2:12), its American like republicanism (Mosiah 29:25 ff.), its Euro-American racism (1 Nephi 12:22–23), its Euro-American anti–Semitism (2 Nephi 25:2), and its Protestant anti–Catholicism (1 Nephi 13:5, 14:3, 10, 17, 22:13–19 2 Nephi 1:7, 6: 12, 26, 29, 25:2, 29:5, 4 Nephi 29). Additionally, as a number of commentators have noted, the references to "secret combinations" in the Book of Mormon likely refer to nineteenth-century conspiracies associated with Freemasons, wealthy elites, elite bankers, and Roman Catholics (Helaman 3:23ff., 6:24ff., 9:28, 11:26ff., *Ether* 8:14 ff.).[40]

Others have argued that the Book of Mormon was a nineteenth-century work of Christian doctrine masquerading as an ancient document. For instance, Alexander Campbell argued in 1831 that the Book of Mormon (and, one might add, the Doctrine and Covenants) dealt "with every error and almost every truth discussed in New York for the last ten years and was best seen as a response to religious and theological pluralism." For him, the Book of Mormon was written by Joseph Smith to provide authoritative answers to every theological dispute then current in the United States including "infant baptism, ordination, the trinity, regeneration, repentance, justification, the fall of man, the atonement, transubstantiation, penance, church government, religious experience, the call to the ministry, the general resurrection, eternal punishment, who may baptize, and even the question of free masonry, republican government, and the rights of man."[41]

While Campbell had a valid point, it must not be forgotten that virtually every one of the doctrinal debates he noted was not novel to nineteenth-century New York. They had been disputed by Christians for hundreds of years. For instance, Anabaptists, since their birth, had opposed the baptism of infants and, by cutting the ties between church and state, undermined Christian theocratism.

Regardless of whether the Book of Mormon is a nineteenth-century document or an ancient one, as Mormon faith-oriented scholars, apologists, and polemicists have claimed, it is clear that not all of the cultural scripts or ideologies found in the Book of Mormon are peculiar to nineteenth-century America. The Book of Mormon is also, at least in part, the product of American and European Christian culture. For instance, the racism, anti–Semitism and anti–Catholicism of the Book of Mormon have long pedigrees that stretch back centuries, as I noted in Chapter One. The notion that churches had fallen into apostasy also has a long history. For instance, Roger Williams (1603?-1683) believed that all the churches of his time were apostate. The notion that America is exceptional and has an exceptional destiny before it, is also a relatively old cultural template. Early Puritans, for example, believed that America had a sacred mission before it. A number of Americans, including the Congregationalist and Presbyterian Lyman Beecher (1775-1863), the Unitarian William Ellery Channing (1780-1842), and the amateur historian George Bancroft (1800-1891), shared Joseph Smith's convictions that America was a special land guided by divine providence.[42]

As a nationalist romance about the lost tribes of Israel, the origins of America's indigenous peoples, and the epic and ancient past of America, the Book of Mormon is not novel either. Nationalist romances were not uncommon in eighteenth- and nineteenth-century America and Europe as the romance novels of Sir Walter Scott, the poetic Arthurian romances, Henry Wadsworth Longfellow's poem Hiawatha, the Finnish *Kalevala*, the Welsh *Mabinogion*, the Grimm's *Kinder- und Hausmarchen* German tales, the Serbo-Slavonic tales of Vuk Karadzic, Rossini's *Guillaume Tell*, Bellini's *Norma*, and Verdi's metaphorical *Nabucco* make clear. All of these mythic romances reflect a European and American fascination with a legendary and heroic past and are linked to the first great age of nation building, an age in which new national identities were being constructed throughout the Atlantic world and throughout Europe particularly in the nineteenth and twentieth century. The Book of Mormon, in this context, was and is a romantic epic that provided an ancient and glorious past for the new United States in the same way the *Mabinogion* did for Wales.[43] It also provided an ancient and glorious past for those who became Mormons to look back on and try to emulate.

Mormonism and North American Zionist Christianity

There is another aspect of the Book of Mormon that stands out to some observers, its Christian Jewishness and Christian Zionism. Alexander

Campbell was among the first to note the Jewishness of Mormon Christianity when he wrote in the 1830s that "[i]n the Book of Mormon Jews are called Christians." The Book of Mormon's Christian Jews, claimed Campbell, keep "the Laws of Moses, the.... Sabbath, and [worship] in their temple...." As a number of commentators since Campbell have noted, Mormonism is, at least in part, a kind of Jewish Christianity. The Book of Mormon tells the tale of a group of Hebrews who left their old Near Eastern world for the new world of what would become America. Over time, America's Hebrews, thanks to their apostasy, forgot, so the Book of Mormon tells us, who they really were.

Smith's Zionist Mormonism was neither the first nor only variety of Judaic Christianity in the Old World or the New. In the sixteenth century, for instance, a group of Protestants in Hungary (one of the centers of early modern Unitarianism) led by Andras Eissi established a Judaizing brand of Christianity. Eissi's Jewish Christians restored Mosaic ceremonial, worshipped on the Jewish Sabbath, abandoned Christian sacraments, and denied the divinity of Christ. In the 1790s Richard Brothers argued that Britons were the descendants of the lost tribes of Israel. In nineteenth-century America, Robert Matthews, the infamous Matthias the Prophet, established his Kingdom of Matthias in New York and preached and proselytized his hybrid brand of Christianity with its Jewish and cultic elements throughout the southern and eastern United States. In late nineteenth- and twentieth-century America, Seventh Day Adventists adopted Jewish practices such as worshiping on the seventh day and Jewish like dietary laws. In Canada an immigrant from New York named David Willson became leader of a community whose purpose was, at least in part, to bring Christians and Jews together in what he called a community of peace.[44]

Willson saw himself as destined to play a special role in bringing Jews into his Christian community in order to, as he put it, "ornament the Christian Church with all the glory of Israel." Willson claimed to be a "Jew in spirit" and his followers claimed that his mind had travelled backwards in time and dwelt with the Jewish patriarchs Abraham, Isaac, and Jacob. Willson and his Children of Peace built a community of mutual aid that was pacifist, apocalyptic, egalitarian, and centered on a temple that was finished in 1831.[45]

The nineteenth-century Christian interest in Hebrew or Jewish religious practices can also be seen in nineteenth and twentieth-century Christian apocalypticism, Christian travels to and interest in the "holy land," and in Christian missionary efforts. Dispensationalist, apocalyptic, and romantic ideologies spurred many nineteenth-century Protestant figures to call for the return of the Jews to Israel. Individuals as diverse as the poet and

Six. Culture Theory and Mormon Origins

painter William Blake (1757–1827), American New England Congregationalist clergyman Ethan Smith (1762–1848), author of the *View of the Hebrews* (1823), who argued that American First Peoples were descended from old world Hebrews, romantic English poet William Wordsworth (1770–1850), romantic Scottish author Walter Scott, (1771–1832), English barrister and Anglican evangelical Lewis Way (1772–1840), who was active in Anglican missionary work among the Jews, romantic English poet George Byron (1788–1824), the Anglo-Irish Plymouth Brethren John Newton Darby (1800–1862), English politician William Gladstone (1809–1898), English poet Robert Browning (1812–1889), and English novelist George Elliot (1819–1880), called for a Jewish return to the Holy Land. Many saw this return of the Jews to the Holy Land as a confirmation of apocalyptic biblical prophecy.

The increasing nineteenth-century Protestant interest in the Holy Land, the Hebrews, and biblical prophecy, led to an increased interest in early Christianity and propelled increasing numbers of Protestants to visit the Holy Land, write about the Holy Land, and do missionary work in the Holy Land. For many of these Protestant visitors to Palestine their travels to the Holy Land gave rise to an increased interest in both Judaism and in the contemporary European Jewish community. This interest in Judaism and Jews led, in turn, to an increase in Protestant hopes for converting Jews to Christianity. Eventually, this Protestant interest in converting the Jews was institutionalized in the formation of the Protestant London Jews Society or the London Society for Promoting Christianity among the Jews, in 1809, and in the United States with the founding of the Protestant American Society for Colonizing and Evangelizing the Jews, later the American Society for Meliorating the Condition of the Jews, in 1820. The American Society eventually purchased a farm near New Paltz, New York, where it hoped to establish a colony for Christianized Jews from Europe. Mormons were also interested Judaism and in missionizing to the Jews, as is clear from the Book of Mormon's title page and various passages in the Book of Mormon including II Nephi 29:13.[46]

In reaction to these Christian missionary efforts, in 1825 Jew Mordecai Noah purchased a tract of land on Grand Island in the Niagara River near Buffalo, New York. His plan was to establish a Jewish colony there to be named Ararat. He envisaged Ararat as a haven for Jews in a world of anti-Semitism. Noah's Ararat, which he saw as the restoration of ancient Israel, was to be theocratic and somewhat democratic with judges elected by the community from its Jewish members.[47]

Noah was aware of the Mormons and the Mormon prophet Joseph Smith and the Mormons were aware of Noah and Ararat. *The Latter-day Saints Messenger and Advocate* numbered Noah amongst the anti–Mormons and reprinted the attack Noah made on Mormonism in his newspaper, the *New York Evening Star*. *The Latter-day Saints Messenger and Advocate* also printed Smith's response to Noah's attack.[48]

Some have seen the parallels between Noah's Jewish restoration and Smith's Jewish Christian restoration as evidence that Smith borrowed heavily from Noah. Like Smith, Noah believed that the American Indians were remnants of the lost tribes of Israel and that they would share in the restoration of Zion. Both shared notions of a New World "new Jerusalem." Noah saw it as a temporary haven for Jews that would play an important role in bringing about millennial Jewish restoration while Smith saw it as the site to which First Peoples and adopted Jews, like the Mormons, would "gather" in the new millennium. Both Noah and Smith shared a theocratic vision, and both praised the United States. Noah saw its role in the Jewish restoration as important and divinely ordained. However, his long-term goal was to establish a Jewish government at Ararat with its own militia. Noah also believed that Ararat might expand westward. Smith saw the existence of the United States and its laws as a pre-requisite to the restoration of the one true Church, the Church of Jesus Christ of Latter-day Saints. In Nauvoo he established a government, the Council of Fifty, whose role after the expected apocalypse would be to rule the United States, He also instituted a Mormon militia in the "City beautiful." Both Noah and Smith saw temples as the centerpiece of their communities. In addition, both Noah and Smith were Masons, and both were very likely influenced by Masonic ritual.[49]

However, there were also significant differences between the ideologies of the Noah and Smith. Noah's kingdom, for instance, was more democratic than Smith's in that "judges" were to be elected from among the people while Smith's was authoritarian and autocratic. "Elections" may have occurred at Mormon General Conferences, but these generally confirmed what Smith, the priest-king of the "new Jerusalem," had already revealed. Smith's Mormon kingdom was more hierarchical than Noah's. Finally, Smith and Noah propounded different doctrines. Noah, for instance, opposed polygamy. Smith saw polygamy as a divine commandment. Smith emphasized the Davidic kingship and the kinship between Jews and the Mormons while Noah did not. Smith interpreted several prophetic biblical passages as predicting that the restoration of apostolic Christianity would also include the restoration of the Davidic kingship. He named his last son David in order, it appears, to fulfill the prophecies that in the last days a righteous king by the name of David would arise and rule in Zion.[50] Given these significant differences, it is most likely that both Noah and Smith were influenced by and drawing upon, cultural currents that were widespread in early America and in Protestant Europe.[51]

Mormonism and New England Puritanism

Others have seen Mormon Zionism as less a product of a Judaic Christian current in nineteenth-century America and Europe than the product of the New England background of most Mormon leaders, including Joseph Smith and his family. Historian David Brion Davis, historical geographer Donald Meinig, historian Rowland Berthoff, and cultural anthropologist Rex Cooper, have pointed out that most Mormon leaders had New England roots and that Mormon theocratic and covenantal practices, with their common emphasis on the New World as a geographic space that would purify, renew, and transmute old European Christianity back into its original apostolic form, on the purified religious community as the "new Israel," on the community as a saved and worthy community, on human progression, and on covenantal obligations, paralleled similar concepts in New England Puritanism.[52] Others have pointed out that both Mormonism and Puritanism regarded families as central, saw marriage as a sacrament, and were patriarchal.[53]

While there are similarities between Mormonism and Puritanism there are also important differences between the two. Given that Mormon arminianism, temples, baptism of the dead, and the doctrine of eternal progression, have no cultural or ideological precedents in primitive Puritanism even those who emphasize the New England roots of Mormonism do not ultimately reduce Mormonism to a purely revived form of New England Puritanism. Additionally, although Mark Grandstaff and Milton Backman and Whitney Cross found that a significant number Kirtland's Saints had a New England background, these converts did not necessarily come from a traditional Puritan background.[54] Val Rust found that most of the early New England Saints had ties to New England separatism and Radical Spiritualists rather than to "mainstream" Puritanism.[55] Among those who were not of "mainstream" Puritan cultural stock were Joseph Smith and his family. The Mormon prophet grew up on the margins of a transformed Puritan culture that was radically different from what it had been during Puritanism's "golden age." Solomon Mack, the prophet's maternal grandfather, became a Congregationalist only when he was 75. Smith's mother, Lucy, briefly became a Presbyterian in 1820. Smith's paternal grandfather, Asael Smith, was a heterodox Unitarian who associated with the Congregational Church from time to time. Smith's father, Joseph, was a seeker who attended church infrequently and who had religious oriented dreams and visions. All of them were critics of traditional Calvinist predestinarian or deterministic ideologies.[56]

Other scholars have drawn attention to links between Puritan, Unitarian, and Mormon perfectionism. Joseph Smith, John Humphry Noyes,

Horace Bushnell, and William Ellery Channing shared "Yankee" backgrounds and a belief that human perfection was tied to specific choices one made during his or her life. Some intellectual Puritans, for instance, argued that there were five stages in the work of redemption in human lives: call, justification, adoption, sanctification, and faith. The Vermont born Noyes, founder of the Oneida Community, delineated "holiness," "free love," "association in labor," and "immortality" as stages in the lives of those Christians on the road to perfection. The nineteenth-century Connecticut-born Congregationalist theologian and minister Horace Bushnell argued that humans were progressing. The Rhode Island–born nineteenth-century Unitarian preacher William Ellery Channing asserted that the individuality, liberty, and self-government present in the United States were working to create eternal men whose progress would surpass that of the angels. The Mormon prophet taught that men could become "as gods" if they made the right choices during their lives.[57]

While each of these schemas share the ideology that human lives can be divided into stages and that one may be sanctified during these life cycle stages, they varied in terms of the stages one traversed as they moved toward perfection or holiness. Moreover, it was polygamy, something none of the Yankees preached or taught should be practiced, that that was central to the Mormon prophet's evolutionary "ladder" of eternal progression. To Smith plural marriage helped create a "kingdom of priests" that, in turn, thanks to being fruitful and multiplying, provided greater opportunities for spirits from "beyond the veil" to come into the world and work out their salvations. Since families in Mormon doctrine are eternal, "the Principle" of polygamy enabled "worthy" heavenly fathers and heavenly mothers, when ensconced in the highest of heavenly domains, the "celestial kingdom," to populate their planetary worlds with spirit children who would come to worship them as their God.[58] In the end it is clear that Smith's conception of human evolution or "eternal progression" and his assertion that there was a plurality of gods, is very different from Noyes's, Bushnell's and Channing's notions of human progression, though clearly the possibility of human progression and perfection was in the air in an America some perceived in utopian hues.

Some commentators have argued and continue to argue that Smith's doctrine of eternal progression with its anti-trinitarianism and polytheism, was the Prophet's attempt to deal with emerging debates about life on other planets. If this is correct, Smith was not alone in speculating on the nature of the universe. Emmanuel Swedenborg (1688–1772) and the Poughkeepsie Spiritualist Andrew Jackson Davis (1826–1910) also attempted to harmonize contemporary science with contemporary religion in their spiritual naturalisms. Other scholars have seen the Mormon doctrine of deity

Six. Culture Theory and Mormon Origins 117

as a cultural response to the cultural debate about the nature of the universe. Klaus Hansen, for instance, argued that "eternal progression," the doctrine of the plurality of gods, and the Mormon conception of the afterlife, were means through which the powerless in this life became powerful in the next. Finally, still others have seen Mormon eternal progression as Smith's attempt to come to grips with nineteenth-century materialistic science. Smith's God was, after all, a materialistic God.[59]

While Puritanism may not have directly impacted primitive Mormonism, there may be more indirect ideological and historical connections between the two. For instance, historian of Puritanism David Hall claimed that there were inherent tensions and ambiguities in colonial and early American Puritanism. Although Puritanism preached the doctrine of the church of "visible saints," it also preached the doctrine that the church and the community should be and were coterminous. Over time, as Hall notes, many Puritans became concerned about whether their children could be members of the church and, by extension, members of the community. That many Puritans shared this concern gradually pushed the Church to make important cultural and ideological changes. Soon it was acceptable for members to baptize their children into the Church, making them members of both the church of "visible saints" and members of the community. While some Puritans were concerned that those who were possibly "unregenerate" were baptizing their children into the church, and uncomfortable with the possibility that "unregenerate" were partaking the sacrament, others accepted these changes because they tamped down the cognitive dissonance that stemmed from the inherent contradictions within. Puritanism.[60]

Mormonism, with its universalist conception of salvation embedded within a hierarchy of worthiness and clear notions as to what constituted saintliness in the first place, may have been a response to these doctrinal and ideological contradictions and ambiguities within New England Puritanism. There was no ambiguity in the Mormon doctrine and practice of continuing revelation about the relationship between church and state. In primitive Mormonism the Mormon Church was the state. Nor was there any ambiguity in Mormon doctrine concerning infant baptism. Mormon young, revelation said, could only be baptized after making a profession of faith.[61]

There may also be an echo of the half-way covenant of transformed Puritanism in Mormonism. As there were, at least for some Puritans, differences between full way and half-way Saints, there were spiritual differences among Mormons treading along the path of eternal salvation and these spiritual differences had different consequences both in the here and now and "beyond the veil." Worthy Mormons were those who made correct choices during the course of lives and were regarded as the most spiritual of Mormons. Only these "worthy" male Mormons and their wives and children could enter the highest of kingdom "beyond the veil," the "celestial kingdom" governed by God in which those Mormons who had progressed could become "as god." Others, the less worthy, ended up in the "terrestrial kingdom" which was governed by Jesus Christ and inhabited by honorable men who had been "blinded by the craftiness of men," and the "telestial kingdom" which was governed by the Holy Spirit or Holy Ghost, and whose inhabitants had not yet received the gospel or the testimony of Jesus.[62]

Nor was there any ambiguity about who were the worthiest of the worthy Saints in this life as there was in Puritan ideology. Mormon discourse maintained that the worthiest of worthy Saints held the highest offices in the church's spherarchical hierarchy. It was only these worthiest of the worthy who could engage in "the Principle" of polygamy. Moreover, only the worthiest of worthy Saints would hold not only the most power in this world but also in the kingdom beyond the veil[63]

Making Mormons

It seems clear, at least to me, that Joseph Smith filtered everything, including nationalism, romanticism, America as utopian promised land, economic change, changing science, Masonic rituals, the first peoples as the lost tribes of Israel, and reflections on long standing Christian cultural scripts such as restorationism, apocalypticism, perfectionism, dispensationalism, theocracy, and universalism, to note a few, through the Bible. In the process of doing so he interpreted them all through the lens of an ever developing and dynamic biblical hermeneutic that became more "Jewish" and more "novel" as Mormonism itself grew and changed between 1830 and 1844. Mormons were a biblical people and Smith was surrounded by a diverse biblical culture. He justified many of Mormonism's supposed doctrinal novelties, such as baptisms for the dead, sealing rituals, and the restored priesthood, by pointing to biblical precedents.[64]

As Jan Shipps noted in her introduction to the published "Journals" of one-time Mormon leader William McLellin, the Bible was of immense importance to Joseph Smith and to the early Latter-day Saints. As Shipps noted, McLellin was privy to discussions of Mormon leaders in the early years of the Church, and according to him, the Bible and biblical precedents were at the heart of these discussions. Additionally, McLellin's "Journals" document the use of biblical texts and biblical topics by Mormon missionaries as they preached their way across the American Northeast, the American Midwest, and southwestern Ontario, in the primitive era of the Church. It is clear from McLellin's journal that the early Mormon missionaries were

Six. Culture Theory and Mormon Origins

not only steeped in the Bible; they were told by the Mormon elite to emphasize their Christian roots by preaching the Bible as they tried to make converts and as they presented their faith to the world. Shipps also noted that Joseph Smith's "Journals" are filled with references to the Bible and contain Talmudic-like expositions on biblical texts. It is clear that Biblicism and a biblical culture were central to primitive Mormon culture, the culture from the founding of the Church to the assassination of Joseph Smith and are central if we are to comprehend the rise of Mormonism and understand the process by which Mormons were created or manufactured.[65]

It was Joseph Smith, the mediator of this biblically filtered culture, who manufactured Mormonism. In the process Smith also manufactured Mormons. As Dickson Bruce argued in his book on the Cane Ridge revival, the revival created new men and new women through symbols and rituals associated with the revival. Utilizing Victor Turner's notion of betwixt and between states, Bruce asserted that in the liminal state of the ritual conversion call, the old cultural baggage individuals carried with them withered away to be replaced by a new identity and entry into a new community.

I would argue that something similar happened in early Mormonism. Impacted by the charisma of Smith and the rituals and symbols associated with Mormonism, particularly its emphasis on continuing revelation and God acting in history, new Mormon men and women who ordered their lives around the revelations Joseph Smith was receiving, were manufactured or created, through liminal resocialization processes.[66]

In Mormonism's primitive era the identities and the community Smith created were incubated in a continuous betwixt-between state in which continuous new revelations, continuing persecutions, and the almost constant chaos that resulted, in large part, from the new revelations and their commands and from subsequent persecutions, met and interacted with the cultural scripts that Smith and those who converted to Mormonism brought with them into this new community. In the process, Mormons were made and transformed into a new Israel replicating, reliving, and repeating what happened to God's Old World chosen people to whom they were, according to Mormon doctrine, tribally related, and who were trying to build "Zion" outside of, but at the same time within, divine and secular space and time all the while surrounded by those who they believed were persecuting them.[67] Smith eventually became the Davidic priest-king of the "new Jerusalem" in the New World.[68]

Karl Marx claimed that humans made their own history but that their ability to do so was bounded by the histories they, or particular the economically, politically, and culturally powerful among them, had already made. Class realities, power differentials, institutional structures, cultural and ideological scripts or templates, and so on, place limits on human world making "creativity." However, those limits do not make such creativity impossible. The pre-existing economic, political, social, and cultural structures and ideologies of Jacksonian America, biblically oriented cultural scripts or templates, and specific forms of a biblically based hermeneutic with elective affinities for each another, when mediated through the prophet, seer, translator, and revelator Joseph Smith, manufactured Mormonism and created Mormons. It was Joseph Smith, the pivot of authority in the nascent Latter-day Saint community, the same Joseph Smith who was told that existing churches were "an abomination in [God's] sight," who provided the authoritative cultural, institutional, economic, political, and cultural-ideological contexts in which Mormonism became Mormonism and Mormons became Mormons.

Those who became Mormons, Shakers, and Oneidans may have been equally affected by the same economic changes and political chaos of the nineteenth century but they responded to them in very different though equally biblical ways. They interpreted the social, economic and political events around them through the specific cultural frames their leaders and they constructed out of the economic, political, geographical, demographic, and particularly cultural environments and interactions that surrounded them.

Paul Conkin, David Hall, and Jon Butler argued that the cultural frames upon which nineteenth-century religious movements of drew on went back at least to the Reformation and centered on debates surrounding the nature of Christian salvation. According to Conkin, nineteenth-century America was characterized, in part, by varying Christian intellectual cultures arguing over the nature of salvation. Calvinists and Lutherans found salvation in the unknowable grace of God. Unitarians and Universalists found it in God's benevolence. Alexander Campbell (1788–1866) found it in the hearing and understanding of the New Testament and in baptism for the remission of sins. Adventist William Miller (1782–1849) found it in the mathematical predictions of the end time in the apocalyptic books of the Bible. Founder of Christian Science Mary Baker Eddy (1821–1910) found it in mind cures. Pentecostals found it in the Holy Spirit and the sanctification and gifts that followed regeneration. Shakers found it in celibacy and communes. Oneidans found it in group marriage and communes. Mormons found it in "eternal progression" and the "plan of salvation" associated with "eternal progression." Cultural differences structured around these key symbols were at the heart of the different social movements and the identities constructed within them.[69]

These cultural divides between early nineteenth-century American religious movements also marked off and distinguished "moderate" Christian social movements from "radical" Christian social movements such as the Mormons, Shakers, and Oneida. Moderate groups tended to be more open and "democratic" and were characterized by a "moderate" arminianized Calvinism making it easier for them to integrate themselves into the mainstream of White, Anglo-Saxon, and Protestant American and middle-class American life. For example, Charles Finney leavened his arminian evangelicalism and perfectionism with a doctrine of sin that did not push the logic of Christian authority, perfectionism, dispensationalism, and apocalypticism to their endpoints.

Many radicals, on the other hand, did push the logic of Christian authority, perfectionism, dispensationalism, and apocalypticism to, or close to, their "extremes" if in somewhat different ways. These more radical Christian communities were, as a result, more totalistic in their identities. They also tended to be more authoritarian, and autocratic, or, as in the Quaker case, more radically democratic, than their more "mainstream" evangelical cousins which tended toward republicanism and even reformist republicanism. The radicals also tended to be more separatist or sectarian in orientation compared to their more "mainstream" evangelical cousins.[70]

Of course, founding father of sociology Max Weber argued that sectarian separatism was the product of formalization, rationalization, and bureaucratization. He contended that as groups become more formal in structure those hoping to return the group to its original primitive state formed social movements to do just that.

Marianne Perciaccante made a similar argument about Mormonism and other groups in the Burned-Over District. Each of these groups can thus be seen as sectarian movements. They were movements of revolt, though they revolted in different ways, against formalization, and they revolted in order to return Christianity to what they saw as its primitive apostolic roots. As Weber noted, movements of primitivist return to a supposed earlier sacred time and sacred space are an inherent aspect of religious social movements, and such movements of eternal return arise again and again throughout religious and Christian social movement history.[71]

It is important to remember that while Pauline Christianity, sixteenth-century Central European Anabaptism, seventeenth-century English Quakerism, Shakerism, the Oneida Community, and Mormonism may have shared primitivist, apocalyptic, and perfectionist cultural scripts or ideologies, this does not mean that there is a direct historical lineage between earlier Christian culture and the groups that came to embody elements of this culture. It simply means that all of these groups shared a biblically oriented Christian background that has historically emphasized that Christ will come again and repeatedly asked themselves what Christ's church should look like and be like until Christ returned, and it also means that Christian social groups shared a belief that they, in whole or in part, were to be numbered among the remnant of the saved. For example, many Anabaptists, Quakers, Mormons, Shakers, Oneidans, and Mormons were millennial and perfectionist because they were simply trying to recover what they believed to be the historic form of primitive and apostolic Christianity.

As many scholars have pointed out and as many diaries, journals, autobiographies, and memoirs foreground, Jacksonian-era Christians of all backgrounds thought about what the apostolic church was and reflected on the doctrinal controversies of the time, including those surrounding free will versus determinism, millennialism, dispensationalism, and perfectionism. Many Jacksonian Americans clearly took their Christianity seriously. As Daniel Walker Howe noted, many sought to remake themselves, to remake their society, or to separate from a fallen society. They believed, as Curtis Johnson pointed out, that salvation was important and that they might be able to impact not only their own salvation but that of others. As John Higham and Mark Noll argued, some of these groups attempted to remake themselves by creating separate communities. Others wanted to remake themselves and wanted simultaneously to remake the broader community or communities in which they lived. They were, in other words, non-worldly sectarians and more worldly sectarians respectively.[72]

That sectarian groups emphasizing Arminianism, apocalypticism, perfectionism, and primitivism or restorationism, among other cultural scripts, can be found in Roman times, in the mediaeval period, during the Reformation, and in Jacksonian America, does, of course, raise questions about arguments that trace these ideologies to the advent of capitalism or to specific political changes of a particular era, such as the increasing democratization of America during the Jacksonian era. However, in the final analysis, recognizing that Christian cultural scripts or templates have long histories does not undercut arguments about the importance of exploring and understanding economic, political, demographic, and geographic factors in the rise of social and cultural movement. What this approach shows instead is that the interpretation and use of longstanding cultural scripts in Christian culture are impacted and bounded by, in different places and at different times, economic, political, geographic, and demographic factors or forces. In terms of the history of Christian culture, this approach also points up the fact, as many researchers now argue, that the protestantization of the West was a much longer process than historians and sociologists thought it to be.[73]

In an approach somewhat similar to that of Weber, social and cultural anthropologist Anthony Wallace argued that periods of social and cultural change often lead to cultural and psychological anxiety. Wallace asserted that movements arise to revitalize or reconstruct a more psychologically

Six. Culture Theory and Mormon Origins   123

satisfying culture in periods of cultural change and innovation. He delineated the stages that social groups go through during such cultural crises. Cultures initially exist in steady states of moving equilibrium. In instances when systems are no longer in steady states, they are unable to accommodate stress resulting in a rise in a sense of anomie and disillusionment. In such stressful periods, cultural distortion results. In the period of cultural distortion some members of society attempt to restore a sense of personal equilibrium by adopting dysfunctional expedients (for example, alcohol, scapegoating others for the problems). Since these are generally ineffective at countering the severe disorientation some are experiencing, the period of cultural distortion will be followed by a period of revitalization if the society is to survive. In this period of revitalization some charismatic individual usually formulates a new utopian image for society. Those who formulate the new code along with their followers usually offer this code to other members of society as a means of cultural salvation. Once the code attracts followers, a new organizational structure arises, and the code's adherents are organized into two distinct groups, leaders and followers. The leaders usually form the executive body of the revitalized group and establish, refine, and sanctify a code that is both timeless and flexible enough to respond to changing circumstances. When the revitalization movement succeeds in capturing a substantial majority of a society's population, culture can be said to have been transformed and a movement for change now becomes a cultural maintenance movement. A new state of societal moving equilibrium has thus been put in place and the process will, at some point, start all over again.[74]

Wallace's perspective is a helpful one. In fact, religious historian William McLoughlin found Wallace's approach so compelling that he interpreted all of America's many revivals as revitalization movements that created and recreated American identity. However, we need to recognize that it is not only societies that experience revitalization. As Victor Turner pointed out in his discussion of social and cultural dynamics, cultures and in particular subcultures or countercultures, can also experience a sense of societal and cultural unease and find ways or restoring a sense of cultural equilibrium. For Turner, cultural change is characterized by four stages: breach between social elements, crisis, adjustment and redress, and finally reintegration of the group, person, or element into the social structure or irreparable breach.[75]

A cultural approach to Mormonism reveals that primitive Mormonism was a product of a number of long and short-term forces. In the long term, Mormonism was the product of a dynamic Christian culture that had long emphasized restorationist, primitivist, dispensationalist, millennial, and holiness themes and was the product of and continuation of a series of related reformations that began in the sixteenth century in Europe and which continued into the nineteenth century and in all likelihood into the twentieth in Europe, North America, Australia, and New Zealand. These reformations eroded and undermined the idea and the reality of a state church and of a unified Christendom and set-in motion attempts to re-Christianize Europe and English settler societies. These reformations also set-in motion attempts to move Christian piety or holiness out of the monasteries and into the world at large (perfectionism) and to recover the apostolic church (restorationism).[76] By eroding the dominance of the Roman Catholic Church in the life of the West both culturally and institutionally, and in the process creating, at the very least, a space for a wider range of religious expression and, by extension religious toleration, these reformations gave rise to cultural contradictions which impacted virtually every Christian group throughout the Protestant dominated regions of North America and Australasia.

That virtually all Christians in Protestant New Worlds believed that there could be only one true Church, conflicted with the reality of the many churches, particularly in the diverse mid–Atlantic colonies and states of New York, New Jersey, and Pennsylvania, that many Christians and religious seekers saw around them. The contradiction between the notion of Christian unity and the reality of Christian cultural and ideological diversity created a sense of cultural and ideological dissonance. Additionally, the conflict between Christian egalitarianism ("the ministry of all believers") and hierarchical understandings of Christianity that emphasized proper authority and ideologically conformity, created ideological dissonance. These tensions impacted the various and sundry attempts to recover and, in turn, institutionalize "Apostolic Christianity" in both the Old and New Worlds, whether it was Luther's attempt at reformism, Calvin's attempt to create a Protestant kingdom, Anabaptist anti-statism, John Wesley's pietistic Methodism, Alexander Campbell's enlightenment Christianity, Virginia's egalitarian Baptist Christianity, or Joseph Smith's spherarchical Mormonism.[77]

Of course, Christianity, has long been impacted by processes associated with dissenting sectarianism. Like post–Reformation Protestant and Anabaptist "seekers" before them, Burned-Over District seekers and seekers beyond the Burned-Over District for that matter, who became Latter-day Saints or Latter Day Saints, experienced a sense of unease that resulted from the cultural tension between the idea that there could only be one true Christian Church and the reality that there were many culturally and ideologically diverse churches in early America, each claiming to be the one true apostolic Church. These seekers went in search of the one true Church and when they found it, collective cultural anxiety declined, and

Six. Culture Theory and Mormon Origins

a new dynamic equilibrium was restored. This does not mean that unease necessarily ended for every seeker once they found a church they, at least, initially, felt at home in. There are numerous examples in the documentary record of Mormons and Shakers, for example, not being fully satisfied with the choices they made. As a result, they left one restorationist Christian group for another and sometimes even another.

What it does mean is that it was through culture that leaders of the restorationist churches restored the collective cultural psychic and social equilibrium of those seekers who were searching for God's one true Church. Leaders of these various restorationist churches drew on longstanding cultural scripts that were familiar to and provided seekers with a sense of psychic and cultural ease.[78]

These biblical cultures were neither novel nor innovative except perhaps in the way the various cultural scripts drawn upon were put together by the charismatic and patriarchal religious leaders of the various restored apostolic churches. As I noted earlier, some of the restored churches, such as the many evangelical influenced churches of the era, more or less fit into the "mainstream" American culture of the time. Others, Mormonism among them, did not. These latter were more radical or "outsider" forms of Christianity in comparison to the more conformist religious "mainstream."[79]

I want to emphasize again that Mormonism and other religiously oriented social movements in Jacksonian America were impacted by short-term economic, political, social, and cultural changes in early nineteenth-century America. I also want to underscore that seekers filtered these economic, political, social, and cultural changes through their cultural and ideological eyes and molded them to reflect their own ideological "realities." Mormons, for instance, responded to economic changes in the early nineteenth-century economic changes by trying to put into effect a communitarian economic system derived from the Book of Acts and from ongoing revelation. They responded to political chaos by trying to establish a theocracy grounded in Tanakh or Old Testament concepts and contemporary revelation. In other words, Mormons tried to establish a Christian society and culture grounded in the Bible and in contemporary revelations written in a biblical language that made them into a metaphorical and literal chosen people or tribe of God.

Perhaps more than anything else it is essential for historians and social scientists to study the specifics of different social movement cultures in a thorough way if they truly want to understand the processes of group formation and of group identity formation. The best way to do this, in my opinion, is via Weberian hermeneutics, via an interpretive strategy, that seeks to understand (*verstehen*) human beliefs and human culture both from the standpoint of the actors themselves ("going native," emics), and from a more distanced critical perspective (etics), and that recognizes that social groups and movements arise, grow, if they survive, and act within specific economic, political, geographical, and, in particular, cultural boundaries. If we are to truly understand and unlock the social and cultural mysteries of social movements and identity construction it is essential that we employ an approach that pays attention to cultural factors, such as the cultural scripts which new social groups draw upon to recreate and partly reimagine symbols and rituals that help structure new social movements, the ways of seeing these symbols produce, and the process by which these ways of seeing are socialized and embodied in believers.

Conclusion: The Acids of Modernity?

The rise of the New Mormon Studies with its "naturalistic" or "positivistic," contextual and theoretical approaches to Mormonism, and particularly to Mormon origins, along with the impact of conflict history, social history, cultural history, and social movement theory on Mormon Studies, would prove to be controversial within Mormon culture and particularly within Mormon intellectual culture. As we will see in Chapter Seven this controversy would lead to a culture war within the power centers of the Mormon Church and within the intellectual and academic circles in the Church, Brigham Young University. It is to this culture war that I now want to turn.

SEVEN

Mormon Studies and Its Discontents
The "New" Mormon Culture War

Introduction

The increasing diversity of approaches in the social sciences, the humanities, history, and Mormon Studies after the 1960s was stimulated by a host of economic, political, cultural, demographic, and geographic changes in the United States and in the core Western world. The post–1960s era not only saw the increasing professionalization of Mormon Studies but also the increasing diversity of the theories Mormon Studies used by scholars to try to unlock the mysteries of Mormonism and of Mormon origins.

A 1990 survey by James Crooks and Sharon Pugsley revealed that from the 1960s onward professional organizations and professional journals that focused on Mormon Studies, most notably the Mormon History Association (MHA) and its *Journal of the Mormon History Association,* brought together new Mormon historians, whether Latter-day Saint, Latter Day Saint, and Gentile, along with substantial numbers of non-academic Mormons who were interested in and who wrote about Mormon history. Crooks and Pugsley found that only twenty-five percent of Mormon Historical Association members were academics.[1] The large number of non-academic members of the MHA reflects the fact that lay interest in the history of Mormonism was high among Mormons, particularly among those Mormons living in the Mormon culture region, and that "amateur historians" continued to play an important role in the research and writing of LDS history. The numbers also reflected the fact that in Mormon culture history has been sacralized; as a result, Mormons see it as being at the heart of the story of Mormonism itself and at the heart of a Mormon evangelicalism that proclaims the "truth" of the Mormon faith, a faith that claimed and claims that god acted in history to restore the one true faith to earth through the medium of

Joseph Smith. Given this sacralization of Mormon history and particularly the sacralization of the history of Mormon origins, it was almost inevitable that an intellectual cultural war between the new Mormon historians, with their "modern" and "postmodern" approaches to Mormon origins and other things Mormon, and those who regarded the story of Mormonism and its origins as sacred, the Mormon leaders, General Authorities, and the Brethren in Salt Lake City and Mormon apologists and polemicists, many of them in Provo and at Brigham Young University (BYU, the Y), would emerge.

The Old Mormon Culture War

The culture war between the Church leaders, Mormon apologists and polemicists, and the practitioners of the New Mormon Studies in the 1980s and after, was not really all that "new." The "naturalism" of some of the social scientific and historical pioneers of the Old Mormon Studies sometimes led to tensions, between Mormon students of Mormonism and the Mormon General Authorities intent upon safeguarding and promoting the faith. For instance, when E.E. Ericksen wanted to implement a social justice program in the LDS Young Men's Improvement Association, the Mormon powers that be in Salt Lake City, found his proposal too theologically neutral and rejected it.[2] In 1934, Church Authorities examined the beliefs of Lowry Nelson who had written extensively and positively about the Mormon village and the social and cultural construction of Mormon ideology. However, as positive as Nelson's portrayal of the Mormon village was something in Nelson's scholarship appears to have troubled some of the Brethren.[3] In 1947, after returning from Cuba, Nelson troubled Church Authorities even further by writing a letter to the First Presidency questioning the Church's exclusion of Blacks, an exclusion that had been put in place in 1849.[4] Nelson's criticisms led Church authorities to once again investigate his faith and Nelson opted to leave the Mormon culture region for the less doctrinally correct environment of the University of Minnesota. In 1946 the Church excommunicated, Fawn Brodie, who was related to Mormon General Authority and later Church President David O. McKay. By that time Brodie, author of a controversial biography on Joseph Smith was excommunicated. In 1959 an article by Leonard Arrington on economic aspects of the "Word of Wisdom" in the first issue of *BYU Studies* led to the suspension of that journal for a year, a foreshadowing, in retrospect, of things to come.[5]

The New Mormon Culture War

With the rise of the New Mormon Studies in the post–WWII era, the conflicts within Mormon culture and Mormon intellectual culture once

Seven. Mormon Studies and Its Discontents

again heated up, particularly in the 1980s and 1990s. For some, particularly outsiders, this Mormon intellectual culture war was a bit odd. Despite the increasing prominence of Gentile scholars such as Jan Shipps, who has referred to herself as a Mormon insider outsider, and Mario DePillis, who, like Shipps was a past president of the Mormon History Association, the New Mormon Studies remained largely a Mormon enterprise. Like most of those who engaged in the old Mormon Studies, most of the practitioners of the New Mormon Studies were and are believing Mormons.

A 1987 survey by *Dialogue*, one of the leading journals in the New Mormon Studies, found that ninety-four percent of its readers were Latter-day Saints, one percent were Latter Day Saints, and four percent were Gentiles. The survey by Crooks and Pugsley cited earlier found that seventy-seven percent of MHA membership was Latter-day Saint, thirteen percent Latter Day Saint, one percent Saints from other LDS sects, and five percent Gentile. The New Mormon Studies, in other words, was a largely Mormon and, more specifically, a largely Utah Mormon enterprise.[6]

Despite the fact that most of the academic and lay researchers engaged in the New Mormon Studies were Mormons and despite the "achievements" of the New Mormon Studies, the New Mormon Studies proved quite controversial in Mormon culture, particularly in the Mormon culture region, and even more specifically in Salt Lake City and Provo. It was not the profusion of scholarship focusing on New Mormon Studies re-evaluations of Mormon polygamy, probably the most controversial aspect of Mormonism in the mid- to late nineteenth century, that made the New Mormon Studies so controversial to the General Authorities in Salt Lake City and to Mormon apologists and polemicists in Provo. Instead, it was the New Mormon Studies re-readings of Mormon origins that were at the center of intellectual controversies within the intellectual culture of the Church.[7]

Initially, Church authorities appeared to view the New Mormon Studies in a relatively favorable light. In January 1966 Leonard Arrington, one of the pioneers of the New Mormon Studies, was interviewed by N. Eldon Tanner, a member of the First Presidency, one of if not the most powerful hierarchy in the Church, about possible reforms he might suggest for the Church Historical Office (CHO). After discussions with Arrington, Tanner named Arrington to a committee advising the CHO on how it might liaise with the historical community, fund research grants for CHO personnel, and on plans for a multivolume history of the Church publishing program to mark the Church's sesquicentennial. In January 1972, in a move that suggested, at least to some at the time that Church leaders had made their peace with "modernist" approaches to Mormon history and to Mormon origins, Arrington was "called" to the office of Church Historian, making him the first non–General Authority to ever serve in that position in the history of the Church. Arrington was, as was traditional when someone was "called" to an office in the Church, "sustained" in his position by the faithful at the General Conference in Salt Lake City in April 1972. Arrington's appointment was coupled with a half-time professorship at BYU something else that suggested that Church authorities had made their peace with "modern" approaches to Mormon history.[8]

As Church Historian, Arrington was in charge of the History Division of a newly created LDS Historical Department and assigned the responsibility for writing Church History. Almost immediately he instituted several reforms at the CHO. The Archives were opened to all including Gentiles interested in Mormon history.[9] Individual Mormon historians were commissioned to write individual volumes of a planned 16-volume history of the Church that was to be published in the Church's sesquicentennial year of 1980. Arrington also commissioned a one-volume history of the Church, urged the development of an oral history program to record the experiences of Mormons, particularly elderly Mormons, and urged Mormon scholars to transcribe and publish Mormon journals, diaries, letters, and scholarly articles and books on Church leaders, Church documents, local and regional studies, gender studies, and studies of everyday Mormon life.

To help him achieve these reform goals Arrington hired BYU history professor James B. Allen and University of Utah specialist in European history Davis Bitton to assist him. He also hired a number of "historical associates." At its zenith Arrington's CHO had eleven full-time "historical associates," all of them young Mormon historians at the beginnings of their professional careers. Among these associates were Maureen Ursenbach Beecher, Bruce D. Blumell, Jill Mulvay Derr, Ronald K. Esplin, William G. Hartley, Gordon Irving, Richard L. Jensen, Dean Jessee, Glen M. Leonard, Carol Cornwall Madsen, D. Michael Quinn, Gene A. Sessions, and Ronald W. Walker, all of whom would become significant figures in the New Mormon history. Finally, Arrington and his two "councilors" initiated grants for young scholars for research in and writing on LDS History.[10]

Arrington's reforms changed the CHO and professionalized it, turning an office in the Church that was once polemical and apologetic into something more akin to an academic organization. Over the years, those connected to the History Division conducted some eight hundred oral history interviews, transcribed three thousand church documents, published three hundred and fifty articles, book chapters, and reviews, seventy of them in Church periodicals like the *Ensign*. They also published twenty books, including Arrington and Bitton's thematically structured *The Mormon Experience: A History of the Latter-Day Saints*, which was aimed at Gentiles, and Allen and Glen M. Leonard's *The Story of the Latter-day Saints*, which was aimed at Latter-day Saints.

The New Mormon Studies and Church Authorities

It would be *The Story of the Latter-day Saints* that would, it appears, lead to the firing off of the opening salvo of an internal culture war between the New Mormon Studies historians and Church leaders and Church apologetic and polemical "faith historians," most of whom were affiliated with BYU[11] While reactions to the book were favorable in professional historical circles, and the book, published by Deseret, the Church publishing house, sold out in its first three years of publication,[12] *Story* was not popular with everyone. Church authorities refused to approve *Story* for use in Seminary, Mormon religious education aimed at secondary school students, Institute, Mormon religious education aimed at college students, or for Church owned college or university class use. Eventually, Deseret Books allowed *Story* to go out of print and remain out of print amidst rumors that Church authorities were concerned about *Story's* broader contextualization of Mormon history in American social, cultural and religious currents and the impact *Story's* popularity and its historical contextualizations might have on the faithful who read it.[13]

Controversies over *Story* apparently exacerbated controversies over the New Mormon Studies and the Church History Division already rumbling through the Church halls of power in Salt Lake City and Provo. For instance, Apostle Ezra Taft Benson, later president and prophet of the Church, warned of the dangers of attempting to reconcile "secular" philosophies with their neutral style, their undermining of "prophetic history," and their dangerous practice of contextualizing early Mormon history in broader nineteenth-century American historical currents, with the "pure gospel" of church leaders. In his "The Mantle is Far, Far Greater than the Intellect," LDS Apostle Boyd D. Packer complained that the New Mormon Studies historians, though he never called them by name, were too "secular" and thus were too ready and eager to ignore the religious motives of believers and focus instead on the "foibles" of Church leaders. Packer also charged the practitioners of the New Mormon Studies with repeating claims made by nineteenth-century "anti–Mormons," an accusation akin to calling someone a supporter of the monarchy in early republican America or calling someone a communist in Cold War America.[14]

Story was not the only publication of the Arrington CHO years that apparently stirred controversy among the powers that be in the Church and in Provo. Arrington's, Feramorz Fox's, and Dean May's *Building the City of God: Community and Cooperation Among the Mormons*, initially published by Deseret in 1976, also proved controversial. *Building*, the story of Mormon communalism, apparently made a number of Church Authorities and faithful Mormons uncomfortable, which is not surprising given that the book, which explores the history of Mormon communalism, was published in a climate of post–World War I and post–World War II American anti–Communism, an anti–Communism which many Mormon leaders and many of the Mormon faithful had deeply imbibed.[15]

All of these controversies eventually led to the downsizing of the Church Historical Division and the cancellation of the sixteen-volume history of the Church. In 1982, the History Division, including Arrington, was transferred to BYU and renamed the Joseph Fielding Smith Institute for Church History. In the wake of this battle, the authorities in Salt Lake City once again restricted access to the Church's archival collections and took steps to control the publication of materials based on research undertaken at the Church Archives. Church employees were now required to submit their writings to the Correlation Committee, which was charged with ensuring that all Church publications were doctrinally sound and correct in interpretation prior to publication. In 1982, G. Homer Durham, holder of a doctorate in political science and history and one of the Church's General Authorities, replaced Arrington as Church Historian.[16]

Within the Mormon community this opening salvo in the culture war over the New Mormon Studies has been variously interpreted. For some, the reaction to the "Camelot" period of the CHO, as some supporters called it, may not have been as nefarious as it seems. They argued that there had always been some ambiguity in Arrington's "calling" as Church Historian and that his appointment should be seen as akin to that of the head of a "secular" library and archives. However, as others have noted, the problem with this argument, is that Arrington had been "sustained" by the faithful, as are all church leaders, at General Conference suggesting that he was more than a "secular" librarian and archivist.[17]

Others have read the demise of "Camelot" differently. For instance, Mormon sociologist Armand Mauss argued that contemporary Mormonism was a divided faith community. He claimed that at the heart of Mormonism was a divide or a contradiction between the Church's angel impulses, the urge to keep Mormonism distinctive and Mormons a peculiar people, and the Church's beehive impulses, the urge for Mormons to assimilate and become part of the broader American mainstream.[18] In this interpretation the mixed angel and beehive messages the Church Authorities sent during the Arrington years at the CHO may simply have been a function of this fundamental tension between the angel and beehive within Mormon intellectual culture.

Whatever the case, the fight over Arrington and the modernized CHO suggests that there may have been a culture war afoot within the inner circles of the Mormon elite. On one side were some Brethren who wanted to professionalize the Church and its institutions. On the other side were Brethren whose conception of history was gained by reading Joseph Fielding Smith's *Essentials of Church History*, a book which emphasized that the Church was a product of divine intervention and divinely inspired humans, and which saw modernization and professionalization as forms of creeping "secularism." The "secular" histories of the new Mormon historians simply did not sit well with those brought up on Joseph Fielding Smith's faith promoting version of Church history.[19]

The New Mormon Faith Studies

As I have noted, negative reactions to New Mormon Studies "revisionism," as some have called it, were not a monopoly of Church leaders. There were also negative reactions to the new Mormon history in the Mormon intellectual and academic world beyond Salt Lake City and particularly in Provo, the beating heart of Mormon orthodoxy.

In the 1980s and 1990s, Mormon Studies came, one might say, full circle as a type of faith history that was little bit old and a little bit new emerged in Mormon academic and intellectual culture. It was a little bit old in that it emphasized the same nationalist, boosterist, and exceptionalist myths that tended to characterize consensus American histories and like them conflated normative mythic history with descriptive history.[20] It was a little bit old in that it took a great men and great events approach to history, with God being among the great men who made Mormon "history" by restoring apostolic Christianity through the medium of another great man, the Mormon prophet, seer, and revelator Joseph Smith. It was a little bit new in that it adopted and adapted aspects of cultural postmodernism. New Mormon faith historians would draw on postmodernist theories that posited that, in the late twentieth-and twenty-first centuries, the cultures of the now deindustrialized core nations had come to be characterized by fragmentation, globalization, and a celebration of multiculturalism. They would use the postmodernist celebration of diversity to critique and condemn what they called the "naturalism," "secularism," "positivism" and elite exclusivity of the New Mormon Studies.

The attack on the New Mormon Studies took several forms. In the wake of Church Authorities' criticisms of the New Mormon Studies, Church-related publications and publishers, such as *BYU Studies* and Deseret Books began to cut back on their publication of works written by the new Mormon historians and began to publish more and more of the books and articles written by new Mormon faith historians.

On the intellectual and academic front, new Mormon faith theorists like Louis Midgley began a theoretical, methodological, and empirical counterattack against the New Mormon Studies. Midgley, a Mormon and professor of political science at BYU, concerned, he claimed, by the "secular" and "positivistic" New Mormon Studies, adopted and adapted the relativism of postmodernist theory and particularly the theories of French Jewish philosopher and Talmudic scholar Emmanuel Levinas, and adopted positive notions of multiculturalism as weapons in a culture war to combat what he deemed New Mormon Studies "positivism." Midgley and the other new faith historians who followed in his footsteps, contended that if all theoretical perspectives were products of particular historical social and cultural forces and that if all perspectives were equally valuable, then a Mormon faith perspective that saw Mormon origins as the product of God's intervention in history was just as valuable and valid as any other. The new Mormon faith historians also took the practitioners of the New Mormon Studies to task for ignoring the emic faith claims contained in Mormon primary source materials and concentrating instead on the etic deep structural economic, political, cultural, and psychological factors they assumed to be the "real" dynamic factors at play in Mormon history and Mormon action.

The New Mormon Faith Studies played a particularly important role at BYU where many of the new faith historians found a comfortable home. They were joined in their crusade against the acids of the New Mormon Studies by members and fellow travelers of the Foundation for Ancient Research and Mormon Studies, FARMS, which had its headquarters in Provo since 1980 and which became a research institution at BYU in 1997. FARMS members, who came from a variety of academic disciplinary backgrounds including religious studies, history, linguistics, anthropology, and Islamic Studies, and FARMS fellow travelers, argued that Mormonism had its origins in the Ancient Near East and that the Book of Mormon was an ancient document. As a group, the devotees of the New Mormon Faith Studies were, like the Church Authorities who had earlier criticized the New Mormon Studies, critical of the argument that the Book of Mormon was the product of nineteenth-century America. Like Church Authorities they were also critical of the fact that the practitioners of the New Mormon Studies sometimes repeated claims made by nineteenth-century anti–Mormon polemical writers such as Eber D. Howe. Many FARMS members and their fellow travelers, in fact, sometimes conflated the practitioners of the New Mormon Studies with evangelical anti–Mormons and atheist critics of religion. Some of them even categorized all three as "anti–Mormons," a rather convenient classification and category and an important tool the practitioners of New Mormon Faith Studies used in their apologetic and polemical battles over Mormon origins and the New Mormon

Seven. Mormon Studies and Its Discontents

Studies, casting those they saw themselves in combat with as "deviant" if not "heretical."[21]

What is, of course, ironic about this culture war, at least from the outside, is that most of the practitioners of the New Mormon Studies saw themselves as faithful Mormons. What is also ironic is the fact that the New Mormon faith historians condemned the practitioners of the New Mormon Studies for contextualism, something they themselves practiced. The two camps differed only on one point. For the practitioners of the New Mormon Faith Studies, the broader context of Mormon origins was Ancient Israel, the Ancient Near East more broadly, and the Ancient Yucatan peninsula, where FARMs members and fellow travelers argued the people of the Book of Mormon settled after their exodus from the ancient Hebrew lands. For the practitioners of the New Mormon Studies, on the other hand, the context of Mormon origins was the seventeenth-, eighteenth-, and nineteenth-century Atlantic World and the Jackson-era United States.

In theory, the practitioners of the New Mormon Faith Studies may have been doing something different from those of the New Mormon Studies "naturalists," but in practice the differences between the two were not always clear.[22] For instance, faith historian Richard Bushman's biography of Joseph Smith, like the work of new Mormon Gentile historian Jan Shipps, whose study of Mormon origins goes native or emic by accepting Smith's claims, places Smith's actions in the context of early nineteenth-century America.[23] Terryl Givens's analysis of the reception history of the Book of Mormon explores academic and intellectual approaches to the "scripture," places the Book of Mormon in its nineteenth-century context, and sympathetically examines approaches to the Book of Mormon that explore its "ancient" contexts, standard operating practice in intellectual and academic "secular" histories of text reception. If contextualization is an element of post–Enlightenment modernism then the practitioners of the New Mormon Faith Studies were and are just as impacted by the very acids of modernity they condemned in the work of the new Mormon historians.[24] Also, somewhat ironically, the practitioners of the New Mormon Faith Studies were not particularly sympathetic to third way cultural approaches to Mormon origins such as those of Shipps. In her studies of early or primitive Mormonism Shipps accepted that Smith *believed* he was doing the work of God and that those who followed him *believed* he was God's prophet. For the Mormon Faith historians even Shipp's ethnographic going native approach of Shipps was unacceptable. For them, the only acceptable approach to Mormon history was one that admitted that God really had acted in history when he restored his one true and only Church, the Church of Jesus Christ of Latter-day Saints, to the earth. Like typical polemicists, they wanted the "naturalists" and "secularists" they inquisited to submit and give obeisance to what was ultimately a metaphysical proposition, a simultaneously postmodernist and modern "traditionalist" metaphysical proposition.[25]

The New Mormon Culture War

The battle over the New Mormon Studies has been contentious at times. As with the culture wars of the late nineteenth- and early twentieth-centuries over the new higher Biblical criticism and Darwinian evolution, the Mormon culture war was fought largely over origins. However, instead of centering upon the origins of the Bible and of human life itself, the Mormon culture war largely revolved around the issue of how to view Mormon origins.[26]

No figure in the New Mormon Studies has been more contentious, particularly with the New Mormon Faith Studies crowd, than Mormon (now ex–Mormon and cultural Mormon) D. Michael Quinn. After receiving a doctorate from Yale University, Quinn taught history at BYU between 1976 and 1988. In his years at the Y Quinn published a number of books and papers, many of them controversial, including one on Church Authority J. Reuben Clark, one on Mormon polygamy, and one on early Mormonism and the magical world view.[27]

Quinn's prominent role as a practitioner of the new Mormon History and as a defender of the new Mormon history faith while at the Y, ultimately brought him into conflict with Mormon Prophet Ezra Taft Benson and Mormon Apostle Boyd K Packer. In the wake of President Benson's and Apostle Packer's 1981 criticisms of the new Mormon history, Quinn challenged both directly in a speech to the BYU Student History Association entitled "On Being a Mormon Historian."[28] In this speech, which was eventually published in pamphlet form, Quinn vigorously defended the New Mormon Studies against Packer's charges that its practitioners were repeating "'sensitive or controversial' charges made by enemies of the Church, and making too much of contextual arguments." The resulting conflict and the controversy that ensued, along with the controversy surrounding Quinn's book on early Mormonism and the magical world view, which echoed a connection "anti–Mormons" had also made since the nineteenth century, led to Quinn's resignation from BYU in 1988.

However, Quinn's trials and travails did not end with his resignation from BYU. Controversy surrounded him until his death in 2021. In 1993, Quinn was one of six Mormon intellectuals and academics excommunicated from the Church by ward authorities. Some believe that his essay arguing that Mormon women were given the priesthood in 1843, was paramount among the reasons for Quinn's excommunication from the Church. At the time, Church Authorities were deeply concerned with the impact of feminism and the small but growing number of women praying to Mother in Heaven. They tended to see both as challenges to their singular authority over the entirety of the Church.[29]

Quinn's troubles continued when in 1996 he published *Same Sex Dynamics Among Nineteenth-century Americans: A Mormon Example* in which he argued that nineteenth-century Mormonism had no conception of sexuality or sexual identity and, thus, did not single out homosexuality for special condemnation thereby allowing for a range of same sex relationships in the Church. It was not until the triumph of homophobia in the Church in the 1950s, he argued, that homosexuality came in for condemnation by Church leaders.[30] In 1996, Quinn announced that he was gay, a very controversial move in a church that, at the time, condemned homosexuality as a "sin."[31] In a letter to Sandra Tanner, New Mormon Faith Studies practitioner Louis Midgley accused the "deeply troubled" Quinn of having a "homosexual agenda" and that this agenda had colored much of his recent work on Mormon history undermining its veracity.[32]

Despite being excommunicated Quinn, who continued to maintain that he still believed in many of the tenants of Mormonism, remained a target for the faithful. According to an April 2006 piece in the *Wall Street Journal* written by Daniel Golden, Quinn became persona non grata at conferences sponsored or co-sponsored by Mormon institutions and at universities with ties to Mormonism and to Mormon donors. In 2003, while Quinn was a visiting professor at Yale University, BYU threatened to withdraw funding for a Yale conference it was co-sponsoring if conference organizers allowed Quinn to give a paper. Noel Reynolds, a long-time BYU administrator and at the time a Mormon mission president in Fort Lauderdale, Florida, said BYU was concerned that the conference would be used to "promote personalities or personal complaints about the church." Yale stood its ground, but Quinn decided to introduce a speaker rather than give a paper, hoping this would diffuse the tense situation.

In 2003, when Quinn was a candidate for a position at the University of Utah, BYU history professor Thomas Alexander wrote Quinn a glowing recommendation but warned the U that if they hired Quinn it might jeopardize state funding given the prominence of faithful Mormons in the Utah legislature and urged the U not to hire him. When the U's history department decided against hiring Quinn, Robert Newman, dean of humanities at the school, claimed the decision was because Quinn's research presentation was not strong enough and that most of Quinn's books were not published by university presses.

In 2004, when the newly formed Religious Studies Department at

Arizona State University (ASU) decided to offer Quinn a one-year appointment, ASU administrators vetoed the recommendation. Several ASU faculty members later admitted to Golden that this was because officials at the university feared alienating ASU's some 3,700 LDS students and offending Ira Fulton, a powerful Mormon donor who referred to Quinn as a "nothing person."[33]

Quinn was not the only casualty of the new Mormon culture war. Some publications and symposia also came in for condemnation by Church General Authorities. In 1986, Church Authorities advised BYU administrators not to publish in *Dialogue* or *Sunstone*.[34] In November 1990, Elbert Peck, editor and publisher of *Sunstone*, which had, over the years published a number of controversial articles on Mormonism including some by Quinn, lost his temple recommend.[35] In August 1991, the First Presidency and the Twelve cautioned Church members, and particularly those teaching at BYU, against attending "symposia" that inappropriately discussed private matters or ridiculed sacred things. It was clear to many observers that the "symposia" Church Authorities were referring to were those sponsored and run by *Sunstone*. The cautions seemed to work as some Mormons subsequently steered clear of symposia associated with the publication. In a March 1992 survey in the BYU student newspaper the *Universe*, forty-two percent of BYU faculty said they would not participate in *Sunstone* symposia.

In April 1992, a draft document on academic freedom that placed what its authors claimed was "reasonable restrictions" on academic freedom began to circulate within the educational community. The statement prohibited contradicting fundamental church policies, deliberate or derisive attacks on the Church and its leaders, and violations of the Honor Code. In a response to the document twenty faculty members of the Y's Department of Sociology signed a letter to President Rex Lee expressing concern about the impact of the statement on academic freedom at BYU.[36] In August of 1992 Church employees were explicitly warned against attending Sunstone symposia.[37]

Academics were not the only ones under surveillance within the Church. As early as 1985, just after the politically and ideologically right wing Ezra Taft Benson ascended to the presidency of the Church, a secret committee called the Strengthening of Church Members Committee was formed to collect information on members who were, in the eyes of Church leaders, moving in the direction of "apostasy" or who were already, in their view, "apostates."[38] In April of 1989 Apostle Dalin Oaks, a former president of BYU, warned Church members against listening to "alternative voices." In November 1991 Apostle Gordon B. Hinckley, repeating a caution he made at General Conference in April of that year, counseled,

Seven. Mormon Studies and Its Discontents   139

during a speech to the women's general firesides or Church evening meetings, female members against praying to Mother in Heaven.[39] Hinckley was responding to the growing number of female members of the Church who were influenced by the New Mormon Studies and recent Mormon feminist theologies and were discussing Mother in Heaven at forums like the Mormon Women's Forum or praying to Mother in Heaven at meetings or retreats.[40] In August 1992 Apostle Neal A. Maxwell criticized Mormon intellectuals during his keynote speech at one of the BYU devotionals or religiously oriented talks.[41] In October 1992 at October General Conference, Apostle M. Russell Ballard and Apostle Boyd Packer cautioned those not "ordained" who were caught up in extreme preparations and warnings of impending economic doom, presumably Mormondom's survivalists.[42] In November 1992, Elder Malcolm S. Jeppesen, president of the Utah South area, cautioned polygamists, feminists, and intellectuals with a "naturalistic" bent during a Utah South area priesthood meeting.[43]

Excommunication, which the Church has never shied away from, became one of the weapons in the culture war against the practitioners of the New Mormon Studies and Mormon feminists. In September 1993, Paul Toscano, Avraham Gileadi, Maxine Hanks, and Lavina Fielding Anderson, were excommunicated, along with Quinn, and Lynne Whitesides's membership was rescinded by the authorities of the wards each attended. Two years later Janice Allred was excommunicated.

The New Mormon Studies, Mormon feminism, and questions about authority in the Church, seemed to be at the top of the list as to the reasons for these excommunications. Whitesides, Allred, Hanks, and Anderson were feminists, Whitesides and Allred gave talks on Heavenly Mother, and Allred wrote on Mother in Heaven. Hanks co-edited the book *Women and Authority: Re-emerging Mormon Feminism*, which contained essays on Mother in Heaven and an article by Quinn arguing that Smith had given the priesthood to women in 1843 when he formed the Relief Society.[44] Anderson contributed to *Women and Authority* and worked with the Mormon Alliance, an organization formed to 1992 to counter "spiritual and ecclesiastical" abuse by Church authorities. Mormon Alliance co-founder Paul Toscano was an attorney and co-author with his wife Margaret of *Strangers in Paradox: Explorations in Mormon Theology*, a book that applied recent developments in the New Mormon Studies to Mormon doctrine. Gileadi was a theologically conservative literary scholar, a Hebraist, a translator, and author of several books touching on Biblical interpretation and Church doctrine.[45]

The modern Mormon culture war was about more than simply how to write Mormon history, how to interpret Mormon scriptures, or about the role of women in the Church. It was also, as I mentioned, a battle over power and authority within the Church. From the outside, there appears to be an inherent paradox in Mormonism. Mormonism preached the priesthood of all (male) believers and is profoundly shaped by communal or collective and democratic impulses, but it, at the same time, ties this priesthood authority to the hierarchical position male priests hold within a particular domain in the Church. Power within the Mormon Church, in other words, is spherarchical. Only certain male priesthood-holding Mormons are given the power and authority to act in particular and specific spheres within the Church. The seven scholars excommunicated by the Church between 1993 and 1995 were apparently perceived as directly or indirectly challenging the power structure of a hierarchical Church and the authority of Church Authorities to correctly and faithfully interpret Mormon history and Mormon doctrine. For example, Quinn's essay on women and the priesthood directly challenged Mormon doctrine that the priesthood was a male preserve. Paul and Margaret Toscano were wading into areas that were largely the preserve of the General Authorities particularly when they raised questions about a patriarchal bias in the Church. Rumor has it that Gileadi's book *The Last Days* was ordered pulled from the shelves of the Church owned Deseret Bookstores because it was seen as challenging the doctrine that only Church Authorities could definitively interpret the Scriptures.

These excommunications did not end the new Mormon culture war. Other excommunications and other forms of disciplining followed. In 1993, BYU fired anthropology professor David Knowlton and English professor Cecilia Farr on the basis of "inadequate academic performance." However, others claimed that both Knowlton and Farr were fired for their political, ideological, and religious views. Some speculated that Knowlton's firing may have had something to do with essays he published in *Sunstone* and his presentations at Sunstone conferences, most of which dealt with the LDS Church and Latin American "terrorism." Farr's firing apparently had everything to do with her feminism and, in particular, with her involvement with the BYU feminist group VOICE, one of the, if not the, largest student group on the BYU campus in the early 1990s. VOICE's co-sponsor, psychology professor and Gentile Tomi-Ann Roberts would leave BYU in 1993. In 1996, BYU fired English faculty member Gail Houston for "contradicting ... church doctrines and attacking the church." In 1997, these attacks on Mormon academics at the Y resulted in the American Association of University Professors (AAUP) censuring BYU for limiting free expression..

The AAUP censure of BYU did not stop the culture war between academics and intellectuals and the Church hierarchy. In 2006, BYU Philosophy Department faculty member Jeffrey Nielsen was fired for an editorial piece he wrote criticizing Church policy on same-sex marriage. In 2014,

Kate Kelly, founder of the website Ordain Women: Mormon Women Seeking Ordination to the Priesthood, was excommunicated for advocating for women's ordination to the priesthood. In 2015, John Dehlin, founder of the website The Mormon Stories: Explaining, Celebrating, and Challenging Mormon Culture Through Stories, was excommunicated for disagreeing with Church beliefs.[46]

This Mormon intellectual culture war, of course, bore similarities, as I mentioned earlier, to previous intellectual culture wars in Atlantic and American history and to broader contemporary English settler society culture wars.[47] It has echoes of nineteenth and early twentieth-century battles over Darwinism in Europe, North America, and Australasia, of battles surrounding "modern" higher biblical criticism in North America, Europe and Australasia, and of battles over feminism and non-normative sexuality particularly in the twentieth-century West. The recent Mormon culture war can be read as yet another battle between the forces of "tradition," a tradition that was constructed in the modern crucibles of the Scientific Revolution and the Enlightenment of the seventeenth century and eighteenth century, just like those approaches which took a more "naturalistic" approach. On the other hand, the traditional versus modern culture wars can be read and have been read as local battles over local issues. Finally, culture wars can be read and understood as being simultaneously cross-cultural, national, and local, all at the same time. Regardless of how one interprets the battle between faithful New Mormon Studies intellectuals and faithful New Faith Studies intellectuals and Church Authorities, this culture war in Mormon intellectual culture played itself out in a language and in symbols that were modern, postmodern, and Mormon.[48]

The Problem with Mormon Exceptionalism

In his essay in *The Great Basin Kingdom Revisited*, Mormon historian Charles S. Peterson argued that the massive influence of Arrington's *Great Basin Kingdom* in Mormon intellectual culture gave rise to an exceptionalist approach to Mormon history by the practitioners of the New Mormon Studies. As a result, he argues, the New Mormon Studies that Leonard Arrington, whose pioneering book is the subject of the collection in which Peterson's essay is found, helped found, has, Peterson contends, remained outside of mainstream history, has been inward looking, and has been focused on what Peterson called the "cult of the Prophet" and Mormon origins.[49] This new Mormon history, he claimed, was an exceptionalist history in which some Mormon intellectuals tried to balance faith with "naturalistic" and "interpretive" scholarship. Like those engaged in Biblical Studies and those semiologists writing in the early twentieth-century Soviet Union, those associated with the New Mormon Studies, consciously or unconsciously, felt that they had to square the circle between "secular" history and faith history.

In retrospect, it is clear that many of those associated with the New Mormon Studies have had at least two masters they were trying to serve. Most of the Latter-day Saint new Mormon historians proclaimed their faith in Mormonism while simultaneously proclaiming their faith in some variety of "secular" history. For example, believing Latter Day Saint, new Mormon historian, and one time Reorganized Church of Jesus Christ of Latter Day Saints Church Historian Robert Flanders, who taught at the Latter Day Saint Graceland College, praised the new Mormon history for its shift from parochial and polemical history to a humanistic history.[50] Latter-day Saint Leonard Arrington claimed that the new Mormon historians took a "naturalistic" approach to Mormon Studies but that this did not mean they were rejecting the "divinity" of Mormonism.[51] Latter-day Saint historian Richard Bushman proclaimed himself a "faithful historian."[52] D. Michael Quinn's approach to Mormon Studies has been described as personal, impressionistic, encyclopedic, humanistic, and faithful, all at the same time.[53] Latter-day Saint historian Thomas Alexander, like his Gentile colleague Jan Shipps, proclaimed his faith in ethnographic, Weberian *verstehen*, or Geertzian "going native" history at the same time that he proclaimed his faith in the Mormon restoration.[54]

The new Mormon historians attempt to balance modern scholarship with religious belief was, of course, a phenomenon as old as the Renaissance, the Enlightenment, and the late nineteenth century, all periods when reformist Roman Catholic and liberal Protestant scholars tried to balance faith with novel theologies. In the nineteenth-, twentieth-, and twenty-first centuries modern Christians of all stripes have tried to balance novel scientific scholarship including so-called higher Biblical criticism and the evolutionary theories of Charles Darwin and his intellectual descendants, with their faith. Balancing faith with a critical approach to Mormon Studies has proven as difficult for the practitioners of the New Mormon Studies as it did for many other Christian "moderns" and "postmoderns." And it had the same result, a culture war. It resulted in a culture war, this one between the practitioners of the New Mormon Studies and the latter-day defenders of the faith, Mormondom's faithful academics. For the new "modern" and "postmodern" Mormon faith historians, the proclamations of faith by the new Mormon historians and social scientists were, just as they were for many other Christian "traditionalist" "moderns" and "postmoderns," simply not sufficient or acceptable.[55]

The debate over how to do the New Mormon Studies has led not only to a division between the practitioners of the New Mormon Studies and the practitioners of the New Mormon Faith Studies; it also gave rise to a division within the ranks of the New Mormon Studies itself. For instance, new Mormons Ronald Walker, David Whittaker, and James Allen, claimed that the New Mormon Studies had resulted in its practitioners losing touch with its faithful audience just as believing higher Biblical critics had lost touch with the believing masses thanks to their practice of "esoteric" higher Biblical criticism.[56] The late Mormon and Queen's University historian Klaus Hansen wondered how a Methodist such as Jan Shipps and Mormons such as Thomas Alexander and Richard Bushman, all of whom took approaches that accepted the statements of Smith and other Mormons at face value, could come to the same conclusions about Mormonism and Joseph Smith despite their differing faith commitments.[57] Circling the wagons, Hansen called on the new Mormon historians to lean more toward the faith history end of the doing history spectrum or continuum than the "naturalist" one, asserted that Mormon intellectuals had been too influenced by their middle-class, secular, liberal, establishmentarian, status seeking, and tolerant academic values, and called on Mormon historians to write "faithful history."[58]

In the end one can, I suppose, ask whether the new Mormon faith historians have a point, if a rather odd one coming, as it does, from those convinced of the absolute truth of their own faith. Was the devotion of "secular" scholars to "secular" methodologies just as much a statement of faith as belief in the Book of Mormon as an ancient document? And if it was, was "secular" scholarship just another form of ideology, an ideology not particularly appealing to the majority of the Mormon faithful?

Conclusion: Ideology and Mormon Studies

From the 1930s through the 2000s, Mormon leaders had been fighting another culture war, one very much like the culture war against the practitioners of the New Mormon Studies, and one which had ebbed and flowed over the years. In the 1930s, in order to counteract the growing Mormon fundamentalist movement, a twentieth-century sectarian social movement that placed the practice of "the Principle" at the core of its restoration of what it regarded as true Mormonism, the Church actively began to excommunicate Mormon fundamentalists and deny them access to Church temples, the places where members engaged in rituals central to their religious life courses and to their "eternal progression" toward godhood. Under the leadership of second counselor in the First Presidency Reuben J. Clark and later Elder Mark E. Peterson, the Church went so far as to demand a loyalty oath from select members, loyalty oaths in which those select members assured the General Authorities that they were not practicing "the Principle" and which asked "worthy Mormons" to denounce both the idea and the practice of polygamy. Monogamy was now the sole sacred marriage pattern for God's Latter-day Saints.

By the 1940s and in to the 1950s, the Church's position on plural marriage had changed to such an extent that it was actively helping state and local law enforcement agencies in the Mormon culture region target Fundamentalist polygamists and raid their communities and residences. As a result, Church leaders supported the raid on the fundamentalist Mormon community of Short Creek on the border between Utah and Arizona on 26 July 1953. This raid turned into a public relations disaster when photographs of children being pulled away from their mothers by law enforcement officials hit the press, leading to a backlash against the raid within the "mainstream" Latter-day Saint community, thanks to its emphasis on the holiness and sacredness of family.[59]

This opposition to polygamy within the very institution that had once argued for its divine origin and centrality to eternal progression and eternal life, the sacred made profane, seems to have been aimed, at least in part, at counteracting the Church's negative public image, the perceived negative impact of plural marriage on this image, and the perceived negative impact of polygamy on church growth. Mormon leaders have long been conscious of how the public has viewed their faith, if for no other reason than that Latter-day Saint leaders have always seen themselves as part of the only one true form of the Christian faith and thus, they have regarded proselytization as immensely important. Church officials presumably believed that there was a tension between the continued practice of "the Principle" and church growth, at least in the early and middle parts of the twentieth century.

The Church's efforts to combat the practice of "the Principle" was part of the broader social and cultural contexts in which Leonard Arrington and Davis Bitton wrote their chapter on the practice of polygamy in the pre-manifesto period in their 1979 history of Mormonism, *The Mormon Experience*. In that book, the new Mormon historians Arrington and Bitton argued that polygamy was practiced by around five percent of Mormon men and twelve percent of Mormon women. However, as I noted in Chapter Four, recent investigations of Mormon polygamy rates in the pre-manifesto period, have raised questions about Arrington and Bitton's estimates of Mormon polygamy rates. The fact that Arrington and Bitton seem to have underemphasized the numbers of Mormons practicing "the Principle" foregrounds the question of whether Arrington and Bitton's estimates were, at least in part, the product of the Mormon ideological climate in which they wrote in the 1970s, a post–World War II ideological climate in which the Church, increasingly concerned with its image, particularly in non–Mormon circles, was engaged in a campaign to de-emphasize polygamy and even, at times, forcefully combat it.[60]

On the surface the "correction" of Arrington and Bitton's low rates of the practice of "the Principle" by a number of the practitioners of the New Mormon Studies, seems to suggest that empirical accuracy will inevitably triumph over the cultural and ideological construction of reality, whatever its source, in the long run. However, this upward revision of the number of individuals practicing "the Principle" in Zion, raises a number of epistemological and theoretical issues and raises the question of whether naturalist "objectivity" or Weberian and Geertzian detached dispassion, are even possible when analyzing that which one values, particularly a faith one values, in some way, shape, or form.[61]

Conclusion
Whither Mormon Studies?

This book has focused on the historical and sociological subdiscipline of Mormon Studies from the early nineteenth century to the end of the twentieth century. Mormon Studies, of course, has not ended with the advent of the new millennium. Scholars both within the Mormon community and, in lesser numbers, outside of it, continue to explore various aspects of Mormon history, society, and culture, including but not exclusively, the exploration of Mormon origins, the study of women and Mormonism, the investigation of Mormon polygamy, the study of early and contemporary Mormon demographics, and the exploration of various and sundry aspects of the Book of Mormon both from a polemical and apologetic perspective and, if in lesser numbers, from a critical perspective. It is not an exaggeration to say that Mormon Studies has become a major subdiscipline and counterculture or subculture within the broader academic disciplines of history and sociology.

What seems clear, at least from the vantage point of the early twenty-first century, is that Mormon Studies continues to operate within the same ideal type and hegemonic paradigms it has operated in since the nineteenth and twentieth centuries: the apologetic-polemical employed by those who explore Mormonism in the context of normative belief, and the scientific-humanistic, utilized by those who explore Mormonism within economic, political, cultural, geographic, and demographic descriptive and interpretive frames. In this, Mormon Studies parallels a similar division found within Biblical Studies, as I noted in Chapter Seven, since the nineteenth century.

The internal Mormon culture war between these two ideal type paradigms continues as it has since the twentieth century, though it also continues to ebb and flow. Both the apologetic-polemical and scientific-humanistic paradigms, though this is not always obvious in the rhetoric each use about their other, invariably seep into one another.

The insider apologetic-polemical side, for instance, sometimes utilizes economic, political, cultural, geographic, and demographic frames in their analysis (Bushman, Givens) while many of the Mormon insider scientific-humanistic analyses are grounded in some way, shape, or form in the apologetic rhetoric of belief and faithfulness (Quinn, Alexander).

So, whither Mormon Studies? If I were to gaze into a crystal ball I would guess that an interest in Mormon history, society, and culture is unlikely to diminish anytime soon and that controversies over many aspects of Mormon history, particularly over Mormon origins, polygamy, and the history and culture of Mormon women, are likely to continue to dominate Mormon Studies in the mid- and late twenty-first century even if they trod over many of the same well-worn paths they long have and even if they offer little in the way of theoretical novelty. Historical, social, and cultural analysis, after all, often seems more cyclical than linear or progressive despite, if not in spite of, the intellectual and academic fads of the academic and intellectual moment. Controversy, after all, just like media sensationalism, sells in the academic status marketplace.

I expect the tensions between the angel of Mormon distinctiveness and the beehive of Mormonism's wish to fit in in broader American society, to continue to ebb and flow, and, as a result, I suspect that this cultural schizophrenia will continue to produce tensions within Mormon culture. I also expect that we will continue to see the ebbing and flowing of tensions within Mormon intellectual culture between the angel, the Mormon belief that God acted in history to restore Mormonism, God's one true apostolic church, and the beehive, the attempts by some Mormon scholars to adopt and adapt the approaches of broader Western intellectual culture and the academy and use them to try to unlock the academic and intellectual mysteries of Mormon history including the mystery of Mormon origins.

With respect to the origins of Mormonism, something this author has tried to extensively explore, I want to reiterate what I said in Chapter Six. Yes, humans and human social groups are impacted by economic factors. Yes, humans and social groups are impacted by political forces. Yes, humans and social groups are impacted by geography. Yes, humans and social groups are impacted by biological or demographic factors. Yes, humans and social groups are impacted by social and cultural social psychological factors. All of these forces have impacted and currently impact human life everywhere at every time and in every place. But none of these alone or in combination can fully help us understand the rise and culture of social and cultural movements like Mormonism.

Social movements such as Mormonism, the Oneida Community, Adventism, and evangelicalism, all of which arose in the same or similar geographies, within the same or similar economic and political contexts, and with similar demographics, do differ, but they differ primarily because their cultures vary. In order to fully understand these social and cultural groups and the similarities and their differences between them, we must thus not only pay attention to economic, political, geographical, and demographic factors, but also to the important and significant ways the cultures of these social movements create different social movements with varying collective identities.

As this book has noted, Mormonism was the product of a number of geographic, economic, political, and demographic factors including the intersection of the economic transformations wrought by the Erie Canal, the rise of a Jacksonian democratic politics, the mostly New England and New York backgrounds of Mormons, and the varying class and status backgrounds of Mormon believers. However, it was also the product of a number of cultural and ideological forces ranging from Hebraic-Christian primitivism, to Hebraic-Christian dispensationalism, to Hebraic-Christian millennialism or apocalypticism, to Hebraic-Christian notions of continuing divine revelation, to Hebraic temples, to Hebraic notions of marriage, to Hebraic patriarchalism and tribalism, and to Christian notions about all things being in common, among other things. The way these varying cultural threads were woven together, most of them initially by the Mormon prophet Joseph Smith, was what, in the end, made Mormonism, Mormonism and made Mormons, Mormon.

Physicist J. Robert Oppenheimer managed to bring together his loves of physics and the desert of New Mexico in the Manhattan Project. I hope I have been able to bring together several of the things I am intellectually fascinated by, including history, culture and meaning, culture wars, religiously oriented social movements, and social and cultural theory, in such a way as to provide a helpful and useful way of conceptualizing and understanding the history of Mormon Studies and the history of Mormonism in general in this monograph.

Chapter Notes

Introduction

1. Alexandra Oleson and John Voss (eds.), *The Organization of Knowledge in Modern America, 1860–1920* (Baltimore, MD: Johns Hopkins University Press, 1979), Roger Geiger, *To Advance Knowledge: The Growth of American Research Universities, 1900–1940* (New York: Oxford University Press, 1986), and Roger Geiger, *Relevant Knowledge: American Research Universities Since World War II* (New York: Oxford University Press, 1993).

2. My approach has been massively influenced by Peter Berger and Thomas Luckman, *The Social Construction of Reality* (Harmondsworth, UK: Penguin, 1966).

3. On these methodological issues I have been influenced by E.H. Carr, *What is History?* (New York: Vintage, 1961), Roy Bhaskar, *A Realist Theory of Science* (Atlantic Highlands, NJ: Humanities Press, 1978), Ernest Gellner, *Postmodernism, Reason, and Religion* (London: Routledge, 1992), and Thomas Kuhn, *The Structure of Scientific Revolutions*, 2d. ed. (Chicago: University of Chicago, 1970) among others.

4. I have been influenced here by a number of people and perspectives but particularly by Clifford Geertz, "The Pinch of Destiny: Religion as Experience, Meaning, Identity, Power" in Clifford Geertz, *Available Light: Anthropological Reflections on Philosophical Topics* (Princeton, NJ: Princeton University Press, 2000), 167–187; Clifford Geertz, *The Interpretation of Cultures: Selected Essays* (New York: Basic, 1973); and Clifford Geertz, *Local Knowledge: Further Essays in Interpretive Anthropology* (New York: Basic, 1983).

5. On the Jacksonian period and particular aspects of Jacksonian America I have been influenced here and elsewhere by Richard D. Brown, *Modernization: The Transformation of American Life 1600–1865* (New York: Hill and Wang, 1976), 122–158; Robert Wiebe, *The Opening of American Society from the Adoption of the Constitution to the Eve of Disunion* (New York: Knopf, 1984), 234–352; Edward Pessen, *Jacksonian America: Society, Personality, and Politics*, revised edition (Champaign: University of Illinois Press, 1978); Michael Lebowitz, "The Jacksonians: Paradox Lost" in Barton Bernstein (ed.), *Toward a New Past: Dissenting Essays in American History* (New York: Vintage, 1968), 65–89; and Daniel Walker Howe, *What Hath God Wrought: The Transformation of America, 1815–1848* (New York: Oxford University Press, 2007).

6. On Jacksonian ideology and symbols see John William Ward, *Andrew Jackson: Symbol for an Age* (New York: Oxford University Press, 1955) and Marvin Meyers, *The Jacksonian Persuasion: Politics and Belief* (Palo Alto, CA: Stanford University Press, 1960). On communications in early America see Richard D. Brown, *Knowledge is Power: The Diffusion of Information in Early America, 1700–1865* (New York: Oxford University Press, 1989). On status and class in Jacksonian America see Sean Wilentz, *Chant's Democratic: New York City and the Rise of the American Working Class, 1788–1850* (New York: Oxford University Press, 1984) and Richard Bushman, *The Refinement of America: Persons, Houses, Cities* (New York: Knopf, 1993). On Jacksonian political culture see Emil Pocock, "Popular Roots of Jacksonian Democracy: The Case of Dayton, Ohio, 1815–1830"

Journal of the Early Republic 9 (Winter 1989), 489-513 and Lee Benson, *The Concept of Jacksonian Democracy: New York as a Test Case* (New York: Atheneum, 1961). On religion and religious culture in the Jacksonian era see Daniel Walker Howe, "Protestantism, Voluntarism, and Personal Identity in Antebellum America" in Harry Stout and D.G. Hart (eds.), *New Directions in American Religious History* (New York: Oxford University Press, 1997), 206-238 and Daniel Walker Howe, *What God Hath Wrought: The Transformation of America, 1815-1848* (New York: Oxford University Press, 2007), 164-202, 285-327, 446-482, and 643-656. On religion and economic issues during the Jacksonian era see Melvin Stokes and Stephen Conway (eds.), *The Market Revolution in America: Social, Political, and Religious Expressions, 1800-1880* (Charlottesville: University Press of Virginia, 1996); Mark Noll (ed.), *God and Mammon: Protestants, Money, and the Market, 1790-1860* (New York: Oxford University Press, 2001); Mark Noll, "Protestant Reasoning About Money and the Economy, 1790-1860" in Mark Noll (ed.), *God and Mammon: Protestants, Money, and the Market, 1790-1860* (New York: Oxford University Press, 2001), 265-295; Daniel Walker Howe, "Charles Sellers, the Market Revolution, and the Shaping of American Identity in Whig-Jacksonian America" in Mark Noll (ed.), *God and Mammon: Protestants, Money, and the Market, 1790-1860* (New York: Oxford University Press, 2001), 54-74; and Richard Carwardine, "Charles Sellers' 'Antinomians' and 'Arminians': Methodists and the Market Revolution" in Mark Noll (ed.), *God and Mammon: Protestants, Money, and the Market, 1790-1860* (New York: Oxford University Press, 2001), 75-98. On religion and ethnic issues in Jacksonian America see John Higham, "Ethnicity and American Protestantism: Collective Identity in the Mainstream" in Harry Stout and D.G. Hart (eds.), *New Directions in Religious History* (New York: Oxford University Press, 1997), 239-259. For the global contexts of early United States history see the interesting and useful brief discussions in Carl Guarneri, *America in the World: United States History in Global Context* (New York: McGraw-Hill, 2007), 115-165 and Thomas Bender, *A Nation Among Nations: America's Place in World History* (New York: Hill and Wang, 2006). As Guarneri notes the democratic, nation-making, economic, transportation, cultural, communication, and religious revolutions of the period were Atlantic and, to some extent, global.

7. George Rawlyk, *The Canada Fire: Radical Evangelicalism in British North America, 1775-1812* (Montreal and Kingston: McGill-Queens University Press, 1994). On global revivalism—they occurred in seventeenth century England, eighteenth-century England, Wales, Scotland, Northern Ireland, British North America, German speaking states, and the Habsburg Empire, in nineteenth-century in England, Wales, Scotland, Northern Ireland, the U.S., Canada, Australia, New Zealand, France, Germany, and Norway—and in the twentieth all across the globe see W.R. Ward, *The Protestant Evangelical Awakening* (Cambridge, UK: Cambridge University Press, 1992); Mark Noll, *The Rise of Evangelicalism: The Age of Edwards, Whitefield, and the Wesley's* (Downers Grove, IL: IVP, 2003); Mark Noll, David Bebbington, and George Rawlyk (eds.), *Evangelicalism: Comparative Studies of Popular Protestantism in North America, the British Isles, and Beyond* (New York: Oxford University Press, 1994); George Rawlyk and Mark Noll (eds.), *Amazing Grace: Evangelicalism in Australia, Britain, Canada, and the United States* (Montreal and Kingston: McGill-Queen's University Press, 1994); Keith Robbins (ed.), *Protestant Evangelicalism: Britain, Ireland, Germany, and America, c. 1750-1850* (Oxford, UK: Oxford University Press, 1990); Edith Blumhofer and Randall Balmer (eds.), *Modern Christian Revivals* (Urbana: University of Illinois Press, 1993); Richard Carwardine, *Transatlantic Revivalism: Popular Evangelicalism in Britain and America, 1790-1865* (Westport, CT: Greenwood Press, 1978); Christopher Clark, "Germany 1815-1848: Restoration or Pre-March?" in Mary Fulbrook (ed.), *German History since 1800* (London: Arnold, 1997), 38-60, especially 58-59; and Leigh Eric Schmidt, *Holy Fairs: Scotland and the Making of American Revivalism*, 2d. ed. (Grand Rapids: Eerdmans, 2001). Schmidt notes the similarities between Scottish Presbyterian Holy Fairs and American camp meetings. On pietistic revivalism see Randall Balmer, "Eschewing the 'Routine of Religion': Eighteenth-Century Pietism and the Revival Tradition in America" in Edith

Blumhofer and Randall Balmer (eds.), *Modern Christian Revivals* (Urbana: University of Illinois Press, 1993), 1-16; F. Ernest Stoeffler, "Pietism" in Daniel Reid, Robert Linder, Bruce Shelly, and Harry Stout (eds.), *Dictionary of Christianity in America* (Downers Grove, IL: IVP Press, 1990), 902-904; F. Ernest Stoeffler (ed.), *Continental Pietism and Early American Christianity* (Grand Rapids: Eerdmans, 1976); J.S. O'Malley, "Revivalism, German-American" in Daniel Reid, Robert Linder, Bruce Shelly, and Harry Stout (eds.), *Dictionary of Christianity in America* (Downers Grove, IL: IVP Press, 1990), 1011-1012; and E. Clifford Nelson (ed.), *The Lutherans in North America*, revised edition (Philadelphia: Fortress, 1980), 62-67 and 71-72. On Pietism in general see Stoeffler, *The Rise of Evangelical Pietism* (Leiden, 1971).

8. On the Kentucky and Tennessee revivals see Dickson Bruce, *And They All Sang Hallelujah: Plain-Folk Camp-Meeting Religion, 1800-1845* (Knoxville: University of Tennessee Press, 1974). On Southern revivals see Christine Leigh Heyrman, *Southern Cross: The Beginnings of the Bible Belt* (Chapel Hill: University of North Carolina Press, 1997). On Southern civil religion see Charles Reagan Wilson, *Baptized in Blood: The Religion of the Lost Cause, 1865-1920* (Athens: University of Georgia Press, 1983).

9. Sydney Ahlstrom, *A Religious History of the American People* (New Haven, CT: Yale University Press, 1972), 425-428.

10. On the Burned-Over District see Whitney Cross, *The Burned-Over District: The Social and Intellectual History of Enthusiastic Religion in Western New York, 1800-1850* (New York: Harper and Row, 1950) and Curtis Johnson, *Islands of Holiness: Revival Religion in Upstate New York* (Ithaca, NY: Cornell University Press, 1989). On antebellum reform see Ronald Walters, *American Reformers 1815-1860*, revised edition (New York: Hill and Wang, 1997).

11. On Adventism see Edwin S. Gaustad (ed.), *The Rise of Adventism: Religion and Society in Mid-Nineteenth-century America* (New York: Harper and Row, 1974) and Ronald Numbers and Jonathan Butler (eds.), *The Disappointed: Millerism and Millenarianism in the Nineteenth-century* (Bloomington: Indiana University Press, 1987).

12. On Shakers see Raymond Lee Muncy, *Sex and Marriage in Utopian Communities: Nineteenth-Century America* (Baltimore, MD: Penguin, 1973), 34-47 and 89-90; Lawrence Foster, *Religion and Sexuality: The Shakers, the Mormons, and the Oneida Community* (Urbana: University of Illinois Press, 1981), 21-71; Patricia Brewer, *Shaker Communities, Shaker Lives* (Hanover, NH: University Press of New England, 1986); Priscilla Brewer, "The Shakers of Mother Ann Lee" in Donald Pitzer (ed.), *America's Communal Utopias* (Chapel Hill: University of North Carolina Press, 1997), 37-56; Stephen Stein, *The Shaker Experience in America: A History of the United Society of Believers* (New Haven, CT: Yale University Press, 1992); Edward Deming Andrews, *The People Called Shakers* (New York: Dover, 1953); Clarke Garrett, *Origins of the Shakers: From the Old World to the New World* (Baltimore MD: Johns Hopkins University Press, 1987); and William Sims Bainbridge, "Shaker Demographics 1840-1900: An Example From the Use of Census Examination Schedules," *Journal for the Scientific Study of Religion* 21:4 (1982), 352-365. For an excellent collection of Shaker documents see Jean M. Humez (ed.), *Mother's First-Born Daughters: Early Shaker Writings on Women and Religion* (Bloomington: Indiana University Press, 1993).

13. On Oneida see Maren Lockwood Carden, *Oneida: Utopian Community to Modern Corporation* (New York: Harper and Row, 1969); Lawrence Foster, "Free Love and Community: John Humphrey Noyes and the Oneida Perfectionists" Donald Pitzer (ed.), *America's Communal Utopias* (Chapel Hill: University of North Carolina Press, 1997), 253-278; Lawrence Foster, *Religion and Sexuality: The Shakers, the Mormons, and the Oneida Community* (Urbana: University of Illinois Press, 1981), 72-122; Robert David Thomas, *The Man Who Would Be Perfect: John Humphrey Noyes and the Utopian Impulse* (Philadelphia: University of Pennsylvania Press, 1977); and Raymond Lee Muncy, *Sex and Marriage in Utopian Communities: Nineteenth-century America* (Baltimore, MD: Penguin, 1974). 160-196. The biblical reference is Acts 2:44-45.

14. Shawn Michael Trimble, "Spiritualism and Channeling" in Timothy Miller (ed.), *America's Alternative Religions* (Albany: State University of New York Press, 1995), 333-334. On Spiritualism see Howard Kerr and Charles Crow (eds.), *The Occult in America: New Historical Perspectives* (Urbana: University of Illinois Press, 1983); R. Laurence Moore, *In Search of White Crows: Spiritualism, Parapsychology, and American Culture* (New York: Oxford University Press, 1977); Bret E Carroll, *Spiritualism in Antebellum America* (Bloomington: Indiana University Press, 1997); and Shawn Michael Trimble, "Spiritualism and Channeling" in Timothy Miller (ed.), *America's Alternative Religions* (Albany: State University of New York Press, 1995), 331-337. On the important role women played in the Spiritualist movement see Ann Braude, *Radical Spirits: Spiritualism and Women's Rights in Nineteenth-Century America* (Boston: Beacon, 1991).

15. Hence the term Burned-Over District. The term references Finney's statement about fires of revival burning across upstate New York and parts of eastern Ohio in the nineteenth-century. See Whitney Cross, *The Burned-Over District: The Social and Intellectual History of Enthusiastic Religion in Western New York, 1800-1850* (Syracuse, NY: Syracuse University Press, 1950).

16. For the texts of the "First Vision" and a discussion of them see *The Papers of Joseph Smith* (hereafter cited as *Papers 1*), Volume 1, edited by Dean Jessee (Salt Lake City: Deseret, 1989) especially pages 6-7, 127, 272-73, 429-30, 444, and 448-49. Primary sources for the first vision include the "1832 Autobiography and History," the "1839 History of the Church," the "Wentworth Letter," and Warren Cowdery's "Kirtland Diary, 1835." The official version of the First Vision, which I am drawing on here, is contained in the Pearl of Great Price's "Extracts from the History of Joseph Smith, The Prophet" (Joseph Smith 2). On the first vision and its variants see Richard Bushman, *Joseph Smith: Rough Stone Rolling* (New York Knopf, 2005), 35-41; Jan Shipps, *Mormonism: The Story of a New Religious Tradition* (Urbana: University of Illinois Press, 1985), 30-32; Milton Backman, *Joseph Smith's First Vision*, 2d. ed. (Salt Lake City: Bookcraft, 1980); James B. Allen, "Emergence of a Fundamental: The Expanding Role of Joseph Smith's First Vision in Mormon Religious Thought" in *Journal of Mormon History* 7 (1980), 437-461; Dean Jessee, "The Early Accounts of Joseph Smith's First Vision," *BYU Studies* 9:3 (Spring 1969), 275-294. By the way, a multivolume collection of the Joseph Smith Papers, some of which have already been published by the Church Historian's Press, is in process as I type in 2021. Once completed this multivolume work will be the standard compilation of the papers of Joseph Smith.

17. On the Book of Mormon see Dan Vogel and Brent Metcalfe (eds.), *American Apocalypse: Essays on the Book of Mormon* (Salt Lake City: Signature, 2002); Brent Metcalfe (ed.), *New Approaches to the Book of Mormon* (Salt Lake City: Signature, 1993); and Terryl Givens, *By the Hand of Mormon: The American Scripture that Created a New Religion* (New York: Oxford University Press, 2002).

18. Doctrine and Covenants 51:16 (1831). In Doctrine and Covenants 82:13 (1832) and 94:1 (1833) Kirtland is referred to as a "stake" of "Zion."

19. On Mormon Kirtland see Jan Shipps, *Mormonism: The Story of a New Religious Tradition* (Urbana: University of Illinois Press, 1985), 119-120, 157-158 and Richard Bushman, *Joseph Smith: Rough Stone Rolling* (New York: Knopf, 2005), 127-176, 251-327.

20. Doctrine and Covenants 57. D&C 84:2-5 reveals that Independence is the "new Jerusalem," the center point and gathering place for the Saints in the Americas.

21. R. Laurence Moore, *Religious Outsiders and the Making of Americans* (New York City, 1986), 25-47.

22. On Kirtland and the bank scandal see Marvin Hill, Keith Rooker, and Larry Wimmer, "The Kirtland Economy Revisited: A Market Critique of Sectarian Economics," *BYU Studies* 17:4 (Summer 1977), 389-476.

23. On Mormon and non-Mormon conflict see Stephen C. LeSueur, *The 1838 Mormon War in Missouri* (Columbia: University of Missouri Press, 1987) and *BYU Studies* 13:1, 14:4, and 26:2. On Mormon communalism see Leonard Arrington, Feramorz Fox, and Dean May, *Building the City of God: Community and Cooperation among the Mormons*, 2d. ed. (Urbana: University of Illinois Press, 1992).

24. On Mormon Nauvoo see Jan Shipps, *Mormonism: The Story of a New Religious Tradition* (Urbana: University of Illinois Press, 1985), 159-161 and Richard Bushman, *Joseph Smith: Rough Stone Rolling* (New York: Knopf, 2006), 501-550. Also see Robert Flanders, *Nauvoo: Kingdom on the Mississippi* (Urbana: University of Illinois Press, 1965); Roger Launius and John Halwas (eds.), *The Kingdom on the Mississippi Revisited* (Urbana: University of Illinois Press, 1996); the special issue of *Dialogue* on Nauvoo, 5:1 (Spring 1970); Benjamin Park, *Kingdom of Nauvoo: The Rise and Fall of a Religious Empire on the American Frontier* (New York: Liveright, 2020); and John Bennett's sensationalistic expose *History of the Saints* (Utah Lighthouse Ministry, 1842).

25. On Mormonism and its background see Dan Vogel, *Religious Seekers and the Advent of Mormonism* (Salt Lake City: Signature, 1988); Vogel, *Indian Origins and the Book of Mormon* (Salt Lake City: Signature, 1986); Leonard Arrington and Davis Bitton, *The Mormon Experience*, 2d. ed. (Urbana: University of Illinois Press, 1992); Douglas Davies, "Mormon History, Identity, and Faith Community" in Elizabeth Tonkin, Maryon McDonald, and Malcolm Chapman (editors), *History and Ethnicity* (London: Routledge, 1989), 168-182; Patricia Nelson Limerick, "Peace Initiative: Using the Mormons to Rethink Culture and Ethnicity in American History" in Patricia Nelson Limerick, *Something in the Soil: Legacies and Reckonings in the New West* (New York: Norton, 2000), 235-255; Jan Shipps, *Mormonism: The Story of a New Religious Tradition* (Urbana: University of Illinois Press, 1985); and Jan Shipps, *Sojourner in the Promised Land: Forty Years Among the Mormons*, Urbana: University of Illinois Press, 2000),

26. The first-hand accounts of Smith's Nauvoo teachings are conveniently collected in Lyndon Cook and Andrew Ehat (eds.), *The Words of Joseph Smith* (Orem, UT: Grandin, 1991). The King Follett Discourse was reported by Willard Richards, Wilford Woodruff, Thomas Bullock, and William Clayton in their journals and diaries. These are reprinted in the Cook and Ehat compilation noted above. A version of it was also printed in the Mormon newspaper *Times and Seasons* 5, 15 August 1844.

For an interesting discussion of Smith's theology see Don Bradley, "The Grand Fundamental Principles of Mormonism: Joseph Smith's Unfinished Reformation," *Sunstone*, April 2006. 32-41.

27. For two somewhat different views of the Council of Fifty see D. Michael Quinn, "The Council of Fifty and Its Members," *BYU Studies* 20 (Winter 1980), 163-197 and Klaus Hansen, *The Political Kingdom of God and the Council of Fifty in Mormon History* (East Lansing: Michigan State University Press, 1967).

28. On doctrinal developments in Nauvoo, including the doctrines of "eternal progression" and "celestial marriage" see Thomas Alexander, "The Reconstruction of Mormon Doctrine: From Joseph Smith to Progressive Theology," *Sunstone* 10:5 (July-August 1980), 24-33. For primary source materials on Smith's doctrinal pronouncements in Nauvoo see Lyndon Cook and Andrew Ehat (eds.), *The Words of Joseph Smith* (Orem, UT: Grandin, 1991). Harold Bloom's *The American Religion: The Emergence of the Post-Christian Nation* (New York: Simon and Schuster, 1992) is a brilliant (if flawed) analysis of Smith's thought.

29. Doctrine and Covenants 28:7 (1830) specified that the "authorities" had been given "the keys to the mysteries."

30. *The Nauvoo Expositor*, 7 June 1844, 1 2.

31. Robert Wiebe has an interesting discussion of Mormon nationalism (and nationalism in general) in his *Who We Are: A History of Popular Nationalism* (Princeton, NJ: Princeton University Press, 2002).

32. Edward Leo Lyman, *Political Deliverance: The Mormon Quest for Statehood* (Urbana: University of Illinois Press, 1986).

33. On the Utah War see Norman Furniss, *The Mormon Conflict, 1850-1859* (New Haven, CT: Yale University Press, 1960) and Richard Poll, "The Move South," *BYU Studies* 29:4 (Fall 1989), 65-88.

34. Tim Heaton, "Vital Statistics" in James T. Duke (ed.), *Latter-Day Saint Social Life: Social Research on the LDS Church and its Members* (Provo, UT: Religious Studies Center, BYU, 1998), 105-132. Heaton estimates that between 1830 and 1840 thirty percent of Mormons were practicing polygamy. Heaton argued that between 1855 and 1859 the percentage declined to

twelve percent while after 1880 it was rare as a result of American government action against the Saints.

35. David Brion Davis, "Some Themes of Countersubversion: An Analysis of Anti-Masonic, Anti-Catholic, and Anti-Mormon Literature," *Mississippi Valley Historical Review* 47:2 (September 1960), 205–224.

36. E.B. Long, *The Saints and the Union* (Urbana: University of Illinois Press, 1981).

37. On *Reynolds v. the United States* see Edwin Firmage and Richard Mangrum, *Zion in the Courts: A Legal History of the Church of Jesus Christ of Latter-day Saints* (Urbana: University of Illinois Press, 1988) and Sarah Barringer Gordon, *The Mormon Question: Polygamy and Constitutional Conflict in Nineteenth-Century America* (Chapel Hill: University of North Carolina Press, 2002). The decision of the Supreme Court, of course, was influenced by ideologies of monogamy grounded in Christian (i.e., Protestant) discourse.

38. On the antipolygamy campaigns see Joan Iverson, "A Debate on the American Home: The Antipolygamy Controversy, 1880–1890," *Journal of the History of Sexuality* 1:4 (1991), 585–602 and Paul Conkin, *American Originals: Homemade Varieties of Christianity* (Chapel Hill: University of North Carolina Press, 1997), 216–223.

39. Doctrine and Covenants 132.

40. Jan Shipps, *Mormonism: The Story of a New Religious Tradition* (Urbana: University of Illinois Press, 1985), 131–149 and Shipps, "In the Presence of the Past: Continuity and Change in Twentieth Century Mormonism" in Thomas Alexander and Jessie Embry (eds.), *After 150 Years: The Latter-day Saints in Sesquicentennial Perspective* (Provo, UT: Charles Redd Center for Western Studies, 1983), 3–35.

41. My discussion of the battle over polygamy after the manifesto has been influenced by D. Michael Quinn, "LDS Church Authority and New Plural Marriages, 1890–1904" *Dialogue* 18:1 (Spring 1985); 9–105, D. Michael Quinn, "Plural Marriages after the 1890 Manifesto," a talk presented at Bluffdale, Utah, 11 August 1991, copy in the author's possession; Kenneth Cannon II, "Beyond the Manifesto: Polygamous Cohabitation Among LDS General Authorities After 1890," *Utah Historical Quarterly* 46:1 (Winter 1978), 24–36; Kenneth Cannon II, "After the Manifesto: Mormon Polygamy, 1890–1906," in D. Michael Quinn (ed.), *The New Mormon History: Revisionist Essays on the Past* (Salt Lake City: Signature, 1992), 201–220; R. Carmon Hardy, *Solemn Covenant: The Mormon Polygamous Passage* (Urbana: University of Illinois Press, 1992); Hardy, "Appendix II: Mormon Polygamous Marriages After the 1890 Manifesto Through 1910: A Tentative List" in R. Carmon Hardy, *Solemn Covenant: The Mormon Polygamous Passage* (Urbana: University of Illinois Press, 1992), 389–426; and Martha Bradley, "Changed Faces: The Official LDS Position on Polygamy," *Sunstone* 14:1 (February 1990), 26–33.

42. On the changing official Mormon positions on polygamy see Martha Bradley, "Changed Faces: The Official LDS Position on Polygamy," *Sunstone* 14:1 (February 1990), 26–33.

43. On the Smoot controversy see Kathleen Flake, *The Politics of Religious Identity: The Seating of Senator Reed Smoot, Mormon Apostle* (Chapel Hill: University of North Carolina Press, 2004).

44. The so-called "second manifesto" can be found at "Official Statement by President Joseph F. Smith," *Improvement Era* 7, 545–546 (Apr. 1904).

45. This letter can be found at the end of Martha Bradley, "Changed Faces: The Official LDS Position on Polygamy," *Sunstone* 14:1 (February 1990), 26–33. A Mormon stake, by the way, is comparable to a diocese in the Catholic Church.

46. It was under prophet and president Heber J. Grant that Mormonism made its transformation from primitive Mormonism with its theocracy and polygamy, to bureaucratic institution. On the Grant era see Thomas Alexander, *Mormonism in Transition: A History of the Latter-day Saints, 1890–1930*, 2d. ed. (Urbana: University of Illinois Press, 1996).

47. My discussion of Mormon fundamentalism has been influenced by D. Michael Quinn, "Plural Marriage and Mormon Fundamentalism" in Martin Marty and R. Scott Appleby (eds.), *Fundamentalisms and Society: Reclaiming the Sciences, the Family, and Education* (Chicago: University of Chicago Press, 1993), 240–293 and Merrill Singer, "Nathaniel Baldwin, Utah Inventor and Patron of the

Fundamentalist Movement," *Utah Historical Quarterly* 47:1 (Winter 1979), 42–53. Also on post-manifesto Mormon fundamentalism see Newell Bringhurst and Craig Foster, *The Persistence of Mormon Polygamy: Fundamentalist Mormon Polygamy from 1890 to the Present* (Independence, MO: John Whitmer Books, 2015).

48. For a range of statistics on contemporary Mormonism see the *2020 LDS Church Almanac* (Salt Lake City: Deseret News, 2020). Recent LDS Church membership numbers are taken from the official Church website.

49. On the Church response to dissidence see Lavina Fielding Anderson, "The LDS Intellectual Community and Church Leadership," *Dialogue* 26:1 (Spring 1993), 7–64.

50. On contemporary Mormonism see the relevant chapters in James B. Allen and Glen M. Leonard, *Story of the Latter-day Saints*, 2d. ed. (Salt Lake City: Deseret, 1992) and Thomas Alexander, *Mormonism in Transition*, 2d. ed. (Urbana: University of Illinois Press, 1996).

51. On Mormon symbology see Jan Shipps, *Mormonism: The Story of a New Religious Tradition* (Urbana: University of Illinois Press, 1985); Douglas Davies, *Introduction to Mormonism* (Cambridge, UK: Cambridge University Press, 2003); O. Kendall White, *Mormon Neo-Orthodoxy: A Crisis Theology* (Salt Lake City: Signature, 1987); Gordon and Gary Shepherd, *A Kingdom Transformed* (Salt Lake City: University of Utah Press, 1984); David John Buerger, *The Mysteries of Godliness: A History of Mormon Temple Worship* (Salt Lake City: Signature, 2002); and Jerald Tanner and Sandra Tanner, *Evolution of the Mormon Temple Ceremony: 1842–1990*, updated edition (Salt Lake City: Utah Lighthouse Ministry 2005). On the evangelicalization and fundamentalization of Mormonism in the twentieth-century see O. Kendall White, *Mormon Neo-Orthodoxy: A Crisis Theology* (Salt Lake City: Signature, 1987).

52. On immigration to Utah see Thomas Alexander, *Utah: The Right Place*, revised and updated edition (Salt Lake City: Gibbs Smith, 2003), 234–241.

53. Tim Heaton, "Vital Statistics" in James T. Duke (ed.), *Latter-Day Saint Social Life: Social Research on the LDS Church and Its Members* (Provo, UT: Religious Studies Center, BYU, 1998), 105–132.

54. On the history of the BYU Honor Code see Gary James Bergera and Ronald Priddis, *Brigham Young University: A House of Faith* (Salt Lake City: Signature, 1985), Chapter Three.

55. General Conference is held twice a year in Salt Lake City. Church leaders give speeches at the conferences on a variety of issues.

56. Gordon and Gary Shepherd, *A Kingdom Transformed: Themes in the Development of Mormonism* (Salt Lake City: University of Utah Press 1984).

57. Jan Shipps, *Mormonism: The Story of a New Religious Tradition* (Urbana: University of Illinois Press, 1985), 131–149; D. Mark Leone, *Roots of Modern Mormonism* (Cambridge, MA: Harvard University Press, 1979); and Michael Quinn, personal communication with author 1993.

58. Dean May, "One Heart and One Mind" in Donald Pitzer (ed.), *America's Communal Utopias* (Chapel Hill: University of North Carolina Press), 153–155.

59. Victor Turner, "Symbols in African Ritual," *Science* Vol. 179, no. 4078, 16 March 1973, 1100–1101.

Chapter One

1. My approach to ethnocentrism, tradition, and culture has been influenced by Richard Handler, *Nationalism and the Politics of Culture in Quebec* (Madison: University of Wisconsin Press, 1988).

2. On the Christian construction of otherness see R.I. Moore, *The Formation of a Persecuting Society: Authority and Deviance in Western Europe 950–1250*, 2d. ed. (Oxford, UK: Blackwell, 2007); Louis Fieldman, *Jew and Gentile in the Ancient World: Attitudes and Interactions from Alexander to Justinian* (Princeton, NJ: Princeton University Press, 1993); Andrew Sharf, *Byzantine Jewry from Justinian to the Fourth Crusade* (New York: Schocken, 1971); David Kertzler, *The Popes Against the Jews: The Vatican's Role in the Rise of Modern Anti-Semitism* (New York: Vintage, 2002); Jonathan Riley-Smith (ed.), *The Oxford Illustrated History of the Crusades* (New York: Oxford University Press, 2002); and Patrick Collinson, *The Reformation: A History* (New York: Modern Library, 2003).

3. On the persecution of Quakers in

Puritan New England see Margaret Bacon, "On the Verge: The Evolution of American Quakerism, in Timothy Miller (ed.), *America's Alternative Religions* (Albany, NY: SUNY Press, 1995), 70 and Peter Williams, *America's Religions: From Their Origins to the Twenty-First Century* (Urbana: University of Illinois Press, 2002), 115.

4. On Anti-Catholicism and Anti-Masonry in the United States see David Brion Davis, "Some Themes of Counter-Subversion," *Journal of American History*, 47: 2, September 1960, 205–224. On American Anti-Catholicism see Roy Billington, *The Protestant Crusade: A Study in the Origins of American Nativism, 1800–1860* (Chicago: Quadrangle, 1952). On "otherness" in the United States see Stephen Stein, *Communities of Dissent: A History of Alternative Religions in America* (New York: Oxford University Press, 2003), 56.

5. On Anti-Shakerism see Elizabeth A. DeWolfe, *Shaking the Faith: Women, Family, and Mary Marshall Dyer's Anti-Shaker Campaign, 1815–1867* (New York: Palgrave, 2002). Dyer's own critiques of Shakerism include *Shakerism Exposed* (Hanover, NH: Dartmouth Press, n.d. [ca. 1852]), *A Brief Statement of the Sufferings of Mary Dyer Occasioned By the Society Called Shakers* (Concord, NH: Joseph Spear, 1818), *A Portraiture of Shakerism...* (Concord, NH: Printed for the Author [by Sylvester Goss], 1822), *Reply to the Shakers* (Concord, [NH]: Printed for the Author, 1824), and, under the pseudonym Mary Mitchell, *The Rise and Progress of the Serpent from the Garden of Eden to the Present Day* (Concord, [NH}: Printed for the Author, 1847). The references to Dyer in the text are from pages 147, 184–185, and 221 of the last.

6. For John Mears' criticisms of Oneida (and the Mormons) see his "Utah and the Oneida Community," *The Independent* 31 (1879), 1584. Mears' anti–Oneida activities were reported in the *New York Times*, 15 February 1879, 1. On anti–Oneida activities see Maren Lockwood Carden, *Oneida: Utopian Community to Modern Corporation* (New York: Harper and Row, 1969) 101, 103; Lawrence Foster, "Free Love and Community: John Humphrey Noyes and the Oneida Perfectionists" in Donald Pitzer (ed.), *America's Communal Utopias* (Chapel Hill: University of North Carolina Press, 1997), 253–278; and Nancy Cott, *Public Vows: A History of Marriage and the Nation* (Cambridge, MA: Harvard University Press, 2002), 124, 128.

7. On new religious movements and cult scare moral panics see Phillip Jenkins' excellent *Mystics and Messiahs: Cults and New Religions in American History* (New York: Oxford University Press, 2001).

8. On Anti-Mormonism see Davis Bitton, "Antimormonism: Periodization, Strategies, Motivation"; 1985, unpublished paper in author's possession; Leonard Arrington and Jon Haupt, "Intolerable Zion: Images of Mormonism in Nineteenth-century Fiction," *Western Humanities Review* 22 (Summer 1968), 37–50; Leonard Arrington and Jon Haupt, "The Missouri and Illinois Mormons in Ante-Bellum Fiction," *Dialogue* 5:1 (1970), 243–260; Gary Bunker and Davis Bitton, *The Mormon Graphic Image, 1834–1914* (Salt Lake City: University of Utah Press, 1983); Terryl Givens; *The Viper in the Hearth: Mormons, Myths, and the Construction of Heresy* (New York: Oxford University Press, 1997); Jan Shipps, "From Satyr to Saint: American Perception of the Mormons, 1860–1960" in Jan Shipps "Sojourner in a Promised Land: Forty Years Among the Mormons" (Urbana: University of Illinois Press, 2000), 51–97; and Jan Shipps, "Surveying the Mormon Image Since 1960," Jan Shipps, *Sojourner in a Promised Land: Forty Years Among the Mormons* (Urbana: University of Illinois Press, 2000), 98–123. On Mormon perceptions of "Gentiles" see Jan Shipps, "From Gentile to Non-Mormon: Mormon Perceptions of the Other" in Jan Shipps, *Sojourner in the Promised Land: Forty Years Among the Mormons* (Urbana: University of Illinois Press, 2000), 124–142. The broad use of the term anti–Mormonism to describe any valid or invalid criticism of Mormonism has become an ideological and political tool in an apologetic and polemical culture war. The term, as used by some apologists and polemicists, conflates valid forms of criticism, those grounded in empirical economic, political, cultural, demographic, and geographical analysis, with invalid forms of criticism, those grounded in emotional and ideological apologetics and polemics. In this regard it has much in common with the apologetics and polemics surrounding the conflation of anti–Semitism with any criticism of Israel

and the conflation of anti-Americanism with any criticism of the United States. That said, there are clear cases of anti-Mormonism, cases where "criticism" of Mormonism is grounded in emotional hatred and theological dispute rather than critical analysis, just as there are clear cases of anti-Semitism.

9. Doctrine and Covenants 1:30, 1971 edition.

10. E.D. Howe, *Mormonism Unvailed or, a Faithful Account of that Singular Imposition and Delusion* (Salt Lake City: Utah Lighthouse Ministry, 1834), 64, 100, 278-290. On the Spaulding hypothesis see Lester Bush, "The Spaulding Theory Then and Now," *Dialogue* 10:4 (Autumn 1977), 40-69.

11. Doctor was his first name not his title.

12. In the early 1820s Smith claimed an ability to use seer stones for locating lost items and buried treasure. Smith's method for finding buried treasure involved putting a stone in a white stovepipe hat and following the information that appeared in the hat thanks to reflections given off by the stone. For one view of Smith and treasure seeking see D. Michael Quinn, *Early Mormonism and the Magic Worldview*, revised and enlarged edition (Salt Lake City: Signature, 1998), 33-74, and 265-266.

13. La Roy Sunderland, *Mormonism Exposed and Refuted* (New York: Piercy and Reed, 1838), iii, 35ff, 49-50.

14. John C. Bennett, *The History of the Saints, or, An Expose of Joe Smith and Mormonism* (Urbana: University of Illinois Press, 2000 [1842]).

15. John A. Clark, *Gleanings by the Way* (Philadelphia: W.J. and J.K. Simon, 1842).

16. Origen Bacheler, *Mormonism Exposed Internally and Externally* (New York: n.p., 1838), 5-6, 11-12, 14, 17, 20, 26, 36, 48. Bachelor also attacked Universalism (Owen Bacheler, *Trial of the Commonwealth, Versus Origen Bacheler, for a Libel on the Character of George B. Beals, Deceased, at the Municipal Court, Boston* (Boston, John H. Belcher 1829), and Owenite communalism (Robert Owen and Owen Bacheler, *Discussion on the authenticity of the Bible, between Origen Bacheler and Robert Dale Owen* (London: J. Watson, 1840 [1832]).

17. Henry Caswall, *The Prophet of the Nineteenth-century, or, The Rise, Progress, and Present State of the Mormons* (London: J.G.F. and J. Rivington, 1843), vi and 8.

18. Pomeroy Tucker, *Origin, Rise, and Progress of Mormonism: Biography of Its Founders and History of Its Church* (Salt Lake City: Utah Lighthouse Ministry, 1867), 16 and 278-279.

19. John Gunnison's *The Mormons, or, Latter-day Saints in the Valley of the Great Salt Lake City* (Philadelphia: Lippincott, 1852), 95-96.

20. Mark Twain, *Roughing It* (Hartford, CT: American Publishing Company, 1872), Appendix A.

21. Arthur Conan Doyle, *A Study in Scarlet* (Oxford, UK: Oxford University Press, 1994 [1888]), 86, 87, 88, 91, 93, 94, 95, 102.

22. John D. Lee *Mormonism Unveiled: or The Life and Confessions of the Late Mormon Bishop John D. Lee* (New York: Bryan, Brand, and Company, 1877), 213-249, especially 221, 224, 245, 247, 249 ("destroying angel"), 250-254, 265.

23. William Hickman, *Brigham's Destroying Angel: Being the Life, Confession, and Startling Disclosures of the Notorious Bill Hickman, Danite Chief of Utah* (New York: George A. Crofutt, 1872), especially 122-185.

24. Bruce Kinney, *Mormonism: The Islam of America* (New York: Fleming Revell, 1912), 55, 32, 127, 136, 36, 125, 141, 147, 247.

25. Bruce Kinney, *Mormonism: The Islam of America* (New York: Fleming Revell, 1912), p. 180. On early American orientalism see Fuad Sha'ban, *Islam and the Arabs in Early American Thought* (Durham, NC: Acorn, 1991).

26. See, for example, Jerald Tanner and Sandra Tanner, *Did Spaulding Write the Book of Mormon?* (Salt Lake City: Modern Microfilms, 1977).

27. On the Tanners see Lawrence Foster, "Career Apostates: Reflections on the Works of Jerald and Sandra Tanner," *Dialogue* 17:2 (Summer 1984), 35-60 and Lawrence Foster, "Apostate Believers: Jerald and Sandra Tanner's Encounter with Mormon History, in Roger D. Launius and Laurel Thatcher (eds.), *Differing Visions: Dissenters in Mormon History* (Urbana: University of Illinois Press, 1994), 343-365. Jerald Tanner and Sandra Tanner, *Mormonism: Shadow or Reality?* (Salt Lake City: Utah Lighthouse Ministry, 1987) brings together in one place the Tanner's criticisms of Mormonism.

28. Both "The God Makers" and "The God Makers II" have been shown in evangelical oriented churches around the world. Decker has published a book based on the films, Ed Decker and Dave Hunt, *The God Makers: The Mormon Quest for Godhood* (Eugene, OR: Harvest House, 1984). On "The Godmakers" see Randall A. Mackey, "'The Godmakers' Examined: Introduction," *Dialogue* 18:2 (Summer 1985), 14–16; Sharon Lee Swenson, "'The Godmakers' Examined: Does the Camera Lie: A Structural Analysis of '"The Godmakers,"' *Dialogue* 18:2 (Summer 1985), 16–23; and Allen D. Roberts, "'The Godmakers': Shadow or Reality? A Content Analysis," *Dialogue* 18:2 (Summer 1985), 24–33.

29. On muckraking and its reformist ideology see Robert Wiebe, *The Search for Order 1877-1920* (New York: Hill and Wang, 1967), 198–199.

30. Frank Q. Cannon and Harvey J. O'Higgins, *Under the Prophet in Utah: The National Menace of a Political Priestcraft* (Boston: C.M. Clark, 1911), 9. The articles were published throughout 1910 and 1911 in nine numbers of the magazine.

31. John Heinerman and Anson Shupe, *The Mormon Corporate Empire* (Boston: Beacon, 1985) and Anson Shupe, *The Darker Side of Virtue: Corruption, Scandal and the Mormon Empire* (Buffalo, NY: Prometheus, 1991).

32. On tensions between Mormons and "Gentiles" see Max Parkin, "Kirtland, A Stronghold for the Kingdom" in F. Mark McKiernan, Alma R. Blair, and Paul M. Edwards (eds.), *The Restoration Movement: Essays in Mormon History*, 2d.ed. (Independence, MO: Herald House, 1992), 99. 77–83; Marvin Hill, *Quest for Refuge: The Mormon Flight from American Pluralism* (Salt Lake City: Signature, 1989), 66, 82–84; Stephen C. LeSueur, *The 1838 Mormon War in Missouri* (Columbia: University of Missouri Press, 1987); F. Mark McKiernan, "Mormonism on the Defensive: Far West, 1838–1839" in Mark McKiernan, Alma Blair, and Paul Edwards (eds.), *The Restoration Movement*, 126–132; Clark Johnson (ed.), *Mormon Redress Petitions: Documents of the 1833-1838 Missouri Conflict* (Provo, UT: BYU Religious Studies Center, 1992); Annette Hampshire, *Mormons in Conflict: The Nauvoo Years* (Edward Mellen, 1985); and John Hallwas and Roger D. Launius (eds.), *Cultures in Conflict: A Documentary History of the Mormon War in Illinois* (Logan: Utah State University Press, 1999).

33. On Anti-Mormonism see Davis Bitton, "Antimormonism: Periodization, Strategies, Motivation," 1985, unpublished paper in author's possession; Terryl Givens, *The Viper in the Hearth: Mormons, Myths, and the Construction of Heresy* (New York: Oxford University Press, 1997); Jan Shipps, "From Gentile to Non-Mormon: Mormon Perceptions of the Other" in Shipps, *Sojourner in the Promised Land: Forty Years Among the Mormons* (Urbana: University of Illinois Press, 2000), 124–142; Gary L. Ward (ed.), *Mormonism I: Evangelical Christian Anti-Mormonism in the Twentieth Century* (New York: Garland, 1990); and Massimo Introvigne, "The Devil Makers: Contemporary Evangelical Fundamentalist Anti-Mormonism," *Dialogue* 27:1 (Spring 1994), 153–169. On negative popular images of Mormonism see, Leonard Arrington and Jon Haupt, "Intolerable Zion: Images of Mormonism in Nineteenth-century Fiction," *Western Humanities Review* 22 (Summer 1968), 37–50; Arrington and Rebecca Cornwall Foster, "Perpetuation of a Myth: Mormon Danites in Western Novels, 1840–90," *BYU Studies* 23:2 (Spring 1983), 147–165; Gary Bunker and Davis Bitton, *The Mormon Graphic Image, 1834-1914* (Salt Lake City: University of Utah Press, 1983); Jan Shipps, "From Satyr to Saint: American Perception of the Mormons, 1860-1960" in Jan Shipps, *Sojourner in the Promised Land: Forty Years Among the Mormons* (Urbana: University of Illinois Press, 2000), 51–97; and Jan Shipps, "Surveying the Mormon Image Since 1960" in Jan Shipps, *Sojourner in the Promised Land: Forty Years Among the Mormons* (Urbana: University of Illinois Press, 2000), 98–123.

34. Oliver Cowdery, "Letter IV," *The Latter Day Saints' Messenger and Advocate* 1 (1835): 77–80 and Cowdery, "Letter VIII," *The Latter Day Saints' Messenger and Advocate* 2 (1835): 195–201. *Latter-Day Saints Messenger and Advocate* was a Mormon newspaper published in Kirtland, Ohio. The eight letters were later published as *Letters of Oliver Cowdery to W.W. Phelps* in Liverpool in 1844.

35. Oliver Cowdery, "Letter 8 to W.W. Phelps," *Latter Day Saints Messenger and Advocate* 2:1, October 1835, 45.

36. Parley Pratt *Mormonism Unveiled: Zion's Watchman Unmasked and Its Editor Mr. L.R. Sunderland Exposed, Truth Vindicated, the Devil Mad, and Priestcraft in Danger*, 2d. ed. (New York: O. Pratt and E. Fordham, 1838), iii and 40.

37. Joseph Smith, "Church History: Wentworth Letter," *Times and Seasons* 3 (1 March 1842), 706–710.

38. On the transformation of Utah and Mormonism see Thomas Alexander, *Utah: The Right Place*, revised and updated edition (Salt Lake City: Gibbs Smith, 2003) particularly 276–402.

39. Hugh Nibley, *No Ma'am That's Not History: A Brief Review of Mrs. Brodie's Reluctant Vindication of a Prophet She Seeks to Expose* (Salt Lake City: Bookcraft, 1946). Nibley is critiquing the first edition of Brodie's book which came out in 1945. Also see Hugh Nibley, "How to Write and Anti-Mormon Book," BYU Speech, Provo, Utah, 17 February 1962. On Nibley see Boyd Jay Petersen, *Hugh Nibley: A Consecrated Life* (Salt Lake City: Greg Kofford Books, 2002).

40. For examples of faithful Mormon critiques of Anti-Mormonism emanating from FARMS see Daniel Peterson, "Reflections on Secular Anti-Mormonism," *FARMS Review*, Volume 17, Number 2 (2005), 423–450; Peterson and Steven Ricks, *Offenders for a Word: How Anti-Mormons Play Word Games to Attack the Latter-day Saints* (Provo, UT: FARMS, 1992); Peterson, "A Modern Malleus malificarum," *FARMS Review* 3:1 (1991), 231–260; Davis Bitton, "Spotting an Anti-Mormon Book": *FARMS Review* 16:1 (2004), 355–360; George L. Mitton, "Introduction: Anti-Mormon Writings: Encountering the Topsy Turvy Approach to Mormon Origins," *FARMS Review* 16:1 (2004), xi–xxxii; Louis Midgley, "The Signature Books Saga" *FARMS Review* 16:1 (2004), 361–406; and William Hamblin, "Basic Methodological Problems with the Anti-Mormon Approach to the Geography and Archaeology of the Book of Mormon" *Journal of Book of Mormon Studies* 2:1 (1993), 161–197.

41. Part of the statement of intent of the Foundation for Apologetic and Information Research (FAIR) website.

42. John Welch, "Chiasmus in the Book of Mormon," *BYU Studies* 10: 3 (1969), pp. 69–83 (chiasms); Steven D. Ricks, "Kingship, Coronation, and Covenant in Mosiah 1–6" in John Welch and Steven D. Ricks (eds.), *King Benjamin's Speech: That Ye May Learn Wisdom* (Provo. UT: FARMS, 1998), 233–275 (evidence of knowledge of ancient coronation ceremonies); Warren P. Aston and Michaela Knoth Aston, *In the Footsteps of Lehi: New Evidence for Lehi's Journey Across Arabia to Bountiful* (Salt Lake City: Deseret, 1994) (evidence of knowledge of ancient geography); Hugh Nibley, *Since Cumorah*, 2d. ed. (Provo, UT: FARMS, 1988) (evidence of Egyptianisms); E. Craig Bramwell, "Hebrew Idioms in the Small Plates of Nephi," unpublished master's thesis, BYU, 1960 (evidence of Hebraisms); and John B. Sorenson, *An Ancient American Setting for the Book of Mormon* (Provo, UT: FARMS, 1985) (the Yucatan peninsula as ancient Book of Mormon lands).

43. Richard Bushman, *Joseph Smith: Rough Stone Rolling* (New York: Knopf, 2005), 92.

44. Brent Lee Metcalfe (ed.), *New Approaches to the Book of Mormon: Explorations in Critical Methodology* (Salt Lake City: Signature, 1993) and Dan Vogel and Metcalfe (eds.), *American Apocrypha: Essays on the Book of Mormon* (Salt Lake City: Signature, 2002).

45. Blake Ostler, "The *Book of Mormon* as a Modern Expansion of an Ancient Source," *Dialogue* 20 (Spring 1987), 66–123; Dan Vogel and Brent Lee Metcalfe (eds.), *American Apocrypha: Essays on the Book of Mormon* (Salt Lake City: Signature, 2002), vii and ix; Vogel, *Indian Origins and the Book of Mormon: Religious Solutions from Columbus to Joseph Smith* (Salt Lake City: Signature, 1986); Vogel, "Echoes of Anti-Masonry: A Rejoinder to the Critics of the Anti-Masonic Thesis" in Vogel and Brent Lee Metcalfe (eds.), *American Apocrypha: Essays on the Book of Mormon* (Salt Lake City: Signature, 2002), 275–320; Vogel, "Anti-Universalist Rhetoric in the *Book of Mormon*" in Metcalfe (ed.), *New Approaches to the Book of Mormon: Explorations in Critical Methodology* (Salt Lake City: Signature, 1993), 21–52; Edward H. Ashment, "'A Record in the Language of My Father': Evidence of Ancient Egyptian and Hebrew in the *Book of Mormon*," in Metcalfe (ed.), *New Approaches to the Book of Mormon: Explorations in*

Critical Methodology (Salt Lake City: Signature Books, 1993), 329–393; Deanne Matheny, "Does the Shoe Fit? A Critique of the Limited Tehuantepec" in Metcalfe (ed.), *New Approaches to the Book of Mormon: Explorations in Critical Methodology* (Salt Lake City: Signature Books, 1993), 269–328; and Earl M. Wunderli, Critique of a Limited Geography for *Book of Mormon* Events," *Dialogue* 35:3 (Fall 2002), 161–197. For a FARMS response to insider Book of Mormon critics see Louis Midgley, "Who Really Wrote the *Book of Mormon*? The Critics and Their Theories" in Noel Reynolds (ed.) *Book of Mormon Authorship Revisited: Evidence for Ancient Origins* (Provo, UT: FARMS, 1997), 101–139.

46. William Hamblin, "An Apologist for the Critics: Brent Lee Metcalfe's Assumptions and Methodology," *Review of Books on the Book of Mormon* 6:1 (1994), 434–523. Hamblin is responding to Brent Lee Metcalfe, "Apologetic and Critical Assumptions about *Book of Mormon* Historicity," *Dialogue* 26:3 (Fall 1993), 154–84. On the Hamblin-Metcalfe cold war see Vern Anderson, "A Challenge to the Origins of the *Book of Mormon*," Associated Press Report, *Los Angeles Times*, 19 June 1993, Metro Section, 4.

47. Carl Mosser and Paul Owen, "Mormon Apologetic Scholarship and Evangelical Neglect: Losing the Battle and Not Knowing It," paper given at the 1997 Evangelical Theological Society Far West Annual Meeting, San Francisco, California, April 25, 1997; Carl Mosser and Paul Owen, "Mormon Apologetic Scholarship and Evangelical Neglect: Losing the Battle and Not Knowing It," *Trinity Journal* 19:2 (Fall 1998), 179–205; and Francis J. Beckwith, Carl Mosser, and Paul Owen, *The New Mormon Challenge: Responding to the Latest Defenses of a Fast-Growing Movement* (Grand Rapids: Zondervan, 2002). For a critique of *The New Mormon Challenge* by a Mormon apologist and polemicist see David L. Paulsen, "A General Response to *The New Mormon Challenge*," *FARMS Review* 14:1 (2002), 99–112. In a move that was novel in the often sometimes acrimonious debate between Evangelicals and Mormons, Musser asked Paulsen to critique his edited collection.

48. Craig Blomberg and Stephen E. Robinson, *How Wide the Divide? A Mormon and an Evangelical in Conversation* (Downers Grove, IL: InterVarsity Press, 1997); Craig Blomberg, "Is Mormonism Christian?" in Francis J. Beckwith, Carl Mosser, and Paul Owen, *The New Mormon Challenge: Responding to the Latest Defenses of a Fast-Growing Movement* (Grand Rapids: Zondervan, 2002), 315–333; E. Robinson, *Are Mormons Christian?* (Salt Lake City: Bookcraft, 1998); Jan Shipps, "Is Mormonism Christian? Reflections on a Complicated Question" in Shipps, *Sojourner in a Promised Land: Forty Years Among the Mormons* (Urbana: University of Illinois Press, 2000), 335–357; Daniel Peterson and Stephen Ricks, *Offenders for a Word: How Anti-Mormons Play Word Games to Attack the Latter-day Saints* (Provo, Utah: FARMS, 1998); Robert Millett and Gerald McDermott, *Claiming Christ: A Mormon-Evangelical Debate* (Grand Rapids: Brazos, 2007); Robert Millett and Gregory Johnson, *Bridging the Divide: The Continuing Conversation Between a Mormon and an Evangelical* (Rhinebeck, NY: Monkfish); and Donald Musser and David Paulsen (ed.), *Mormonism in Dialogue with Contemporary Christian Theologies* (Macon, GA: Mercer University Press, 2008).

49. Terryl Givens, *By the Hand of Mormon: The American Scripture that Launched a World Religion* (New York: Oxford University Press, 2002) and Givens, *The Book of Mormon: A Very Short Introduction* (New York: Oxford University Press, 2009).

50. Jerald Tanner and Sandra Tanner, *Problems in The Godmakers II* (Salt Lake City: Utah Lighthouse Ministry, 1993) and Rhonda Abrams, "Letter to Richard Lindsay," 25 May 1984, FAIR.

Chapter Two

1. Robert Baird, *Religion in America, or An Account of the Origin, Progress, Relation to the State, and the Present Condition of the Evangelical Churches of the United States: With Notices of the Unevangelical Denominations* (New York: Harper, 1844), 273–274, 269–291, and 318–338.

2. H. Richard Niebuhr, *The Social Sources of Denominationalism* (Cleveland, OH: Meridian, 1929), 160.

3. Klaus Hansen, *Mormonism and the*

American Experience (Chicago: University of Chicago Press, 1981), 205-211.

4. Mark Noll, *A History of Christianity in the United States and Canada* (Grand Rapids: Eerdmans, 1992), 191-217.

5. Jan Shipps: *Mormonism: The Story of a New Religious Tradition* (Urbana: University of Illinois Press, 1985), ix-x, 67-85, and 87-107 and Shipps, "Is Mormonism Christian? Reflections on a Complicated Question" in Jan Shipps, *Sojourner in a Promised Land: Forty Years Among the Mormons* (Urbana: University of Illinois Press, 2000), 335-357, especially 335-338.

6. Rodney Stark, "The Rise of a New World Faith" in James T. Duke (ed.), *Latter-Day Saint Social Life: Social Research on the LDS Church and its Members* (Provo, UT: Religious Studies Center, BYU, 1998), 9-27.

7. Fawn Brodie, *No Man Knows My History: The Life of Joseph Smith*, 2d. ed. (New York: Knopf, 1971), 91.

8. Thomas O'Dea, *The Mormons* (Chicago: University of Chicago Press, 1957), p. 115.

9. Mario DePillis, The Quest for Religious Authority and the Rise of Mormonism," *Dialogue* 1:1 (Spring 1966), 68-88.

10. John L. Brooke, *The Refiner's Fire: The Making of Mormon Cosmology, 1644-1844* (New York: Cambridge University Press, 1994).

11. Catherine Albanese, *America: Religions and Religion*, 4th. ed. (Belmont, CA: Thomson, fourth edition, 2007), 159.

12. Harold Bloom, *The American Religion: The Emergence of the Post-Christian Nation* (New York: Simon and Schuster, 1992).

13. For the debate over whether Mormonism is Christian or not see Jan Shipps, "Is Mormonism Christian: Reflections on a Complicated Question" in Jan Shipps, *Sojourner in a Promised Land: Forty Years Among the Mormons* (Urbana: University of Illinois Press, 2000), 347-354.

14. Fawn Brodie, *No Man Knows My History: The Life of Joseph Smith* (New York: Knopf, 1945), Fawn Brodie, *No Man Knows My History: The Life of Joseph Smith*, 2d. ed. (New York: Knopf. 1971), 412-413, 418-421.

15. Alice Felt Tyler, *Freedom's Ferment: Phases of American Social History from the Colonial Period to the Outbreak of the Civil War* (Minneapolis: University of Minnesota Press, 1944), 86-107; Louis Kern, *An Ordered Love: Sex Roles and Sexuality in Victorian Utopias: The Shakers, the Mormons, and the Oneida Community* (Chapel Hill: University of North Carolina Press, 1981), Part III, especially Chapters 7 and 10; Charles Sellers, *The Market Revolution: Jacksonian America 1815-1846* (New York: Oxford University Press, 1991), 217-225; and Lawrence Foster, "The Psychology of Religious Genius: Joseph Smith and the Origins of New Religious Movements," in Bryan Waterman, *The Prophet Puzzle* (Salt Lake City: Signature, 1999), 183-208. Sellers' psychological assessment of Smith is probably influenced by the work of Fawn Brodie. For excellent critiques of Sellers see Daniel Ward Howe, "Charles Sellers, the Market Revolution, and the Shaping of American Identity in Whig-Jacksonian America," 54-74 in Mark Noll (ed.), *God and Mammon: Protestants, Money, and the Market, 1790-1860* (New York: Oxford, 2001) and David Carwardine, "Charles Sellers' "Antinomians" and "Arminians": Methodists and the Market Revolution," 75-98 in Mark Noll (ed.), *God and Mammon: Protestants, Money, and the Market, 1790-1860* (New York: Oxford, 2001).

16. Parts of this chapter are heavily indebted to a number of books and essays on the history of intellectuals, the history of professionalization, the history of social science, and the history of history. These include Lewis Coser, *Men of Ideas: A Sociologists View* (Glencoe, IL: Free Press, 1965); Edward Shils, "The Intellectuals and the Powers" in Edward Shils, *The Constitution of Society* (Chicago: University of Chicago Press, 1982), 197-201; David Hollinger, "Historians and the Discourse of Intellectuals" in John Higham and Paul Conkin (eds.), *New Directions in American Intellectual History* (Baltimore, MD: Johns Hopkins University Press), 42-63; Ellen Messer-Davidow, David Shumway, and David Sylvan (eds.), *Knowledges: Historical and Critical Studies in Disciplinarity* (Charlottesville: University Press of Virginia, 1993); Burton Bledstein, *The Culture of Professionalism: The Middle Class and the Development of Higher Education in America* (New York: Norton, 1978); Laurence Veysey, *The Emergence of the American University* (Chicago: University of Chicago

Press, 1965); Clyde Barrow, *Universities and the Capitalist State: Corporate Liberalism and the Reconstruction of American Higher Education, 1894–1928* (Madison: University of Wisconsin Press, 1990); Thomas Haskell (ed.), *The Authority of Experts: Studies in History and Theory* (Bloomington: Indiana University Press, 1984); Robin Blackburn (ed.), *Ideology in Social Science: Readings in Critical Social Theory* (New York: Vintage, 1972); Dorothy Ross, *The Origins of American Social Science* (New York: Cambridge University Press, 1991); Mary Furner, *Advocacy and Objectivity: A Crisis in the Professionalization of American Social Science, 1865–1905* (Lexington: University Press of Kentucky, 1975); Thomas Haskell, *The Emergence of Professional Social Science: The American Social Science Association and the Nineteenth-century Crisis of Authority* (Urbana: University of Illinois Press, 1977); Dorothy Ross (ed.), *Modernist Impulses in the Human Sciences 1870–1930* (Baltimore, MD: Johns Hopkins University Press, 1994); Edward Silva and Sheila Slaughter, *Serving Power: The Making of the Academic Social Science Expert* (Westport, CT: Greenwood Press, 1984); Mark Smith, *Social Science in the Crucible: The American Debate Over Objectivity and Purpose, 1918–1941* (Durham, NC: Duke University Press, 1994); Robert Lynd, *Knowledge for What? The Place of Social Science in American Culture* (Princeton, NJ: Princeton University Press, 1939); Bruce Kuklick, "The Organization of Social Science in America: A Review Essay," *American Quarterly* 28 (Spring 1976), 124–141; Kuklick, "Restructuring the Past: Toward an Appreciation of the Social Context of Social Science," *Sociological Quarterly* 21 (Winter 1980), 5–21; Tom Bottomore and Robert Nisbet (eds.), *A History of Sociological Analyses* (New York: Basic, 1978); Bruce Kuklick, "Boundary Maintenance in American Sociology," *Journal of the History of the Behavioral Sciences* 16 (July 1980), 201–219; Roger Bannister, *Sociology and Scientism: The American Quest for Objectivity* (Chapel Hill: University of North Carolina Press, 1987); Christopher Simpson (ed.), *Universities and Empire: Money and Politics in the Social Sciences During the Cold War* (New York: New Press, 1998); Noam Chomsky, Ira Katznelson, R.C. Lewontin, David Montgomery, Laura Nader, Richard Ohmann, Ray Siever, Immanuel Wallerstein, and Howard Zinn (eds.), *The Cold War and the University* (New York: New Press, 1997); Arthur Vidich and Stanford Lyman, *American Sociology: Worldly Rejections of Religion and Their Directions* (New Haven, CT: Yale University Press, 1985); L.L. Bernard and Jessie Bernard, *Origins of American Sociology: The Social Science Movement in America* (New York: Thomas Y. Crowell, 1943); Joel Pfister and Nancy Schnog (eds.), *Inventing the Psychological: Toward a Cultural History of Emotional Life in America* (New Haven, CT: Yale University Press, 1997); James Capshew, *Psychologists on the March: Science, Practice, and Professional Identity in America, 1929–1969* (New York: Cambridge University Press, 1999); Ellen Herman, *The Romance of American Psychology: Political Culture in the Age of Experts* (Berkeley: University of California Press, 1995); D.G. Hart, *The University Gets Religion: Religious Studies in American Higher Education* (Baltimore, MD: Johns Hopkins University Press, 1999); Sean McCloud, *Making the American Religious Fringe: Exotics, Subversives, and Journalists, 1955–1993* (Chapel Hill: University of North Carolina Press, 2004); Michel Foucault, *The Order of Things: An Archaeology of the Human Sciences* (New York: Pantheon, 1970); and Michel Foucault, *The Archaeology of Knowledge* (New York: Pantheon, 2002).

17. Max Weber, *Economy and Society: An Outline of Interpretive Sociology* (Berkeley: University of California Press, 1968), especially Chapter Six. Also see Max Weber, *Protestant Ethic and the Spirit of Capitalism* (London: Routledge, 1930), 144–154.

18. Ernst Troeltsch, *The Social Teachings of the Christian Churches*, two volumes (Louisville, KY: Westminster/John Knox, 1960), 461–465.

19. H. Richard Niebuhr, *The Social Sources of Denominationalism* (Cleveland, OH: Meridian, 1929), 17–21. Niebuhr saw class, nationalism, region, and ethnicity as the social forces that divided Christianity.

20. Howard Becker, *Through Values to Social Interpretation* (Durham, NC: Duke University Press, 1950), 627–628 and Becker, *Systematic Sociology on the Basis of the Beziehungslehre and Gebildelehre of Leopold Van Wiese* (New York: Wiley, 1932). On the history of the term cult see Stephen Stein, *Communities of Dissent: A History of*

Alternative Religions in America (New York: Oxford University Press, 2003), 4-5. On sociological typologies see Thomas Robbins, *Cults, Charisma, and the Sociology of New Religious Movements* (London: Sage, 1988) and Meredith McGuire, *Religion: The Social Context* (Belmont, CA: Wadsworth, third edition, 1992), 134-172.

21. Rodney Stark and William Sims Bainbridge, *The Future of Religion: Secularisation, Revivals, and Cult Formation* (Berkeley: University of California Press, 1986), 19-37.

22. Jan Shipps, *Mormonism: The Story of a New Religious Tradition* (Urbana: University of Illinois Press, 1985), 47-48.

23. I am heavily indebted to Rodney Stark and Roger Finke, *Acts of Faith: Explaining the Human Side of Religion* (Berkeley: University of California Press, 2000), 15-17 for my analysis on the rise of professional organizations and professional journals focused on the sociology of religion.

24. On the history of social science see Dorothy Ross, *The Origins of American Social Science* (New York: Cambridge University Press, 1991); Mary Furner, *Advocacy and Objectivity: A Crisis in the Professionalization of American Social Science, 1865-1905* (Lexington: University Press of Kentucky, 1975); Thomas Haskell, *The Emergence of Professional Social Science: The American Social Science Association and the Nineteenth-century Crisis of Authority* (Urbana: University of Illinois Press, 1977); Dorothy Ross (ed.), *Modernist Impulses in the Human Sciences 1870-1930* (Baltimore, MD: Johns Hopkins University Press, 1994); Edward Silva and Sheila Slaughter, *Serving Power: The Making of the Academic Social Science Expert* (Westport, CT: Greenwood Press, 1984); Mark Smith, *Social Science in the Crucible: The American Debate Over Objectivity and Purpose, 1918-1941* (Durham, NC: Duke University Press, 1994); Bruce Kuklick, "The Organization of Social Science in America: A Review Essay," *American Quarterly* 28 (Spring 1976), 124-141; Kuklick, "Restructuring the Past: Toward an Appreciation of the Social Context of Social Science," *Sociological Quarterly* 21 (Winter 1980), 5-21; Tom Bottomore and Robert Nisbet (eds.), *A History of Sociological Analyses* (New York: Basic, 1978); Kuklick, "Boundary Maintenance in American Sociology," *Journal of the History of the Behavioral Sciences*, 16 (July 1980), 201-219; and Roger Bannister, *Sociology and Scientism: The American Quest for Objectivity* (Chapel Hill: University of North Carolina Press, 1987).

25. For examples of Christensen's early research see Harold Christensen, "The Time Interval between Marriage of Parents and the Birth of Their First Child in Utah County, Utah," *American Journal of Sociology* 44 (January 1939), 518-525 and Christensen, "Mormon Fertility: A Survey of Student Opinion," *American Journal of Sociology* 53 (January 1948), 270-275.

26. Glenn Vernon, "An Inquiry Into the Scalability of Church Orthodoxy," *Sociology and Social Research* 39 (May/June 1955), 324-327; Vernon, "Background Factors Related to Church Orthodoxy," *Social Forces* 34 (March 1956), 252-254; and Evon Vogt and Ethel Albert (eds.), *People of Rimrock; A Study of Values in Five Cultures* (Cambridge, MA: Harvard University Press, 1966).

27. O'Dea, Thomas, *The Mormons* (Chicago: University of Chicago Press, 1957). On O'Dea see Robert Michaelson, "Thomas O'Dea and the Mormons: Retrospect and Assessment," *Dialogue* 11:1 (Spring 1978), 44-57.

28. Information on the history of the SSSML, now the MSSA, was gleaned from its website.

29. Harold Christensen, "Cultural Relativism and Premarital Sex Norms," *American Sociological Review* 25 (1960), 31-39; Christensen and George Carpenter, "Value-Behavior Discrepancies Regarding Premarital Coitus in Three Western Cultures," *American Sociological Review* 27 (1962), 66-74; Tim Heaton, Kristen Goodman, and Thomas Holman, "In Search of a Peculiar People: Are Mormon Families Really Different" in Marie Cornwall, Tim Heaton, and Lawrence Young, *Contemporary Mormonism: Social Science Perspectives* (Urbana: University of Illinois Press, 1994), 87-117, especially 88, 113 and 114; Tim Heaton, "Vital Statistics" in James T. Duke (ed.), *Latter-day Saint Social Life: Social Research on the LDS Church and its Members* (Provo, UT: Religious Studies Center, 1998), 105-132, especially 111-115 and 124-125; Tim Heaton "Religious Influences on Mormon Fertility: Cross National

Comparisons," *Review of Religious Research* 30 (1989), 401–411; and Tim Heaton and Kristen Goodman, "Religion and Family Formation," *Review of Religious Research* 26 (1985), 343–359.

30. Stan Albrecht, "The Consequential Dimensions of Mormon Religiosity" in James T. Duke (ed.), *Latter-day Saint Social Life: Social Research on the LDS Church and its Members* (Provo, UT: Religious Studies Center, 1998), 285–292, especially 281–286.

31. Tim Heaton, Kristen Goodman, and Thomas Holman, "In Search of a Peculiar People: Are Mormon Families Really Different" in Marie Cornwall, Tim Heaton, and Lawrence Young, *Contemporary Mormonism: Social Science Perspectives* (Urbana: University of Illinois Press, 1994), 87–117 and Stan Albrecht, "The Consequential Dimensions of Mormon Religiosity" in James T. Duke (ed.), *Latter-day Saint Social Life: Social Research on the LDS Church and its Members* (Provo, UT: Religious Studies Center, 1998), 285–292, especially 286.

32. Robert Anderson, *Inside the Mind of Joseph Smith: Psychobiography and the Book of Mormon* (Salt Lake City: Signature, 1999), xvii–xl and 1–14, and "The Testimony of the Three Witnesses, and The Testimony of the Eight Witnesses" in the Book of Mormon. These statements were originally found in the back of the 1830 edition. In modern editions they can be found in the front of the book.

33. Rodney Stark and William Bainbridge: *The Future of Religion: Secularisation, Revivals, and Cult Formation* (Berkeley: University of California Press, 1986), 65, 193–194, 198, 200, 204, 245–251, 256, especially 245 and Sydney Ahlstrom, *The Religious History of the American People* (New Haven, CT: Yale University Press, 1972), 509.

34. Linda Woodhead, *Christianity: A Very Short Introduction* (New York: Oxford University Press, 2004), particularly 1–5 and 46–88.

35. James Beckford, "Explaining Religious Movements," *International Social Science Journal*, 29:2 (1977), 135–249. One can argue that the terms developed to study religion can be used to study other organizational forms *a la* Weber.

36. Roy Wallis, "The Cult and Its Transformation" in Rou Wallis (ed.), *Sectarianism: Analysis of Religious and non-Religious Sects* (New York: Wiley), 35–49 and Wallis, "Three Types of New Religious Movement" in Lorne Dawson (ed.), *Cults and New Religious Movements* (Oxford, UK: Blackwell, 2003), 36–58.

37. For an interesting discussion of the social and cultural construction of the American religious "mainstream" and "fringe" (note the binarism here) see Sean McCloud, *Making the American Religious Fringe: Exotics, Subversives, and Journalists, 1955–1993* (Chapel Hill: University of North Carolina Press, 2004).

38. Tim Heaton, Kristen Goodman, and Thomas Holman, "In Search of a Peculiar People: Are Mormon Families Really Different" in Marie Cornwall, Tim Heaton, and Lawrence Young, *Contemporary Mormonism: Social Science Perspectives* (Urbana: University of Illinois Press, 1994), 87–117, especially 114.

Chapter Three

1. On Mormon perceptions of themselves as the new Israel see Melodie Moench Charles, "Nineteenth-Century Mormons: The New Israel," *Dialogue* 12 (Spring 1979), 42–54.

2. Doctrine and Covenants 21:1. All references to the D&C are to the 1981 edition unless otherwise noted.

3. D&C 47 and 123:1–7.

4. On the office of Church Historian see Dean Jessee, "Joseph Smith and the Beginning of Mormon Record Keeping" in Larry C. Porter and Susan Easton Black (eds.), *The Prophet Joseph* (Salt Lake City: Deseret, 1988), 138–160 and Charles Adams and Gustave Larson, "A Study of the LDS Church Historians Office, 1830–1900," *Utah Historical Quarterly* 40 (Fall 1972), 370–389.

5. Cowdery discusses these particularly in Letter VIII, *Latter-Day Saints Messenger and Advocate*, Kirtland, Ohio, October 1835, 197. The *Latter-Day Saints Messenger and Advocate* ran from October 1834 to September 1837.

6. Orson Pratt, *Interesting Account of Several Remarkable Visions, And of the Late Discovery of Ancient American Records* (Edinburgh, UK: Ballantyne and Hughes, 1840).

7. Dean Jessee, "The Writing of Joseph

Smith's History," *BYU Studies* 11 (Summer 1971), 439-473; Dean Jessee, "The Reliability of Joseph Smith's History," *Journal of Mormon History* 3 (1976), 23-46; and Howard Coray, "Howard Coray's Recollections of Joseph Smith's History," edited by Dean Jessee, *BYU Studies* 11 (Summer 1971), 1-7.

8. Howard Coray, "The Autobiography of Howard Coray," typescript, Harold B. Lee Library, BYU.

9. *Times and Seasons*, Nauvoo, Illinois, November 1839 to February 1846, *Latter-Day Saints Millennial Star*, Liverpool, England, May 1840-1970 and the *Deseret News*, Salt Lake City, Utah, June 1850.

10. *History of the Church of Jesus Christ of Latter-day Saints: Period 1, History of Joseph Smith, the Prophet, by himself*, six volumes, edited by B.H. Roberts (Salt Lake City: Deseret, 1902-1912). This is commonly referred to as the *Documentary History of the Church (DHC)*. Roberts made his corrections, deletions, and emendations without giving a rationale for them. On the making of Roberts as historian see Davis Bitton, "B.H. Roberts as Historian," *Dialogue* 3 (Winter 1968), 25-44.

11. Joseph Fielding Smith, *Essentials in Church History: A History of the Church from the Birth of Joseph Smith Until the Present Times with Introductory Chapters on the Antiquity of the Gospel and the "Falling Away"* (Salt Lake City: Deseret News, 1922). On *Essentials* see Ronald W. Walker, David K. Whittaker, and James B. Allen, *Mormon History* (Urbana: University of Illinois Press, 2000), p. 35. Smith published one of the earliest books critical of evolution in Mormon culture, Joseph Fielding Smith, *Man, His Origin and Destiny* (Salt Lake City: Deseret, 1954).

12. Ralph Waldo Emerson, "An After-clap of Puritanism" in William Mulder and Russell Mortensen (eds.), *Among the Mormons—Historic Accounts by Contemporary Observers* (New York: Knopf, 1958), 382-384 and Alexander Campbell, "Delusions," *Millennial Harbinger*, 7 February 1831, 85-96.

13. Charles Mackay, *The Mormons, or Latter-day Saints, with Memoirs of the Life and Death of Joseph Smith, or the American "Mahomet"* (London: Office of the National Illustrated Library, 1851).

14. H.H. Bancroft, *History of Utah, 1540-1886* (San Francisco: History Company, 1889). On Bancroft's history of Utah see S. George Ellsworth, "Hubert Howe Bancroft and the History of Utah," *Utah Historical Quarterly* 22 (April 1954), 99-124.

15. B.H. Roberts, *Comprehensive History of the Church: Century I*, six volumes (Salt Lake City: Deseret News, 1930). On Roberts see Ronald W. Walker, David K. Whittaker, and James B. Allen, *Mormon History* (Urbana: University of Illinois Press, 2000), 36 and Kenneth Godfrey, "Comprehensive History of the Church, A" in Arnold Garr, Donald Q. Cannon, and Richard O. Cowan (eds.), *Encyclopedia of Latter-day Saint History* (Salt Lake City: Deseret Book, 2000), 232-233. On Roberts as historian see Davis Bitton, "B.H. Roberts as Historian," *Dialogue* 3:4 (Winter 1968), 25-44. On the Mountain Meadows massacre see Juanita Brooks, *The Mountain Meadows Massacre*, revised edition (Norman: University of Oklahoma Press, 1991); Will Bagley, *Blood of the Prophets: Brigham Young and the Massacre at Mountain Meadows* (Norman: University of Oklahoma Press, 2004); Ronald Walker, Richard Turley, and Glen Leonard, *Massacre at Mountain Meadows* (New York: Oxford University Press, 2008); and John D. Lee, *The Confessions of John D. Lee* (Salt Lake City: Utah Lighthouse Ministry, 1877).

16. On the transformation of Utah see Thomas Alexander, *Utah: The Right Place*, 2d ed. (Salt Lake City: Gibbs Smith, 2003), 218-361. On the rise of the scholarly study of Mormonism in the twentieth-century see Leonard Arrington, "Scholarly Studies of Mormonism in the Twentieth-Century," *Dialogue* 1 (Spring 1966), 15-32.

17. Richard Ely, "Economic Aspects of Mormonism," *Harper's Monthly* 106 (April 1903), 667-678. Ely praises the Mormon command economy on page 668. On Ely see Sidney Fine, "Richard T. Ely, Forerunner of Progressivism, 1880-1901," *Mississippi Valley Historical Review* 37:4 (March 1951), 599-624 and Benjamin G. Rader, "Richard T. Ely: Lay Spokesman for the Social Gospel," *Journal of American History* 53:1 (June 1966), 61-74

18. Ephraim Edward Ericksen, "The Psychological and Ethical Aspects of Mormonism," unpublished Ph.D. dissertation, University of Chicago, 1922, especially

28 and 99. On Ericksen see Ephraim Edward Ericksen, *Memories and Reflections: The Autobiography of E.E. Ericksen*, edited by Scott Kenney (Salt Lake City: Signature, 1987) and Scott Kenney, "E.E. Ericksen-Loyal Heretic, *Sunstone* 3 (July-August 1978), 16–27.

19. Lowry Nelson, *The Mormon Village: A Pattern and Technique of Land Settlement* (Salt Lake City: University of Utah Press, 1952); Nelson, "A Social Survey of Escalante, Utah," *BYU Studies* 1 (1925), 1–44; Nelson, "The Utah Farm Village of Ephraim," *BYU Studies* 2 (1928), 1–41; Nelson "The Mormon Village: A Study in Social Origins," *Proceedings of the Utah Academy of Science* 7 (1930), 11–37; and Nelson "Some Social and Economic Features of American Fork, Utah, *BYU Studies* 4 (1933), 5–73. On Nelson see Lowry Nelson, *In the Direction of His Dreams: Memoirs* (New York: Philosophical Society, 1985). On the Mormon doctrine on Blacks see Lester Bush, "Mormonism's Negro Doctrine: A Historical Overview," *Dialogue* 8:1 (Spring 1973), 11–68; Bush and Armand Mauss (eds.), *Neither White Nor Black: Mormon Scholars Confront the Race Issue in a Universal Church* (Midvale, UT: Signature, 1984); and Mauss, *All Abraham's Children: Changing Mormon Conceptions of Race and Lineage* (Urbana: University of Illinois Press, 2003. On Mormon whiteness and Mormon racism see Joanna Brooks, *Mormonism and White Supremacy: American Religion and the Problem of Racial Innocence* (New York: Oxford University Press, 2020).

20. Nels Anderson, *The Hobo: The Sociology of the Homeless Man* (Chicago: University of Chicago Press, 1923).

21. Nels Anderson, *Desert Saints: The Mormon Frontier in Utah* (Chicago: University of Chicago Press, 1942).

22. I. Woodbridge Riley, *The Founder of Mormonism: A Psychological Study of Joseph Smith* (New York: Dodd, Mead, 1902); Walter F. Prince, "Psychological Tests for the Authorship of the Book of Mormon," *American Journal of Psychology* 28 (July 1917), 373–389; Franklin D. Daines, "Separatism in Utah, 1847–1870," *Annual Report of the American Historical Association for the Year 1917* (Washington: The Association, 1920), 333–343; Hamilton Gardner, "Cooperation Among the Mormons," *Quarterly Journal of Economics* 31 (May 1917), 461–469; Gardner, "Communism Among the Mormons," *Quarterly Journal of Economics* 37 (1923), 134–174; Joseph Geddes, "The United Order Among the Mormons," unpublished Ph.D. dissertation, Columbia University, 1924; Feramorz Fox, "The Mormon Land System: A Study of the Settlement and Utilization of Land Under the Direction of the Mormon Church," unpublished Ph.D. dissertation, Northwestern University, 1932; Arden Beal Olsen, "The History of Mormon Mercantile Cooperation in Utah," unpublished Ph.D. dissertation, University of California, Berkeley, 1935; William McNiff, "The Part Played by the Mormon Church in the Cultural Development of Early Utah," unpublished Ph.D. dissertation, The Ohio State University, 1929; Kimball Young, *Isn't One Wife Enough?: The Story of Mormon Polygamy* (New York: Henry Holt and Company, 1954); and Austin E. and Alta Fife, *Saints of Sage and Saddle: Folklore Among the Mormons* (Bloomington: Indiana University Press 1956).

23. Fawn Brodie, *No Man Knows My History: The Life of Joseph Smith* (New York: Knopf, 1945). On Brodie see Newell Bringhurst, *Fawn McKay Brodie: A Biographers Life* (Norman: University of Oklahoma Press, 1999).

24. Dale Morgan, *The State of Deseret* (Salt Lake City: Utah State Historical Society, 1940) and Morgan, *The Great Salt Lake City* (Indianapolis: Bobbs Merrill, 1947. Morgan's history of early Mormonism was never published in his lifetime. Material related to the history can be found in Dale Morgan, *Dale Morgan on Early Mormonism: Correspondence and a New History*, edited by John Phillip Walker (Salt Lake City: Signature, 1986). Morgan wrote, uncredited, *A History of Ogden* (Ogden, UT: Ogden City Commission, 1940), *Utah: A Guide to the State* (New York: Hastings House, 1941), and *Provo: Pioneer Mormon City* (Portland, OR: Binfords and Mort, 1942) for the Works Progress Administration. On Morgan see Richard Saunders, "The Strange Mixture of Emotion and Intellect: A Social History of Dale Morgan, 1933–1942," *Dialogue* 28 (Winter 1995), 30–58 and Charles S. Peterson, "Dale Morgan, Writers Project, and Mormon History as a Regional Study," *Dialogue* 24 (Summer 1991), 47–63.

25. Brooks wrote a number of books

and articles relating to Mormon Studies including Juanita Brooks, "A Close-Up of Polygamy," *Harper's* 168 (February 1934), 299–307; Brooks, *The Mountain Meadows Massacre* (Palo Alto, CA: Stanford University Press, 1950); and Brooks, *John Doyle Lee: Zealot, Pioneer Builder, Scapegoat* (Logan: Utah State University Press, 1992). On Brooks see Levi S. Peterson, *Juanita Brooks: Mormon Woman Historian* (Salt Lake City: University of Utah Press, 1988) and Brooks's autobiography *Quicksand and Cactus: A Memoir of the Southern Mormon Frontier* (Logan: Utah State University Press, 1992).

26. On Ferguson see Stan Larson, *Quest for the Gold Plates: Thomas Stuart Ferguson's Archaeological Search for the Book of Mormon* (Herriman, UT: Freethinker Press, 2004) and Terryl Givens, *By the Hand of Mormon: The American Scripture that Launched a New World Religion* (New York: Oxford University Press, 2002), 112–116. Ferguson wrote and co-wrote several books on Book of Mormon archaeology including Thomas Ferguson, *One Fold and One Shepherd* (San Francisco: Books of California, 1958) and Milton Hunter and Ferguson, *Ancient America and the Book of Mormon* (Oakland, CA: Kolob, 1950). Hunter was a member of the Quorum of the Seventies. Ferguson would eventually lose faith in both Book of Mormon archaeology and Mormonism. On the NWAF see Daniel Peterson, "The New World Archaeology Foundation," *FARMS Review*, 16 (1): 221–233.

27. Ronald W. Walker, David J. Whittaker, and James B. Allen, *Mormon History* (Urbana: University of Illinois Press, 2000), 56. On the Utah State Historical Society and its organ, the *Utah Historical Quarterly*, see Gary Topping, "One Hundred Years at the Utah State Historical Society," *Utah Historical Quarterly*, 65 (Summer 1997), 223–232.

Chapter Four

1. Moses Rischin, "Beyond the Great Divide: Immigration and the Last Frontier," *Journal of American History* 55 (June 1968), p. 49 and Rischin, "The New Mormon History," *American West* 6 (March 1969), 49. On the transformation and Americanization of Utah after World War II and the expansion and professionalization of Utah's universities see Thomas Alexander, *Utah: The Right Place* (Salt Lake City: Gibbs Smith, revised and updated edition, 2003), 362–459.

2. S. George Ellsworth, "History of Mormon Missions in the United States and Canada, 1830–1860," unpublished Ph.D. dissertation, University of California at Berkeley, 1950.

3. Eugene E. Campbell, "History of the Church of Jesus Christ of Latter-day Saints in California, 1846–1946," unpublished Ph.D. dissertation, University of Southern California, 1952.

4. Arrington reflects on his influences in Leonard Arrington, "In Praise of Amateurs," *Journal of Mormon History* 17 (1991), 35–42. On regionalism in the U.S. and Southern regionalism see Robert Dorman, *The Revolt of the Provinces: The Regionalist Movement in America, 1920–1945* (Chapel Hill: University of North Carolina Press, 1993) and Paul Challen, *A Sociological Analysis of Southern Regionalism: The Contributions of Howard W. Odum* (Lewiston, NY: Edward Mellen, 1993). On the influence of regionalism on Arrington see Rebecca Cornwall, *From Chicken Farmer to History* (Salt Lake City: Privately Published, 1976), 78–79 and Arrington, "In Praise of Amateurs," *Journal of Mormon History* 17 (1991), 36–37. Chapel Hill, as Arrington noted, was a center of Southern regionalism from the 1920s through the 1950s and remains so today. The notion that Mormons are a product of Yankee New England is, of course, a form of intellectual and academic regionalism. On the influence of Ely on Arrington see Arrington, *Adventures of a Church Historian* (Urbana: University of Illinois Press, 1998), 26.

5. Richard Poll, "Book Review: Leonard J. Arrington. *Great Basin Kingdom: An Economic History of the Latter-day Saints, 1830–1900*. Cambridge: Harvard University Press, 1958. 534 pp. $9.00," *BYU Studies* 3:1, 1961), 65.

6. Leonard Arrington, "Historian as Entrepreneur: A Personal Essay," *BYU Studies* 17 (Winter 1977), 193–209 and William Hartley, "The Founding of the LDS Church History Department, 1972," *Journal of Mormon History* 18:2 (Fall 1992), 51.

7. On the MHA see Leonard Arrington, "Reflections on the Founding and Purpose of the Mormon History Association, 1965–1983," *Journal of Mormon History* 10 (Fall 1992), 41–56; Davis Bitton, "Taking Stock:

The Mormon History Association after Twenty-Five Years," *Journal of Mormon History* 17 (1991), 1–27; and Maureen Ursenbach Beecher, "Entre Nous: An Intimate History of the MHA," *Journal of Mormon History* 12 (1985), 43–52.

8. Ronald W. Walker, David J. Whittaker, and James B. Allen, *Mormon History* (Urbana: University of Illinois Press, 2000), 82, 89–91, 164–165; Lee Bean, Dean May, and Mark Skolnik, "The Mormon Historical Demography Project," *Historical Methodology* 11 (1978), 45–53; and James T. Duke, "Introduction" in James T. Duke (ed.) *Latter-day Saint Social Life: Social Research on the LDS Church and its Members* (Provo, UT: Religious Studies Center, BYU, 1998), 4–5.

9. Clinton E. Larson, "The Founding Vision of BYU Studies, 1959–1967," *BYU Studies* 31 (Fall 1991), 5–10 and G. Wesley Johnson, "Editorial Preface," *Dialogue* 1 (Spring 1966), 1. For a history of *Dialogue* see Devery Anderson, "A History of *Dialogue*, Part One: The Early Years, 1965–1971," *Dialogue* 32:2 (Summer 1999), 15–67; Anderson, "A History of *Dialogue*, Part Two: Struggle Toward Maturity, 1971–1982," *Dialogue* 33:2 (Summer 2000), 1–96; and Anderson, "A History of *Dialogue*, Part Three: "Coming of Age" in Utah, 1982–1987," *Dialogue* 35: 2 (Summer 2002), 1–71. On *Sunstone* see Lee Warthen, "History of *Sunstone*: The Scott Kenney Years, Summer 1974–June 1978," *Sunstone* 22 (June 1999), 48–61. On *Exponent II* see Carrel Hilton Sheldon, "Launching *Exponent II*," *Exponent II* 22:4 (Summer 1999) (at the Exponent II website) and Claudia Bushman, "Editorial: *Exponent II* Is Born," *Exponent II* 1 (July 1978), 2. On Eugene England see Terryl Givens, *Stretching the Heavens: The Life of Eugene England and the Crisis of Modern Mormonism* (Chapel Hill: University of North Carolina Press, 2021).

10. The following give a sense of the depth and breadth of the New Mormon Studies: Lawrence Foster, *Religion, and Sexuality: Three American Communal Experiments in the Nineteenth-Century* (New York: Oxford University Press, 1981); Mark Leone, *Roots of Modern Mormonism* (Cambridge, MA: Harvard University Press, 1977); Thomas O'Dea, *The Mormons* (Chicago: University of Chicago Press, 1957); Jan Shipps, *Mormonism: The Story of a New Religious Tradition* (Urbana: University of Illinois Press, 1985); Shipps, "Making Saints: In the Early Days and the Latter Days" in Marie Cornwall, Tim B. Heaton, and Lawrence A. Young, *Contemporary Mormonism: Social Science Perspectives* (Urbana: University of Illinois Press, 1994), 64–83; Dean May, "Mormons" in Stephen Thernstrom (ed.), *Harvard Encyclopedia of American Ethnic Groups* (Cambridge, MA: Harvard University Press, 1980), 720–731; Patricia Nelson Limerick, "Peace Initiative: Using Mormons to Rethink Culture and Ethnicity in American History" in Limerick, *Something in the Soil: Legacies and Reckonings in the New West* (New York: Norton, 2000), 235–255; James B. Allen and Glen M. Leonard, *The Story of the Latter-day Saints* (Salt Lake City: Deseret, 1976); Leonard Arrington and Davis Bitton, *The Mormon Experience: A History of the Latter-day Saints* (New York: Knopf, 1979); Richard P. Howard, *The Church Through the Years, Volume 1: RLDS Beginnings to 1860, Volume 2: The Reorganization Comes of Age 1860–1992* (Independence, MO: Herald House, 1992, 1993); Donald Meinig, "The Mormon Culture Region: Strategies and Patterns in the Geography of the American West," *Annals of the Association of American Geographers* 55 (June 1965), 191–220; Dean May, "A Demographic Portrait of the Mormons, 1830–1980 in D. Michael Quinn (ed.), *The New Mormon History: Revisionist Essays on the Mormon Past* (Salt Lake City: Signature, 1992), 121–135; Philip Barlow, *Mormons and the Bible: The Place of the Latter-day Saints in American Religion* (New York: Oxford University Press, 1991); David John Buerger, "The Adam-God Doctrine, *Dialogue* 15:1 (Spring 1982), 4–58; Buerger, *Mysteries of Godliness: A History of Mormon Temple Worship* (Salt Lake City: Signature, 2002); Dean May, *Three Frontiers: Family, Land, and Society in the American West, 1850–1900* (New York: Cambridge University Press, 1997); Evon Vogt and Ethel M. Albert (eds.), *People of Rimrock: A Study of Values in Five Cultures* (Cambridge, MA: Harvard University Press, 1966); Quinn, *Early Mormonism and the Magic World View*, 2d. ed. (Salt Lake City: Signature, 1998); Jon Butler, "Magic, Astrology, and the Early American Religious Heritage, 1600–1700," *American Historical Review* 84:2 (April 1979), 317–346; Butler, *Awash in a Sea of Faith: Christianizing the American People* (Cambridge, MA: Harvard

University Press, 1992), 67–97; Robert Flanders, *Nauvoo: Kingdom on the Mississippi* (Urbana: University of Illinois Press, 1965); Leonard J. Arrington, Feramorz Fox, and Dean L. May, *Building the City of God: Community and Cooperation Among the Mormons* (Salt Lake City: Deseret, 1976); Thomas Alexander, *Mormonism in Transition: A History of the Latter-day Saints, 1890–1930* (Urbana: University of Illinois Press, 1985); Richard Bushman, *Joseph Smith: Rough Stone Rolling* (New York: Knopf, 2005); Arrington, *Brigham Young: American Moses* (New York: Knopf, 1985); Thomas Alexander, *Things in Heaven and Earth: The Life and Times of Wilford Woodruff* (Salt Lake City: Signature, 1991); William Hartley, *"They are My Friends": A History of the Joseph Knight Family, 1825–1850* (Provo, UT: Grandin, 1986); Maureen Ursenbach Beecher, *Eliza and her Sisters* (Salt Lake City: Aspen, 1991); Jill Mulvay Derr, Janath Russell Cannon, and Beecher, *Women of Covenant: The Story of the Relief Society* (Salt Lake City: Deseret, 1992); Beecher and Lavina Fielding Anderson (eds.), *Sisters in Spirit: Mormon Women in Historical and Cultural Perspective* (Urbana: University of Illinois Press, 1992); Joseph Smith, *The Personal Writings of Joseph Smith*, edited and compiled by Dean Jessee (Salt Lake City: Deseret, 1984); Joseph Smith, *The Papers of Joseph Smith*, two volumes, Volume 1: *Autobiographical and Historical Writings*, Volume 2: *Journal, 1832–1842* (Salt Lake City: Deseret, 1989, 1992); Eliza Roxey Snow, *The Personal Writings of Eliza Roxey Snow*, edited by Maureen Ursenbach Beecher (Salt Lake City: University of Utah Press, 1995); Richard L. Jensen and Malcolm R. Thorp (eds.), *Mormons in Victorian Britain* (Salt Lake City: University of Utah Press, 1989); Brigham Card, Herbert C. Northcott, and John Foster (eds.), *The Mormon Presence in Canada* (Edmonton: University of Alberta Press, 1990); William Mulder, *Homeward to Zion: The Mormon Migration from Scandinavia* (New York: Knopf, 1958); Leo Edward Lyman, *Political Deliverance: The Mormon Quest for Statehood* (Urbana: University of Illinois Press, 1986); Charles S. Peterson, *"Take Up Your Mission": Mormon Colonizing along the Little Colorado River, 1870–1900* (Tucson: University of Arizona Press, 1973); Jessie Embry, *Black Saints in a White Church: Contemporary African American Mormons* (Salt Lake City: Signature, 1994); Embry, *'In His Own Language': Mormon Spanish Speaking Congregations in the United States* (Provo, UT: Charles Redd Center for Western Studies, 1997); Embry, *Asian American Mormons: Bridging Cultures* (Provo, UT: Charles Redd Center for Western Studies, 1999); Gustave Larson, *The Americanization of Utah for Statehood* (San Marino, CA: Huntington Library, 1971); Armand Mauss, *The Angel and the Beehive: The Mormon Struggle with Assimilation* (Urbana: University of Illinois Press, 1994); Gordon and Gary Shepherd, *The Kingdom Transformed: Themes in the Development of Mormonism* (Salt Lake City: University of Utah Press, 1984); O. Kendall White, *Mormon Neo-Orthodoxy: A Crisis Theology* (Salt Lake City: Signature, 1987); Grant Underwood, *The Millenarian World of Early Mormonism* (Urbana: University of Illinois Press, 1993); Klaus Hansen, *Quest for Empire: The Political Kingdom of God and the Council of Fifty in Mormon History* (East Lansing: Michigan State University Press, 1967); D. Michael Quinn, *The Mormon Hierarchy: Origins of Power* (Salt Lake City: Signature, 1994); Quinn, *The Mormon Hierarchy: Extensions of Power* (Salt Lake City: Signature, 1997); Quinn, *Same-Sex Dynamics Among Nineteenth-Century Americans: A Mormon Example* (Urbana: University of Illinois Press, 1996); Ronald Walker, *Wayward Saints: The Godbeites and Brigham Young* (Urbana: University of Illinois Press, 1999); Davis Bitton, *Guide to Mormon Diaries and Autobiographies* (Provo: BYU Press, 1977); Thomas Alexander, *Utah, the Right Place: The Official Centennial History* (Salt Lake City: Gibbs Smith, 1993); Daniel H. Ludlow (ed.), *The Encyclopedia of Mormonism*, five volumes (New York: Macmillan, 1992); Tim Heaton, "Vital Statistics." In James T. Duke (ed.), *Latter-Day Saint Social Life: Social Research on the LDS Church and its Members* (Provo: Religious Studies Center, BYU, 1998), 105–132; and Lawrence A. Young, "Confronting Turbulent Environments: Issues in the Organizational Growth and Globalization of Mormonism" in Marie Cornwall, Tim B. Heaton, and Lawrence A. Young, *Contemporary Mormonism: Social Science Perspectives* (Urbana: University of Illinois Press, 1994), 43–63.

11. Lawrence Foster, *Religion and Sexuality: The Shakers, the Mormons and the

Oneida Community (Urbana: University of Illinois Press, 1981), 146-151.

12. Eugene Campbell and Bruce Campbell, "Divorce Among Mormon Polygamists: Extent and Explanations," *Utah Historical Quarterly* 46 (Winter 1978), 4-23.

13. Julie Roy Jeffrey, *Frontier Women: Civilizing the West? 1840 to 1880*, revised edition (New York: Hill and Wang, 1998), 179-213; Joan Iverson, "A Debate on the American Home: The Antipolygamy Controversy, 1880-1890," *Journal of the History of Sexuality* 1:4 (1991), 585-602; Maureen Ursenbach Beecher, "'The Leading Sisters': A Female Hierarchy in Nineteenth-Century Mormon Society," *Journal of Mormon History* 9 (1982), 26-39; and Julie Dunfey; "'Living the Principle' of Plural Marriage: Mormon Women, Utopia, and Female Sexuality in the Nineteenth-Century, *Feminist Studies* 10:3 (1984), 523-536.

14. J.E. Hullett; "The Social Role of the Mormon Polygamous Male," *American Sociological Review* 8 (June 1943), 279-287.

15. Jessie Embry, "Effects of Polygamy on Mormon Women," *Frontier—A Journal of Women Studies*, 7, 1984, 56-61.

16. For an excellent review of the problems associated with the study of Mormon polygamy see R. Carmon Hardy, "Lying for the Lord: An Essay" in R. Carmon Hardy, *Solemn Covenant: The Mormon Polygamous Passage* (Urbana: University of Illinois Press, 1992), 363-388. For an excellent review of scholarly work on Mormon polygamy up to 1977 see Davis Bitton, "Mormon Polygamy: A Review Article" *Journal of Mormon History* 4 (1977), 101-118.

17. Daniel Bachman, "New Light on an Old Hypothesis: The Ohio Origins of the Revelation on Eternal Marriage," *Journal of Mormon History* 5 (1978), 19-32. Also see Lawrence Foster, *Religion and Sexuality: The Shakers, the Mormons, and the Oneida Community* (Urbana: University of Illinois Press, 1981); R. Carmon Hardy, *Solemn Covenant: The Mormon Polygamous Passage* (Urbana: University of Illinois Press, 1992); Brian Hales, *Joseph Smith's Polygamy, Volume I: History* (Salt Lake City: Greg Kofford Books, 2013), Hales, *Joseph Smith's Polygamy, Volume 2: History* (Salt Lake City: Greg Kofford Books, 2013), and Hales, *Joseph Smith's Polygamy, Volume 3: Theology* (Salt Lake City: Greg Kofford Books, 2013).

18. On Gentile opposition to polygamy see Richard Van Wagoner, *Mormon Polygamy: A History*, 2d. ed. (Salt Lake City: Signature, 1989), 105-114; Charles A. Cannon, "The Awesome Power of Sex: The Polemical Campaign Against Mormon Polygamy," *Pacific Historical Review*, 43:1 (February 1974), 61-82; and Peggy Pascoe, *Relations of Rescue: The Search for Female Moral Authority in the American West, 1874-1939* (New York: Oxford University Press, 1993), 22-23 and 61-62.

19. On Emma Smith's opposition to polygamy see Linda Newell and Valeen Tippetts, *Mormon Enigma: Emma Hale Smith—Prophet's Wife*, 2d. ed. (Urbana: University of Illinois Press, 1993), 97-99.

20. For the relationship between polygamy and Mormon power see D. Michael Quinn, *The Mormon Hierarchy: Origins of Power* (Salt Lake City: Signature, 1994), and Quinn, *The Mormon Hierarchy: The Extensions of Power* (Salt Lake City: Signature, 1997).

21. Fawn Brodie, *'No Man Knows My History: The Life of Joseph Smith, the Mormon Prophet*, 2d. ed. (New York: Knopf, 1971), 334-337 and 457-488.

22. Stanley Ivins's list can be found in Jerald Tanner and Sandra Tanner, *Joseph Smith and Polygamy* (Salt Lake City: Modern Microfilms, 1967), 41-47. On Smith's wives see Todd Compton, *In Sacred Loneliness: The Plural Wives of Joseph Smith* (Salt Lake City: Signature, 1997).

23. Lawrence Foster, *Religion and Sexuality: The Shakers, the Mormons, and the Oneida Community* (Urbana: University of Illinois Press, 1981), 159-166.

24. On the ideologies underlying plural marriage see Lawrence Foster, *Religion and Sexuality: The Shakers, the Mormons, and the Oneida Community* (Urbana: University of Illinois Press, 1981), 142-146

25. On unilinear evolution and its impact see George Stocking, Jr., *Race, Culture, and Evolution: Essays in the History of Anthropology* (Chicago: University of Chicago Press, 1982). On how the ideologies of civilizational and racial superiority worked their way out in the U.S. in the late nineteenth and early twentieth centuries see Matthew Frye Jacobson, *Barbarian Virtues: The United States Encounters Foreign Peoples at Home and Abroad, 1876-1917* (New York: Hill and Wang, 2000).

26. James Edward Hulett, Jr., "The

Sociological and Social Psychological Aspects of the Mormon Polygamous Family" (Ph.D. diss., University of Wisconsin, 1939); Hulett, "Social Role and Personal Security in Mormon Polygamy," *American Journal of Sociology* 44:4 (January 1940), 542–553; Hulett, "The Social Role of the Mormon Polygamous Male," *American Sociological Review* 8 (June 1943), 279–287; Nels Anderson, *Desert Saints: The Mormon Frontier in Utah* (Chicago: University of Chicago Press, 1942); and Kimball Young, *Isn't One Wife Enough? The Story of Mormon Polygamy* (New York: Holt, 1954). Young drew extensively on Hulett's work in his analysis of Mormon polygamy.

27. Stanley Ivins, "Notes on Mormon Polygamy," *Western Humanities Review* 10 (Summer 1956), 229–239.

28. Julie Roy Jeffrey, *Frontier Women: Civilizing the West, 1840–1880*, revised edition (New York: Hill and Wang, 1998), 197.

29. Eugene Campbell and Bruce Campbell, "Divorce Among Mormon Polygamists: Extent and Explanations," *Utah Historical Quarterly* 46 (Winter 1978), 4–23.

30. Leonard Arrington and Davis Bitton, *The Mormon Experience: A History of the Latter-day Saints*, 2d. ed. (Urbana: University of Illinois Press, 1992), 199 and 204.

31. Leonard Arrington and Davis Bitton, *The Mormon Experience: A History of the Latter-day Saints*, 2d. ed. (Urbana: University of Illinois Press, 1992), 199 and 204. The first edition of *The Mormon Experience* was published by Knopf in 1979.

32. Leonard Arrington and Davis Bitton, *The Mormon Experience: A History of the Latter-day Saints*, 2d. ed. (Urbana: University of Illinois Press, 1992), 199 and 204.

33. James Smith and Phillip Kunz, "Polygyny and Fertility in Nineteenth-Century America," *Population Studies* 30 (1976), 465–480.

34. Lowell "Ben" Bennion, "The Incidence of Mormon Polygamy in 1880: "Dixie" versus Davis Stake," *Journal of Mormon History* 11 (1984), 27–42. Bennion also found that there were variations in polygamy rates in the regions themselves. In Davis County, for instance, rates of polygamy ranged from five percent to thirty-two percent. Bennion believes that even his more sophisticated analysis probably underestimated the extent of plural marriage in the regions he studied. Orderville also happened to be the most communal of the "United Order" cooperative settlements established in Utah. Mormon communes were regarded by many of the faithful as a return to the commands made to the Lord's People in the revelations received by their Prophet Joseph Smith. The connection between communal living and polygamic practice would not have been a surprise or a mystery to them.

35. Larry Logue, "A Time of Marriage: Monogamy and Polygamy in a Utah Town," *Journal of Mormon History* 11 (1984), 3–26. When analyzed in household terms, Logue's rates rose to thirty-four percent in 1870 and 38.5 percent in 1880. Like Bennion, Logue also found variation in incidence rates within Utah's "Dixie."

36. Marie Cornwall, Camela Courtright, and Laga Van Beek, "How Common the Principle? Women as Plural Wives in 1860," *Dialogue* 26:2 (Summer 1993), 139–153 and Jan Shipps, Cheryl May, and Dean May, "Sugar House Ward: A Latter-day Saint Congregation," in James Wind and James Lewis (editors), *American Congregations: Volume I, Portraits of Twelve Religious Communities* (Chicago: University of Chicago Press, 1994), 293–348.

37. On the 1960s, which really, of course, began in the 1950s and ended in the 1970s, see Mark Hamilton Lytle, *America's Uncivil Wars: The Sixties from Elvis to the Fall of Richard Nixon* (New York: Oxford University Press, 2006) and Maurice Isserman and Michael Kazin, *America Divided: The Civil War of the 1960s* (New York: Oxford University Press, 2000).

38. Leonard J. Arrington, "'Persons for All Seasons': Women in Mormon History," *BYU Studies* 20 (Fall 1979), 39–58; Arrington, "Historian as Entrepreneur: A Personal Essay," *BYU Studies* 17 (Winter 1977), 193–209; and William Hartley, "The Founding of the LDS Church History Department, 1972," *Journal of Mormon History* 18:2 (Fall 1992), 51.

39. Leonard J. Arrington, "'Persons for All Seasons': Women in Mormon History," *BYU Studies* 20 (Fall 1979), 39–58; Maureen Ursenbach Beecher and Lavina Fielding Anderson (eds.), *Sisters in Spirit: Mormon Women in Historical and Cultural Perspective* (Urbana: University of Illinois Press, 1992); Lawrence Foster (1979), "From Frontier Activism to Neo-Victorian

Domesticity: Mormon Women in the Nineteenth and Twentieth Centuries," *Journal of Mormon History* (6, 1979), 3–22; Carol Cornwall Madsen, *In Their Own Words: Women and the Story of Nauvoo* (Salt Lake City: Deseret, 2002); Maureen Ursenbach Beecher, "Women's Work on the Mormon Frontier," *Utah Historical Quarterly* 49 (Summer 1981), 276–290; Linda King Newell and Valeen Tippetts Avery, *Mormon Enigma: Emma Hale Smith* (New York: Doubleday, 1984); Carol Cornwall Madsen, "Mormon Women and the Struggle for Definition: The Nineteenth-Century Church," *Sunstone* 6 (Nov.-Dec. 1981), 7–11; Jill Mulvay Derr and C. Brooklyn Derr, "Outside the Mormon Hierarchy: Alternative Aspects of Institutional Power," *Dialogue* 15 (Winter 1982), 21–43; Maxine Hanks (ed.), *Women and Authority: Re-emerging Mormon Feminism* (Salt Lake City: Signature, 1992); Marie Cornwall (1994), "The Institutional Role of Mormon Women," in Marie Cornwall, Tim B. Heaton, Lawrence Alfred Young (eds.), *Contemporary Mormonism: Social Science Perspectives* (Urbana: University of Illinois Press, 1994), 239–264; Jill Derr, Janath Russell Cannon, and Maureen Ursenbach Beecher, *Women of Covenant: The Story of the Relief Society* (Salt Lake City: Deseret, 1992); Lola Van Wagenen, "In Their Own Behalf: The Politicization of Mormon Women and the 1870 Franchise," *Dialogue* 24 (Winter 1991), 31–43; Leonard Arrington, "Modern Lysistratas: Mormon Women in the International Peace Movement," *Journal of Mormon History* 15 (1989), 89–104; Neil J. Young, "'The ERA Is a Moral Issue': The Mormon Church, LDS Women, and the Defeat of the Equal Rights Amendment," *American Quarterly* 59: 3 (September 2007), 623–644; Jessie Embry (1987), *Mormon Polygamous Families: Life in the Principle* (Salt Lake City: University of Utah Press, 1987); B. Carmon Hardy, *Solemn Covenant: The Mormon Polygamous Passage* (Urbana: University of Illinois Press, 1992), 84–126; Richard Van Wagoner, *Mormon Polygamy: A History* (Salt Lake City: Signature Books, 1986); B. Carmon Hardy, "'Lords of Creation': Polygamy, the Abrahamic Household, and the Mormon Patriarchy," *Journal of Mormon History* 20 (1, 1994), 119–152; Lawrence Foster, *Religion and Sexuality: The Shakers, the Mormons, and the Oneida Community* (Urbana: University of Illinois Press, 1981); Kimball Young, *Isn't One Wife Enough? The Story of Mormon Polygamy* (New York: Holt, 1954); Carol Cornwall Madsen, "At Their Peril': Utah Law and the Case of Plural Wives, 1850–1900" *Western Historical Quarterly* 21 ((November 1990), 425–43; Phillip Kunz; "One Wife or Several: A Comparative Study of Late Nineteenth-Century Marriage in Utah" in Thomas Alexander (ed.), *The Mormon People: Their Character and Traditions* (Provo, UT: Brigham Young University Press, 1980), 53–73; James Smith and Phillip Kunz, "Polygyny and Fertility in Nineteenth-Century America," *Population Studies*, 30 (1976), 465–480; Eugene E. Campbell and Bruce L. Campbell. "Divorce Among Mormon Polygamists: Extent and Explanations," *Utah Historical Quarterly* 46 (Winter 1978), 4–23; D. Michael Quinn, "LDS Church Authority and New Plural Marriages, 1890–1904" *Dialogue* 18 (Spring 1985), 9–105; and Martha Bradley, "The Women of Fundamentalism: Short Creek, 1953," *Dialogue* 23:2 (Summer 1990), 15–37.

40. Julie Roy Jeffrey, *Frontier Women: Civilizing the West?, 1840–1880*, revised edition (New York: Hill and Wang, 1998), 179–213; Joan Iverson, "A Debate on the American Home: The Antipolygamy controversy, 1880–1890," *Journal of the History of Sexuality*, 1 (4), 585–602; Maureen Ursenbach Beecher, "The 'Leading Sisters': A Female Hierarchy in Nineteenth-Century Mormon Society," *Journal of Mormon History* 9 (1982), 25–39; and Lola Van Wagenen; "In Their Own Behalf: The Politicization of Mormon Women and the 1870 Franchise," *Dialogue* 24 (Winter 1991), 31–43, especially 35 and 41. For the broader context of early American women see Carroll Smith-Rosenberg's *Disorderly Conduct: Visions of Gender in Victorian America* (New York: Oxford, 1985).

41. Julie Dunfey; "'Living the Principle' of Plural Marriage: Mormon Women, Utopia, and Female Sexuality in the Nineteenth-Century," *Feminist Studies*, 10 (3, 1984), 523–536; B. Carmon Hardy, *Solemn Covenant: The Mormon Polygamous Passage* (Urbana: University of Illinois Press, 1992), 84–126; B. Carmon Hardy, "'Lords of Creation': Polygamy, the Abrahamic Household, and the Mormon

Patriarchy," *Journal of Mormon History* 20 (1, 1994), 119-152; Richard Van Wagoner, *Mormon Polygamy: A History* (Salt Lake City: Signature, 1986), 109; Beverly Benton, *Women Vote in the West* (New York: Garland, 1986), 37; and Anne Firor Scott, "Mormon Women, Other Women" *Journal of Mormon History* 13 (1986-1987), 3-19, especially 10.

42. J.E. Hullett; "Social Role and Personal Security in Mormon Polygamy," *American Journal of Sociology* 44:4 (January 1940), 542-553.

43. D. Michael Quinn, "Mormon Women Have Had the Priesthood Since 1843"; in Maxine Hanks (ed.), *Women and Authority: Re-emerging Mormon Feminism* (Salt Lake City: Signature, 1992), 365-410. Quinn references Joseph Smith's "Journal" for 1842-1843. Smith's papers can be found in the Archives of the Church of Jesus Christ of Latter-day Saints in Salt Lake City.

44. Jill Mulvay Derr, Janeth Russell Cannon, and Maureen Ursenbach Beecher, *Women of Covenant: The Story of Relief Society* (Salt Lake City: Deseret Book, 1992), particularly chapter one. Anne Firor Scott argued that the Relief Society is yet other nineteenth-century female benevolent organization whose purpose was fundamentally the relief of the poor and that the Relief Society was male dominated in her "Mormon Women, Other Women" *Journal of Mormon History* 13 (1986-1987), 7.

45. Ronald W. Walker, David J. Whittaker, and James B. Allen, *Mormon History* (Urbana: University of Illinois Press, 2000), 91-92.

Chapter Five

1. Karl Marx, *Capital: A Critique of Political Economy*, three volumes (Harmondsworth: Penguin, 1993); Max Weber, *Economy and Society: An Outline of Interpretive Sociology* (Berkeley: University of California Press, 1968); Émile Durkheim, *The Division of Labor in Society* (New York: Free Press, 1893); and Ferdinand Tönnies, *Community and Society* (New York: Harper Torchbooks, 1935).

2. James Mooney, *The Ghost Dance Religion and the Sioux Outbreak of 1890* (Lincoln: University of Nebraska Press, 1896).

3. Peter Worsley, *The Trumpet Shall Sound* (New York: Schocken, 1957) and Norman Cohn, *The Pursuit of the Millennium*, revised edition (New York: Oxford University Press, 1971). See particularly Cohn's Introduction.

4. George Rudé, *Revolutionary Europe, 1783-1815*, 2d. ed. (Oxford, UK: Blackwell, 2000).

5. Paul Johnson, *A Shopkeeper's Millennium: Society and Revivals in Rochester, New York, 1915-1817* (New York: Hill and Wang, 1978); Mary Ryan, *Cradle of the Middle Class: The Family in Oneida County, New York, 1790-1865* (New York: Cambridge University Press, 1981); Carroll Smith-Rosenberg, *Disorderly Conduct: Visions of Gender in Victorian America* (New York: Oxford University Press, 1985); Smith-Rosenberg, "Women and Religious Revivals: Anti-Ritualism, Liminality, and the Emergence of the American Bourgeoisie" in Leonard Sweet (ed.), *The Evangelical Tradition in America* (Macon, GA: Mercer University Press, 1984), 199-231; and Charles Sellers, *The Market Revolution: Jacksonian America 1815-1846* (New York: Oxford University Press, 1991), 217-225.

6. Paul Johnson; *A Shopkeeper's Millennium: Society and Revivals in Rochester, New York, 1915-1817* (New York: Hill and Wang, 1978); Mary Ryan, *Cradle of the Middle Class: The Family in Oneida County, New York, 1790-1865* (New York: Cambridge University Press, 1981); and Carroll Smith-Rosenberg, *Disorderly Conduct: Visions of Gender in Victorian America* (New York: Oxford University Press, 1985). In her introduction to Part Two of the essays in *Disorderly Conduct*, "Bourgeois Discourse in the Age of Jackson: An Introduction," 79-89, and in the essay "The Cross and the Pedestal: Women, Anti-Ritualism, and the Emergence of the American Bourgeoisie," 129-164, Smith-Rosenberg nicely summarizes and lays out the view that economic transformations wrought by the building of the Erie Canal and the traffic it brought generated changes in religion, the family, and gave birth to an American bourgeoisie.

7. Richard Hofstadter, *The Age of Reform from Bryan to FDR* (New York: Vintage, 1955) and Hofstadter, *The Paranoid Style in American Politics and Other Essays* (Cambridge, MA: Harvard University Press, 1965).

8. David G. Hackett, *The Rude Hand of Innovation: Religion and Social Order in Albany, New York, 1652-1836* (New York: Oxford University Press, 1991).

9. Richard D. Brown, *Modernization: The Transformation of American Life 1600-1865* (New York: Hill and Wang, 1976).

10. Rowland Berthoff, *An Unsettled People: Social Order and Disorder in American History* (New York: Harper and Row, 1971).

11. John McCarthy and Mayer Zald, "Resource Mobilization and Social Movements: A Partial Theory," *American Journal of Sociology* 82: 6 (1977), 1212-1241.

12. Jan Shipps, "The Reality of the Restoration in LDS Theology and Mormon Experience" in Shipps, *Sojourner in the Promised Land: Forty Years Among the Mormons* (Urbana: University of Illinois Press, 2000), 229-240; Shipps, *Mormonism: The Study of a New Religious Tradition* (Urbana: University of Illinois Press, 1985), 45-65; Mark Noll, *A History of Christianity in the United States and Canada* (Grand Rapids: Eerdmans, 1992), 196; Jon Butler *Awash in a Sea of Faith Christianizing the American People* (Cambridge, MA: Harvard University Press, 1992), 242 and 244-246; Lawrence Foster, *Religion and Sexuality: The Shakers, the Mormons, and the Oneida Community* (Urbana: University of Illinois Press, 1981), 128-130; Kenneth Winn, *Exiles in a Land of Liberty: Mormons in America, 1830-1846* (Chapel Hill: University of North Carolina Press, 1989); Mario DePillis, "The Quest for Religious Authority and the Rise of Mormonism," *Dialogue* 1:1 (Spring 1966), 68-88; Whitney Cross, *The Burned-Over District: The Social and Intellectual History of Enthusiastic Religion in Western New York, 1800-1850* (New York: Harper and Row, 1950), Chapter 8; Marvin Hill, "Quest for Refuge: An Hypothesis as to the Social Origins and Nature of the Mormon Political Kingdom," *Journal of Mormon History* 2 (1975), 3-20; Rowland Berthoff, *An Unsettled People: Social Order and Disorder in American History* (New York: Harper and Row, 1971), 247-250; Gordon Wood, "Evangelical America and Early Mormonism" *New York History* 41 (October 1980), 359-386; Gordon Wood, "Religion and the American Revolution" in Harry Stout and D.G. Hart (eds.), *New Directions in American Religious History* (New York: Oxford University Press, 1997), 195; Louis Kern, *An Ordered Love: Sex Roles and Sexuality in Victorian Utopias—The Shakers, the Mormons, and the Oneida Community* (Chapel Hill: University of North Carolina Press, 1981), especially Part III; Fawn Brodie, *No Man Knows My History: The Life of Joseph Smith*, 2d. ed. (New York: Knopf, 1971); Alice Felt Tyler, *Freedom's Ferment: Phases of American Social History from the Colonial Period to the Outbreak of the Civil War* (New York: Harper and Row, 1944), 86-107; Lawrence Foster, "The Psychology of Religious Genius: Joseph Smith and the Origins of New Religious Movements," in Bryan Waterman, *The Prophet Puzzle* (Salt Lake City: Signature, 1999), 183-208; Robert Anderson, *Inside the Mind of Joseph Smith: Psychobiography and the Book of Mormon* (Salt Lake City: Signature, 2002); Newell Bringhurst, "Joseph Smith, the Mormons, and Antebellum Reform: A Closer Look," *John Whitmer Historical Association Journal* 14 (1994), 73-92; John Brooke, *The Refiner's Fire: The Making of Mormon Cosmology, 1644-1844* (New York: Cambridge University Press, 1994); Marianne Perciaccante, "Backlash Against Formalism: Early Mormonism's Appeal in Jefferson County," *Journal of Mormon History* 19:2 (Fall 1993), 35-63; Nathan Hatch, *The Democratization of American Christianity* (New Haven, CT: Yale University Press, 1989), 113-122; Hatch, "Mormon and Methodist: Popular Religion in the Crucible of the Free Market," *Journal of Mormon History* 20: 1 (Spring 1994), 24-44; Michael Barkun, *Crucible of the Millennium: The Burned-Over District of New York in the 1840s* (Syracuse, NY: Syracuse University Press, 1986), 63-89; Ralph Waldo Emerson, "An After-clap of Puritanism" in William Mulder and Russell Mortensen (eds.), *Among the Mormons—Historic Accounts by Contemporary Observers* (New York: Knopf, 1958), 382-384; David Brion Davis, "The New England Origins of Mormonism," *New England Quarterly* XXVI (June 1953), 143-168; Rex Cooper, *Promises Made to the Fathers: Mormon Covenant Organization* (Salt Lake City: University of Utah Press, 1990); Donald Meinig, *The Shaping of American Volume 3: Transcontinental America, 1850-1915* (New Haven, CT: Yale University Press, 1998), 89-112; Leonard Arrington, *The Great Basin Kingdom: An Economic History of the Latter-Day Saints*

(Lincoln: University of Nebraska Press, 1959), viii; Cushing Strout, *The New Heavens and the New Earth: Political Religion in America* (New York: Harper and Row, 1974); Harold Bloom, *The American Religion: The Emergence of the Post-Christian Nation* (New York: Simon and Schuster, 1992); Marvin Hill, "The Role of Christian Primitivism in the Origin and Development of the Mormon Kingdom," unpublished Ph.D. dissertation, University of Chicago, 1968; Hill, "The Rise of Mormonism in the Burned-Over District: Another View," *New York History* LXI:4 (October 1980), 411-430; Richard Hughes and Leonard Allen, *Illusions of Innocence: Protestant Primitivism in America, 1630-1875* (Chicago: University of Chicago Press, 1988), 133-152; and Timothy Smith, "The Book of Mormon in a Biblical Culture," *Journal of Mormon History* 7 (1980), 3-21.

13. Whitney Cross, *The Burned-Over District: The Social and Intellectual History of Enthusiastic Religion in Western New York, 1800-1850* (Ithaca, NY: Cornell University Press, 1950), 138-150. For a critique of Cross see Judith Wellman (Judith Wellman, "Crossing Over Cross: Whitney Cross's Burned-Over District as Social History," *Reviews in American History* 17:1 (March 1989), 159-174.

14. Charles Sellers, *The Market Revolution: Jacksonian America 1815-1846* (New York: Oxford University Press, 1991), 217-225.

15. Nathan Hatch, *The Democratization of American Christianity* (New Haven, CT: Yale University Press, 1989), 113-122 and Hatch, "Mormon and Methodist: Popular Religion in the Crucible of the Free Market," *Journal of Mormon History* 20: 1 (Spring 1994), 24-44.

16. Marvin Hill, "Quest for Refuge: An Hypothesis as to the Social Origins and Nature of the Mormon Political Kingdom," *Journal of Mormon History* 2 (1975), 3-20.

17. Kenneth Winn, *Exiles in a Land of Liberty: Mormons in America, 1930-1846* (Chapel Hill: University of North Carolina Press, 1989).

18. Newell Bringhurst, "Joseph Smith, the Mormons, and Antebellum Reform: A Closer Look," *John Whitmer Historical Association Journal* 14 (1994), 73-92. Bringhurst draws on an earlier work by Geoffrey Spencer, which traces the Mormon reformist impulse to socio-economic strains in the Smith family ("Anxious Saints: The Early Mormons, Social Reform, and Status Anxiety, *John Whitmer Historical Association Journal* 1 (1981), 43-53). The "Word of Wisdom" can be found in Section 89 of the most recent editions of the Doctrine and Covenants. It was section 80 in the 1835 edition. On reform in general during the era see Ronald Walters, *American Reformers 1815-1860* (New York: Hill and Wang, 1978).

19. Michael Barkun, *Crucible of the Millennium: The Burned-Over District of New York in the 1840s* (Syracuse, NY: Syracuse University Press, 1986). Modernization theory, like economic theory in general, emphasizes the primary role economic factors play in historical dynamics.

20. For interesting discussions of intellectual attempts to understand religious experience and revivalism and a critique of them see Ann Taves, *Fits, Trances, and Visions: Experiencing Religion and Explaining Experience from Wesley to James* (Princeton, NJ: Princeton University Press, 1999) and Leigh Eric Schmidt, *Hearing Things: Religion, Illusion, and the American Enlightenment* (Cambridge, MA: Harvard University Press, 2002).

21. James Mooney, *The Ghost Dance Religion and the Sioux Outbreak of 1890* (Lincoln: University of Nebraska Press, 1896). On millennialism as the ideology of the oppressed and poor see John Gager, *Kingdom and Community: The Social World of Early Christianity* (Englewood Cliffs, NJ: Prentice-Hall, 1975); the essays in Sylvia L. Thrupp (ed.), *Millennial Dreams in Action* (New York: Schocken, 1962); Peter Worsley, *The Trumpet Shall Sound: A Study of Cargo Cults in Melanesia*, 2d. ed. (New York: Schocken, 1968); Vittorio Lantenari, *The Religion of the Oppressed: A Study of Modern Messianic Movements* (New York: Knopf, 1963); Eric Hobsbawm, *Primitive Rebels: Studies in Archaic Forms of Social Movement in the 19th and 20th Centuries* (London: Abacus, 1959); and Anthony Wallace, "Revitalization Movements" *American Anthropologist* 58 (1956), 264-281.

22. Nathan Hatch, *The Democratization of American Christianity* (New Haven,

CT: Yale University Press, 1989), 113–122 and Hatch, "Mormon and Methodist: Popular Religion in the Crucible of the Free Market," *Journal of Mormon History* 20: 1 (Spring 1994), 24–44.

23. Nathan Hatch, *The Democratization of American Christianity* (New Haven, CT: Yale University Press, 1989), 113. On the "marginality" of the Smith family also see Richard Bushman, *The Refinement of America: Persons, Houses, Cities* (New York: Knopf, 1993), 425–427.

24. David S. Katz and Richard H. Popkin, *Messianic Revolution: Radical Religious Politics to the End of the Second Millennium* (Harmondsworth, UK: Allen Lane, 1999), xix–xxv; Linda Woodhead, *An Introduction to Christianity* (Cambridge, UK: Cambridge University Press, 2004), 133; Violet Rowe, *Sir Henry Vane the Younger* (London: Athlone, 1970), 202–206; Christopher Hill, *The Antichrist in the Seventeenth-Century* (London: Verso, 1971); Frank Manuel, *The Religion of Isaac Newton* (New York: Oxford University Press, 1974); and Austin Dobbins, *Milton and the Book of Revelation: The Heavenly Cycle* (Tuscaloosa: University of Alabama Press, 1975).

25. Mark Grandstaff and Milton Backman, "The Social Origins of Kirtland Mormons"; *BYU Studies* 30:2 (1990), 47–66 and Stephen C. Harper, "Infallible Proofs, Both Human and Divine: The Persuasiveness of Mormonism for Early Converts," *Religion and American Culture*, 10:1 (Winter 2000), 114.

26. David Rowe, "Millerites: A Shadow Portrait" in Ronald Numbers and Jonathan M. Butler (eds.), *The Disappointed: Millerism and Millenarianism in Nineteenth-Century America* (Knoxville: University of Tennessee Press, 1993), 6–11; Henri Desroche, *The American Shakers: From Neo-Christianity to Presocialism* (Amherst: University of Massachusetts Press, 1971), 101–115 and 125–138; and Robert Sutton, *Communal Utopias and the American Experience: Religious Communities, 1722-2000* (Westport: CT: Praeger, 2003), 74.

27. On Methodist demographics see John Wigger, "Fighting Bees: Methodist Itinerants and the Dynamics of Methodist Growth, 1770–1820" in Nathan Hatch (ed.), *Methodism and the Shaping of American Culture* (Nashville: Kingswood Press, 2001), 88–91 and Dee Andrews, *The Methodists in Revolutionary America, 1760-1800: The Shaping of an Evangelical Culture* (Princeton, NJ: Princeton University Press, 2000), 155–184. On Methodist economic thinking see David Carwardine, "Charles Sellers' "Antinomians" and "Arminians" in Mark Noll (ed.), *God and Mammon: Protestants, Money, and the Market, 1790–1860* (New York: Oxford University Press, 2001), 75–98.

28. Edward Pessen, *Jacksonian America: Society, Personality, and Politics*, revised edition (Champaign: University of Illinois Press, 1978), Chapter 5; Michael Lebowitz, "The Jacksonians: Paradox Lost" in Barton Bernstein (ed.), *Toward a New Past: Dissenting Essays in American History* (New York: Vintage, 1968), 65–89; and Lee Benson, *The Concept of Jacksonian Democracy: New York as a Test Case* (New York: Atheneum, 1961).

29. Clifford Griffin, "Religious Benevolence as Social Control, 1815–1860, *Mississippi Valley Historical Review*, XLIV (December 1957), 432–444 and Griffin, *Their Brothers Keepers: Moral Stewardship in the United States, 1800–1865* (New Brunswick, NJ: Rutgers University Press, 1960). Also see John Bodo, *The Protestant Clergy and Public Issues 1812-1848* (Princeton, NJ: Princeton University Press, 1954); Charles Foster, *An Errand of Mercy: The Evangelical United Front, 1790–1837* (Chapel Hill: University of North Carolina Press, 1960); and Charles Cole, *The Social Ideas of the Northern Evangelists* (New York: Columbia University Press, 1954).

30. For critiques of the status anxiety/social control thesis see especially Nathan Hatch, *The Democratization of American Christianity* (New Haven, CT: Yale University Press, 1989) and Lois Banner, "Religious Benevolence as Social Control: A Critique" *Journal of American History* 60 (1973) 23–41.

31. Joseph Gusfield, *Symbolic Crusade: Status Politics and the American Temperance Movement* (Urbana: University of Illinois Press, 1963).

32. Whitney Cross, *The Burned-Over District: The Social and Intellectual History of Enthusiastic Religion in Western New York, 1800–1850* (New York: Harper and Row, 1950), 138–139 and Newell Bringhurst, "Joseph Smith, the Mormons, and Antebellum Reform: A Closer Look," *John*

Whitmer Historical Association Journal 14 (1994), 73–92.

33. Newell Bringhurst, "Joseph Smith, the Mormons, and Antebellum Reform: A Closer Look," *John Whitmer Historical Association Journal* 14 (1994), 73–92.

34. Norman Cohn, *The Pursuit of the Millennium*, revised edition (New York: Oxford University Press, 1971). Richard Vann argued that early Quakers came primarily from the yeoman status groups or classes of England (*The Social Development of English Quakerism: 1655–1755* (Cambridge, MA: Harvard University Press, 1969). Vann's work has not gone unchallenged. For the debates over the issue of early Quaker demographics and social status see the various essays on the subject in *Past and Present*, number 48, August 1970.

35. On the Reformation see Thomas A. Brady, Heiko Oberman, and James D. Tracy, *Handbook of European History, 1400–1600*, two volumes (Grand Rapids: Eerdmans, 1995); Steven Ozment, *The Age of Reform 1250–1550: An Intellectual and Religious History of Late Medieval and Reformation Europe* (New Haven, CT: Yale University Press, 1980); Lewis Spitz, *The Protestant Reformation 1517–1559* (New York: Harper and Row, 1985); Euen Cameron, *The European Reformation* (New York: Oxford University Press, 1991); Diarmaid MacCulloch, *The Reformation: A History* (New York: Penguin Press, 2003); Robert Scribner, Roy Porter, and Mikulas Teich (eds.), *The Reformation in National Context* (Cambridge, MA: Cambridge University Press, 1994); Carter Lindberg, *The European Reformations* (Oxford, UK: Blackwell, 1996); and George Williams, *The Radical Reformation*, 3d. ed. (Kirksville, MO: Sixteenth Century Journal Publishers, 1992).

36. John McCarthy and M. Zald, "Resource Mobilization and Social Movements: A Partial Theory," *American Journal of Sociology* 82: 6 (1977), 1212–1241.

37. Conversion from one group to another does not lessen commitment; it heightens it. Those who become Quakers or Mormons, for instance, generally do so because the movement appeals to them. In some instances, "consent" members prove more committed to their new group's values than "descent" members. On this see Jan Shipps, "Making Saints: In the Early Days and Latter Days" in Marie Cornwall, Tim Heaton, and Larry A. Young (eds.), *Contemporary Mormonism: Social Science Perspectives* (Urbana: University of Illinois Press, 1994), 64–83. By the way, the same argument, I would suggest, holds for those who voluntarily change nationalities.

38. Frederick Turner, *The Significance of the Frontier in American History* (New York: Penguin, 1893); Whitney Cross, *The Burned-Over District: The Social and Intellectual History of Enthusiastic Religion in Western New York, 1800–1850* (New York: Harper and Row, 1950), 55–77; Curtis Johnson, *Islands of Holiness; Rural Religion in Upstate New York, 1790–1860* (Ithaca, NY: Cornell University Press, 1989), 67–69; and Marianne Perciaccante, "Backlash Against Formalism: Early Mormonism's Appeal in Jefferson County," *Journal of Mormon History* 19:2 (Fall 1993), 35–63. Johnson studied Cortland County, New York, Perciaccante, Jefferson County, New York.

39. On Christian primitivism and its various flavors see Ernest Troeltsch, *The Social Teachings of the Christian Churches*, two volumes (Louisville, KY: Westminster, 1931), 355–356, 465–484, 694–699, 706–712, 703–706. 712–714, 714–719, 780–783, and 784–787; Bill Leonard, *Baptists in America* (New York: Columbia University Press, 2005), 7–9 (Baptist ideology); Linda Woodhead, *An Introduction to Christianity* (Cambridge, UK: Cambridge University Press, 2004), 138, 169–179, 194–196, 220, 221–225, 225–227, and 235; Michael Mullett, "Radical Sects and Dissenting Churches, 1600–1750," in Sheridan Gilley and W.J. Sheils (eds.), *A History of Religion in Britain: Practice and Belief from Pre-Roman Times to the Present* (Oxford, UK: Blackwell, 1994),188–210 and especially 192 and 200; Christopher Hill, *Society and Puritanism in Pre-Revolutionary England* (London: Mercury, 1964); Nicholas Tyacke, "Puritanism, Arminianism, and Counter-Revolution" in Richard Cust and Ann Hughes (eds.), *The English Civil War* (London: Arnold, 1997), 136–159 (Puritanism and Arminianism); Priscilla Brewer, "The Shakers of Mother Ann Lee" in Donald Pitzer (ed.), *America's Communal Utopias* (Chapel Hill: University of North Carolina Press, 1997), 38–40 (Shaker); Lawrence Foster, "Free Love and Community: John Humphrey Noyes and the Oneida Perfectionists" in Donald

Pitzer (ed.), *America's Communal Utopias* (Chapel Hill: University of North Carolina Press, 1997), 255–256; and J.J. Woltjer and M.E.H.N. Mout, "Settlements: The Netherlands" in Thomas Brady, Heiko Oberman, and James D. Tracy, *Handbook of European History, 1400-1600: Late Middle Ages, Renaissance, and Reformation, Volume 2: Visions, Programs, and Outcomes* (Grand Rapids: Eerdmans), 405.

There has long been a tension in Christian thought and practice between "freedom" and "the law." Paul's letters to Corinth (I and II Corinthians), for instance, apparently attempt, in part, to counter a group of Christians who felt that since they were no longer bound by the Jewish law of circumcision they were sanctified and hence could do anything they wanted. On Paul's letters to the Corinthians see Morton Scott Enslin, *Christian Beginnings* (New York: Harper & Brothers, 1938), 249–250 and L. Michael White, *From Jesus to Christianity: How Four Generations of Visionaries and Storytellers Created the New Testament and the Christian Faith* (San Francisco: Harper San Francisco, 2004), 181–182.

40. Paul Johnson, *A Shopkeepers Millennium: Society and Revivals in Rochester, New York, 1815-1837* (New York: Hill and Wang, 1978); Mark Noll, "Protestant Reasoning About Money and the Economy" in Mark Noll (ed.), *God and Mammon: Protestants, Money, and the Market, 1790-1860* (New York: Oxford University Press), 278; Charles Finney, "Lecture XIII: Being in Debt," *The Oberlin Evangelist* 1, number 17 (31 July 1839), 129–131; and Charles Finney, "Lecture XX: How to Prevent our Employments from Injuring our Souls," *The Oberlin Evangelist* 1, number 24 (6 November 1839), 185–187.

41. Charles Sellers, *Market Revolution: Jacksonian America, 1815-1846* (New York: Oxford University Press, 1991), 217–225.

42. George Thomas, *Revivalism and Cultural Change: Christianity, Nation Building, and the Market in the Nineteenth-Century United States* (Chicago: University of Chicago Press, 1989).

43. Charles Sellers, *Market Revolution: Jacksonian America, 1815-1846* (New York: Oxford University Press, 1991), 217–225; George Thomas, *Revivalism and Cultural Change: Christianity, Nation Building, and the Market in Nineteenth-Century America* (Chicago: University of Chicago Press, 1989); Daniel Walker Howe, "Charles Sellers, the Market Revolution, and the Shaping of American Identity in Whig-Jacksonian America" in Mark Noll (ed.), *God and Mammon: Protestants, Money, and the Market, 1790-1860* (New York: Oxford University Press), 54–74; Richard Carwardine, "Charles Sellers' "Antinomians" and "Arminians": Methodists and the Market Revolution" in Mark Noll (ed.), *God and Mammon: Protestants, Money, and the Market, 1790-1860* (New York: Oxford University Press), 75–98; Melvyn Stokes and Stephen Conway (eds.), *The Market Revolution in America: Social, Political, and Religious Expression, 1800-1880* (Charlottesville: University of Virginia Press, 1996); and Curtis Johnson, *Islands of Holiness: Rural Religion in Upstate New York, 1790-1860* (Ithaca, NY: Cornell University Press, 1989) 82–85. According to Johnson, Methodism grew most rapidly in areas already penetrated by market capitalism.

44. Carroll Smith-Rosenberg, *Disorderly Conduct: Visions of Gender in Victorian America* (New York: Oxford University Press, 1985) and Smith-Rosenberg, "Women and Religious Revivals: Anti-Ritualism, Liminality, and the Emergence of the American Bourgeoisie" in Leonard Sweet (ed.), *The Evangelical Tradition in America* (Macon, GA: Mercer University Press, 1984), 199–231.

45. Robert Wiebe, *Who We Are: A History of Popular Nationalism* (Princeton, NJ: Princeton University Press, 2002), 88–92. As Wiebe points out, Mormons were unable to act on their theocratic impulses because the more powerful American state was arrayed against them.

46. R. Laurence Moore; *Religious Outsiders and the Making of Americans* (New York: Oxford University Press, 1987) and Clarke Garrett, *Origins of the Shakers: From the Old World to the New World* (Baltimore, MD: Johns Hopkins University Press, 1987).

47. Clarke Garrett, *Origins of the Shakers: From the Old World to the New World* (Baltimore, MD: Johns Hopkins, 1987); Mark Grandstaff and Milton Backman, "The Social Origins of Kirtland Mormons"; *BYU Studies* 30:2 (1990), 47–66; and Lawrence Foster, "Free Love and Community: John Humphrey Noyes and the Oneida Perfectionists" in Donald Pitzer (ed.),

America's Communal Utopias (Chapel Hill: University of North Carolina Press, 1997), 255-256.

48. Mark Grandstaff and Milton Backman, "The Social Origins of Kirtland Mormons"; *BYU Studies* 30:2 (1990), 47-66; David Rowe, "Millerites: A Shadow Portrait" in Ronald Numbers and Jonathan Butler (eds.), *The Disappointed: Millerism and Millenarianism in Nineteenth-Century America* (Knoxville: University of Tennessee Press, 1993), 6-11; Henri Desroche, *The American Shakers: From Neo-Christianity to Presocialism* (Amherst: University of Massachusetts Press, 1971), 101-115 and 125-138; and Robert Sutton, *Communal Utopias and the American Experience: Religious Communities, 1722-2000* (Westport: CT: Praeger, 2003), 74.

49. Curtis Johnson, *Islands of Holiness: Rural Religion in Upstate New York, 1790-1860* (Ithaca, NY: Cornell University Press, 1989) and Richard Carwardine, "Charles Sellers' "Antinomians" and "Arminians": Methodists and the Market Revolution" in Mark Noll (ed.), *God and Mammon: Protestants, Money, and the Market, 1790-1860* (New York: Oxford University Press), 84-85.

50. Rowland Berthoff, *An Unsettled People: Social Order and Disorder in American History* (New York: Harper and Row, 1971) 243-244.

Chapter Six

1. For a review of recent literature that explores the connection between economic factors and Protestant religious groups and ideology see Robert Wuthnow and Tracy Scott, "Protestants and Economic Behavior" in Harry Stout and D.G. Hart, *New Directions on American Religious History* (New York: Oxford University Press, 1997), 260-295.

2. John Brooke nicely makes the point in his *The Refiner's Fire: The Making of Mormon Cosmology, 1844-1844* (New York: Cambridge University Press, 1994), xv-xvi, that if it was not mobility or class and status that made some "seekers" Mormons, Oneidans, Shakers, Campbellites, or Adventists. In this chapter I have been extensively influenced here by Clifford Geertz, "Religion as a Cultural System" in Michael Banton (ed.), *Anthropological Approaches to the Study of Religion* (London: Tavistock), 1-46 and Peter Berger, *The Sacred Canopy: Elements of a Sociological Theory of Religion* (Garden City, NJ: Anchor, 1967). Works which emphasize the importance of culture in the analysis of religion and religious groups include Gordon Wood, "Religion and the American Revolution" in Harry Stout and D.G. Hart (eds.), *New Directions in American Religious History* (New York: Oxford University Press, 1997), 173-205; Rhys Isaac, *The Transformation of Virginia, 1740-1790* (Chapel Hill: University of North Carolina Press, 1999); and Robert Wuthnow and Tracy L. Scott, "Protestants and Economic Behavior" in Harry Stout and D.G. Hart (eds.), *New Directions in American Religious History* (New York: Oxford University Press, 1997), 260-295.

3. Dickson Bruce, *And They All Sang Hallelujah: Plain Folk Camp Meeting Religion, 1800-1845* (Knoxville: University of Tennessee Press, 1974).

4. Daniel Walker Howe, "Protestantism, Volunteerism, and Personal Identity" in Harry Stout and D.G. Hart (eds.), *New Directions in American Religious History* (New York: Oxford University Press, 1997), 206-238, especially pages 215 and following.

5. Timothy Smith, "The Book of Mormon in a Biblical Culture," *Journal of Mormon History* 7 (1980), 3-21. Biblicism refers to the central role of the Bible in forming the ideological worldview of these groups and their leaders.

6. Lawrence Foster, *Religion and Sexuality: The Shakers, the Mormons, and the Oneida Community* (Urbana: University of Illinois Press, 1981), 128-130 and 132-134. Also see Foster, *Women, Family, and Utopia: Communal Experiments of the Shakers, the Oneida Community, and the Mormons* (Syracuse, NY: Syracuse University Press, 1991). Julie Dunfey ("'Living the Principle' of Plural Marriage: Mormon Women, Utopia, and Female Sexuality in the Nineteenth-Century," *Feminist Studies* 10:3 (Fall 1984), 523-536) and Julie Roy Jeffrey (*Frontier Women: Civilizing the West? 1840 to 1880*, revised edition (New York: Hill and Wang, 1998), 179-213) have also emphasized the role of the frontier in the rise of Mormon polygamy.

7. Marvin Hill, "The Role of Christian

Primitivism in the Origin and Development of the Mormon Kingdom," unpublished Ph.D. dissertation, University of Chicago, 1968. Hill offers an expanded version of this thesis in his essay "The Rise of Mormonism in the Burned-Over District: Another View," *New York History* LXI:4 (October 1980), 411-430.

8. Mario DePillis, "The Quest for Religious Authority and the Rise of Mormonism," *Dialogue* 1:1 (Spring 1966), 68-88.

9. Richard Hughes, "Soaring With the Gods: Early Mormons and the Eclipse of Religious Pluralism in Richard Hughes and Leonard Allen, *Illusions of Innocence: Protestant Primitivism in America, 1630-1875* (Chicago: University of Chicago Press, 1988), 133-152 and Hughes, "Two Restoration Traditions: Mormons and Churches of Christ in the Nineteenth-Century," in Michael Casey and Douglas Foster (eds.), *The Stone Campbell Movement: An International Religious Tradition* (Knoxville: University of Kentucky Press, 2002), 348-363. On romanticism see Roy Porter and Mikulas Teich (eds.), *Romanticism in National Context* (Cambridge, UK: Cambridge University Press, 1988). George Marsden argues that one can and should distinguish between Biblicism, a return to the faith and organizational forms perceived in the Bible, and primitivism, an experimental return to origins that goes beyond the Bible and which characterized Quakerism and Mormonism in his article "By Primitivism Possessed: How Useful is the Concept "Primitivism" for Understanding American Fundamentalism" in Richard Hughes, *Primitivism in the Modern Church* (Urbana: University of Illinois Press, 1995), 34-46.

10. Jan Shipps, "The Reality of the Restoration in LDS Theology and Mormon Experience" in Shipps, *Sojourner in the Promised Land: Forty Years Among the Mormons* (Urbana: University of Illinois Press, 2000), 229-240 and Shipps, *Mormonism: The Study of a New Religious Tradition* (Urbana: University of Illinois Press, 1985), 64, 69-72, 120, and 154.

11. David Brion Davis, "The New England Origins of Mormonism," *New England Quarterly* XXVI (June 1953), 143-168.

12. Donald Meinig, *The Shaping of America Volume 3: Transcontinental America, 1850-1915* (New Haven, CT: Yale University Press, 1998), 89-112, especially. 90-91; Meinig "The Mormon Cultural Region: Strategies and Patterns in the Geography of the American West, 1847-1964," *Annals of the Association of American Geographers* 55, 1965, 191-220; and Rex Cooper, *Promises Made to the Fathers: Mormon Covenant Organization* (Salt Lake City: University of Utah Press, 1990). Cooper sees similarities between Mormon covenantal theologies and Puritan covenantal theologies. There are social constructionist approaches to geography, on the other hand, like those of Larry Wolf, *Inventing Eastern Europe: The Map of Civilization and the Mind of the Enlightenment* (Palo Alto, CA.: Stanford University Press, 1994) and Martin W. Lewis and Karen E. Wigen, *The Myth of Continents: A Critique of Metageography* (Berkeley: University of California Press, 1997), that argue that geographies are, at least in part, constructed.

13. Marianne Perciaccante, "Backlash against Formalism: Early Mormonism's Appeal in Jefferson County," *Journal of Mormon History* 19:2 (Fall 1993), 35-63. Also see Perciaccante's *Calling Down Fire: Charles Grandison Finney and Revivalism in Jefferson County, New York, 1800-1840* (Albany: State University of New York Press, 2003). Jefferson County is in the north central part of upstate New York in the area near the eastern portion of Lake Ontario.

14. R. Laurence Moore, *Religious Outsiders and the Making of Americans* (New York: Oxford University Press, 1986), 25-47. Martin Marty's *A Nation of Behavers* (Chicago: University of Chicago Press, 1976) makes the point that religion has and always has played an important role in identity construction in the United States.

15. Mormon bloc voting was not unique. A number of scholars have noted that bloc voting was a common, or at least a common criticism, leveled by one party, group, or clique against another, in Jacksonian America. Mob action, likewise, was also far from uncommon at the time. Mormons, Shakers, the Oneida Community, abolitionists, bankers, and Catholics, suffered at the hands of mobs in Ohio, Missouri, and Illinois. On mobs in Jacksonian America see Leonard Richards, *'Gentlemen of Property and Standing': Anti-Abolition Mobs in Jacksonian America* (New York: Oxford

University Press, 1970); David Grimstead, "Rioting in Its Jacksonian Setting" in *American Historical Review* 77 (1972), 361–397; Grimstead, "Democratic Rioting: A Case Study of the Baltimore Bank Mob of 1835" in William O'Neill (ed.), *Insights and Parallels: Problems and Issues of American Social History* (Minneapolis: Burgess, 1973), 125–149; and Michael Feldberg, *The Turbulent Era: Riot and Disorder in Jacksonian America* (New York: Oxford University Press, 1980). On prejudice in the United States see Ray Billington, *The Protestant Crusade: A Study in the Origins of American Nativism, 1800–1860* (Chicago: Quadrangle, 1952). As to Methodists, Carwardine noted Methodist support for Jackson was tenuous. Jacksonian laissez-faire attitudes and Catholic, immigrant, and irreligious support for the Democrats led more and more Methodist leaders to leave the Democratic Party for the Whigs as time wore on in his "Methodist Ministers and the Second Party System" in Russell Richey, Kenneth Rowe, and Jean Miller Schmidt (eds.), *Perspectives on American Methodism: Interpretive Essays* (Nashville, TN: Kingwood, 1993), 309–342 and his, "Charles Sellers's 'Antinomians' and 'Arminians': Methodists and the Market Revolution" in Mark Noll (ed.), *God and Mammon: Protestants, Money, and the Market, 1790–1860* (New York: Oxford University Press, 2001), 89–92.

16. On the Kirtland Anti-Safety Society (the Kirtland Safety Bank) and its consequences both within and outside of the Mormon Community see Marvin Hill, Keith Rooker, and Larry Wimmer, "The Kirtland Economy Revisited: A Market Critique of Sectarian Economics," *BYU Studies* 17:4 (Summer 1977), 389–476. On Mormon Kirtland see Milton Backman, *The Heavens Resound: A History of the Latter-day Saints in Ohio 1830–1838* (Salt Lake City: Deseret, 1983); and Max Parkin, "Kirtland, A Stronghold for the Kingdom" in F. Mark McKiernan, Alma Blair, and Paul M. Edwards (eds.), *The Restoration Movement: Essays in Mormon History*, 2d. ed. (Independence, MO: Herald House, 1992), 61–96. Brooke (*The Refiner's Fire: The Making of Mormon Cosmology, 1644–1944* (New York: Cambridge University Press, 1994), 106–108. and 221–226), rather problematically, in my opinion, argued that the Kirtland Anti-Safety Society shows Mormonism's ties to hermeticism by suggesting that the counterfeiting that was taking place at the Kirtland Bank was a form of alchemy.

17. On Mormon communalism see Leonard Arrington, Feramorz Fox, and Dean May, *Building the City of God: Community and Cooperation Among the Mormons*, 2d. ed. (Urbana: University of Illinois Press, 1992) and Dean May, "One Heart and Mind: Communal Life and Values Among the Mormons" in Donald E. Pitzer (editor), *America's Communal Utopias* (Chapel Hill: University of North Carolina Press, 1997), 135–158. Revelations relating to the "Law of Consecration and Stewardship" can be found in *Evening and Morning Star* 1 (July 1832), Book of Commandments XLIV, Doctrine and Covenants 13 (1835 edition), Doctrine and Covenants 1:14–16, 13, 38:27, 42, and 58:55 (contemporary editions). On the Church's welfare system see Garth Mangum and Bruce Blummel, *The Mormons' War on Poverty: A History of LDS Welfare, 1830–1990* (Salt Lake City: University of Utah Press, 1993).

18. That Mormon migration, politics, economic communalism, and cultural differences led to tensions and attacks on Mormons should not be surprising nor were they unusual in the context. Migration, in Jacksonian America, was as common among non-Mormons as among Mormons. Mormons were on the move but so were many Jacksonian Americans. Grandstaff and Backman (Mark Grandstaff and Milton Backman, "The Social Origins of Kirtland Mormons"; *BYU Studies* 30:2 (1990), 50–54) found that Mormons were more stable in their settlement patterns than were their non-Mormon neighbors. According to them fifty percent of Mormon converts living in Kirtland had not moved prior to their migration to Kirtland. On the other hand, eighty percent of those traveling westward by the Overland Trail in the mid-nineteenth-century had moved at least once before migrating.

19. On Mormonism in Missouri see Stephen C. LeSueur, *The 1838 Mormon War in Missouri* (Columbia: University of Missouri Press, 1987) and the following issues of *BYU Studies*: 13:1, 14:4, and 26:2. For primary documents relating to the Mormon Missouri period see Donald Cannon and Lyndon Cook (eds.), *Far West Record: Minutes*

of the Church of Jesus Christ of Latter-day Saints, 1830–1844 (Salt Lake City: Deseret, 1983) and Clark Johnson (ed.), *Mormon Redress Petitions: Documents of the 1833–1838 Missouri Conflict* (Provo, UT: BYU Religious Studies Center, 1992). Vinson Knight's letter to William Cooper, 3 February 1835, Typescript, Harold B. Lee Library, BYU, gives a first-hand account of the conflict from the Mormon side. On American nativism and xenophobia see David Bennett, *The Party of Fear: The American Far Right from Nativism to the Militia Movement*, revised and updated edition (New York: Vintage, 1995) and Erika Lee, *America for Americans: A History of Xenophobia in the United States* (New York: Basic, 2019).

20. On Mormon Nauvoo see Robert Flanders, *Nauvoo: Kingdom on the Mississippi* (Urbana: University of Illinois Press, 1965); Roger Launius and John Halwas (eds.), *The Kingdom on the Mississippi Revisited* (Urbana: University of Illinois Press, 1996); David and Della Miller, *Nauvoo: The City of Joseph* (Salt Lake City: Peregrine Smith, 1974); Richard and Jeni Holzapfeel, *Women of Nauvoo* (Salt Lake City: Bookcraft, 1992); Annette Hampshire, *Mormons in Conflict: The Nauvoo Years* (Edward Mellen, 1985); the following issues of *BYU Studies* 15:4 (Summer 1975). 18:2 (Winter 1978), 19:3 (Spring 1979), and 31:1 (Winter 1991); and *Dialogue* 5:1 (Spring 1970); and Benjamin Park, *Kingdom of Nauvoo: The Rise and Fall of a Religious Empire on the American Frontier* (New York: Liveright, 2020).

21. Harold Bloom, *The American Religion: The Emergence of the Post-Christian Nation* (New York: Simon and Schuster, 1992).

22. Harold Bloom, *The American Religion: The Emergence of the Post-Christian Nation* (New York: Simon and Schuster, 1992) and John Brooke, *The Refiner's Fire: The Making of Mormon Cosmology, 1844–1844* (New York: Cambridge University Press, 1994). For a critique of Brooke see the review by William Hamblin, Dan Peterson, and George Mitton, "Mormon in the Fiery Furnace, or Loftes Tryck Goes to Cambridge" in *Review of Books on the Book of Mormon* 6:2 (1994), 1–58 and Jan Shipps, "Thoughts about the Academic Community's Response to John Brooke's *Refiner's Fire*" in Shipps, *Sojourner in the Promised Land: Forty Years Among the Mormons* (Urbana: University of Illinois Press, 2000), 204–217. On the American occult tradition, see the essays in Howard Kerr and Charles Crow (eds.), *The Occult in America: New Historical Perspectives* (Urbana: University of Illinois Press, 1983). On Mormonism and the occult see D. Michael Quinn, *Early Mormonism and the Magic Worldview*, revised and enlarged edition (Salt Lake City: Signature, 1998).

23. On Munster Anabaptism see R. Po-chia Hsia, "Munster and the Anabaptists" in R. Po-chia Hsia (ed.), *The German People and the Reformation* (Ithaca, NY: Cornell University Press, 1988), 51–69, especially 55; James Stayer, *The German Peasants War and Anabaptist Community of Goods* (Montreal and Kingston, Ontario: McGill-Queens University Press, 1991); and Anthony Arthur, *The Tailor-King: The Rise and Fall of the Anabaptist Kingdom of Munster* (New York: St. Martin's, 1999). On the Davidic ideologies associated with Munster Anabaptism see Patrick Collinson, *The Reformation: A History* (New York: Modern Library, 2003), 82.

24. Charlotte Haven, "Letter 8 September 1843" in William Mulder and Russell Mortensen (eds.), *Among the Mormons: Historical Accounts by Contemporary Observers* (New York: Knopf, 1958), 126–127 and Udney Hay Jacob, *An Extract from a Manuscript Entitled the Peace Maker, or the Doctrines of the Millennium* (Nauvoo, IL: J. Smith, 1842). Jacob's pamphlet was the first attempt to justify polygamy published by a member of the Church. On the pamphlet see Larry Foster, "A Little Known Defense of Polygamy from the Mormon Press in 1842," *Dialogue* 9 (Winter 1974), 21–34. For the revelation on plural marriage see Doctrine and Covenants 132.

25. D. Michael Quinn, *Early Mormonism and the Magic Worldview*, revised and enlarged edition (Salt Lake City: Signature, 1998).

26. On Christian Biblicism see Linda Woodhead, *An Introduction to Christianity* (Cambridge, UK: Cambridge University Press, 2004), 173–174 (Luther's Biblicism), 183–184 (Calvin's Biblicism), 220 (Baptist Biblicism). On Zwinglian Biblicism see Patrick Collinson, *The Reformation: A History* (London: Phoenix, 2003), 73. On Anabaptist Biblicism see Carter Lindberg, *The European Reformations* (Oxford, UK:

Blackwell, 1996), 202–203. On the importance of the Bible in America see Mark Noll and Nathan Hatch (eds.), *The Bible in America: Essays in Cultural History* (New York: Oxford University Press, 1982) and Ernest Sandeen (ed.), *The Bible and Social Reform* (Philadelphia: Fortress, 1982). On Mormon Biblicism see Timothy Smith, "The Book of Mormon in a Biblical Culture," *Journal of Mormon History* 7 (1980), 3–21; Gordon Irving, "Mormons and the Bible in the 1830s," *BYU Studies* 13 (Summer 1973), 473–478; and Phillip Barlow, *Mormons and the Bible: The Place of Latter-day Saints in American Religion* (New York: Oxford University Press, 1991).

27. Linda Woodhead, *An Introduction to Christianity* (Cambridge, UK: Cambridge University Press, 2004), 133 and Frederic J. Baumgartner, *Longing for the End: A History of Millennialism in Western Civilization* (New York: Palgrave, 1999), 63–67. According to David S. Katz and Richard Popkin (*Messianic Revolution: Radical Religious Politics to the End of the Second Millennium* (London: Penguin, 1998) the apocalypticisms of all the radical Christian messianic movements that followed in Joachim's wake can be traced back to Fiore (252–253). Christianity has, during its long history, been characterized by two major types or forms of millennialism: premillennialism and postmillennialism. Premillennialists hold that the second coming of Christ will occur before the millennium. Postmillennialists believe that the "Kingdom of God" is already present in the world and can be extended through preaching and evangelization. Puritans, like Jonathan Edwards (1703–1758), were postmillennialists. So were Congregationalist Lyman Beecher (1775–1863), revivalist Charles Finney (1792–1875), and most Social Gospelers. The Mormons and William Miller (1782–1849), on the other hand, were premillennialists. Apocalypticism, by the way, is not a purely Christian phenomenon. Judaism, likely thanks to the influence of Zoroastrianism on it during the Persian exile, Islam, particularly Shia Islam, and the Bahai Faith, are apocalyptic as well.

28. On Christian perfectionism see Linda Woodhead, *An Introduction to Christianity* (Cambridge, UK: Cambridge University Press, 2004), 82–83, 138, and 323. On Roman Catholic perfectionism see Lawrence McCrank, "Religious Orders and Monastic Communalism in the United States" in Donald Pitzer (ed.), *America's Communal Utopias* (Chapel Hill: University of North Carolina Press, 1997), 204–253. On the Anabaptist extension of monastic and holiness ideologies into everyday life see Cornelius Dyck (ed.), *Introduction to Mennonite History: A Popular History of the Anabaptists and Mennonites* (Scottsdale, PA: Herald Press, third edition, 1993), 33–49. On Oneida perfectionism see Lawrence Foster, *Religion and Sexuality: The Shakers, Mormons, and the Oneida Community* (Urbana: University of Illinois Press, 1981), 76–78; Foster, "Free Love and Community" in Donald Pitzer (ed.), *America's Communal Utopias* (Chapel Hill: University of North Carolina Press, 1997), 255–256, 272–273; and J. William Frost, "Christianity and Culture in America" in Howard Clark Kee, Emily Albu, Carter Lindberg, J. William Frost, and Dana Robert, *Christianity: A Social and Cultural History*, 2d. ed. (Upper Saddle River, NJ: Prentice-Hall, 1998), 438. On Shaker perfectionism see Patricia Brewer, "The Shakers of Mother Ann Lee" in Donald Pitzer (ed.), *America's Communal Utopias* (Chapel Hill: University of North Carolina Press, 1997), 38, 40, and 42, and J. William Frost, "Christianity and Culture in America" in Howard Clark Kee, Emily Albu, Carter Lindberg, J. William Frost, and Dana Robert, *Christianity: A Social and Cultural History*, 2d. ed. (Upper Saddle River, NJ: Prentice-Hall, 1998), 438. On Mormon perfectionism see Douglas Davies, *An Introduction to Mormonism* (Cambridge, UK: Cambridge University Press, 2003), 192. On holiness and perfectionism in American religious life see Timothy Smith, *Revivalism and Social Reform* (New York: Harper and Row, 1957). On the theme that the United States was the new Eden and that its men were new Adam's see R.W.B. Lewis, *The American Adam: Innocence, Tragedy, and Tradition in the Nineteenth-Century* (Chicago: University of Chicago Press, 1955). For an insider perspective on Mormon doctrine see Bruce McConkie, *Mormon Doctrine: A Compendium of the Gospel* (Salt Lake City: Bookcraft, 1958).

29. On Mormon dispensationalism see Lawrence Foster, *Religion and Sexuality: The Shakers, Mormons, and the Oneida Community* (Urbana: University of Illinois

Press, 1981), 132, 133, 156 and J. William Frost, "Christianity and Culture in America" in Howard Clark Kee, Emily Albu, Carter Lindberg, J. William Frost, and Dana Robert, *Christianity: A Social and Cultural History* 2d. ed. (Upper Saddle River, NJ: Prentice-Hall, 1998), 438. On Shaker dispensationalism see J. William Frost, "Christianity and Culture in America" in Howard Clark Kee, Emily Albu, Carter Lindberg, J. William Frost, and Dana Robert, *Christianity: A Social and Cultural History*, 2d. ed. (Upper Saddle River, NJ: Prentice-Hall, 1998), 438. Dispensationalism, by the way, is not only a Christian cultural script. Islam asserted and asserts that it had succeeded Judaism and Christianity and brought about a new age on earth and the Baha'i Faith asserts that it had succeeded Judaism, Christianity, and Islam and that its prophet, Bahaullah, is the prophet of the new age or the new dispensation. On Islamic dispensationalism see Gisela Webb, "Expressions of Islam in America" in Timothy Miller (ed.), *America's Alternative Religions* (Albany: State University of New York Press, 1995), 234. On Baha'i dispensationalism see Robert Stockman, "The American Baha'i Community in the Nineties" in Timothy Miller (ed.), *America's Alternative Religions* (Albany: State University of New York Press, 1995) 243–244.

30. On Christian primitivism see Richard Hughes (ed.), *The American Quest for the Primitive Church* (Urbana: University of Illinois Press, 1988) and Hughes and Leonard Allen, *Illusions of Innocence: Protestant Primitivism in America, 1630–1875* (Chicago: University of Chicago Press, 1988). On Puritan primitivism see T.D. Bozeman, *To Live Ancient Lives: The Primitivist Dimension of New England Puritanism* (Chapel Hill: University of North Carolina Press, 1988). On common sense and Republicanism in American Christian theology see Mark Noll, *America's God: From Jonathan Edwards to Abraham Lincoln* (New York: Oxford University Press, 2005) and Nathan Hatch, *The Democratization of American Christianity* (New Haven, CT: Yale University Press, 1989), 82–83 and 167–170.

31. A contemporary Shaker document brings out the character of this early nineteenth-century culture war between groups each claiming to be God's one true Church quite clearly. Shaker Asbel Kitchell's Journal reports that Mormon missionaries visiting his Shaker community informed their hosts that Mormonism was clearly superior to Shakerism because Mormons alone were privy to God's instructions through their Prophet Joseph Smith. In other words, for Mormons it was revelation and the authority of Joseph Smith that proved that the Shaker preaching and practice of celibacy was wrong and that marriage was right. Unsurprisingly Shakers agreed to disagree. For them, their revelations and their celibate communities were clearly superior to those of the Mormons. The relevant excerpt from Asbel Kitchell's "Journal" can be most conveniently found in the *Historian's Corner* section of *BYU Studies* 20:1, 94–99 under the title "A Shaker View of a Mormon Mission" edited by Chad Flake. The journal is at the Shaker Museum at Old Chatham, New York. The Mormon missionaries who visited the Shaker settlement were Oliver Cowdery and Leman Copley. The revelation criticizing Shaker celibacy can be found in Doctrine and Covenants 49:15. This revelation is also aimed at other nineteenth-century health reformers and health reform movements and criticizes vegetarianism.

Shakers weren't the only targets of Mormon cultural polemics. In his "Diary and Journal" Smith counter-pointed pagans, Baptists, Methodists, Presbyterians, and Millerites to the one true faith of Mormonism. For Smith the Millerite Church couldn't be God's true church because Miller didn't' receive continuing revelations and because he did perform the signs and wonders which signified evidence of the one true Church, namely miracles. Smith was not above pointing out the apocalyptic failures of Millerites. In one entry in his "Diary and Journal" he noted that the great day predicted by Miller had failed to come. Smith interpreted this as yet another sign of the fact that Milleritism was not true Christianity. In another example of Smith's condemnation of false prophets, Smith found Robert Matthews or Matthias or "Joshua the Priest," as he called himself during his visit to Kirtland, to be preaching false doctrines. On this see Joseph Smith, *An American Prophet's Record: The Diaries and Journals of Joseph Smith* edited by Scott Faulring (Salt Lake City: Signature, 1987) entries for 22 October 1833, 9 November 1835, 10 November 1835, 29 December 1835, 29 January 1843,12 February 1843, 21 February 1843, 3 April 1843, 7 April 1843, 10 March 1844, 13 March 1844, and 6 May 1944. Matthias or Joshua, the Jewish priestly name by which Matthias called himself when he visited Smith and spoke with him about Christian theology, had predicted the destruction of Albany, New York and had been tried for murder. For a somewhat reductive account of the Matthias "cult" see Paul Johnson and Sean Wilentz, *The Kingdom of Matthias: A Story of Sex and Salvation in 19th-Century America* (New York: Oxford University Press, 1995).

All of this, of course, raises issues of identity construction and ethnocentrism. Identity groups, in general, tend to believe themselves to be superior to those they mark themselves off against. In marking themselves off from others they draw from a menu of binary oppositions and similarities in which their own superiority (in good ethnocentric manner) is marked off against the other. For an interesting attempt to ground anti-Semitism in ethnocentrism and historical context see Frederic Cople Jaher, *A Scapegoat in the Wilderness: The Origins and Rise of Anti-Semitism in America* (Cambridge, MA: Harvard University Press, 1994).

32. According to Robert Fogerty ("Oneida: A Utopian Search for Religious Security," *Labor History* 14: 2 (Spring 1973), 206) Oneida converts included Congregationalists, Methodists, Baptists, Dutch Reformed, Millerite, Lutheran, Quaker, "Tobiasite," Universalist, and the Free Church of New Haven. According to David Rowe ("Millerites: A Shadow Portrait" in Ronald Numbers and Jonathan M. Butler (eds.), *The Disappointed: Millerism and Millenarianism in the Nineteenth-Century* (Bloomington: Indiana University Press, 1993), 8–9) Adventist converts included Methodists (forty-four percent), Baptists (twenty-seven percent), "Christianites" (nine percent), Presbyterians (seven percent), and a smattering of Dutch Reformed, Quakers, Episcopalians, and Lutherans.

33. On Joseph Smith's first vision see Richard Bushman, *Joseph Smith and the Beginnings of Mormonism* (Urbana: University of Illinois Press, 1988), 53–59 and Marvin Hill, "The First Vision: A Critique and Reconciliation," *Dialogue* 15 (Summer 1982), 31–46. The quotes are from Brigham Young *Journal of Discourses* III and VIII, Solomon Chamberlain; "Short Sketch" found in Larry Porter, "A Study of the Origins of the Church of Jesus Christ of Latter-Day Saints in the States of New York and Pennsylvania, 1816-1831" Ph.D. dissertation, Brigham Young University, 1971; Parley Pratt, *The Autobiography of Parley Pratt, One of the Twelve Apostles*, edited by Parley Pratt (Salt Lake City: Deseret, 1874); and Wilford Woodruff to Aphek Woodruff, 15 March 1834, copy of original in Aphek Woodruff Collection, LDS Archives (Woodruff would become the third Prophet and President of the Church).

34. Mark Grandstaff and Milton Backman, "The Social Origins of Kirtland Mormons"; *BYU Studies* 30:2 (1990), 57–63. The writings of Smith reveal how important important dreams and visions were in early Mormonism, Joseph Smith, *Personal Writings of Joseph Smith*, edited by Dean Jessee (Salt Lake City: Deseret, 1984), 63, 93, 94, 101–103, 104, 129–130, 163, 294–296, 662. Grant Underwood ("The Meaning and Attraction of Mormonism Reexamined" *Thetan* (March 1977), 1–15) and Steven Harper ("Infallible Proofs, Both Human and Divine: The Persuasiveness of Mormonism for Early Converts," *Religion and American Culture*, 10:1 (2000) 106–112) explore the role the Book of Mormon played in early Mormon missionary work and proselytization. Contemporary sources reveal how important the Book of Mormon, continuing revelation, dreams and visions, and Smith were for those seekers who converted to Mormonism. For the impact of these ideologies on believers see Joseph Holbrook, "Autobiography," typescript, Harold B. Lee Library (HBLL), Brigham Young University (BYU); Mary Pulsipher, "Autobiography, typescript, HBLL, BYU; Mary Lightner, "Autobiography," *Utah Genealogical and Historical Magazine*, 17 July 1926, 193–205; Sarah Studevant Leavitt, *History of S.S. Leavitt*, edited by Juanita C. Pulsipher, n.p., 1919; Bathsheba Wilson Bigler Smith, "Autobiography," typescript, HBLL, BYU; Ezra Taft Benson, "Autobiography," *The Instructor* 80, 145; John Lowe Butler, "Autobiography," typescript, HBLL, BYU; Harrison Burgess, "Autobiography" in Kenneth Glynn Hales

(ed. and comp.), *Windows: A Mormon Family* (Tucson: Skyline, 1985); Henry William Bigler, "Autobiography," typescript, HBLL, BYU; William Adams, "Autobiography," typescript, HBLL, BYU; Henry G. Boyle, "Autobiography," typescript, HBLL, BYU; Milo Andrus, "Autobiography," typescript, HBLL, BYU; Benjamin Brown, "Autobiography" in *Testimony for the Truth* (Liverpool: S.W. Richards, 1854); Thomas B. Marsh, *History of Thomas Baldwin Marsh by Himself*, Latter-day Saints *Millennial Star*, 29 (1864), 359–360, 375–376, 390–392, 406; Levi Hancock, "Autobiography," typescript, HBLL, BYU; Elizabeth Ann Whitney, "Biography" in Edward Tullidge, *The Women of Mormondom* (New York: Tullidge and Drandell, 1877), 32–35, 41–42; Phoebe W. Carter Woodruff, "Biography" in Edward Tullidge, *The Women of Mormondom* (New York: Tullidge and Crandall, 1877), 399–400, 411–414; Parley Pratt, "The Millennium" and "Letter to the Queen" in Pratt, *The Writings of Parley Parker Pratt* (Salt Lake City: Parker Pratt Robertson, 1952); Pratt, *Voice of Warning* (Salt Lake City: Hawkes Publishing, 1837); and Pratt, *Key to the Science of Theology* (Salem, UT: Pioneer Press, 1855). Pratt's books are among the earliest published explications and defense of LDS doctrine.

According to Grandstaff and Backman (Mark Grandstaff and Milton Backman; "The Social Origins of Kirtland Mormons"; *BYU Studies* 30:2 (1990), 47–66), Mormon converts came from the following religious communities: Methodist and Reformed Methodist (twenty-four percent), Presbyterian (eighteen percent), Baptist and Reformed Baptist (twenty-eight percent), Campbellite (three percent), Universalist (three percent), Dutch Reformed (three percent), Congregationalist (three percent), and Episcopal and Lutheran (one percent). However, the highest percentage were "unchurched" (twenty-seven percent). Documentary sources also indicate that Shakers and Quakers converted to Mormonism.

35. For Paul's claims of apostolic authority see *Galatians* 1:13–17.

36. Linda Woodhead, *An Introduction to Christianity* (Cambridge, UK: Cambridge University Press, 2004), 133 (Joachim); Robert Scribner, *The German Reformation* (London: Macmillan, 1986), 4 (Luther as *reformator*); David Durnbaugh, "Communitarian Societies in Colonial America" in Donald Pitzer (ed.), *America's Communal Utopias* (Chapel Hill: University of North Carolina Press, 1997), 23 (Muntzer); Ben Pink Dandelion, *An Introduction to Quakerism* (Cambridge, UK: University of Cambridge Press, 2007), 18 (Quakers and revelations); Patricia Brewer, "The Shakers of Mother Ann Lee" in Donald Pitzer (ed.), *America's Communal Utopias* (Chapel Hill: University of North Carolina Press, 1997), 40 and 41 (Shaker revelation); Eugene Taylor, "Swedenborgianism" in Timothy Miller (ed.), *America's Alternative Religions* (Albany: State University of New York Press, 1995), 78 (Swedenborg); Jon Butler, *Awash in a Sea of Faith: Christianizing the American People* (Cambridge, MA: Harvard University Press, 1992), 222 and 238–239 (Garritson); Nathan Hatch, *The Democratization of American Christianity* (New Haven, CT: Yale University Press, 1989), 33 (Barlow); Shawn Michael Trimble, "Spiritualism and Channeling" in Timothy Miller (ed.) *America's Alternative Religions* (Albany: State University of New York Press, 1995), 332 (the Poughkeepsie Seer); and William John McIntyre, *Children of Peace* (Montreal and Kingston: McGill-Queen's University Press, 1994), 30–47 (Willson). The debate over proper authority and the foundation of this proper authority, by the way, was not only a Christian debate. Muhammad, the founder "prophet' of Islam, for instance, was believed by devotees, to have received revelations from Allah in the seventh-century. The Nineteenth-century Persian prophet Baha'u'llah claimed to be a messenger of God. Seneca charismatic leader Handsome Lake believed he was receiving communications from the divine.

37. The revelation on priesthood and priesthood structure can be found at Doctrine and Covenants 84 (September 1832).

38. On the Book of Mormon see Terryl Givens, *The Book of Mormon: A Very Short Introduction* (New York: Oxford University Press, 2009); Givens, *By the Hand of Mormon: The American Scripture that Launched a New World Religion* (New York: Oxford University Press, 2002); B.H. Roberts, *Studies of the Book of Mormon*, 2d. ed. (Salt Lake City: Signature, 1992); and Dan Vogel (ed.),

The Word of God: Essays on Mormon Scriptures (Salt Lake City: Signature, 1990). For the Spaulding manuscript see Solomon Spaulding, *The Complete Original Spaulding Manuscript Found*, edited by Kent Jackson (Provo, UT: Religious Studies Center, BYU, 1996). On the Spaulding hypothesis see Lester Bush, "The Spaulding Theory Then and Now"; *Dialogue* 10:4 (Autumn 1977), 40–69. For years Spaulding's tale of ancient peoples in the new world was thought lost. It was rediscovered in Honolulu in 1884. With its rediscovery it became clear, given the differences between the Book of Mormon and the Spaulding manuscript, that the claim that Smith borrowed from the Spaulding manuscript when writing the Book of Mormon was false.

39. For the *View of the Hebrews* see Ethan Smith, *View of the Hebrews*, edited by Charles Tate (Provo, UT: BYU Religious Studies Center, 1825).

40. On Mormonism and Masonry see Dan Vogel, "Mormonism's 'Anti-Masonic Bible,'" *John Whitmer Historical Society Journal* 9 (1989), 17–30; Vogel, "Echoes of Anti-Masonry: A Rejoinder to Critics of the Anti-Masonic Thesis" in Vogel and Brent Lee Metcalfe (eds.), *American Apocalypse: Essays in the Book of Mormon* (Salt Lake City: Signature, 2002), 275–320; Clyde Forsberg, *Equal Rites: The Book of Mormon, Masonry, Gender, and American Culture* (New York: Columbia University Press, 2003); Forsberg, "By Study and Also by Blood: Mormonism, Masonry, Father Abraham, and Race," unpublished paper presented at the Mormon History Association Conference, Kirtland, Ohio, 2003; and Michael Homer, "'Similarity of Priesthood in Masonry': The Relationship Between Freemasonry and Mormonism" *Dialogue* 27 (Fall 1994), 1–113. The following Book of Mormon passages are often cited as evidence of Smith's early opposition to Masonry: *Helaman* 6:24ff (where the Gadiantons are Masons), 8:28, 11:10, *3 Nephi* 6:29 and 9:8, *Mormon* 8:27ff, and *Ether* 8:18.

Not everyone agrees that the nineteenth-century environment is crucial to understanding the Book of Mormon. For the argument that the Book of Mormon is an ancient document see Richard Bushman *Joseph Smith: Rough Stone Rolling* (New York: Knopf, 2005) 65–66; Noel Reynolds (ed.), *Book of Mormon Authorship* (Provo, UT: BYU Religious Studies Center, 1982); Reynolds (ed.), *Book of Mormon Authorship Revisited: The Evidence for Ancient Origins* (Provo: FARMS, 1997). On Book of Mormon archaeology see Hugh Nibley, *Lehi in the Desert/The World of the Jaredites/They Were the Jaredites* (Provo, UT: FARMS, 1988); Nibley, *An Approach to the Book of Mormon* (Provo, UT: FARMS, 1988); Nibley, *Since Cumorah*, 2d. ed. (Provo, UT: FARMS, 1988); and John Sorenson, *An Ancient American Setting for the Book of Mormon* (Provo, UT: FARMS, 1985). On Zelph, a "white Nephite" found by Smith and a group of Saints in a native mound in Missouri during Zion's March, see Kenneth Godfrey, "The Zelph Story" *BYU Studies* 29:2 (Spring 1989), 32–56 and B.H. Roberts (ed.), *Documentary History of the Church of Jesus Christ of Latter-day Saints (DHC)*, volume 2 (Salt Lake: Deseret News, 1904), 115–116. For work that is critical of this ancient hypothesis see Brent Metcalfe (ed.), *New Approaches to the Book of Mormon* (Salt Lake City: Signature, 1993) and Dan Vogel and Metcalfe (eds.), *American Apocalypse: Essays on the Book of Mormon* (Salt Lake City: Signature, 2002). On mnemonic devices in oral literature see Alfred Lord, *The Singer of Tales* (Cambridge, MA: Harvard University Press, 1960) and Moses Finley, *The World of Odysseus* (Harmondsworth, UK: Penguin, 1979). On chiasms see John Welch, *Chiasmus in Antiquity* (Provo, UT: Utah Research Press, 1999). On literary and narrative chiasms see Max Nänny, "Chiasmus in Literature: Ornament of Function?" *Word and Image* 4 (January-March 1988), 51–59. Analysts over the years claim to have found chiasms in Ovid, Shakespeare, Carlos Fuentes, Frederick Douglas, Herman Melville, and James Joyce to name just a few.

41. Alexander Campbell, "Delusions," *Millennial Harbinger*, 7 February 1831.

42. Ernest Lee Tuveson, *Redeemer Nation: The Idea of America's Millennial Role* (Chicago: University of Chicago Press, 1968) and Yehoshua Arieli, *Individualism and Nationalism in American Ideology* (Baltimore, MD: Penguin, 1968).

43. Eric Hobsbawm and Terrence Ranger (eds.), *The Invention of Tradition* (Cambridge, UK: Cambridge University Press, 1983); Robert Gildea, *Barricades and Borders: Europe 1800–1914*, 2d. ed. (New York: Oxford University Press, 1996);

Yehoshua Arieli, *Individualism and Nationalism in American Ideology* (Baltimore, MD: Penguin, 1968); Michael Rogin, *Ronald Reagan, the Movie and Other Episodes in Political Demonology* (Berkeley: University of California Press, 1987); Richard Drinnon, *Facing West: The Metaphysics of Indian Hatred and Empire Building* (New York: Schocken, 1980); Thomas Gossett, *Race: The History of an Idea in America* (New York: Schocken, 1965); Roy Billington, *The Protestant Crusade: A Study in the Origins of American Nativism, 1800-1860* (Chicago: Quadrangle, 1952); and John Higham, *Strangers in the Land: Patterns of American Nativism, 1860-1925* (New York: Vintage, 1963).

44. Alexander Campbell, "Delusions," *Millennial Harbinger*, 7 February 1831. On Matthias see Paul Johnson and Sean Wilentz, *The Kingdom of Matthias: A Story of Sex and Salvation in 19th-Century America* (New York: Oxford University Press, 1995).

45. On the Children of Peace see William John McIntyre, *Children of Peace* (Montreal and Kingston, Ontario: McGill-Queens University Press, 1994).

46. On American Christian attempts to missionize the Jews see Yaakov S. Ariel, *Evangelizing the Chosen People: Missions to the Jews in America, 1880-2000* (Chapel Hill: University of North Carolina Press, 1999).

47. On Noah see Jonathan Sarna, *Jacksonian Jew: The Two Worlds of Mordecai Manuel Noah* (New York: Holmes and Meier, 1981). For an example of Noah's writing itself see Mordecai Noah, *Discourse on the Restoration of the Jews* (New York: Harper and Brothers, 1845). On Puritan views of Israel see Peter Toon (ed.), *Puritans, the Millennium and the Future of Israel: Puritan Eschatology 1600 to 1660*, new edition (Cambridge, UK: James Clarke, 2002).

48. *The Latter-day Saints Messenger and Advocate* Volume 2, Number 3 (1835) *DHC* Vol. II, p. 351.

49. Mordecai Noah, *Discourse on the Restoration of the Jews* (New York: Harper and Brothers, 1945) and Mordecai Noah, *Discourse on the Evidences on the American Indians Being the Descendants of the Lost Tribes of Israel* (New York: James Van Noorden, 1837).

50. Biblical references to Mormon Zionism and Mormon Davidic kingship include *Isaiah* 11:1, 10, *Hosea* 3:5, *Jeremiah* 30:9, *Ezekiel* 34:23–24, *Isaiah* 2:2, *Joseph Smith Translation (JST) Genesis* 50:26–33, and *Nephi* 3:6-15. On controversies in prophetic succession in Mormonism see D. Michael Quinn, "The Mormon Succession Crisis of 1844," *BYU Studies* 16: 2, 187–234; Quinn, *The Mormon Hierarchy: The Origins of Power* (Salt Lake City: Signature, 1994), and Quinn, *The Mormon Hierarchy: Extensions of Power* (Salt Lake City: Signature, 1997).

51. Mordecai Noah, *Discourse on the Evidences on the American Indians Being the Descendants of the Lost Tribes of Israel* (New York: James Van Noorden, 1837).

52. David Brion Davis, "The New England Origins of Mormonism," *New England Quarterly* XXVI (June 1953), 143–168; Rex Cooper, *Promises Made to the Fathers: Mormon Covenant Organization* (Salt Lake City: University of Utah Press, 1990); Donald Meinig, *The Shaping of America: A Geographical Perspective on 500 Years of History, Volume 3: Transcontinental America, 1850-1915* (New Haven, CT: Yale University Press, 1998). 89–112; Rowland Berthoff, *An Unsettled People: Social Order and Disorder in American History* (New York: Harper and Row, 1971), 247–250); and Marvin Hill, "The Shaping of the Mormon Mind in New England and New York" *BYU Studies* 9 (Spring 1989), 351–372. David Hall's historiographic essay on Puritanism ("Narrating Puritanism") in Stout and Hart's edited collection *New Directions in American Religious History* (New York: Oxford University Press, 1997), is an excellent state of the art introduction to controversies surrounding Puritanism and its theological and experiential aspects.

53. Edmund Morgan, *The Puritan Family: Religion and Domestic Relations in Seventeenth-Century New England*, revised edition (New York: Harper and Row, 1966).

54. Whitney Cross, *The Burned-Over District: The Social and Intellectual History of Enthusiastic Religion in Western New York, 1800-1850* (New York: Harper and Row, 1950), particularly Chapter Eight, and Mark Grandstaff and Milton Backman, "The Social Origins of Kirtland Mormons"; *BYU Studies* 30:2 (1990), 47–66.

55. Val Rust, "Mormonism and the Radical Religious Movement in Colonial New England," *Dialogue* 33:1 (Spring 2000), 23–55. Rust's bases his analysis on direct line ancestral sources of 1,583 individuals

who converted to Mormonism prior to 1835.

56. Richard Bushman, *Joseph Smith: Rough Stone Rolling* (New York: Knopf, 2005), 37, 17, 25, 199–200.

57. William Ellery Channing, *Unitarian Christianity and Other Essays*, edited by Irving Bartlett (Indianapolis: Bobbs-Merrill, 1957). The Smith quote is from his King Follett Discourse printed in *Times and Seasons*, 5 (15 August 1844), 612–17.

58. D. Michael Quinn, *The Mormon Hierarchy: The Origins of Power* (Salt Lake City: Signature, 1994).

59. Robert Paul, *Science, Religion, and Mormon Cosmology* (Urbana: University of Illinois Press, 1992), 75–126; Paul, "Joseph Smith and the Plurality of Worlds Idea" *Dialogue* 19:2 (Summer 1986), 15–36; and Klaus Hansen, *Mormonism and the American Experience* (Chicago: University of Chicago Press, 1981).

60. David Hall, "Narrating Puritanism" in Harry Stout and D.G. Hart; *New Directions in American Religious History* (New York: Oxford University Press, 1997), 51–83.

61. Doctrine and Covenants 22.

62. On the celestial, terrestrial, and telestial kingdoms see Doctrine and Covenants 76. Smith justified this conception of the afterlife by referencing the Bible, especially I Corinthians.

63. On power in primitive Mormonism see D. Michael Quinn, *The Mormon Hierarchy: The Origins of Power* (Salt Lake City: Signature, 1994) and Quinn, *The Mormon Hierarchy: Extensions of Power* (Salt Lake City: Signature, 1997).

64. Mormon baptisms for the dead, with their conception that human consciousness continues in the afterlife, and the Mormon conception that marriage can continue "beyond the veil," share much with Spiritualist conceptions of the dead, Spiritualist proxy marriages for the dead, and popular cultural conceptions of the afterlife. On this see Colleen McDannel and Bernhard Lang, *Heaven: A History* (New Haven, CT: Yale University Press, 1995), 313–322. Revelations related to baptism of the dead can be found in Doctrine and Covenants 124 (1841) and 128 (1842). On the biblical justification of baptism for the dead see, for example, *1 Corinthians*: 15:29 and 1 Peter 3:19. Baptisms for the dead were also grounded in a universalist view of human salvation that had much in common with arminian varieties of Anglo-American Christianity such as Finney's Presbyterianism, Noyes's Oneida Community, and Hosea Ballou's Universalism. Smith believed that all but a few could be "saved."

65. William McLellin, *The Journals of William E. McLellin, 1831-1836*, edited by Jan Shipps and John Welch (Urbana: University of Illinois Press, 1994) and Shipps, "Thoughts about the Academic Community's Response to John Brooke's *Refiner's Fire*" in Shipps, *Sojourner in the Promised Land: Forty Years Among the Mormons* (Urbana: University of Illinois Press, 2000), 204–218. Biblical references can be found throughout McLellin's journals. For examples see pages. 14, 15, 16, 17, 18, 25, 54 123, 124, 157, 158, 161, 179, 180, 202, and 204. For examples of Biblical references and exegesis in Smith's Journals see pages 266, 305, 340, 349, 356, 357, and 541 in Joseph Smith, *An American Prophet's Record: The Diaries and Journals of Joseph Smith*, edited by Scott Faulring (Salt Lake City: Signature, 1987).

66. Dickson Bruce, *And They All Sang Hallelujah: Plain Folk Camp Meeting Religion, 1800-1845* (Knoxville: University of Tennessee Press, 1974), 61–95 and Victor Turner, "Betwixt and Between: The Liminal Period in Rites of Passage" in Victor Turner, *The Forest of Symbols* (Ithaca, NY: Cornell University Press, 1967), 93–111. On the Mormon conception of Zion see Dean May, "Rites of Passage: The Gathering as Cultural Credo," *Journal of Mormon History* 29:1 (Spring 2003), 1–41.

67. R. Laurence Moore, *Religious Outsiders and the Making of Americans* (New York: Oxford University Press, 1986). The problem with Moore's book, as Robert Wiebe (*Who We Are: A History of Popular Nationalism* (Princeton, NJ: Princeton University Press, 2002), 88–92) notes, is that he seems to assert that Mormon distinctives were the inventions of Smith whose sole purpose in manufacturing them was to give rise to a distinctive Mormon identity formed through the crucible of persecution. This perspective ignores the critical role Biblicism and other Christian ideologies (rather than persecution) played in Smith's construction of Mormon culture and the issue of why some "Gentiles" persecuted Mormons.

68. On Mormon Israelitism see Jan Shipps, *Mormonism: The Story of a New Religious Tradition* (Urbana: University of Illinois Press, 1985), 38; Melodie Moench Charles, "Nineteenth-Century Mormons: The New Israel," *Dialogue* 12:1 (Spring 1979), 42–54; and Donald Meinig, *The Shaping of America: A Geographical Perspective on 500 Years of History, Volume 3: Transcontinental America, 1850–1915* (New Haven, CT: Yale University Press, 1998), 96 and 104.

69. On key symbols see Clifford Geertz, *The Interpretation of Cultures: Selected Essays* (New York: Basic Books, 1973), particularly Chapter Fifteen, "Deep Play: Notes on the Balinese Cockfight," pages 435–474, and Sherry Ortner, "On Key Symbols," *American Anthropologist*, 75:5, October 1973, 1338–1346.

70. Paul Conkin, *American Originals: Homemade Varieties of Christianity* (Chapel Hill: University of North Carolina Press, 1997), vii–xv; David Hall, *Worlds of Wonder, Days of Judgment: Popular Religious Belief in New England* (Cambridge, MA: Harvard University Press, 1990), 8–10; and Jon Butler, *Awash in a Sea of Faith: Christianizing the American People* (New Haven, CT: Yale University Press 1992), 7–36. For an excellent history of Christian culture and its ideologies see Linda Woodhead, *An Introduction to Christianity* (Cambridge, UK: Cambridge University Press, 2004).

71. Max Weber, *Economy and Society: An Outline of Interpretive Sociology* (Berkeley: University of California Press, two volumes, 1968), 399–634 and 1111–1157.

72. Linda Woodhead, *An Introduction to Christianity* (Cambridge, UK: Cambridge University Press, 2004); John Higham, "Ethnicity and American Protestantism: Collective Identity in the Mainstream" in Harry Stout and D.G. Hart, *New Directions in American Religious History* (New York: Oxford University Press, 1997), 239–259; Mark Noll, "Protestant Reasoning About Money and Economics, 1790–1860" in Noll (ed.), *God and Mammon: Protestants, Money, and the Markets, 1790–1860* (New York: Oxford University Press, 2001), 265–295; and Daniel Walker Howe, "Protestantism, Voluntarism, and Personal Identity in Antebellum America" in Stout and Hart (eds.), *New Directions in American Religious History* (New York: Oxford University Press, 1997), 206–238. Howe emphasizes the important role culture and doctrinal discussions and debates played in Antebellum America. These were all part of the popular intellectual culture of Biblicism in Jacksonian America.

73. As several scholars have recognized, the protestantization of the West was a long process that began before the Reformation and stretches into the seventeenth, eighteenth, nineteenth, twentieth, and twenty-first centuries. On this see Christopher Haigh, *English Reformations: Religion, Politics, and Society under the Tudors* (New York: Oxford University Press, 1993). Susan Juster (Juster, "The Spirit and the Flesh: Gender, Language, and Sexuality in American Protestantism" in Harry Stout and D.G. Hart [eds.], *New Directions in American Religious History* [New York: Oxford University Press, 1997], 334–361), emphasizes the role marginality, particularly gender and racial marginality, has played in American history. Sectarianization, it should be noted, is not a monopoly of religious groups. As Greil Marcus's *Lipstick Traces: A Secret History of the Twentieth Century* (Cambridge, MA: Harvard University Press, 1990) shows, sectarian subcultural and countercultural movements beyond the sphere of religion have existed throughout history. So have other groups whose *raison d'etre* seems more political and economic. History, for example, is littered with the attempts of socialists to recover the spirit and form of the golden days of the past, with the attempts of economists to find that one interpretive key to economic truth, and American presidents who promise to return America to its past glories.

74. Anthony F.C. Wallace, *Culture and Personality* (New York: Random House, 1961).

75. William McLoughlin, *Revivals, Awakenings, and Reform* (Chicago: University of Chicago Press, 1980) and Victor Turner, "Liminal to Liminoid, in Play, Flow, and Ritual: An Essay in Comparative Symbology," *Rice University Studies* 60 (Summer 1974), 53–92.

76. On Christian worldviews and ideologies see Linda Woodhead, *An Introduction to Christianity* (Cambridge, UK: Cambridge University Press, 2004). On the Reformation see Robert Scribner, *The German Reformation* (Basingstoke, UK: Macmillan, 1986)

and Patrick Collinson, *The Reformation: A History* (London: Phoenix, 2003). On the Reformation as Christianization see Scott Hendrix, *Recultivating the Vineyard: The Reformation Agendas of Christianization* (Louisville, KY: Westminster John Knox, 2004). Dissent within Christian culture did not, of course, begin with the Reformation, Martin Luther, or Jean Calvin. On early forms of religious dissent in Europe see R.I. Moore, *The Origins of European Dissent* (Toronto: University of Toronto Press, 1994) and his *The Formation of a Persecuting Society: Power and Deviance in Western Europe, 950-1250* (Oxford, UK: Blackwell, 1987). I (obviously) wouldn't subscribe to Moore's thesis that European dissent is reducible to social anxieties and frustrations. The European Reformation had its antecedents and foreshadowing in European Humanism, Lollardy, and the Hussite Movement. On this see Robert Scribner; "A Comparative Overview" in Robert Scribner, Roy Porter, and Mikulas Teich (eds.), *The Reformation in National Context* (Cambridge, UK: Cambridge University Press, 1994), 217 and 225 and Patrick Collinson, "England" in Scribner, Roy Porter, and Mikulas Teich (eds.), *The Reformation in National Context* (Cambridge, UK: Cambridge University Press, 1994), 85-86.

77. My formulation of the contradictions inherent in the Enlightenment has been influenced by Tony Judt, *Past Imperfect: French Intellectuals, 1944-1956* (Berkeley: University of California Press, 1992) and Francois Furet, *The Passing of an Illusion: The Idea of Communism in the Twentieth Century* (Chicago: University of Chicago Press, 1999), 1-33. Furet notes that so much of the dynamics of the Enlightenment were the product of the contradiction between an Enlightenment emphasis on individual freedom, on the one hand, and equality, on the other. The emphasis by some on individual freedom, he points out, led to inequalities which those committed to equality (ideology creating activism) such as Socialists, Anarchists, and Marxists, reacted against and attempted to heal. In this formulation, liberals, of both the libertarian and social varieties, Socialists, Anarchists, and Marxists, are all part of the same Enlightenment cultural and ideological fraternity and sorority.

78. Mark Grandstaff and Milton Backman, "The Social Origins of Kirtland Mormons"; *BYU Studies* 30:2 (1990), 47-66. For an interesting attempt to explore the geographical and cultural background of North American British groups each of whom, it is claimed, were heavily influenced by their religious ideologies see David Hackett Fischer, *Albion's Seed: Four British Folkways in America* (New York: Oxford University Press, 1989).

79. On religious outsiders in the United States see R. Laurence Moore, *Religious Outsiders and the Making of Americans* (New York: Oxford University Press, 1986).

Chapter Seven

1. Patricia Lynn Scott, James E. Crooks, and Sharon G. Pugsley: "'A Kinship of Interest': The Mormon History Association's Membership," *Journal of Mormon History* 18:1 (Spring 1992), 158-159.

2. Scott Kenney, "E.E. Ericksen-Loyal Heretic," *Sunstone* 3 (July-August 1978), 20.

3. On the controversies surrounding Lowry Nelson see Ronald W. Walker, David J. Whittaker, and James B. Allen, *Mormon History* (Urbana: University of Illinois, 2000), 41 and 54 (note 30).

4. The ban on Blacks in the priesthood was overturned in 1978 by a revelation received by then Church President Spencer W. Kimball. On issues surrounding Blacks and Mormonism see Lester Bush and Armand Mauss (eds.), *Neither Black Nor White: Mormon Scholars Confront the Race Issue in a Universal Church* (Salt Lake City: Signature, 1984) particularly Bush's long essay in the book "Mormonism's Negro Doctrine: A Historical Overview." The race issue is a complicated one in Mormonism. Though the Book of Mormon notes that the sinful Lamanites were cursed by God with a skin of blackness (II Nephi 5:21), it also preached, drawing on Saint Paul (Galatians 3:28), that the Lord "denieth none that come unto him, black and white, bond and free, male and female" (II Nephi 26:33), and three Black males, Elijah Abel, Joseph Ball, and Walker Lewis, were members of the Mormon priesthood before Smith's assassination.

5. Fawn McKay Brodie, An Oral History Interview" *Dialogue* 14 (Summer 1981), 100 and 106. On Arrington's essay on the Word of Wisdom see Gary Bergera

and Ronald Priddis, *Brigham Young University: A House of Faith* (Salt Lake: Signature, 1985) p. 87. Arrington's offending article, titled "The Economic Aspects of the Word of Wisdom" was published in the Winter 1959 issue of *BYU Studies* on pages 37–49.

6. Patricia Lynn Scott, James E. Crooks, and Sharon G. Pugsley, "'A Kinship of Interest': The Mormon History Association's Membership," *Journal of Mormon History* 18:1 (Spring 1992), 158–159. The results of the *Dialogue* survey can be found in Armand L. Mauss, John R. Tarjan, and Martha D. Esplin, "The Unfettered Faithful: An Analysis of the Dialogue Subscribers Survey," *Dialogue* 20 (Spring 1987), p. 28. On "outsiders" and outsider insiders in Mormon Studies see Jan Shipps, "An 'Insider-Outsider' in Zion," *Dialogue* 15:1 (Spring 1982), 138-161 and Lawrence Foster, "A Personal Odyssey: My Encounter with Mormon History," *Dialogue* 16 (Autumn 1983), 87-98.

7. I am drawing, in part, on conversations and interviews I had with many of the participants in the Mormon intellectual culture war and several LDS observers of this culture war. These conversations and interviews were conducted between 1991 and 1994 and 2000 and included interviews with D. Michael Quinn, David Knowlton, Paul Toscano, Margaret Toscano, John Clark, Lynn England, Larry Young, and Louis Midgley.

8. On the Church Historical Division and the controversies surrounding Arrington's "calling" as Church Historian see William Hartley, "The Founding of the LDS Church Historical Division, 1972," *Journal of Mormon History* 18 (Fall 1992), 41–47; Arrington, *Adventures of a Church Historian* (Urbana: University of Illinois Press, 1998), Chapters 5 through 14; Davis Bitton, "Ten Years in Camelot: A Personal Memoir," *Dialogue* 16 (Autumn 1983), 9–33; Ronald W. Walker, David K. Whittaker, and James B. Allen, *Mormon History* (Urbana: University of Illinois Press, 2000), 64–68; Jan Shipps, *Mormonism: The Story of a New Religious Tradition* (Urbana: University of Illinois Press, 1985), 88–91; and Shipps: "Gentiles, Mormons, and the History of the American West" in Shipps, *Sojourner in the Promised Land: Forty Years Among the Mormons* (Urbana: University of Illinois Press, 2000), 26–33.

9. Jan Shipps, "Gentiles, Mormons, and the History of the American West" in Shipps, *Sojourner in the Promised Land: Forty Years Among the Mormons* (Urbana: University of Illinois Press, 2000), 24.

10. Ronald W. Walker, David J. Whittaker, and James B. Allen, *Mormon History* (Urbana: University of Illinois Press, 2000), 98.

11. Ronald W. Walker, David J. Whittaker, and James B. Allen, *Mormon History* (Urbana: University of Illinois Press, 2000), 66-67.

12. According to Jan Shipps *Story* sold 10,000 copies in its first week, Shipps, "Gentiles, Mormons, and the History of the American West" in Shipps, *Sojourner in a Promised Land: Forty Years Among the Mormons* (Urbana: University of Illinois Press, 2000), p. 33.

13. Deseret eventually published a second edition of *Story* in 1992.

14. Ezra Taft Benson, *The Gospel Teacher and His Message*, Address to CES Religious Educators, 17 September 1976, Temple Square Assembly Hall (Salt Lake City[?]: Intellectual Reserve, 1976), 1–9, especially 4 and 5, and Boyd K. Packer, "The Mantle Is Far, Far Greater Than the Intellect," *BYU Studies* 21 (Summer 1981), 259–271, especially p. 268.

15. On the *Building of the City of God* controversy see Leonard Arrington, *Adventures of a Church Historian* (Urbana: University of Illinois Press, 1998), 150–153. *Building* was republished by the University of Illinois Press in 1992. On the history of Mormon politics, right wingism, and anti-communism see Gregory A. Prince, "The Red Peril, the Candy Maker, and the Apostle: David O. McKay's Confrontation with Communism, *Dialogue* 37:2 (summer 2004), 37–94; D. Michael Quinn, "Ezra Taft Benson and Mormon Political Conflicts," *Dialogue* 26:2 (summer 1993), 1–87; Alexander Zaitchik, "Meet the Man Who Changed Glenn Beck's Life" *Salon*, 16 Sept 2009 (available online); Neil J. Young, "'The ERA Is a Moral Issue': The Mormon Church, LDS Women, and the Defeat of the Equal Rights Amendment," *American Quarterly* 59: 3 (September 2007), 623–644; and O. Kendall White, "Mormonism and the Equal Rights Amendment," *Journal of Church and State* 31:2 (1989), 249–267.

16. Ronald W. Walker, David J.

Whittaker, and James B. Allen, *Mormon History* (Urbana: University of Illinois Press, 2000), p. 68 and Jan Shipps, *Mormonism: The Story of a New Religious Tradition* (Urbana: University of Illinois Press, 1985), 89.

17. Jan Shipps, "Gentiles, Mormons, and the History of the American West" in Shipps, *Sojourner in a Promised Land: Forty Years Among the Mormons* (Urbana: University of Illinois Press, 2000), 27.

18. Armand Mauss, *The Angel and the Beehive: The Mormon Struggle with Assimilation* (Urbana: University of Illinois Press, 1994).

19. Jan Shipps, "Gentiles, Mormons, and the History of the American West" in Shipps, *Sojourner in a Promised Land: Forty Years Among the Mormons* (Urbana: University of Illinois Press, 2000), 32.

20. On the culture wars over history see Gary Nash, Charlotte Crabtree, and Ross Dunn, *History on Trial: Culture Wars and the Teaching of the Past* (New York: Knopf, 1997).

21. On the conflation of New Mormon Studies scholars, apostates, and anti-Mormons see the paper of one prominent FARMS member and BYU academic Daniel Peterson, "Reflections on Secular Anti-Mormonism" at the FAIR website.

22. For essays arguing for and against the new Mormon faith history see George Smith (ed.), *Faithful History: Essays on Writing Mormon History* (Salt Lake City: Signature, 1992). For critiques of the New Mormon Studies see Louis Midgley, "The Acids of Modernity and the Crisis in Mormon Historiography" in George Smith (ed.), *Faithful History: Essays on Writing Mormon History* (Salt Lake City: Signature, 1992), 189-226; Midgley, "The Challenge of Historical Consciousness and the Encounter with Secular Modernity" in John M. Lindquist and Stephen D. Ricks (eds.), *By Study and Also By Faith: Essays in Honor of Hugh Nibley*, volume 2 (Provo, UT: FARMS, 1990), 502-551; David Bohn, "Unfounded Claims and Impossible Expectations: A Critique of New Mormon History" in Smith (ed.), *Faithful History: Essays on Writing Mormon History* (Salt Lake City: Signature, 1992), 227-261; Bohn, "Our Own Agenda: A Critique of the Methodology of the New Mormon History," *Sunstone* 14 (June 1990), 45-49; Bohn, "No Higher Ground: Objective History is an Elusive Chimera," *Sunstone* 8 (May-June 1983), 26-32; and Gary Novak, "Naturalistic Claims and the Book of Mormon," *BYU Studies* 30 (Summer 1990), 23-40.

23. For an interesting critical biography of Shipps by two Mormon sociologists see Gordon and Gary Shepherd, *Jan Shipps: A Social and Intellectual Portrait* (Salt Lake City: Greg Kofford Books, 2019).

24. Richard Bushman, *Joseph Smith: Rough Stone Rolling* (New York: Knopf, 2005) and Terryl Givens, *By the Hand of Mormon: The American Scripture that Launched a New World Religion* (New York: Oxford University Press, 2002).

25. For FARMS approaches to early Mormonism see Noel B Reynolds (ed.), *Book of Mormon Authorship Revisited: The Evidence for Ancient Origins* (Provo, UT: Foundation for Ancient Research and Mormon Studies, 1997); John Welch, "Chiasmus in the Book of Mormon," *BYU Studies* 10: 3 (1969), pp. 69-83; and John Sorenson, *An Ancient American Setting for the Book of Mormon* (Provo, UT: FARMS, 1985).

26. On the fundamentalist controversy see Norman Furniss, *The Fundamentalist Controversy, 1918-1931* (New Haven, CT: Yale University Press, 1963).

27. D. Michael Quinn, *J. Reuben Clark: The Church Years* (Provo, UT: Brigham Young University Press, 1983); Quinn, "LDS Church Authorities and New Plural Marriages, 1890-1904," *Dialogue* 18:1 (Spring 1985), 9-105; and Quinn, *Early Mormonism and the Magic Worldview* (Salt Lake City: Signature, 1987).

28. D. Michael Quinn, "On Being a Mormon Historian," BYU Student History Association Lecture, Fall 1981. Quinn's talk, with an added afterward, can also be found in George Smith (ed.), *Faithful History: Essays on Writing Mormon History* (Salt Lake City: Signature, 1992) 69-111.

29. D. Michael Quinn, "Mormon Women Have Had the Priesthood Since 1843," in Maxine Hanks (ed.), *Women and Authority: Re-emerging Mormon Feminism* (Salt Lake City: Signature, 1992), 365-410. On the excommunications see Lavina Fielding Anderson, "The LDS Intellectual Community and Church Leadership: A Contemporary Chronology." *Dialogue* 26:1 (Spring 1993), 7-64. On Quinn see Lavina Fielding Anderson, "DNA Mormon: D.

Michael Quinn" in John Sillitoe and Susan Staker (eds.), *Mormon Mavericks: Essays on Dissenters* (Salt Lake City: Signature Books, 2002) 329–363. Discussions of Church Authority concerns over feminism in the Church and Mormon women praying to Mother in Heaven can be found in Lavina Fielding Anderson, "The LDS Intellectual Community and Church Leadership: A Contemporary Chronology." *Dialogue* 26:1 (Spring 1993), 31–32, 35–36, 39–40, 49, and 66. On Church Authority responses to Mormon feminism, Mormon writing on Mother in Heaven, and Mormon praying to Mother in Heaven see Gordon B. Hinckley, "Daughters of God," *Ensign*, November 1991, 98–100. This speech was delivered at the LDS General Women's Conference in October of 1991. In 1992 Loren C. Dunn, a member of the Church's First Council, ordered quotations from Joseph Smith, Bathsheba Smith, and Eliza R. Snow removed from a sesquicentennial exhibit at the LDS Museum of Church History because they referred to women as "queens and priestesses." He defended his actions saying that he did this because the quotations were "too sacred" to be placed on public view, "Relief Society Exhibit Censure," *Sunstone* 16 (February 1992), 66.

30. D. Michael Quinn, *Same Sex Dynamics Among Nineteenth-Century Americans: A Mormon Example* (Urbana: University of Illinois Press, 2001).

31. Official Church pronouncements and publications, including in official Church guides issued to Ward Bishops, have, on a number of occasions, condemned homosexuality as sinful. One of the most prominent is Apostle Boyd K. Packer's, "To Young Men Only," a speech given to the General Conference Priesthood Session on 2 October 1976. This speech was later published by the Church and circulated quite widely in the Church.

32. Louis Midgley, Letter to Sandra Tanner, 2 July 1997.

33. Daniel Golden, "In Religion Studies, Universities Bend to Views of Faithful: Scholar of Mormon History, Expelled from Church, Hits a Wall in Job Search," *Wall Street Journal*, A1, 6 April 2006.

For an analysis of the intellectual culture war in Mormonism since the advent of the New Mormon Studies see Lavina Fielding Anderson, "The LDS Intellectual Community and Church Leadership: A Contemporary Chronology." *Dialogue* 26:1 (Spring 1993), 7–64. On the controversies over academic freedom at BYU see Bryan Waterman and Brian Kagel, *The Lord's University: Freedom and Authority at BYU* (Salt Lake City: Signature, 1998). On the firings of Farr and Knowlton see "BYU Fires Two Controversial Faculty Members" *Sunstone*, July 1993, 74–77. On the firing of Nielsen see Todd Hollingshead, "BYU Fires Teacher Over Op-Ed Stance," *Salt Lake City Tribune*, 14 June 2006.

34. Lavina Fielding Anderson, "The LDS Intellectual Community and Church Leadership: A Contemporary Chronology." *Dialogue* 26:1 (Spring 1993), 28.

35. On the confiscation of Peck's temple recommend see Lavina Fielding Anderson, "The LDS Intellectual Community and Church Leadership: A Contemporary Chronology." *Dialogue* 26:1 (Spring 1993), 34.

36. On the history of *Sunstone* and the controversy over Sunstone symposia see Elbert Peck, "The Origin and Evolution of the Sunstone Species: 25 Years of Creative Adaptation," *Sunstone*, December 1999, 5–14. On the investigation of Sunstone and Sunstone symposia see Lavina Fielding Anderson, "The LDS Intellectual Community and Church Leadership: A Contemporary Chronology." *Dialogue* 26:1 (Spring 1993), 38. On the results of the *Sunstone* survey see Lavina Fielding Anderson, "The LDS Intellectual Community and Church Leadership: A Contemporary Chronology." *Dialogue* 26:1 (Spring 1993), 42. On academic freedom at BYU see Bryan Waterman and Brian Kagel, *The Lord's University: Freedom and Authority at BYU* (Salt Lake City: Signature, 1998), 177–202; "Statement on Academic Freedom at BYU, 14 September 1992; and Lavina Fielding Anderson, "The LDS Intellectual Community and Church Leadership: A Contemporary Chronology." *Dialogue* 26:1 (Spring 1993), 41–42. Church warnings against apostasy and symposia can be found in *Church Handbook of Instructions: Book 1, Stake Presidents and Bishoprics* (Salt Lake City: Church of Jesus Christ of Latter-day Saints, 1998), 95–95 and 153. The BYU Honor Code is a set of standards that students, faculty, and staff agree to abide by while at "the Y."

37. Peggy Fletcher Stack, "Despite Church Warnings, 1500 Attended Sunstone Symposia," *Salt Lake City Tribune*, 15 August 1992, A-5 and A-7.

38. D. Michael Quinn, *The Mormon Hierarchy: Extensions of Power* (Salt Lake City: Signature Books, 1997), p. 311. The existence of the Strengthening of Church Members Committee was revealed in a 1990 memo from General Authority Glen Pace that was leaked and published by the Tanners.' On the memo see Patty Henetz, "Church Evaluating Reports of Satanic Cults in Utah," [Salt Lake City] *Deseret News*, October 25, 1991, B1–B2. For an excellent article on Benson and political conflicts within the LDS Church between the 1950s and 1980s see D. Michael Quinn's "Ezra Taft Benson and Mormon Political Conflicts," *Dialogue* 26 (2, summer 1993), 1–87. Benson, who was secretary of agriculture under President Dwight D. Eisenhower, was a cold warrior and outspoken critic of communism and socialism and had ties to the John Birch Society though he was never a member. Some, of course, have seen a bit of McCarthyism in all of this.

39. Lavina Fielding Anderson, "The LDS Intellectual Community and Church Leaders: A Chronology," *Dialogue* 26 (1, spring 1993), 30 (Oaks), 64 (Hinckley). The Hinckley talk "Daughters of God" can be found in the Church magazine *Ensign*, 21 November 1991.

40. On the history of the Mormon concept of Mother in Heaven see Linda Wilcox, "The Mormon Concept of Mother in Heaven" in Maureen Ursenbach Beecher and Lavina Fielding Anderson (eds.), *Sisters in Spirit: Mormon Women in Historical and Cultural Perspective* (Urbana: University of Illinois Press, 1987), 64–77. The Mormon Women's Forum was founded in 1988 "to encourage open and honest discussion among people with diverse opinions and promotes gender equity and social justice in the context of the worldwide Mormon community" (Mormon Women's Forum webpage).

41. "Knowledge Alone is Not Enough, Apostle Says," *Deseret News*, 19 August 1992.

42. Lavina Fielding Anderson, "The LDS Intellectual Community and Church Leaders: A Chronology," *Dialogue* 26 (1, spring 1993), 51.

43. Lavina Fielding Anderson, "The LDS Intellectual Community and Church Leaders: A Chronology," *Dialogue* 26 (1, spring 1993), 55–56.

44. On the intellectual culture war in Mormonism over feminism see Jan Shipps, "Dangerous History: Laurel Thatcher Ulrich and Her Sisters" in Shipps, *Sojourner in a Promised Land: Forty Years Among the Mormons* (Urbana: University of Illinois Press, 2000), 193–203. On the founding of the Mormon Alliance see Peggy Fletcher Stack, "LDS Intelligentsia is Grouping to Fight Defamation," *Salt Lake City Tribune*, 27 June 1992, A-7.

45. Lavina Fielding Anderson, "The LDS Intellectual Community and Church Leadership: A Contemporary Chronology," *Dialogue* 26:1 (Spring 1993), 52–64; Maxine Hanks and D. Michael Quinn (eds.), *Women and Authority: Re-emerging Mormon Feminism* (Salt Lake City: Signature, 1992); Paul Toscano and Margaret Toscano, *Strangers in Paradox: Explorations in Mormon Theology* (Salt Lake City: Signature, 1990); and Avraham Gileadi, *The Last Days: Types and Shadows from the Bible and the Book of Mormon* (Salt Lake City: Deseret, 1991). Gileadi re-joined the Church in 1996 and was rebaptized in 1996 after all charges against him were expunged. Hanks rejoined the Church in 2012.

46. Lavina Fielding Anderson, "The LDS Intellectual Community and Church Leadership: A Contemporary Chronology," *Dialogue* 26:1 (Spring 1993), 36, 44 and 66; AAUP, Report: Academic Freedom and Tenure: Brigham Young University, *Academe*, September-October 1997, 52–71; Amanda Holpuch, "Mormon Church Excommunicates Kelly Over Women's Advocacy Work," *The Guardian*, 23 June 2014 (at *The Guardian* website), and Associated Press, Mormon Church Excommunicates Man Who Ran Forum for Doubting Members," *The Guardian*, 10 February 2015 (at *The Guardian* website).

47. The literature on the moderns or secularists versus traditionalists or fundamentalists culture wars is massive. For a brief overview see Malise Ruthven, *Fundamentalism: A Very Short Introduction* (Oxford, UK: Oxford University Press, 2007). Ruthven, rightly in my mind, links fundamentalisms, patriarchy, and nationalisms.

48. On the battles over Darwinism in

the UK and US see James R. Moore, *The Post-Darwinian Controversies: A Study of the Protestant Struggle to Come to Terms with Darwin in Great Britain and America, 1870-1900* (Cambridge, Eng: Cambridge University Press, 1979); Edward J. Larson, *Summer for the Gods: The Scopes Trial and America's Continuing Debate Over Science and Religion* (New York City: Basic Books, 1997); and Paul Conkin, *When All the Gods Trembled: Darwinism, Scopes, and American Intellectuals* (Lanham, MD: Rowman and Littlefield, 2001). On the battles over the Bible in Canada see Barry Mack, "Of Canadian Presbyterians and Guardian Angels" and David R. Elliott, "Knowing No Borders: Canadian Contributions to American Fundamentalism" both in George Rawlyk and Mark Noll (eds.), *Amazing Grace: Evangelicalism in Australia, Britain, Canada, and the United States* (Kingston, Ont and Montreal, Que: McGill-Queens University Press, 1995), particularly pages 279-280 and 355-359. On the battles over the Bible in the U.S. see Mark Noll, *A History of Christianity in the United States and Canada* (Grand Rapids: Eerdmans, 1992), 368-386. On the fundamentalist and modernist controversies within one American denomination see Bradley J. Longfield, *The Presbyterian Controversy: Fundamentalists, Modernists, and Moderates* (New York: Oxford University Press, 1991).

49. Charles S. Peterson, "Beyond the Problems of Exceptionalist History" in Thomas Alexander, *The Great Basin Kingdom Revisited* (Logan: Utah State University Press, 1991), 143-148. One might profitably explore Mormon exceptionalism as a variant of American exceptionalism.

50. For arguments for the New Mormon Studies see Robert Flanders, "Some Reflections on the New Mormon History," *Dialogue* 9 (Spring 1974), 35.

51. Leonard Arrington, "Scholarly Studies of Mormonism in the Twentieth-Century," *Dialogue* (Spring 1966), 28.

52. Leonard Arrington, *Adventures of a Church Historian* (Urbana: University of Illinois Press, 1998); Arrington, "Faith and Intellect as Partners in Mormon History" in "The Collected Leonard J. Arrington Mormon History Lectures" Special Collections & Archives, Utah State University Libraries, Logan, 2005; Richard Bushman, "My Faith" in Bushman, *Believing History: Latter-day Saint Essays* (New York: Columbia University Press, 2004), 20-29; and Bushman, "Faithful History" Dialogue 4 (Winter 1969), 16 and 25.

53. D. Michael Quinn's "testimony" about the truth of Mormonism and his "testimony" about the rightness of doing New Mormon history can be found in D. Michael Quinn, "On Being a Mormon Historian (and the Aftermath)" in George Smith (ed.), *Faithful History: Essays on Writing Mormon History* (Salt Lake City: Signature, 1992), 69-111, particularly p. 72-74. I am borrowing this description of Quinn's approach from Ronald W. Walker, David J. Whittaker, and James B. Allen, *Mormon History* (Urbana: University of Illinois Press, 200), 87.

54. Thomas Alexander, *Things in Heaven and Earth: The Life and Times of Wilford Woodruff* (Salt Lake City: Signature, 1991), Introduction.

55. Conversation between Ronald Helfrich and Louis Midgley, Provo, Utah, 1993.

56. Ronald W. Walker, David J. Whittaker, and James B. Allen, *Mormon History* (Urbana: University of Illinois Press, 2000), p. 93.

57. Thomas Alexander, "Historiography and the New Mormon History: A Historians Perspective," *Dialogue* 19 (Fall 1986), 25-49. For a discussion of the approach of Alexander and his critics see M. Gerald Bradford, "The Case of the New Mormon History: Thomas G. Alexander and His Critics," *Dialogue* 21 (Winter 1988), 143-150.

58. Richard Bushman, "Faithful History," *Dialogue* (Winter 1969), 16 and 25.

59. On the Short Creek raid see Martha Bradley, *Kidnapped from That Land: The Government Raids on the Short Creek Polygamists* (Salt Lake City: University of Utah Press, 1993). Interestingly, despite the anti-polygamy campaigns of the Church's enemies between the 1850s and early 1900s, Church growth was not hurt, probably, in large part, because Saints were "gathering to Zion" from overseas. The demise of Zionist rhetoric was likewise, in part, related to public relations concerns. However, like the supposed death of plural marriage, the demise of commanding Mormons to gather to Zion was more rhetorical than

actual since the draw of the Mormon culture region remains strong for many Mormons who live outside of it.

60. Leonard Arrington and Davis Bitton, *The Mormon Experience*, 2d. ed. (Urbana: University of Illinois Press, 1992), 199 and 204. Arrington and Bitton's analysis of Mormon polygamy can be found on pages 194 to 205. On Mormon plural marriage in general see R. Carmon Hardy, *Solemn Covenant: The Mormon Polygamous Passage* (Urbana: University of Illinois Press, 1992) and Kathleen Daynes, *More Wives than One: The Transformation of the Mormon Marriage System, 1840–1910* (Urbana: University of Illinois Press, 2001). Ironically, the Book of Mormon condemned plural marriage ("Jacob" 1:15, 2:24). On Mormon Fundamentalism and the Church campaign against Mormon fundamentalists see Martha Bradley, "Changed Faces: The Official LDS Position on Polygamy," *Sunstone* 14:1 (February 1990), 26–33; D. Michael Quinn, *Elder Statesman: A Biography of Reuben J. Clark* (Salt Lake City: Signature, 2002); Merrill Singer, "Nathaniel Baldwin, Utah Inventor and Patron of the Fundamentalist Movement," *Utah Historical Quarterly* 47:1 (Winter 1979), 42–53; Quinn, "Plural Marriage and Mormon Fundamentalism," *Dialogue* 31:2 (Summer 1998), 1–68; and Bradley, "The Women of Fundamentalism: Short Creek, 1953," *Dialogue* 23:2 (Summer 1990), 15–38.

61. Max Weber, *The Methodology of the Social Sciences* (New York: Free Press, 1949).

Bibliography

AAUP, Report: Academic Freedom and Tenure: Brigham Young University, Academe, September-October 1997.

AAUP, "Statement on Academic Freedom at BYU," 14 September 1992.

Abrams, Rhonda, "Letter to Richard Lindsay," 25 May 1984, FAIR.

Adams, Charles, and Gustave Larson, "A Study of the LDS Church Historians Office, 1830-1900," *Utah Historical Quarterly* 40 (Fall 1972), 370-389.

Adams, William, "Autobiography," typescript, Harold B. Lee Library (HBLL), Brigham Young University (BYU).

Ahlstrom, Sydney, *A Religious History of the American People* (New Haven, CT: Yale University Press, 1972).

Albanese, Catherine, *America: Religions and Religion*, 4th. ed. (Belmont, CA: Thomson, 2007).

Albrecht, Stan, "The Consequential Dimensions of Mormon Religiosity" in James T. Duke (ed.), *Latter-day Saint Social Life: Social Research on the LDS Church and its Members* (Provo, UT: Religious Studies Center, 1998), 285-292.

Alexander, Thomas, "Historiography and the New Mormon History: A Historians Perspective," *Dialogue* 19 (Fall 1986), 25-49.

Alexander, Thomas, *Mormonism in Transition*, 2d. ed. (Urbana: University of Illinois Press, 1996).

Alexander, Thomas, *Mormonism in Transition: A History of the Latter-day Saints, 1890-1930* (Urbana: University of Illinois Press, 1985).

Alexander, Thomas, "The Reconstruction of Mormon Doctrine: From Joseph Smith to Progressive Theology," *Sunstone* 10:5 (July-August 1980), 24-33.

Alexander, Thomas, *Things in Heaven and Earth: The Life and Times of Wilford Woodruff* (Salt Lake City: Signature, 1991).

Alexander, Thomas, *Utah: The Right Place*, revised and updated edition (Salt Lake City: Gibbs Smith, 2003).

Allen, James B., "Emergence of a Fundamental: The Expanding Role of Joseph Smith's First Vision in Mormon Religious Thought" in *Journal of Mormon History* 7 (1980), 437-461.

Allen, James B., and Glen M. Leonard, *The Story of the Latter-day Saints* (Salt Lake City: Deseret, 1976).

Allen, James B., and Glen M. Leonard, *Story of the Latter-day Saints*, 2d. ed. (Salt Lake City: Deseret, 1992).

Anderson, Devery, "A History of Dialogue, Part One: The Early Years, 1965-1971," *Dialogue* 32:2 (Summer 1999), 15-67.

Anderson, Devery, "A History of Dialogue, Part Two: Struggle toward Maturity, 1971-1982," *Dialogue* 33:2 (Summer 2000), 1-96.

Anderson, Devery, "A History of Dialogue, Part Three: "Coming of Age" in Utah, 1982-1987," *Dialogue* 35: 2 (Summer 2002), 1-71.

Anderson, Lavina Fielding, "DNA Mormon: D. Michael Quinn" in John Sillitoe and Susan Staker (eds.), *Mormon Mavericks: Essays on Dissenters* (Salt Lake City: Signature Books, 2002) 329-363.

Anderson, Lavina Fielding, "The LDS Intellectual Community and Church Leadership," *Dialogue* 26:1 (Spring 1993), 7-64.

Anderson, Nels, *Desert Saints: The Mormon Frontier in Utah* (Chicago: University of Chicago Press, 1942).

Anderson, Nels, *The Hobo: The Sociology of*

the Homeless Man (Chicago: University of Chicago Press, 1923).

Anderson, Robert, *Inside the Mind of Joseph Smith: Psychobiography and the Book of Mormon* (Salt Lake City: Signature, 2002).

Anderson, Vern, "A Challenge to the Origins of the Book of Mormon," Associated Press Report, *Los Angeles Times*, 19 June 1993, Metro Section, 4.

Andrews, Dee, *The Methodists in Revolutionary America, 1760-1800: The Shaping of an Evangelical Culture* (Princeton, NJ: Princeton University Press, 2000).

Andrews, Edward Deming, *The People Called Shakers* (New York: Dover, 1953).

Andrus, Milo, "Autobiography," typescript, HBLL, BYU.

Ariel, Yaakov S., *Evangelizing the Chosen People: Missions to the Jews in America, 1880-2000* (Chapel Hill: University of North Carolina Press, 1999).

Arieli, Yehoshua, *Individualism and Nationalism in American Ideology* (Baltimore, MD: Penguin, 1968).

Arrington, Leonard, *Adventures of a Church Historian* (Urbana: University of Illinois Press, 1998).

Arrington, Leonard, *Brigham Young: American Moses* (New York: Knopf, 1985).

Arrington, Leonard, "Faith and Intellect as Partners in Mormon History" in "The Collected Leonard J. Arrington Mormon History Lectures" Special Collections & Archives, Utah State University Libraries, Logan, 2005.

Arrington, Leonard, *The Great Basin Kingdom: An Economic History of the Latter-Day Saints* (Lincoln: University of Nebraska Press, 1959).

Arrington, Leonard, "Historian as Entrepreneur: A Personal Essay," *BYU Studies* 17 (Winter 1977), 193-209.

Arrington, Leonard, "In Praise of Amateurs," *Journal of Mormon History* 17 (1991), 35-42.

Arrington, Leonard, "Modern Lysistratas: Mormon Women in the International Peace Movement," *Journal of Mormon History* 15 (1989), 89-104.

Arrington, Leonard, "'Persons for All Seasons': Women in Mormon History," *BYU Studies* 20 (Fall 1979), 39-58.

Arrington, Leonard, "Reflections on the Founding and Purpose of the Mormon History Association, 1965-1983," *Journal of Mormon History* 10 (Fall 1992), 41-56.

Arrington, Leonard, "Scholarly Studies of Mormonism in the Twentieth-Century," *Dialogue* 1 (Spring 1966), 15-32.

Arrington, Leonard, and Davis Bitton, *The Mormon Experience*, 2d. ed. (Urbana: University of Illinois Press, 1992).

Arrington, Leonard, and Davis Bitton, *The Mormon Experience: A History of the Latter-day Saints* (New York: Knopf, 1979).

Arrington, Leonard, and Jon Haupt, "Intolerable Zion: Images of Mormonism in Nineteenth-Century Fiction," *Western Humanities Review* 22 (Summer 1968), 37-50.

Arrington, Leonard, and Jon Haupt, "The Missouri and Illinois Mormons in Ante-Bellum Fiction," *Dialogue* 5:1 (1970), 243-260.

Arrington, Leonard, and Rebecca Cornwall Foster, "Perpetuation of a Myth: Mormon Danites in Western Novels, 1840-90," *BYU Studies* 23:2 (Spring 1983), 147-165.

Arrington, Leonard, Feramorz Fox, and Dean May, *Building the City of God: Community and Cooperation Among the Mormons* (Urbana: University of Illinois Press, second edition, 1992).

Arthur, Anthony, *The Tailor-King: The Rise and Fall of the Anabaptist Kingdom of Munster* (New York: St. Martin's, 1999).

Ashment, Edward H., "'A Record in the Language of My Father': Evidence of Ancient Egyptian and Hebrew in the Book of Mormon," in Brent Lee Metcalfe (ed.), *New Approaches to the Book of Mormon: Explorations in Critical Methodology* (Salt Lake City: Signature Books, 1993), 329-393.

Associated Press, Mormon Church Excommunicates Man Who Ran Forum for Doubting Members," *The Guardian*, 10 February 2015 (online).

Aston, Warren P., and Michaela Knoth Aston, *In the Footsteps of Lehi: New Evidence for Lehi's Journey Across Arabia to Bountiful* (Salt Lake City: Deseret, 1994).

Bacheler, Origen, *Mormonism Exposed Internally and Externally* (New York: n.p., 1838).

Bachman, Daniel, "New Light on an Old Hypothesis: The Ohio Origins of the Revelation on Eternal Marriage," *Journal of Mormon History* 5 (1978), 19-32.

Backman, Milton, *The Heavens Resound: A History of the Latter-day Saints in Ohio 1830-1838* (Salt Lake City: Deseret, 1983).

Backman, Milton, *Joseph Smith's First Vision*, 2d. ed. (Salt Lake City: Bookcraft, 1980).

Bacon, Margaret, "On the Verge: The Evolution of American Quakerism," in Timothy Miller (ed.), *America's Alternative Religions* (Albany: SUNY Press, 1995), 69-76.

Bagley, Will, *Blood of the Prophets: Brigham Young and the Massacre at Mountain Meadows* (Norman: University of Oklahoma Press, 2004).

Bainbridge, William Sims, "Shaker Demographics 1840-1900: An Example From the Use of Census Examination Schedules," *Journal for the Scientific Study of Religion* 21:4 (1982), 352-365.

Baird, Robert, *Religion in America, or An Account of the Origin, Progress, Relation to the State, and the Present Condition of the Evangelical Churches of the United States: With Notices of the Unevangelical Denominations* (New York: Harper, 1844).

Balmer, Randall, "Eschewing the 'Routine of Religion': Eighteenth-Century Pietism and the Revival Tradition in America" in Edith Blumhofer and Randall Balmer (eds.), *Modern Christian Revivals* (Urbana: University of Illinois Press, 1993), 1-16.

Bancroft, H.H., *History of Utah, 1540-1886* (San Francisco: History Company, 1889).

Banner, Lois, "Religious Benevolence as Social Control: A Critique" *Journal of American History* 60 (1973) 23-41.

Bannister, Roger, *Sociology and Scientism: The American Quest for Objectivity* (Chapel Hill: University of North Carolina Press, 1987).

Barkun, Michael, *Crucible of the Millennium: The Burned-Over District of New York in the 1840s* (Syracuse: Syracuse University Press, 1986).

Barlow, Phillip, *Mormons and the Bible: The Place of Latter-day Saints in American Religion* (New York: Oxford University Press, 1991).

Barrow, Clyde, *Universities and the Capitalist State: Corporate Liberalism and the Reconstruction of American Higher Education, 1894-1928* (Madison: University of Wisconsin Press, 1990).

Baumgartner, Frederick J., *Longing for the End: A History of Millennialism in Western Civilization* (New York: Palgrave, 1999).

Bean, Lee, Dean May, and Mark Skolnik, "The Mormon Historical Demography Project," *Historical Methodology* 11 (1978), 45-53.

Becker, Howard, *Systematic Sociology on the Basis of the Beziehungslehre and Gebildelehre of Leopold Van Wiese* (New York: Wiley, 1932).

Becker, Howard, *Through Values to Social Interpretation* (Durham, NC: Duke University Press, 1950).

Beckford, James, "Explaining Religious Movements," *International Social Science Journal*, 29:2 (1977), 135-249.

Beckwith, Francis J., Carl Mosser, and Paul Owen, *The New Mormon Challenge: Responding to the Latest Defenses of a Fast-Growing Movement* (Grand Rapids: Zondervan, 2002).

Beecher, Maureen Ursenbach, *Eliza and her Sisters* (Salt Lake City: Aspen, 1991).

Beecher, Maureen Ursenbach, "Entre Nous: An Intimate History of the MHA," *Journal of Mormon History* 12 (1985), 43-52.

Beecher, Maureen Ursenbach, "'The Leading Sisters': A Female Hierarchy in Nineteenth-Century Mormon Society," *Journal of Mormon History* 9 (1982), 26-39.

Beecher, Maureen Ursenbach, "Women's Work on the Mormon Frontier," *Utah Historical Quarterly* 49 (Summer 1981), 276-290.

Beecher, Maureen Ursenbach, and Lavina Fielding Anderson (eds.), *Sisters in Spirit: Mormon Women in Historical and Cultural Perspective* (Urbana: University of Illinois Press, 1992).

Bender, Thomas, *A Nation Among Nations: America's Place in World History* (New York: Hill and Wang, 2006).

Bennett, David, *The Party of Fear: The American Far Right from Nativism to the Militia Movement*, revised and updated edition (New York: Vintage, 1995).

Bennett, John, *History of the Saints* (Utah Lighthouse Ministry, 1842).

Bennett, John C., *The History of the Saints, or, An Expose of Joe Smith and Mormonism* (Urbana: University of Illinois Press, 2000 [1842]).

Bennion, Lowell, "The Incidence of

Mormon Polygamy in 1880: 'Dixie' versus Davis Stake," *Journal of Mormon History* 11 (1984), 27–42.

Benson, Ezra Taft, "Autobiography," *The Instructor* 80, 145.

Benson, Ezra Taft, *The Gospel Teacher and His Message*, Address to CES Religious Educators, 17 September 1976, Temple Square Assembly Hall (Salt Lake City: Intellectual Reserve, 1976), 1–9.

Benson, Lee, *The Concept of Jacksonian Democracy: New York as a Test Case* (New York: Atheneum, 1961).

Benton, Beverly, *Women Vote in the West* (New York: Garland, 1986).

Berger, Peter, *The Sacred Canopy: Elements of a Sociological Theory of Religion* (Garden City, NJ: Anchor, 1967).

Berger, Peter, and Thomas Luckman, *The Social Construction of Reality* (Harmondsworth: Penguin, 1966).

Bergera, Gary James, and Ronald Priddis, *Brigham Young University: A House of Faith* (Salt Lake City: Signature, 1985).

Bernard, L.L., and Jessie Bernard, *Origins of American Sociology: The Social Science Movement in America* (New York: Thomas Y. Crowell, 1943).

Berthoff, Rowland, *An Unsettled People: Social Order and Disorder in American History* (New York: Harper and Row, 1971).

Bhaskar Roy, *A Realist Theory of Science* (Atlantic Highlands, NJ: Humanities Press, 1978).

Bigler, Henry William, "Autobiography," typescript, HBLL, BYU.

Billington, Roy, *The Protestant Crusade: A Study in the Origins of American Nativism, 1800–1860* (Chicago: Quadrangle, 1952).

Bitton, Davis, "Antimormonism: Periodization, Strategies, Motivation," 1985, unpublished paper in author's possession.

Bitton, Davis, "B.H. Roberts as Historian," *Dialogue* 3 (Winter 1968), 25–44.

Bitton, Davis, *Guide to Mormon Diaries and Autobiographies* (Provo, UT: BYU Press, 1977).

Bitton, Davis, "Mormon Polygamy: A Review Article" *Journal of Mormon History* 4 (1977), 101–118.

Bitton, Davis, "Spotting an Anti-Mormon Book": *FARMS Review* 16:1 (2004), 355–360.

Bitton, Davis, "Taking Stock: The Mormon History Association after Twenty-Five Years," *Journal of Mormon History* 17 (1991), 1–27.

Bitton, Davis, "Ten Years in Camelot: A Personal Memoir," *Dialogue* 16 (Autumn 1983), 9–33.

Blackburn, Robin (ed.), *Ideology in Social Science: Readings in Critical Social Theory* (New York: Vintage, 1972).

Bledstein, Burton, *The Culture of Professionalism: The Middle Class and the Development of Higher Education in America* (New York: Norton, 1978).

Blomberg, Craig, "Is Mormonism Christian?" in Francis J. Beckwith, Carl Mosser, and Paul Owen, *The New Mormon Challenge: Responding to the Latest Defenses of a Fast-Growing Movement* (Grand Rapids: Zondervan, 2002), 315–333.

Blomberg, Craig, and Stephen E. Robinson, *How Wide the Divide? A Mormon and an Evangelical in Conversation* (Downers Grove, IL: InterVarsity Press, 1997).

Bloom, Harold, *The American Religion: The Emergence of the Post-Christian Nation* (New York: Simon & Schuster, 1992).

Blumhofer, Edith, and Randall Balmer (eds.), *Modern Christian Revivals* (Urbana: University of Illinois Press, 1993).

Bodo, John, *The Protestant Clergy and Public Issues 1812–1848* (Princeton, NJ: Princeton University Press, 1954).

Bohn, David, "No Higher Ground: Objective History Is an Elusive Chimera," *Sunstone* 8 (May-June 1983), 26–32.

Bohn, David, "Our Own Agenda: A Critique of the Methodology of the New Mormon History," *Sunstone* 14 (June 1990), 45–49.

Bohn, David, "Unfounded Claims and Impossible Expectations: A Critique of New Mormon History" in George Smith (ed.), *Faithful History: Essays on Writing Mormon History* (Salt Lake City: Signature, 1992), 227–261.

Book of Mormon (Salt Lake City: Deseret, 1971 [1830]).

Bottomore, Tom, and Robert Nisbet (eds.), *A History of Sociological Analyses* (New York: Basic, 1978).

Boyle, Henry G., "Autobiography," typescript, HBLL, BYU.

Bozeman, T.D., *To Live Ancient Lives: The*

Primitivist Dimension of New England Puritanism (Chapel Hill: University of North Carolina Press, 1988).

Bradford, M. Gerald, "The Case of the New Mormon History: Thomas G. Alexander and His Critics," *Dialogue* 21 (Winter 1988), 143-150.

Bradley, Don, "The Grand Fundamental Principles of Mormonism: Joseph Smith's Unfinished Reformation," *Sunstone*, April 2006. 32-41.

Bradley, Martha, "Changed Faces: The Official LDS Position on Polygamy," *Sunstone* 14:1 (February 1990), 26-33.

Bradley, Martha, *Kidnapped from That Land: The Government Raids on the Short Creek Polygamists* (Salt Lake City: University of Utah Press, 1993).

Bradley, Martha, "The Women of Fundamentalism: Short Creek, 1953," *Dialogue* 23:2 (Summer 1990), 15-38.

Brady, Thomas A., Heiko Oberman, and James D. Tracy, *Handbook of European History, 1400-1600*, two volumes (Grand Rapids: Eerdmans, 1995).

Bramwell, E. Craig, "Hebrew Idioms in the Small Plates of Nephi," unpublished master's thesis, BYU, 1960.

Braude, Ann, *Radical Spirits: Spiritualism and Women's Rights in Nineteenth-Century America* (Boston: Beacon, 1991).

Brewer, Patricia, *Shaker Communities, Shaker Lives* (Hanover, NH: University Press of New England, 1986).

Brewer Priscilla, "The Shakers of Mother Ann Lee" in Donald Pitzer (ed.), *America's Communal Utopias* (Chapel Hill: University of North Carolina Press, 1997), 37-56.

Bringhurst, Newell, *Fawn McKay Brodie: A Biographers Life* (Norman, University of Oklahoma Press, 1999).

Bringhurst, Newell, "Joseph Smith, the Mormons, and Antebellum Reform: A Closer Look," *John Whitmer Historical Association Journal* 14 (1994), 73-92.

Bringhurst, Newell, and Craig Foster, *The Persistence of Mormon Polygamy: Fundamentalist Mormon Polygamy from 1890 to the Present* (Independence, MO: John Whitmer Books, 2015).

Brodie, Fawn, *No Man Knows My History: The Life of Joseph Smith* (New York: Knopf, 1945).

Brodie, Fawn, *No Man Knows My History: The Life of Joseph Smith*, 2d. ed. (New York: Knopf, 1971).

Brodie, Fawn, "An Oral History Interview" *Dialogue* 14 (Summer 1981), 99-116.

Brooke, John, *The Refiner's Fire: The Making of Mormon Cosmology, 1644-1844* (New York: Cambridge University Press, 1994).

Brooks, Joanna, *Mormonism and White Supremacy: American Religion and the Problem of Racial Innocence* (New York: Oxford University Press, 2020).

Brooks, Juanita, "A Close-Up of Polygamy," *Harper's* 168 (February 1934), 299-307.

Brooks, Juanita, *John Doyle Lee: Zealot, Pioneer Builder, Scapegoat* (Logan: Utah State University Press, 1992).

Brooks, Juanita, *The Mountain Meadows Massacre* (Palo Alto, CA: Stanford University Press, 1950).

Brooks, Juanita, *Quicksand and Cactus: A Memoir of the Southern Mormon Frontier* (Logan: Utah State University Press, 1992).

Brown, Benjamin, "Autobiography" in Testimony for the Truth (Liverpool: S.W. Richards, 1854).

Brown, Richard D., *Knowledge Is Power: The Diffusion of Information in Early America, 1700-1865* (New York: Oxford University Press, 1989).

Brown, Richard D., *Modernization: The Transformation of American Life 1600-1865* (New York: Hill and Wang, 1976).

Bruce, Dickson, *And They All Sang Hallelujah: Plain Folk Camp Meeting Religion, 1800-1845* (Knoxville: University of Tennessee Press, 1974).

Buerger, David John, "The Adam-God Doctrine," *Dialogue* 15:1 (Spring 1982), 4-58.

Buerger, David John, *The Mysteries of Godliness: A History of Mormon Temple Worship* (Salt Lake City: Signature, 2002).

Bunker, Gary, and Davis Bitton, *The Mormon Graphic Image, 1834-1914* (Salt Lake City: University of Utah Press, 1983).

Burgess, Harrison, "Autobiography" in Kenneth Glynn Hales (ed. and comp.), *Windows: A Mormon Family* (Tucson: Skyline, 1985) (available online).

Bush, Lester, "Mormonism's Negro Doctrine: A Historical Overview," *Dialogue* 8:1 (Spring 1973), 11-68.

Bush, Lester, "The Spaulding Theory Then and Now," *Dialogue* 10:4 (Autumn 1977), 40-69.

Bush, Lester, and Armand Mauss (eds.),

Neither White Nor Black: Mormon Scholars Confront the Race Issue in a Universal Church (Midvale, UT: Signature, 1984).

Bushman, Claudia, "Editorial: Exponent II is Born," *Exponent II* 1 (July 1978), 2.

Bushman, Richard, "Faithful History," *Dialogue* (Winter 1969), 11–28.

Bushman, Richard, *Joseph Smith and the Beginnings of Mormonism* (Urbana: University of Illinois Press, 1988).

Bushman, Richard, *Joseph Smith: Rough Stone Rolling* (New York: Knopf, 2005).

Bushman, Richard, "My Faith" in Richard Bushman, *Believing History: Latter-day Saint Essays* (New York: Columbia University Press, 2004.

Bushman, Richard, *The Refinement of America: Persons, Houses, Cities* (New York: Knopf, 1993).

Butler, John Lowe, "Autobiography," typescript, HBLL, BYU.

Butler, Jon, *Awash in a Sea of Faith: Christianizing the American People* (New Haven, CT: Yale University Press 1992).

Butler, Jon, "Magic, Astrology, and the Early American Religious Heritage, 1600–1700," *American Historical Review* 84:2 (April 1979), 317–346.

"BYU Fires Two Controversial Faculty Members" *Sunstone*, July 1993, 74–77.

BYU Studies, 13:1, 14:4, and 26:2.

BYU Studies, 15:4. 18:2, 19:3, and 31:1.

Cameron, Euen, *The European Reformation* (New York: Oxford University Press, 1991).

Campbell, Alexander, "Delusions," *Millennial Harbinger*, 7 February 1831, 85–96.

Campbell, Eugene E., "History of the Church of Jesus Christ of Latter-day Saints in California, 1846–1946," unpublished Ph.D. dissertation, University of Southern California, 1952.

Campbell, Eugene E., and Bruce L. Campbell. "Divorce Among Mormon Polygamists: Extent and Explanations," *Utah Historical Quarterly* 46 (Winter 1978), 4–23.

Cannon, Donald, and Lyndon Cook (eds.), *Far West Record: Minutes of the Church of Jesus Christ of Latter-day Saints, 1830–1844* (Salt Lake City: Deseret, 1983).

Cannon, Frank Q., and Harvey J. O'Higgins, *Under the Prophet in Utah: The National Menace of a Political Priestcraft* (Boston: C.M. Clark, 1911).

Cannon, Kenneth II, "After the Manifesto: Mormon Polygamy, 1890–1906," in D. Michael Quinn (ed.), *The New Mormon History: Revisionist Essays on the Past* (Salt Lake City: Signature, 1992), 201–220.

Cannon, Kenneth II, "Beyond the Manifesto: Polygamous Cohabitation Among LDS General Authorities after 1890," *Utah Historical Quarterly* 46:1 (Winter 1978), 24–36.

Cannon Charles A., "The Awesome Power of Sex: The Polemical Campaign Against Mormon Polygamy," *Pacific Historical Review*, 43:1 (February 1974), 61–82.

Capshew, James, *Psychologists on the March: Science, Practice, and Professional Identity in America, 1929–1969* (New York: Cambridge University Press, 1999).

Card, Brigham, Herbert C. Northcott, and John Foster (eds.), *The Mormon Presence in Canada* (Edmonton: University of Alberta Press, 1990).

Carden, Maren Lockwood, *Oneida: Utopian Community to Modern Corporation* (New York: Harper and Row, 1969).

Carr, E.H., *What is History?* (New York: Vintage, 1961).

Carroll, Bret E., *Spiritualism in Antebellum America* (Bloomington: Indiana University Press, 1997).

Carwardine, David, "Charles Sellers' "Antinomians" and "Arminians" in Mark Noll (ed.), *God and Mammon: Protestants, Money, and the Market, 1790–1860* (New York: Oxford University Press, 2001), 75–98.

Carwardine, David, "Methodist Ministers and the Second Party System" in Russell Richey, Kenneth Rowe, and Jean Miller Schmidt (eds.), *Perspectives on American Methodism: Interpretive Essays* (Nashville: Kingwood, 1993), 309–342.

Carwardine, Richard, *Transatlantic Revivalism: Popular Evangelicalism in Britain and America, 1790–1865* (Westport, CT: Greenwood Press, 1978).

Caswall, Henry, *The Prophet of the Nineteenth-Century, or, The Rise, Progress, and Present State of the Mormons* (London: J.G.F. and J. Rivington, 1843).

Challen, Paul, *A Sociological Analysis of Southern Regionalism: The Contributions of Howard W. Odum* (Lewiston, NY: Edward Mellen, 1993).

Channing, William Ellery, *Unitarian Christianity and Other Essays*, edited by Irving

Bartlett (Indianapolis: Bobbs-Merrill, 1957).

Charles, Melodie Moench, "Nineteenth-Century Mormons: The New Israel," *Dialogue* 12 (Spring 1979), 42–54.

Chomsky, Noam, Ira Katznelson, R.C. Lewontin, David Montgomery, Laura Nader, Richard Ohmann, Ray Siever, Immanuel Wallerstein, and Howard Zinn (eds.), *The Cold War and the University* (New York: New Press, 1997).

Christensen, Harold, "Cultural Relativism and Premarital Sex Norms," *American Sociological Review* 25 (1960), 31–39.

Christensen, Harold, "Mormon Fertility: A Survey of Student Opinion," *American Journal of Sociology* 53 (January 1948), 270–275.

Christensen, Harold, "The Time Interval between Marriage of Parents and the Birth of Their First Child in Utah County, Utah," *American Journal of Sociology* 44 (January 1939), 518–525.

Christensen, Harold, and George Carpenter, "Value-Behavior Discrepancies Regarding Premarital Coitus in Three Western Cultures," *American Sociological Review* 27 (1962), 66–74.

Church Handbook of Instructions: Book 1, Stake Presidents and Bishoprics (Salt Lake City: Church of Jesus Christ of Latter-day Saints, 1998).

Clark, Christopher, "Germany 1815–1848: Restoration or Pre-March?" in Mary Fulbrook (ed.), *German History since 1800* (London: Arnold, 1997), 38–60.

Clark, John A., *Gleanings by the Way* (Philadelphia: W.J. and J.K. Simon, 1842).

Coe, Michael, "Mormons and Archaeology: An Outside View," *Dialogue* 8:2 (1972), pp. 40–48.

Cohn, Norman, *The Pursuit of the Millennium*, revised edition (New York: Oxford University Press, 1971).

Cole, Charles, *The Social Ideas of the Northern Evangelists* (New York: Columbia University Press, 1954).

Collinson, Patrick, "England" in Robert Scribner, Roy Porter, and Mikulas Teich (eds.), *The Reformation in National Context* (Cambridge, UK: Cambridge University Press, 1994), 80–94.

Collinson, Patrick, *The Reformation: A History* (New York: Modern Library, 2003).

Compton, Todd, *In Sacred Loneliness: The Plural Wives of Joseph Smith* (Salt Lake City: Signature, 1997).

Conan Doyle, Arthur, *A Study in Scarlet* (New York: Oxford University Press, 1994 [1888]).

Conkin, Paul, *American Originals: Homemade Varieties of Christianity* (Chapel Hill: University of North Carolina Press, 1997).

Conkin, Paul, *When All the Gods Trembled: Darwinism, Scopes, and American Intellectuals* (Lanham, MD: Rowman and Littlefield, 2001).

Cook, Lyndon, and Andrew Ehat (eds.), *The Words of Joseph Smith* (Orem, UT: Grandin, 1991).

Cooper, Rex, *Promises Made to the Fathers: Mormon Covenant Organization* (Salt Lake City: University of Utah Press, 1990).

Coray, Howard, "The Autobiography of Howard Coray," typescript, HBLL, BYU.

Coray, Howard, "Howard Coray's Recollections of Joseph Smith's History," edited by Dean Jessee, *BYU Studies* 11 (Summer 1971), 1–7.

Cornwall, Marie, "The Institutional Role of Mormon Women," in Marie Cornwall, Tim B. Heaton, Lawrence Alfred Young (eds.), *Contemporary Mormonism: Social Science Perspectives* (Urbana: University of Illinois Press, 1994), 239–264.

Cornwall, Marie, Camela Courtright, and Laga Van Beek, "How Common the Principle? Women as Plural Wives in 1860," *Dialogue* 26:2 (Summer 1993), 139–153.

Cornwall, Rebecca, *From Chicken Farmer to History* (Salt Lake City: Privately Published, 1976).

Coser, Lewis, *Men of Ideas: A Sociologists View* (Glencoe, IL: Free Press, 1965).

Cott, Nancy, *Public Vows: A History of Marriage and the Nation* (Cambridge, MA: Harvard University Press, 2002).

Cowdery, Oliver. "Letter IV," *The Latter Day Saints' Messenger and Advocate* 1 (1835): 77–80.

Cowdery, Oliver, "Letter IV to W.W. Phelps," *Latter Day Saints Messenger and Advocate* 1:5, February 1835, 18–19.

Cowdery, Oliver. "Letter VIII," *The Latter Day Saints' Messenger and Advocate* 2 (1835): 195–201.

Cross, Whitney, *The Burned-Over District: The Social and Intellectual History of Enthusiastic Religion in Western New York, 1800–1850* (New York: Harper and Row, 1950).

Daines, Franklin D., "Separatism in Utah, 1847–1870." *Annual Report of the*

American Historical Association for the Year 1917 (Washington: The Association, 1920), 333–343.

Dandelion, Ben Pink, *An Introduction to Quakerism* (Cambridge, UK: University of Cambridge Press, 2007).

Davies, Douglas, *An Introduction to Mormonism* (Cambridge, UK: Cambridge University Press, 2003).

Davies, Douglas, "Mormon History, Identity, and Faith Community" in Elizabeth Tonkin, Maryon McDonald, and Malcolm Chapman (eds.), *History and Ethnicity* (London: Routledge, 1989), 168–182.

Davis, David Brion, "The New England Origins of Mormonism," *New England Quarterly* XXVI (June 1953),143–168.

Davis, David Brion, "Some Themes of Counter-Subversion," *Journal of American History*, 47: 2, September 1960, 205–224.

Daynes, Kathleen, *More Wives than One: The Transformation of the Mormon Marriage System, 1840–1910* (Urbana: University of Illinois Press, 2001).

Decker, Ed, and Dave Hunt, *The God Makers: The Mormon Quest for Godhood* (Eugene, OR: Harvest House, 1984).

DePillis, Mario, "The Quest for Religious Authority and the Rise of Mormonism," *Dialogue* 1:1 (Spring 1966), 68–88.

Derr, Jill Mulvay, and C. Brooklyn Derr, "Outside the Mormon Hierarchy: Alternative Aspects of Institutional Power," *Dialogue* 15 (Winter 1982), 21–43.

Derr, Jill Mulvay, Janath Russell Cannon, and Ursenbach Beecher, *Women of Covenant: The Story of the Relief Society* (Salt Lake City: Deseret, 1992).

Desroche, Henri, *The American Shakers: From Neo-Christianity to Presocialism* (Amherst: University of Massachusetts Press, 1971).

DeWolfe, Elizabeth A., *Shaking the Faith: Women, Family, and Mary Marshall Dyer's Anti-Shaker Campaign, 1815–1867* (New York: Palgrave, 2002).

Dobbins, Austin, *Milton and the Book of Revelation: The Heavenly Cycle* (Tuscaloosa: University of Alabama Press, 1975).

Doctrine and Covenants (Salt Lake City: Deseret, 1971 [1921]).

Dorman, Robert, *The Revolt of the Provinces: The Regionalist Movement in America, 1920–1945* (Chapel Hill: University of North Carolina Press, 1993).

Drinnon, Richard, *Facing West: The Metaphysics of Indian Hatred and Empire Building* (New York: Schocken, 1980).

Duke, James T., "Introduction" in James T. Duke (ed.) *Latter-day Saint Social Life: Social Research on the LDS Church and Its Members* (Provo, UT: Religious Studies Center, BYU, 1998), 4–5.

Dunfey, Julie "'Living the Principle' of Plural Marriage: Mormon Women, Utopia, and Female Sexuality in the Nineteenth-Century," *Feminist Studies* 10:3 (Fall 1984), 523–536.

Durkheim, Émile, *The Division of Labor in Society* (New York: Free Press, 1933 [1893]).

Durnbaugh, David, "Communitarian Societies in Colonial America" in Donald Pitzer (ed.), *America's Communal Utopias* (Chapel Hill: University of North Carolina Press, 1997), 14–36.

Dyck, Cornelius (ed.), *Introduction to Mennonite History: A Popular History of the Anabaptists and Mennonites* (Scottdale, PA: Herald Press, third edition, 1993).

Dyer, Mary, *A Brief Statement of the Sufferings of Mary Dyer Occasioned By the Society Called Shakers* (Concord, NH: Joseph Spear, 1818).

Dyer, Mary, *A Portraiture of Shakerism...* (Concord, NH: Printed for the Author [by Sylvester Goss], 1822).

Dyer, Mary, *Reply to the Shakers* (Concord, NH: Printed for the Author, 1824).

Dyer, Mary, *Shakerism Exposed* (Hanover, NH: Dartmouth Press, n.d [ca. 1852]).

[Dyer], Mary Mitchell, *The Rise and Progress of the Serpent from the Garden of Eden to the Present Day* (Concord, NH: Printed for the Author, 1847).

Elliott, David R., "Knowing No Borders: Canadian Contributions to American Fundamentalism" in George Rawlyk and Mark Noll (eds.), *Amazing Grace: Evangelicalism in Australia, Britain, Canada, and the United States* (Kingston, Ont.: McGill-Queens University Press, 1995), 349–374.

Ellsworth, S. George, "History of Mormon Missions in the United States and Canada, 1830–1860," unpublished Ph.D. dissertation, University of California at Berkeley, 1950.

Ellsworth, S. George, "Hubert Howe Bancroft and the History of Utah," *Utah Historical Quarterly* 22 (April 1954), 99–124.

Ely, Richard, "Economic Aspects of Mormonism," *Harper's Monthly* 106 (April 1903), 667–678.

Embry, Jessie, *Asian American Mormons: Bridging Cultures* (Provo, UT: Charles Redd Center for Western Studies, 1999).

Embry, Jessie, *Black Saints in a White Church: Contemporary African American Mormons* (Salt Lake City: Signature, 1994).

Embry, Jessie, "Effects of Polygamy on Mormon Women," *Frontier—A Journal of Women Studies*, 7, 1984, 56–61.

Embry, Jessie, *"In His Own Language": Mormon Spanish Speaking Congregations in the United States* (Provo, UT: Charles Redd Center for Western Studies, 1997).

Embry, Jessie, *Mormon Polygamous Families: Life in the Principle* (Salt Lake City: University of Utah Press, 1987).

Emerson, Ralph Waldo, "An After-clap of Puritanism" in William Mulder and Russell Mortensen (eds.), *Among the Mormons—Historic Accounts by Contemporary Observers* (New York: Knopf, 1958), 382–384.

Enslin Morton Scott, *Christian Beginnings* (New York: Harper & Brothers, 1938).

Ericksen, Ephraim Edward, *Memories and Reflections: The Autobiography of E.E. Ericksen*, edited by Scott Kenney (Salt Lake City: Signature, 1987).

Ericksen, Ephraim Edward, "The Psychological and Ethical Aspects of Mormonism," unpublished Ph.D. dissertation, University of Chicago, 1922.

Feldberg, Michael, *The Turbulent Era: Riot and Disorder in Jacksonian America* (New York: Oxford University Press, 1980).

Ferguson, Thomas, *One Fold and One Shepherd* (San Francisco: Books of California, 1958).

Fieldman, Louis, *Jew and Gentile in the Ancient World: Attitudes and Interactions from Alexander to Justinian* (Princeton, NJ: Princeton University Press, 1993).

Fife, Austin E., and Alta Fife, *Saints of Sage and Saddle: Folklore Among the Mormons* (Bloomington: Indiana University Press 1956).

Fine, Sidney, "Richard T. Ely, Forerunner of Progressivism, 1880–1901," *Mississippi Valley Historical Review* 37:4 (March 1951), 599–624.

Finley, Moses, *The World of Odysseus* (Harmondsworth, UK: Penguin, 1979).

Finney, Charles, "Lecture XIII: Being in Debt," *The Oberlin Evangelist* 1, number 17 (31 July 1839), 129–131.

Finney, Charles, "Lecture XX: How to Prevent our Employments from Injuring our Souls," *The Oberlin Evangelist* 1, number 24 (6 November 1839), 185–187.

Firmage, Edwin and Richard Mangrum, *Zion in the Courts: A Legal History of the Church of Jesus Christ of Latter-day Saints* (Urbana: University of Illinois Press, 1988).

Fischer, David Hackett, *Albion's Seed: Four British Folkways in America* (New York: Oxford University Press, 1989).

Flake, Kathleen, *The Politics of Religious Identity: The Seating of Senator Reed Smoot, Mormon Apostle* (Chapel Hill: University of North Carolina Press, 2004).

Flanders, Robert, *Nauvoo: Kingdom on the Mississippi* (Urbana: University of Illinois Press, 1965).

Flanders, Robert, "Some Reflections on the New Mormon History," *Dialogue* 9 (Spring 1974), 34–41.

Fogerty, Robert, "Oneida: A Utopian Search for Religious Security," *Labor History* 14: 2 (Spring 1973), 202–227

Forsberg, Clyde, "By Study and Also by Blood: Mormonism, Masonry, Father Abraham, and Race," unpublished paper presented at the Mormon History Association Conference, Kirtland, Ohio, 2003.

Forsberg, Clyde, *Equal Rites: The Book of Mormon, Masonry, Gender, and American Culture* (New York: Columbia University Press, 2003).

Foster, Charles, *An Errand of Mercy: The Evangelical United Front, 1790–1837* (Chapel Hill: University of North Carolina Press, 1960).

Foster, Lawrence, "Apostate Believers: Jerald and Sandra Tanner's Encounter with Mormon History," in Roger D. Launius and Laurel Thatcher (eds.), *Differing Visions: Dissenters in Mormon History* (Urbana: University of Illinois Press, 1994), 343–365.

Foster, Lawrence, "Career Apostates: Reflections on the Works of Jerald and Sandra Tanner," *Dialogue* 17:2 (Summer 1984), 35–60.

Foster, Lawrence, "Free Love and Community: John Humphrey Noyes and the Oneida Perfectionists" in Donald Pitzer (ed.), *America's Communal Utopias* (Chapel Hill: University of North Carolina Press, 1997), 253–278.

Foster, Lawrence, "From Frontier Activism to Neo-Victorian Domesticity: Mormon Women in the Nineteenth and Twentieth Centuries," *Journal of Mormon History* (6, 1979), 3–22.

Foster, Lawrence, "A Little Known Defense of Polygamy from the Mormon Press in 1842" *Dialogue* 9 (Winter 1974), 21–34.

Foster, Lawrence, "A Personal Odyssey: My Encounter with Mormon History," *Dialogue* 16 (Autumn 1983), 87–98.

Foster, Lawrence, "The Psychology of Religious Genius: Joseph Smith and the Origins of New Religious Movements," in Bryan Waterman (ed.), *The Prophet Puzzle* (Salt Lake City: Signature, 1999), 183–208.

Foster, Lawrence, *Religion and Sexuality: The Shakers, the Mormons and the Oneida Community* (Urbana: University of Illinois Press, 1981).

Foster, Lawrence, *Religion, and Sexuality: Three American Communal Experiments in the Nineteenth-Century* (New York: Oxford University Press, 1981).

Foster, Lawrence, *Women, Family, and Utopia: Communal Experiments of the Shakers, the Oneida Community, and the Mormons* (Syracuse: Syracuse University Press, 1991).

Foucault, Michel, *The Archaeology of Knowledge* (New York: Pantheon, 2002).

Foucault, Michel, *The Order of Things: An Archaeology of the Human Sciences* (New York: Pantheon, 1970).

Fox, Feramorz Y., "The Mormon Land System: A Study of the Settlement and Utilization of Land Under the Direction of the Mormon Church," unpublished Ph.D. dissertation, Northwestern University, 1932.

Frost, J. William, "Christianity and Culture in America" in Howard Clark Kee, Emily Albu, Carter Lindberg, J. William Frost, and Dana Robert, *Christianity: A Social and Cultural History*, 2d. ed. (Upper Saddle River, NJ: Prentice-Hall, 1998), 387–519.

Furet, Francois, *The Passing of an Illusion: The Idea of Communism in the Twentieth Century* (Chicago: University of Chicago Press, 1999).

Furner, Mary, *Advocacy and Objectivity: A Crisis in the Professionalization of American Social Science, 1865–1905* (Lexington: University Press of Kentucky, 1975).

Furniss, Norman, *The Fundamentalist Controversy, 1918–1931* (New Haven, CT: Yale University Press, 1963).

Furniss, Norman, *The Mormon Conflict, 1850–1859* (New Haven, CT: Yale University Press, 1960).

Gager, John, *Kingdom and Community: The Social World of Early Christianity* (Englewood Cliffs, NJ: Prentice-Hall, 1975).

Gardner, Hamilton, "Communism Among the Mormons," *Quarterly Journal of Economics* 37 (1923), 134–174.

Gardner, Hamilton, "Cooperation Among the Mormons," *Quarterly Journal of Economics* 31 (May 1917), 461–469.

Garrett, Clarke, *Origins of the Shakers: From the Old World to the New World* (Baltimore, MD: Johns Hopkins University Press, 1987).

Gaustad, Edwin S. (ed.), *The Rise of Adventism: Religion and Society in Mid-Nineteenth-Century America* (New York: Harper and Row, 1974).

Geddes, Joseph, "The United Order Among the Mormons," unpublished Ph.D. dissertation, Columbia University, 1924.

Geertz, Clifford, *The Interpretation of Cultures: Selected Essays* (New York: Basic, 1973).

Geertz, Clifford, *Local Knowledge: Further Essays in Interpretive Anthropology* (New York: Basic, 1983).

Geertz, Clifford, "The Pinch of Destiny: Religion as Experience, Meaning, Identity, Power" in Clifford Geertz (ed.), *Available Light: Anthropological Reflections on Philosophical Topics* (Princeton, NJ: Princeton University Press, 2000), 167–187.

Geertz, Clifford, "Religion as a Cultural System" in Michael Banton (ed.), *Anthropological Approaches to the Study of Religion* (London: Tavistock), 1–46.

Geiger, Roger, *Relevant Knowledge: American Research Universities Since World War II* (New York: Oxford University Press, 1993).

Geiger, Roger, *To Advance Knowledge: The Growth of American Research Universities, 1900–1940* (New York: Oxford University Press, 1986).

Gellner, Ernest, *Postmodernism, Reason, and Religion* (London: Routledge, 1992).

Gildea, Robert, *Barricades and Borders: Europe 1800-1914*, 2d. ed. (New York: Oxford University Press, 1996).

Gileadi, Avraham, *The Last Days: Types and Shadows from the Bible and the Book of Mormon* (Salt Lake City: Deseret, 1991).

Givens, Terryl, *The Book of Mormon: A Very Short Introduction* (New York: Oxford University Press, 2009).

Givens, Terryl, *By the Hand of Mormon: The American Scripture that Created a New Religion* (New York: Oxford University Press, 2002).

Givens, Terryl, *The Viper in the Hearth: Mormons, Myths, and the Construction of Heresy* (New York: Oxford University Press, 1997).

Godfrey, Kenneth, "Comprehensive History of the Church, A" in Arnold Garr, Donald Q. Cannon, and Richard O. Cowan (eds.), *Encyclopedia of Latter-day Saint History* (Salt Lake City: Deseret Book, 2000), 232-233.

Godfrey, Kenneth, "The Zelph Story." *BYU Studies* 29:2 (Spring 1989), 32-56.

Golden, Daniel, "In Religion Studies, Universities Bend to Views of Faithful: Scholar of Mormon History, Expelled from Church, Hits a Wall in Job Search," *Wall Street Journal*, A1, 6 April 2006.

Gordon, Sarah Barringer, *The Mormon Question: Polygamy and Constitutional Conflict in Nineteenth-Century America* (Chapel Hill: University of North Carolina Press, 2002).

Gossett, Thomas, *Race: The History of an Idea in America* (New York: Schocken, 1965).

Grandstaff, Mark, and Milton Backman, "The Social Origins of Kirtland Mormons"; *BYU Studies* 30:2 (1990), 47-66.

Griffin, Clifford, "Religious Benevolence as Social Control, 1815-1860, *Mississippi Valley Historical Review*, XLIV (December 1957), 432-444.

Griffin, Clifford, *Their Brothers Keepers: Moral Stewardship in the United States, 1800-1865* (New Brunswick, NJ: Rutgers University Press, 1960).

Grimstead, David, "Democratic Rioting: A Case Study of the Baltimore Bank Mob of 1835" in William O'Neill (ed.), *Insights and Parallels: Problems and Issues of American Social History* (Minneapolis: Burgess, 1973), 125-149.

Grimstead, David, "Rioting in Its Jacksonian Setting" in *American Historical Review* 77 (1972), 361-397.

Guarneri, Carl, *America in the World: United States History in Global Context* (New York: McGraw-Hill, 2007).

Gunnison, John, *The Mormons, or, Latter-day Saints in the Valley of the Great Salt Lake City* (Philadelphia: Lippincott, 1852).

Gusfield, Joseph, *Symbolic Crusade: Status Politics and the American Temperance Movement* (Urbana: University of Illinois Press, 1963).

Hackett, David G., *The Rude Hand of Innovation: Religion and Social Order in Albany, New York, 1652-1836* (New York: Oxford University Press, 1991).

Haigh, Christopher, *English Reformations: Religion, Politics, and Society Under the Tudors* (New York: Oxford University Press, 1993).

Hales, Brian, *Joseph Smith's Polygamy, Volume 1: History* (Salt Lake City: Greg Kofford Books, 2013).

Hales, Brian, *Joseph Smith's Polygamy, Volume 2: History* (Salt Lake City: Greg Kofford Books, 2013).

Hales, Brian, *Joseph Smith's Polygamy, Volume 3: Theology* (Salt Lake City: Greg Kofford Books, 2013).

Hall, David, "Narrating Puritanism" in Harry Stout and D.G. Hart (eds.), *New Directions in American Religious History* (New York: Oxford University Press, 1997), 51-83.

Hall, David, *Worlds of Wonder, Days of Judgment: Popular Religious Belief in New England* (Cambridge, MA: Harvard University Press, 1990).

Hallwas, John, and Roger D. Launius (eds.), *Cultures in Conflict: A Documentary History of the Mormon War in Illinois* (Logan: Utah State University Press, 1999).

Hamblin, William, "An Apologist for the Critics: Brent Lee Metcalfe's Assumptions and Methodology," *Review of Books on the Book of Mormon* 6:1 (1994), 434-523.

Hamblin, William, "Basic Methodological Problems with the Anti-Mormon Approach to the Geography and Archaeology of the Book of Mormon" *Journal of Book of Mormon Studies* 2:1 (1993), 161-197.

Hamblin, William, Dan Peterson, and

George Mitton, "Mormon in the Fiery Furnace, or Loftes Tryck Goes to Cambridge," *Review of Books on the Book of Mormon* 6:2 (1994), 1–58.

Hampshire, Annette, *Mormons in Conflict: The Nauvoo Years* (Edward Mellen, 1985).

Hancock, Levi, "Autobiography," typescript, HBLL, BYU.

Handler, Richard, *Nationalism and the Politics of Culture in Quebec* (Madison: University of Wisconsin Press, 1988).

Hanks, Maxine, and D. Michael Quinn (eds.), *Women and Authority:Re-emerging Mormon Feminism* (Salt Lake City: Signature, 1992).

Hanks, Maxine (ed.), *Women and Authority: Re-emerging Mormon Feminism* (Salt Lake City: Signature, 1992).

Hansen, Klaus, *Mormonism and the American Experience* (Chicago: University of Chicago Press, 1981).

Hansen, Klaus, *The Political Kingdom of God and the Council of Fifty in Mormon History* (East Lansing: Michigan State University Press, 1967).

Hansen, Klaus, *Quest for Empire: The Political Kingdom of God and the Council of Fifty in Mormon History* (East Lansing: Michigan State University Press, 1967).

Hardy, R. Carmon, "Appendix II: Mormon Polygamous Marriages After the 1890 Manifesto Through 1910: A Tentative List" in R Carmon Hardy, *Solemn Covenant: The Mormon Polygamous Passage* (Urbana: University of Illinois Press, 1992), 389–426.

Hardy, B. Carmon, "'Lords of Creation': Polygamy, the Abrahamic Household, and the Mormon Patriarchy," *Journal of Mormon History* 20 (1, 1994), 119–152.

Hardy, R. Carmon, "Lying for the Lord: An Essay" in Hardy *Solemn Covenant: The Mormon Polygamous Passage* (Urbana: University of Illinois Press, 1992), 363–388.

Hardy, R. Carmon, *Solemn Covenant: The Mormon Polygamous Passage* (Urbana: University of Illinois Press, 1992).

Harper, Stephen C., "Infallible Proofs, Both Human and Divine: The Persuasiveness of Mormonism for Early Converts," *Religion and American Culture*, 10:1 (Winter 2000), 99–118.

Hart, D.G., *The University Gets Religion: Religious Studies in American Higher Education* (Baltimore, MD: Johns Hopkins University Press, 1999).

Hartley, William, "The Founding of the LDS Church History Department, 1992," *Journal of Mormon History*, 18:2 (Fall 1992), 6–40.

Hartley, William, *"They Are My Friends": A History of the Joseph Knight Family, 1825–1850* (Provo, UT: Grandin, 1986).

Haskell, Thomas, *The Emergence of Professional Social Science: The American Social Science Association and the Nineteenth-Century Crisis of Authority* (Urbana: University of Illinois Press, 1977).

Haskell, Thomas (ed.), *The Authority of Experts: Studies in History and Theory* (Bloomington: Indiana University Press, 1984).

Hatch, Nathan, *The Democratization of American Christianity* (New Haven, CT: Yale University Press, 1989).

Hatch, Nathan, "Mormon and Methodist: Popular Religion in the Crucible of the Free Market," *Journal of Mormon History* 20: 1 (Spring 1994), 24–44.

Haven, Charlotte, "Letter 8 September 1843" in William Mulder and Russell Mortensen (eds.), *Among the Mormons: Historical Accounts by Contemporary Observers* (New York: Knopf, 1958), 126–127.

Heaton, Tim "Religious Influences on Mormon Fertility: Cross National Comparisons," *Review of Religious Research* 30 (1989), 401–411.

Heaton, Tim, "Vital Statistics," in James T. Duke (ed.), *Latter-Day Saint Social Life: Social Research on the LDS Church and its Members* (Provo, UT: Religious Studies Center, BYU, 1998), 105–132.

Heaton, Tim, and Kristen Goodman, "Religion and Family Formation," *Review of Religious Research* 26 (1985), 343–359.

Heaton, Tim, Kristen Goodman, and Thomas Holman, "In Search of a Peculiar People: Are Mormon Families Really Different" in Marie Cornwall, Tim Heaton, and Lawrence Young (eds.), *Contemporary Mormonism: Social Science Perspectives* (Urbana: University of Illinois Press, 1994), 87–117.

Heinerman, John, and Anson Shupe, *The Mormon Corporate Empire* (Boston: Beacon, 1985).

Hendrix, Scott, *Recultivating the Vineyard:*

The Reformation Agendas of Christianization (Louisville, KY: Westminster John Knox, 2004).

Henetz, Patty, "Church Evaluating Reports of Satanic Cults in Utah," [Salt Lake City] *Deseret News*, October 25, 1991, B1-B2.

Herman, Ellen, *The Romance of American Psychology: Political Culture in the Age of Experts* (Berkeley: University of California Press, 1995).

Heyrman, Christine Leigh, *Southern Cross: The Beginnings of the Bible Belt* (Chapel Hill: University of North Carolina Press, 1997).

Hickman, William, *Brigham's Destroying Angel: Being the Life, Confession, and Startling Disclosures of the Notorious Bill Hickman, Danite Chief of Utah* (New York: George A. Crofutt, 1872).

Higham, John, "Ethnicity and American Protestantism: Collective Identity in the Mainstream" in Harry Stout and D.G. Hart (eds.), *New Directions in Religious History* (New York: Oxford University Press, 1997), 239-259.

Higham, John, *Strangers in the Land: Patterns of American Nativism, 1860-1925* (New York: Vintage, 1963).

Hill, Christopher, *The Antichrist in the Seventeenth-Century* (London: Verso, 1971).

Hill, Christopher, *Society and Puritanism in Pre-Revolutionary England* (London: Mercury, 1964).

Hill, Marvin, "The First Vision: A Critique and Reconciliation," *Dialogue* 15 (Summer 1982), 31-46.

Hill, Marvin, "Quest for Refuge: An Hypothesis as to the Social Origins and Nature of the Mormon Political Kingdom," *Journal of Mormon History* 2 (1975), 3-20.

Hill, Marvin, *Quest for Refuge: The Mormon Flight from American Pluralism* (Salt Lake City: Signature, 1989).

Hill, Marvin, "The Rise of Mormonism in the Burned-Over District: Another View," *New York History* LXI:4 (October 1980), 411-430.

Hill, Marvin, "The Role of Christian Primitivism in the Origin and Development of the Mormon Kingdom," unpublished Ph.D. dissertation, University of Chicago, 1968.

Hill, Marvin, "The Shaping of the Mormon Mind in New England and New York" *BYU Studies* 9 (Spring 1989), 351-372.

Hill, Marvin, Keith Rooker, and Larry Wimmer, "The Kirtland Economy Revisited: A Market Critique of Sectarian Economics," *BYU Studies* 17:4 (Summer 1977), 389-476.

Hinckley, Gordon B., "Daughters of God," *Ensign*, November 1991, 98-100.

History of the Church of Jesus Christ of Latter-day Saints: Period 1, History of Joseph Smith, the Prophet, by himself, six volumes, edited by B.H. Roberts (Salt Lake City: Deseret, 1902-1912).

Hobsbawm, Eric, *Primitive Rebels: Studies in Archaic Forms of Social Movement in the 19th and 20th Centuries* (London: Abacus, 1959).

Hobsbawm, Eric, and Terrence Ranger (eds.), *The Invention of Tradition* (Cambridge, UK: Cambridge University Press, 1983).

Hofstadter Richard, *The Age of Reform from Bryan to FDR* (New York: Vintage, 1955).

Hofstadter, Richard, *The Paranoid Style in American Politics and Other Essays* (Cambridge, MA: Harvard University Press, 1965).

Holbrook, Joseph, "Autobiography," typescript, HBLL, BYU.

Hollinger, David, "Historians and the Discourse of Intellectuals" in John Higham and Paul Conkin (eds.), *New Directions in American Intellectual History* (Baltimore, MD, Johns Hopkins University Press), 42-63.

Hollingshead, Todd, "BYU Fires Teacher Over Op-Ed Stance," *Salt Lake City Tribune*, 14 June 2006 (online).

Holpuch, Amanda, "Mormon Church Excommunicates Kelly Over Women's Advocacy Work," *The Guardian*, 23 June 2014 (online).

Holzapfeel, Richard, and Jeni Holzapfeel, *Women of Nauvoo* (Salt Lake City: Bookcraft, 1992).

Homer, Michael, "'Similarity of Priesthood in Masonry': The Relationship Between Freemasonry and Mormonism" *Dialogue* 27 (Fall 1994), 1-113.

Howard, Richard P., *The Church Through the Years Volume 1: RLDS Beginnings to 1860, Volume 2: The Reorganization Comes of Age 1860-1992* (Independence, MO: Herald House, 1992, 1993).

Howe, Daniel Walker, "Charles Sellers, the Market Revolution, and the Shaping of American Identity in Whig-Jacksonian

America" in Mark Noll (ed.), *God and Mammon: Protestants, Money, and the Market, 1790-1860* (New York: Oxford University Press, 2001), 54-74.

Howe, Daniel Walker, "Protestantism, Voluntarism, and Personal Identity in Antebellum America" in Harry Stout and D.G. Hart (eds.), *New Directions in American Religious History* (New York: Oxford University Press, 1997), 206-238.

Howe, Daniel Walker, *What Hath God Wrought: The Transformation of America, 1815-1848* (New York: Oxford University Press, 2007).

Howe, E.D., *Mormonism Unvailed or, a Faithful Account of that Singular Imposition and Delusion* (Salt Lake City: Utah Lighthouse Ministry, 1834).

Hsia, R. Po-chia, "Munster and the Anabaptists" in R. Po-chia Hsia (ed.), *The German People and the Reformation* (Ithaca, NY: Cornell University Press, 1988), 51-69.

Hughes, Richard, "Soaring with the Gods: Early Mormons and the Eclipse of Religious Pluralism," in Richard Hughes and Leonard Allen (eds.), *Illusions of Innocence: Protestant Primitivism in America, 1630-1875* (Chicago: University of Chicago Press, 1988), 133-152.

Hughes, Richard, "Two Restoration Traditions: Mormons and Churches of Christ in the Nineteenth-Century," in Michael Casey and Douglas Foster (eds.), *The Stone Campbell Movement: An International Religious Tradition* (Knoxville: University of Kentucky Press, 2002), 348-363.

Hughes, Richard (ed.), *The American Quest for the Primitive Church* (Urbana: University of Illinois Press, 1988).

Hughes, Richard, and Leonard Allen, *Illusions of Innocence: Protestant Primitivism in America, 1630-1875* (Chicago: University of Chicago Press, 1988).

Hulett, James Edward, "Social Role and Personal Security in Mormon Polygamy," *American Journal of Sociology* 44:4 (January 1940), 542-553.

Hulett, James Edward, "The Social Role of the Mormon Polygamous Male," *American Sociological Review* 8 (June 1943), 279-287.

Hulett, James Edward, Jr., "The Sociological and Social Psychological Aspects of the Mormon Polygamous Family," Ph.D. dissertation, University of Wisconsin, 1939.

Humez, Jean M. (ed.), *Mother's First-Born Daughters: Early Shaker Writings on Women and Religion* (Bloomington: Indiana University Press, 1993).

Hunter, Milton, and Thomas Ferguson, *Ancient America and the Book of Mormon* (Oakland, CA: Kolob, 1950).

Introvigne, Massimo, "The Devil Makers: Contemporary Evangelical Fundamentalist Anti-Mormonism," *Dialogue* 27:1 (Spring 1994), 153-169.

Irving, Gordon, "Mormons and the Bible in the 1830s," *BYU Studies* 13 (Summer 1973), 473-478.

Isaac, Rhys, *The Transformation of Virginia, 1740-1790* (Chapel Hill: University of North Carolina Press, 1999 new edition).

Isserman, Maurice, and Michael Kazin, *America Divided: The Civil War of the 1960s* (New York: Oxford University Press, 2000).

Iverson, Joan, "A Debate on the American Home: The Antipolygamy Controversy, 1880-1890," *Journal of the History of Sexuality* 1:4 (1991), 585-602.

Ivins, Stanley, "Notes on Mormon Polygamy," *Western Humanities Review* 10 (Summer 1956), 229-239.

Jacob, Udney Hay, *An Extract from a Manuscript Entitled the Peace Maker, or the Doctrines of the Millennium* (Nauvoo, IL: J. Smith, 1842).

Jacobson, Matthew Frye, *Barbarian Virtues: The United States Encounters Foreign Peoples at Home and Abroad, 1876-1917* (New York: Hill and Wang, 2000).

Jaher, Frederic Cople, *A Scapegoat in the Wilderness: The Origins and Rise of Anti-Semitism in America* (Cambridge, MA: Harvard University Press, 1994).

Jeffrey, Julie Roy, *Frontier Women: Civilizing the West?, 1840-1880*, revised edition (New York: Hill and Wang, 1998).

Jenkins, Phillip, *Mystics and Messiahs: Cults and New Religions in American History* (New York: Oxford University Press, 2001).

Jensen, Richard L., and Malcolm R. Thorp (eds.), *Mormons in Victorian Britain* (Salt Lake City: University of Utah Press, 1989).

Jessee, Dean, "The Early Accounts of Joseph Smith's First Vision," *BYU Studies* 9:3 (Spring 1969), 275-294.

Jessee, Dean, "Joseph Smith and the Beginning of Mormon Record Keeping" in Larry C. Porter and Susan Easton Black (eds.), *The Prophet Joseph* (Salt Lake City: Deseret, 1988), 138–160.

Jessee, Dean, "The Reliability of Joseph Smith's History," *Journal of Mormon History* 3 (1976), 23–46.

Jessee, Dean, "The Writing of Joseph Smith's History," *BYU Studies* 11 (Summer 1971), 439–473.

Johnson, Clark (ed.), *Mormon Redress Petitions: Documents of the 1833-1838 Missouri Conflict* (Provo, UT: BYU Religious Studies Center, 1992).

Johnson, Curtis, *Islands of Holiness; Rural Religion in Upstate New York, 1790-1860* (Ithaca, NY: Cornell University Press, 1989).

Johnson, G. Wesley, "Editorial Preface," *Dialogue* 1 (Spring 1966), 1.

Johnson, Paul, *A Shopkeeper's Millennium: Society and Revivals in Rochester, New York, 1915-1817* (New York: Hill and Wang, 1978).

Johnson, Paul, and Sean Wilentz, *The Kingdom of Matthias: A Story of Sex and Salvation in 19th-Century America* (New York: Oxford University Press, 995).

Judt, Tony, *Past Imperfect: French Intellectuals, 1944-1956* (Berkeley: University of California Press, 1992).

Juster, Susan, "The Spirit and the Flesh: Gender, Language, and Sexuality in American Protestantism" in Harry Stout and D.G. Hart (eds.), *New Directions in American Religious History* (New York: Oxford University Press, 1997), 334–361.

Katz, David S., and Richard H. Popkin, *Messianic Revolution: Radical Religious Politics to the End of the Second Millennium* (Harmondsworth, Allen Lane, 1999).

Kenney, Scott, "E.E. Ericksen-Loyal Heretic, *Sunstone* 3 (July-August 1978), 16–27.

Kern, Louis, *An Ordered Love: Sex Roles and Sexuality in Victorian Utopias: The Shakers, the Mormons, and the Oneida Community* (Chapel Hill: University of North Carolina Press, 1981).

Kerr, Howard, and Charles Crow (eds.), *The Occult in America: New Historical Perspectives* (Urbana: University of Illinois Press, 1983).

Kertzler, David, *The Popes Against the Jews: The Vatican's Role in the Rise of Modern Anti-Semitism* (New York: Vintage, 2002).

Kinney, Bruce, *Mormonism: The Islam of America* (New York: Fleming Revell, 1912).

Kitchell, Asabel, "Asbel Kitchell's 'Journal,' Historian's Corner," *BYU Studies* 20:1, 94–99.

Knight, Vinson, "Letter to William Cooper," 3 February 1835, typescript, HBLL, BYU.

"Knowledge Alone Is Not Enough, Apostle Says," *Deseret News*, 19 August 1992.

Kuhn, Thomas, *The Structure of Scientific Revolutions*, 2d. ed. (Chicago: University of Chicago, second edition, 1970).

Kuklick, Bruce, "Boundary Maintenance in American Sociology," *Journal of the History of the Behavioral Sciences* 16 (July 1980), 201–219.

Kuklick, Bruce, "The Organization of Social Science in America: A Review Essay," *American Quarterly* 28 (Spring 1976), 124–141.

Kuklick, Bruce, "Restructuring the Past: Toward an Appreciation of the Social Context of Social Science," *Sociological Quarterly* 21 (Winter 1980), 5–21.

Kunz, Phillip; "One Wife or Several: A Comparative Study of Late Nineteenth-Century Marriage in Utah" in Thomas Alexander (ed.), *The Mormon People: Their Character and Traditions* (Provo, UT: Brigham Young University Press, 1980), 53–73.

Lantenari, Vittorio, *The Religion of the Oppressed: A Study of Modern Messianic Movements* (New York: Knopf, 1963).

Larson, Clinton E., "The Founding Vision of BYU Studies, 1959-1967," *BYU Studies* 31 (Fall 1991), 5–10.

Larson, Edward J., *Summer for the Gods: The Scopes Trial and America's Continuing Debate Over Science and Religion* (New York: Basic Books, 1997).

Larson, Gustave, *The Americanization of Utah for Statehood* (San Marino, CA: Huntington Library, 1971).

Larson, Stan, *Quest for the Gold Plates: Thomas Stuart Ferguson's Archaeological Search for the Book of Mormon* (Herriman, UT: Freethinker Press, 2004).

Latter-day Saints Messenger and Advocate Volume 2, Number 3 (1835).

Launius, Roger, and John Halwas (eds.), *The Kingdom on the Mississippi Revisited* (Urbana: University of Illinois Press, 1996).

LDS Church Almanac (Salt Lake City: Deseret News, 2020).

Leavitt, Sarah Studevant, *History of S.S. Leavitt*, edited by Juanita C. Pulsipher, n.p., 1919.

Lebowitz, Michael, "The Jacksonians: Paradox Lost" in Barton Bernstein (ed.), *Toward a New Past: Dissenting Essays in American History* (New York: Vintage, 1968), 65–89.

Lee, Erika, *America for Americans: A History of Xenophobia in the United States* (New York: Basic, 2019).

Lee, John D., *The Confessions of John D. Lee* (Salt Lake City: Utah Lighthouse Ministry, 1877).

Lee, John D., *Mormonism Unveiled: or The Life and Confessions of the Late Mormon Bishop John D. Lee* (New York: Bryan, Brand, and Company, 1877).

Leonard, Bill, *Baptists in America* (New York: Columbia University Press, 2005).

Leone, D. Mark, *Roots of Modern Mormonism* (Cambridge, MA: Harvard University Press, 1979).

LeSueur, Stephen C., *The 1838 Mormon War in Missouri* (Columbia: University of Missouri Press, 1987).

Lewis, Martin W., and Karen E. Wigen *The Myth of Continents: A Critique of Metageography* (Berkeley: University of California Press, 1997).

Lewis, R.W.B., *The American Adam: Innocence, Tragedy, and Tradition in the Nineteenth-Century* (Chicago: University of Chicago Press, 1955).

Lightner, Mary, "Autobiography," Utah Genealogical and Historical Magazine, 17 July 1926, 193–205.

Limerick, Patricia Nelson, "Peace Initiative: Using Mormons to Rethink Culture and Ethnicity in American History" in Patricia Nelson Limerick, *Something in the Soil: Legacies and Reckonings in the New West* (New York: Norton, 2000), 235–255.

Lindberg, Carter, *The European Reformations* (Oxford, UK: Blackwell, 1996).

Logue, Larry, "A Time of Marriage: Monogamy and Polygamy in a Utah Town," *Journal of Mormon History* 11 (1984), 3–26.

Long, E.B., *The Saints and the Union* (Urbana: University of Illinois Press, 1981).

Longfield, Bradley J., *The Presbyterian Controversy: Fundamentalists, Modernists, and Moderates* (New York: Oxford University Press, 1991).

Lord, Alfred, *The Singer of Tales* (Cambridge, MA: Harvard University Press, 1960).

Ludlow, Daniel H. (ed.), *The Encyclopedia of Mormonism*, five volumes (New York: Macmillan, 1992).

Lyman, Leo Edward, *Political Deliverance: The Mormon Quest for Statehood* (Urbana: University of Illinois Press, 1986).

Lynd, Robert, *Knowledge for What? The Place of Social Science in American Culture* (Princeton, NJ: Princeton University Press, 1939).

Lytle, Mark Hamilton, *America's Uncivil Wars: The Sixties from Elvis to the Fall of Richard Nixon* (New York: Oxford University Press, 2006).

MacCulloch, Diarmaid, *The Reformation: A History* (New York: Penguin, 2003).

Mack, Barry, "Of Canadian Presbyterians and Guardian Angels" in George Rawlyk and Mark Noll (eds.), *Amazing Grace: Evangelicalism in Australia, Britain, Canada, and the United States* (Kingston, Ont.: McGill-Queens University Press, 1995), 269–292.

Mackay, Charles, *The Mormons, or Latter-day Saints, with Memoirs of the Life and Death of Joseph Smith, or the American "Mahomet"* (London: Office of the National Illustrated Library, 1851).

Mackey, Randall A., "'The Godmakers' Examined: Introduction," Dialogue 18:2 (Summer 1985), 14–16.

Madsen, Carol Cornwall, "'At Their Peril': Utah Law and the Case of Plural Wives, 1850–1900" Western Historical Quarterly 21 (November 1990), 425–43.

Madsen, Carol Cornwall, *In Their Own Words: Women and the Story of Nauvoo* (Salt Lake City: Deseret, 2002).

Madsen, Carol Cornwall, "Mormon Women and the Struggle for Definition: The Nineteenth-Century Church," Sunstone 6 (Nov.-Dec. 1981), 7–11.

Mangum, Garth, and Bruce Blummel, *The Mormons' War on Poverty: A History of LDS Welfare, 1830–1990* (Salt Lake City: University of Utah Press, 1993).

Manuel, Frank, *The Religion of Isaac Newton* (New York: Oxford University Press, 1974).

Marcus, Greil, *Lipstick Traces: A Secret History of the Twentieth Century* (Cambridge, MA: Harvard University Press, 1990).

Marsden, George, "By Primitivism Possessed: How Useful is the Concept 'Primitivism' for Understanding American Fundamentalism" in Richard Hughes, *Primitivism in the Modern Church* (Urbana: University of Illinois Press, 1995), 34–46.

Marsh, Thomas B., *History of Thomas Baldwin Marsh by Himself*, *Latter-day Saints Millennial Star*, 29 (1864), 359–360, 375–376, 390–392, 406.

Marty, Martin, *A Nation of Behavers* (Chicago: University of Chicago Press, 1976).

Marx, Karl, *Capital: A Critique of Political Economy*, three volumes (Harmondsworth, UK: Penguin, 1993).

Matheny, Deanne, "Does the Shoe Fit? A Critique of the Limited Tehuantepec" in Brent Lee Metcalfe (ed.), *New Approaches to the Book of Mormon: Explorations in Critical Methodology* (Salt Lake City: Signature Books, 1993), 269–328.

Mauss, Armand, *All Abraham's Children: Changing Mormon Conceptions of Race and Lineage* (Urbana: University of Illinois Press, 2003).

Mauss, Armand, *The Angel and the Beehive: The Mormon Struggle with Assimilation* (Urbana: University of Illinois Press, 1994).

Mauss, Armand L., John R. Tarjan, and Martha D. Esplin, "The Unfettered Faithful: An Analysis of the Dialogue Subscribers Survey," *Dialogue* 20 (Spring 1987), 27–53.

May, Dean, "A Demographic Portrait of the Mormons, 1830–1980" in D. Michael Quinn (ed.), *The New Mormon History: Revisionist Essays on the Mormon Past* (Salt Lake City: Signature, 1992), 121–135.

May, Dean, "Mormons" in Stephen Thernstrom (ed.), *Harvard Encyclopedia of American Ethnic Groups* (Cambridge, MA: Harvard University Press, 1980), 720–731.

May, Dean, "One Heart and One Mind" in Donald Pitzer (ed.), *America's Communal Utopias* (Chapel Hill: University of North Carolina Press), 135–158.

May, Dean, "Rites of Passage: The Gathering as Cultural Credo," *Journal of Mormon History* 29:1 (Spring 2003), 1–41.

May, Dean, *Three Frontiers: Family, Land, and Society in the American West, 1850–1900* (New York: Cambridge University Press, 1997).

McCarthy, John, and M. Zald, "Resource Mobilization and Social Movements: A Partial Theory," *American Journal of Sociology* 82: 6 (1977), 1212–1241.

McCloud, Sean, *Making the American Religious Fringe: Exotics, Subversives, and Journalists, 1955–1993* (Chapel Hill: University of North Carolina Press, 2004).

McConkie, Bruce, *Mormon Doctrine: A Compendium of the Gospel* (Salt Lake City: Bookcraft, 1958).

McCrank, Lawrence, "Religious Orders and Monastic Communalism in the United States" in Donald Pitzer (ed.), *America's Communal Utopias* (Chapel Hill: University of North Carolina Press, 1997), 204–253.

McDannel, Colleen, and Bernhard Lang, *Heaven: A History* (New Haven, CT: Yale University Press, 1995).

McGuire, Meredith, *Religion: The Social Context* (Belmont, CA: Wadsworth, 1992).

McIntyre, William John, *Children of Peace* (Kingston, Ont.: McGill-Queens University Press, 1994).

McKiernan, F. Mark, "Mormonism on the Defensive: Far West, 1838–1839" in F. Mark McKiernan, Alma Blair, and Paul M. Edwards (eds.), *The Restoration Movement: Essays in Mormon History*, 2d. ed. (Independence, MO: Herald House, 1992), 126–132.

McKiernan, F. Mark, Alma Blair, and Paul M. Edwards (eds.), *The Restoration Movement: Essays in Mormon History*, 2d. ed. (Independence, MO: Herald House, 1992).

McLellin, William, *The Journals of William E. McLellin, 1831–1836*, edited by Jan Shipps and John Welch (Urbana: University of Illinois Press, 1994).

McLoughlin, William, *Revivals, Awakenings, and Reform* (Chicago: University of Chicago Press, 1980).

McNiff, William, "The Part Played by the Mormon Church in the Cultural Development of Early Utah," unpublished Ph.D. dissertation, Ohio State University, 1929.

Mears, John, "Utah and the Oneida Community," *The Independent* 31 (1879), 1584.

Meinig, Donald "The Mormon Cultural Region: Strategies and Patterns in the Geography of the American West, 1847–1964," *Annals of the Association of American Geographers* 55, 1965, 191–220.

Meinig, Donald, *The Shaping of America: A Geographical Perspective on 500 Years of History, Volume 3: Transcontinental America, 1850–1915* (New Haven, CT: Yale University Press, 1998).

Messer-Davidow, Ellen, David Shumway, and David Sylvan (eds.), *Knowledges: Historical and Critical Studies in Disciplinarity* (Charlottesville: University Press of Virginia, 1993).

Metcalfe, Brent Lee, "Apologetic and Critical Assumptions about Book of Mormon Historicity," *Dialogue* 26:3 (Fall 1993), 154–84.

Metcalfe, Brent Lee (ed.), *New Approaches to the Book of Mormon: Explorations in Critical Methodology* (Salt Lake City: Signature, 1993).

Meyers, Marvin, *The Jacksonian Persuasion: Politics and Belief* (Palo Alto, CA: Stanford University Press, 1960).

Michaelson, Robert, "Thomas O'Dea and the Mormons: Retrospect and Assessment," *Dialogue* 11:1 (Spring 1978), 44–57.

Midgley, Louis, "The Acids of Modernity and the Crisis in Mormon Historiography" in George Smith (ed.), *Faithful History: Essays on Writing Mormon History* (Salt Lake City: Signature, 1992), 189–226.

Midgley, Louis, "The Challenge of Historical Consciousness and the Encounter with Secular Modernity" in John M. Lindquist and Stephen D. Ricks (eds.), *By Study and Also By Faith: Essays in Honor of Hugh Nibley*, volume 2 (Provo, UT: FARMS, 1990), 502–551.

Midgley, Louis, Conversation between Ronald Helfrich and Louis Midgely, Provo, Utah, 1993.

Midgley, Louis, Letter to Sandra Tanner, 2 July 1997.

Midgley, Louis, "The Signature Books Saga" *FARMS Review* 16:1 (2004), 361–406.

Midgley, Louis, "Who Really Wrote the Book of Mormon? The Critics and Their Theories" in Noel B. Reynolds (ed.) *Book of Mormon Authorship Revisited: Evidence for Ancient Origins* (Provo, UT: FARMS, 1997), 101–139.

Miller, David, and Della S. Miller, *Nauvoo: The City of Joseph* (Salt Lake City: Peregrine Smith, 1974).

Millett, Robert, and Gerald McDermott, *Claiming Christ: A Mormon-Evangelical Debate* (Grand Rapids: Brazos, 2007).

Millett, Robert, and Gregory Johnson, *Bridging the Divide: The Continuing Conversation Between a Mormon and an Evangelical* (Rhinebeck, NY: Monkfish).

Mitton, George L., "Introduction: Anti-Mormon Writings: Encountering the Topsy Turvy Approach to Mormon Origins," *FARMS Review* 16:1 (2004), xi–xxxii.

Mooney, James, *The Ghost Dance Religion and the Sioux Outbreak of 1890* (Lincoln: University of Nebraska Press, 1896).

Moore, James R., *The Post-Darwinian Controversies: A Study of the Protestant Struggle to Come to Terms with Darwin in Great Britain and America, 1870–1900* (Cambridge, UK: Cambridge University Press, 1979).

Moore, R. Laurence, *In Search of White Crows: Spiritualism, Parapsychology, and American Culture* (New York: Oxford University Press, 1977).

Moore, R. Laurence, *Religious Outsiders and the Making of Americans* (New York: Oxford University Press, 1986).

Moore, R.I., *The Formation of a Persecuting Society: Authority and Deviance in Western Europe 950–1250*, 2d. ed. (Oxford, UK: Blackwell, 2007).

Moore, R.I., *The Formation of a Persecuting Society: Power and Deviance in Western Europe, 950–1250* (Oxford, UK: Blackwell, 1987).

Moore, R.I., *The Origins of European Dissent* (Toronto: University of Toronto Press, 1994).

Morgan, Dale, *Dale Morgan on Early Mormonism: Correspondence and a New History*, edited by John Phillip Walker (Salt Lake City: Signature, 1986).

Morgan, Dale, *The Great Salt Lake City* (Indianapolis: Bobbs Merrill, 1947).

Morgan, Dale, *The State of Deseret* (Salt Lake City: Utah State Historical Society, 1940).

Morgan, Edmund, *The Puritan Family: Religion and Domestic Relations in Seventeenth-Century New England*, revised edition (New York: Harper and Row, 1966).

Mosser, Carl, and Paul Owen, "Mormon

Apologetic Scholarship and Evangelical Neglect: Losing the Battle and Not Knowing It," *Trinity Journal* 19:2 (Fall 1998), 179–205.

Mosser, Carl, and Paul Owen, "Mormon Apologetic Scholarship and Evangelical Neglect: Losing the Battle and Not Knowing It," paper given at the 1997 Evangelical Theological Society Far West Annual Meeting, San Francisco, California, April 25, 1997.

Mulder, William, *Homeward to Zion: The Mormon Migration from Scandinavia* (New York: Knopf, 1958).

Mullett, Michael, "Radical Sects and Dissenting Churches, 1600–1750," in Sheridan Gilley and W.J. Sheils (eds.), *A History of Religion in Britain: Practice and Belief from Pre-Roman Times to the Present* (Oxford, UK: Blackwell, 1994),188–210.

Muncy, Raymond Lee, *Sex and Marriage in Utopian Communities: Nineteenth-Century America* (Baltimore, MD: Penguin, 1974).

Musser, Donald and David Paulsen (ed.), *Mormonism in Dialogue with Contemporary Christian Theologies* (Macon, GA: Mercer University Press, 2008).

Nänny, Max, "Chiasmus in Literature: Ornament of Function?" *Word and Image* 4 (January-March 1988), 51–59.

Nash, Gary, Charlotte Crabtree, and Ross Dunn, *History on Trial: Culture Wars and the Teaching of the Past* (New York: Knopf, 1997).

Nauvoo Expositor, 7 June 1844, pp. 1–2.

Nelson, E. Clifford (ed.), *The Lutherans in North America*, revised edition (Philadelphia: Fortress, 1980), 62–67 and 71–72.

Nelson, Lowry, *In the Direction of His Dreams: Memoirs* (New York: Philosophical Society, 1985).

Nelson, Lowry, *The Mormon Village: A Pattern and Technique of Land Settlement* (Salt Lake City: University of Utah Press, 1952).

Nelson, Lowry, "The Mormon Village: A Study in Social Origins," *Proceedings of the Utah Academy of Science* 7 (1930), 11–37.

Nelson, Lowry "A Social Survey of Escalante, Utah," *BYU Studies* 1 (1925), 1–44.

Nelson, Lowry, "Some Social and Economic Features of American Fork, Utah," *BYU Studies* 4 (1933), 5–73.

Nelson, Lowry, "The Utah Farm Village of Ephraim," BYU Studies 2 (1928), 1–41.

Newell, Linda, and Valeen Tippetts, *Mormon Enigma: Emma Hale Smith—Prophet's Wife*, 2d. ed. (Urbana: University of Illinois Press, 1993).

Newell, Linda, and Valeen Tippetts Avery, *Mormon Enigma: Emma Hale Smith* (New York: Doubleday, 1984).

Nibley, Hugh, *An Approach to the Book of Mormon* (Provo, UT: FARMS, 1988).

Nibley, Hugh, "How to Write an Anti-Mormon Book," BYU Speech, Provo, UT, 17 February 1962.

Nibley, Hugh, *Lehi in the Desert/The World of the Jaredites/They Were the Jaredites* (Provo, UT: FARMS, 1988).

Nibley, Hugh, *No Ma'am That's Not History: A Brief Review of Mrs. Brodie's Reluctant Vindication of a Prophet She Seeks to Expose* (Salt Lake City: Bookcraft, 1946).

Nibley, Hugh, *Since Cummorah*, 2d. ed. (Provo, UT: FARMS, 1988).

Niebuhr, H. Richard, *The Social Sources of Denominationalism* (Cleveland, OH: Meridian, 1929).

Noah, Mordecai, *Discourse on the Evidences on the American Indians Being the Descendants of the Lost Tribes of Israel* (New York: James Van Noorden, 1837).

Noah, Mordecai, *Discourse on the Restoration of the Jews* (New York: Harper and Brothers, 1945).

Noll, Mark, *America's God: From Jonathan Edwards to Abraham Lincoln* (New York: Oxford University Press, 2005).

Noll, Mark, *A History of Christianity in the United States and Canada* (Grand Rapids: Eerdmans, 1992).

Noll, Mark, "Protestant Reasoning About Money and Economics, 1790–1860" in Mark Noll (ed.), *God and Mammon: Protestants, Money, and the Markets, 1790–1860* (New York: Oxford University Press, 2001), 265–295.

Noll, Mark, *The Rise of Evangelicalism: The Age of Edwards, Whitefield, and the Wesley's* (Downers Grove, IL: IVP, 2003).

Noll, Mark, and Nathan Hatch (eds.), *The Bible in America: Essays in Cultural History* (New York: Oxford University Press, 1982).

Noll, Mark (ed.), *God and Mammon: Protestants, Money, and the Market, 1790–1860*

(New York: Oxford University Press, 2001).

Noll, Mark, David Bebbington, and George Rawlyk (eds.), E*vangelicalism: Comparative Studies of Popular Protestantism in North America, the British Isles, and Beyond* (New York: Oxford University Press, 1994).

Novak, Gary, "Naturalistic Claims and the Book of Mormon," *BYU Studies* 30 (Summer 1990), 23–40.

Numbers, Ronald, and Jonathan Butler (eds.), *The Disappointed: Millerism and Millenarianism in the Nineteenth-Century* (Bloomington: Indiana University Press, 1987).

O'Dea, Thomas, *The Mormons* (Chicago: University of Chicago Press, 1957).

"Official Statement by President Joseph F. Smith," *Improvement Era* 7, 545–546 (Apr. 1904).

Oleson, Alexandra, and John Voss (eds.), *The Organization of Knowledge in Modern America, 1860–1920* (Baltimore: Johns Hopkins University Press, 1979).

Olsen, Arden Beal, "The History of Mormon Mercantile Cooperation in Utah," unpublished Ph.D. dissertation, University of California, Berkeley, 1935.

O'Malley, J.S., "Revivalism, German-American" in Daniel Reid, Robert Linder, Bruce Shelly, and Harry Stout (eds.), *Dictionary of Christianity in America* (Downers Grove, IL: IVP Press, 1990), 1011–1012.

Ortner, Sherry, "On Key Symbols," *American Anthropologist*, 75:5, October 1973, 1338–1346.

Ostler, Blake, "The Book of Mormon as a Modern Expansion of an Ancient Source," *Dialogue* 20 (Spring 1987), 66–123.

Ozment, Steven, *The Age of Reform 1250–1550: An Intellectual and Religious History of Late Medieval and Reformation Europe* (New Haven, CT: Yale University Press, 1980).

Packer, Boyd K., "The Mantle Is Far, Far Greater Than the Intellect," *BYU Studies* 21 (Summer 1981), 259–271.

Packer, Boyd K., "To Young Men Only," a speech given to the General Conference Priesthood Session on 2 October 1976.

Park, Benjamin, *Kingdom of Nauvoo: The Rise and Fall of a Religious Empire on the American Frontier* (New York: Liveright, 2020).

Parkin, Max, "Kirtland, A Stronghold for the Kingdom" in F. Mark McKiernan, Alma Blair, and Paul M. Edwards (eds.), *The Restoration Movement: Essays in Mormon History*, 2d. ed. (Independence, MO: Herald House, 1992), 61–96.

Pascoe, Peggy, *Relations of Rescue: The Search for Female Moral Authority in the American West, 1874–1939* (New York: Oxford University Press, 1993).

Past and Present number 48, August 1970.

Paul, Robert, "Joseph Smith and the Plurality of Worlds Idea" *Dialogue* 19:2 (Summer 1986), 15–36.

Paul, Robert, *Science, Religion, and Mormon Cosmology* (Urbana: University of Illinois Press, 1992), 75–126.

Paulsen, David L., "A General Response to The New Mormon Challenge," *FARMS Review* 14:1 (2002), 99–112.

Peck, Elbert, "The Origin and Evolution of the *Sunstone* Species: 25 Years of Creative Adaptation," *Sunstone*, December 1999, 5–14.

Perciaccante, Marianne, "Backlash Against Formalism: Early Mormonism's Appeal in Jefferson County," *Journal of Mormon History* 19:2 (Fall 1993), 35– 63.

Perciaccante, Marianne, *Calling Down Fire: Charles Grandison Finney and Revivalism in Jefferson County, New York, 1800–1840* (Albany: State University of New York Press, 2003).

Pessen, Edward, *Jacksonian America: Society, Personality, and Politics,* revised edition (Champaign: University of Illinois Press, 1978).

Petersen, Boyd Jay, *Hugh Nibley: A Consecrated Life* (Salt Lake City: Greg Kofford Books, 2002).

Peterson, Charles S., "Beyond the Problems of Exceptionalist History" in Thomas Alexander, *The Great Basin Kingdom Revisited* (Logan: Utah State University Press, 1991), 143–148.

Peterson, Charles S., "Dale Morgan, Writers Project, and Mormon History as a Regional Study," *Dialogue* 24 (Summer 1991), 47–63.

Peterson, Charles S., *"Take Up Your Mission': Mormon Colonizing along the Little Colorado River, 1870–1900* (Tucson: University of Arizona Press, 1973).

Peterson, Daniel, "A Modern Malleus maleficarum," *FARMS Review* 3:1 (1991), 231–260.

Peterson, Daniel, "The New World Archaeology Foundation," *FARMS Review*, 16 (1): 221–233.

Peterson, Daniel, "Reflections on Secular Anti-Mormonism," *FARMS Review*, Volume 17, Number 2 (2005), 423–450.

Peterson, Daniel, and Steven Ricks, *Offenders for a Word: How Anti-Mormons Play Word Games to Attack the Latter-day Saints* (Provo, UT: FARMS, 1992).

Peterson, Levi S., *Juanita Brooks: Mormon Woman Historian* (Salt Lake City: University of Utah Press, 1988).

Pfister, Joel, and Nancy Schnog (eds.), *Inventing the Psychological: Toward a Cultural History of Emotional Life in America* (New Haven, CT: Yale University Press, 1997).

Pocock, Emil, "Popular Roots of Jacksonian Democracy: The Case of Dayton, Ohio, 1815–1830" *Journal of the Early Republic* 9 (Winter 1989), 489–513.

Poll, Richard, "Great Basin Kingdom: An Economic History of the Latter-day Saints, 1930–1900 Leonard J. Arrington," *BYU Studies* 3:1, 1961, 65–69.

Poll, Richard, "The Move South," *BYU Studies* 29:4 (Fall 1989), 65–88.

Porter, Larry, "A Study of the Origins of the Church of Jesus Christ of Latter-Day Saints in the States of New York and Pennsylvania, 1816–1831" Ph.D. dissertation, Brigham Young University, 1971.

Porter, Roy, and Mikulas Teich (eds.), *Romanticism in National Context* (Cambridge, MA: Cambridge University Press, 1988).

Pratt, Orson, *Interesting Account of Several Remarkable Visions, And of the Late Discovery of Ancient American Records* (Edinburgh, UK: Ballantyne and Hughes, 1840).

Pratt, Parley, *The Autobiography of Parley Pratt, One of the Twelve Apostles*, edited by Parley Pratt (Salt Lake City: Deseret, 1874).

Pratt, Parley, *Key to the Science of Theology* (Salem, UT: Pioneer Press, 1855).

Pratt, Parley, *Mormonism Unveiled: Zion's Watchman Unmasked and Its Editor Mr. L.R. Sunderland Exposed, Truth Vindicated, the Devil Mad, and Priestcraft in Danger*, 2d. ed. (New York: O. Pratt and E. Fordham, 1838).

Pratt, Parley, *Voice of Warning* (Salt Lake City: Hawkes Publishing, 1837).

Pratt, Parley, *The Writings of Parley Parker Pratt* (Salt Lake City: Parker Pratt Robertson, 1952).

Prince, Gregory A., "The Red Peril, the Candy Maker, and the Apostle: David O. McKay's Confrontation with Communism," *Dialogue* 37:2 (summer 2004), 37–94.

Prince, Walter F., "Psychological Tests for the Authorship of the Book of Mormon," *American Journal of Psychology* 28 (July 1917), 373–389.

Pulpisher, Mary, "Autobiography," typescript, HBLL, BYU.

Quinn, D. Michael, "The Council of Fifty and its Members," *BYU Studies* 20 (Winter 1980), 163–197.

Quinn, D. Michael, *Early Mormonism and the Magic Worldview* (Salt Lake City: Signature, 1987).

Quinn, D. Michael, *Early Mormonism and the Magic World View*, 2d. ed. (Salt Lake City: Signature, 1998).

Quinn, D. Michael, *Elder Statesman: A Biography of Reuben J. Clark* (Salt Lake City: Signature, 2002).

Quinn, D. Michael, "Ezra Taft Benson and Mormon Political Conflicts," *Dialogue* 26:2 (Summer 1993), 1–87.

Quinn, D. Michael, "LDS Church Authorities and New Plural Marriages, 1890–1904," *Dialogue* 18:1 (Spring 1985), 9–105.

Quinn, D. Michael, *The Mormon Hierarchy: Extensions of Power* (Salt Lake City: Signature, 1997).

Quinn, D. Michael, *The Mormon Hierarchy: Origins of Power* (Salt Lake City: Signature, 1994).

Quinn, D. Michael, "The Mormon Succession Crisis of 1844," *BYU Studies* 16: 2, 187–234.

Quinn, D. Michael, "Mormon Women Have Had the Priesthood Since 1843," in Maxine Hanks (ed.), *Women and Authority: Re-emerging Mormon Feminism* (Salt Lake City: Signature, 1992), 365–410.

Quinn, D. Michael, "On Being a Mormon Historian," BYU Student History Association Lecture, Fall 1981.

Quinn, D. Michael, "On Being a Mormon Historian," in George Smith (ed.), *Faithful History: Essays on Writing Mormon History* (Salt Lake City: Signature, 1992) 69–111.

Quinn, D. Michael, "Plural Marriage and Mormon Fundamentalism," *Dialogue* 31:2 (Summer 1998), 1–68.

Quinn, D. Michael, "Plural Marriage and Mormon Fundamentalism" in Martin Marty and R. Scott Appleby (eds.), *Fundamentalisms and Society: Reclaiming the Sciences, the Family, and Education* (Chicago: University of Chicago Press, 1993), 240–293.

Quinn, D. Michael, "Plural Marriages After the 1890 Manifesto," a talk presented at Bluffdale, Utah, 11 August 1991, copy in the author's possession.

Quinn, D. Michael, *Same Sex Dynamics Among Nineteenth-Century Americans: A Mormon Example* (Urbana: University of Illinois Press, 2001).

Quinn, D. Michael, *J. Reuben Clark: The Church Years* (Provo, UT: Brigham Young University Press, 1983).

Rader, Benjamin G., "Richard T. Ely: Lay Spokesman for the Social Gospel," *Journal of American History* 53:1 (June 1966), 61–74.

Rawlyk, George, *The Canada Fire: Radical Evangelicalism in British North America, 1775–1812* (Kingston, Ont.: McGill-Queens University Press, 1994).

Rawlyk, George, and Mark Noll (eds.), *Amazing Grace: Evangelicalism in Australia, Britain, Canada, and the United States* (Kingston, Ont.: McGill-Queen's University Press, 1994).

"Relief Society Exhibit Censure," *Sunstone* 16 (February 1992), 66.

Reynolds, Noel (ed.), *Book of Mormon Authorship* (Provo, UT: BYU Religious Studies Center, 1982).

Reynolds, Noel (ed.), *Book of Mormon Authorship Revisited: The Evidence for Ancient Origins* (Provo, UT: FARMS, 1997).

Richards, Leonard, *"Gentlemen of Property and Standing": Anti-Abolition Mobs in Jacksonian America* (New York: Oxford University Press, 1970).

Ricks, Steven D., "Kingship, Coronation, and Covenant in Mosiah 1–6" in John W. Welch and Steven D. Ricks (eds.), *King Benjamin's Speech: That Ye May Learn Wisdom* (Provo, UT: FARMS, 1998), 233–275.

Riley, I. Woodbridge, *The Founder of Mormonism: A Psychological Study of Joseph Smith* (New York: Dodd, Mead, 1902).

Riley-Smith, Jonathan (ed.), *The Oxford Illustrated History of the Crusades* (New York: Oxford University Press, 2002).

Rischin, Moses, "Beyond the Great Divide: Immigration and the Last Frontier," *Journal of American History* 55 (June 1968), 42–53.

Rischin, Moses, "The New Mormon History," *American West* 6 (March 1969), 49.

Robbins, Keith (ed.), *Protestant Evangelicalism: Britain, Ireland, Germany, and America, c. 1750–1850* (New York: Oxford University Press, 1990).

Robbins, Thomas, *Cults, Charisma, and the Sociology of New Religious Movements* (London: Sage, 1988).

Roberts, Allen D., "'The Godmakers': Shadow or Reality? A Content Analysis," *Dialogue* 18:2 (Summer 1985), 24–33.

Roberts, B.H., *Comprehensive History of the Church: Century I*, six volumes (Salt Lake City: Deseret News, 1930).

Roberts, B.H., *Studies of the Book of Mormon* (Salt Lake City: Signature, 1992).

Robinson, Stephen E., *Are Mormons Christian?* (Salt Lake City: Bookcraft, 1998).

Rogin, Michael, *Ronald Reagan, the Movie and Other Episodes in Political Demonology* (Berkeley: University of California Press, 1987).

Ross, Dorothy, *The Origins of American Social Science* (Cambridge, UK: Cambridge University Press, 1991).

Ross, Dorothy (ed.), *Modernist Impulses in the Human Sciences 1870–1930* (Baltimore: Johns Hopkins University Press, 1994).

Rowe, David, "Millerites: A Shadow Portrait" in Ronald Numbers and Jonathan M. Butler (eds.), *The Disappointed: Millerism and Millenarianism in the Nineteenth-Century* (Bloomington: Indiana University Press, 1993), 1–16.

Rowe, Violet, *Sir Henry Vane the Younger* (London: Athlone, 1970).

Rude, George, *Revolutionary Europe, 1783–1815*, 2d. ed. (Oxford, UK: Blackwell, 2000).

Rust, Val, "Mormonism and the Radical Religious Movement in Colonial New England," *Dialogue* 33:1 (Spring 2000), 23–55.

Ruthven, Malise, *Fundamentalism: A Very Short Introduction* (New York: Oxford University Press, 2007).

Ryan, Mary, *Cradle of the Middle Class: The Family in Oneida County, New York, 1790–1865* (New York: Cambridge University Press, 1981).

Sandeen, Ernest (ed.). *The Bible and Social Reform* (Philadelphia: Fortress, 1982).

Sarna, Jonathan, *Jacksonian Jew: The Two Worlds of Mordecai Manuel Noah* (New York: Holmes and Meier, 1981).

Saunders, Richard, "The Strange Mixture of Emotion and Intellect: A Social History of Dale Morgan, 1933-1942," *Dialogue* 28 (Winter 1995), 30-58.

Schmidt, Leigh Eric, *Hearing Things: Religion, Illusion, and the American Enlightenment* (Cambridge, MA: Harvard University Press, 2002).

Schmidt Leigh Eric, *Holy Fairs: Scotland and the Making of American Revivalism*, 2d. ed. (Grand Rapids: Eerdmans, 2001).

Scott, Anne Firor, "Mormon Women, Other Women" *Journal of Mormon History* 13 (1986-1987), 3-19.

Scott, Patricia Lynn, James E. Crooks, and Sharon G. Pugsley: "'A Kinship of Interest': The Mormon History Association's Membership," *Journal of Mormon History* 18:1 (Spring 1992), 153-176.

Scribner, Robert. *The German Reformation* (Basingstoke, UK: Macmillan, 1986).

Scribner, Robert, Roy Porter, and Mikulas Teich (eds.), *The Reformation in National Context* (Cambridge, UK: Cambridge University Press, 1994).

Scribner, Robert, "A Comparative Overview" in Robert Scribner, Roy Porter, and Mikulas Teich (eds.), *The Reformation in National Context* (Cambridge, UK: Cambridge University Press, 1994), 215-227.

Sellers, Charles, *Market Revolution: Jacksonian America, 1815-1846* (New York: Oxford University Press, 1991).

Sha'ban, Fuad, *Islam and the Arabs in Early American Thought* (Durham, NC: Acorn, 1991).

Sharf, Andrew, *Byzantine Jewry from Justinian to the Fourth Crusade* (New York: Schocken, 1971).

Sheldon, Carrel Hilton, "Launching Exponent II," *Exponent II* 22:4 (Summer 1999) (online).

Shepherd, Gordon, and Gary Shepherd, *Jan Shipps: A Social and Intellectual Portrait* (Salt Lake City: Greg Kofford Books, 2019).

Shepherd, Gordon, and Gary Shepherd, *A Kingdom Transformed: Themes in the Development of Mormonism* (Salt Lake City: University of Utah Press 1984).

Shils, Edward, "The Intellectuals and the Powers" in Edward Shils, *The Constitution of Society* (Chicago: University of Chicago Press, 1982), 197-201.

Shipps, Jan, "Dangerous History: Laurel Thatcher Ulrich and Her Sisters" in Jan Shipps, *Sojourner in a Promised Land: Forty Years Among the Mormons* (Urbana: University of Illinois Press, 2000), 193-203.

Shipps, Jan, "From Gentile to Non-Mormon: Mormon Perceptions of the Other" in Jan Shipps, *Sojourner in the Promised Land: Forty Years Among the Mormons* (Urbana: University of), 124-142.

Shipps, Jan, "From Satyr to Saint: American Perception of the Mormons, 1860-1960" in Jan Shipps, *Sojourner in the Promised Land: Forty Years Among the Mormons* (Urbana: University of Illinois Press, 2000), 51-97.

Shipps, Jan, "Gentiles, Mormons, and the History of the American West" in Jan Shipps, *Sojourner in a Promised Land: Forty Years Among the Mormons* (Urbana: University of Illinois Press, 2000), 17-44.

Shipps, Jan, "In the Presence of the Past: Continuity and Change in Twentieth-Century Mormonism" in Thomas Alexander and Jessie Embry (eds.), *After 150 Years: The Latter-day Saints in Sesquicentennial Perspective* (Provo, UT: Charles Redd Center for Western Studies, 1983), 3-35.

Shipps, Jan, "An 'Insider-Outsider' in Zion," *Dialogue* 15:1 (Spring 1982), 138-161.

Shipps, Jan, "Is Mormonism Christian? Reflections on a Complicated Question" in Jan Shipps, *Sojourner in a Promised Land: Forty Years Among the Mormons* (Urbana: University of Illinois Press, 2000), 335-357.

Shipps, Jan, "Making Saints: In the Early Days and Latter Days" in Marie Cornwall, Tim Heaton, and Larry A. Young (eds.), *Contemporary Mormonism: Social Science Perspectives* (Urbana: University of Illinois Press, 1994), 64-83.

Shipps, Jan, *Mormonism: The Story of a New Religious Tradition* (Urbana: University of Illinois Press, 1985).

Shipps, Jan, "The Reality of the Restoration in LDS Theology and Mormon Experience" in Jan Shipps, *Sojourner in the Promised Land: Forty Years Among the Mormons* (Urbana: University of Illinois Press, 2000), 229-240.

Shipps, Jan, *Sojourner in the Promised Land: Forty Years Among the Mormons* (Urbana: University of Illinois Press, 2000).

Shipps, Jan, "Surveying the Mormon Image Since 1960" in Jan Shipps, *Sojourner in the Promised Land: Forty Years Among the Mormons* (Urbana: University of Illinois Press, 2000), 98–123.

Shipps, Jan, "Thoughts about the Academic Community's Response to John Brooke's Refiner's Fire" in Jan Shipps, *Sojourner in the Promised Land: Forty Years Among the Mormons* (Urbana: University of Illinois Press, 2000), 204–217.

Shipps, Jan, Cheryl May, and Dean May, "Sugar House Ward: A Latter-day Saint Congregation," in James Wind and James Lewis (editors), *American Congregations: Volume I, Portraits of Twelve Religious Communities* (Chicago: University of Chicago Press, 1994), 293–348.

Shupe, Anson, *The Darker Side of Virtue: Corruption, Scandal and the Mormon Empire* (Buffalo, NY: Prometheus, 1991).

Silva, Edward, and Sheila Slaughter, *Serving Power: The Making of the Academic Social Science Expert* (Westport, CT: Greenwood Press, 1984).

Simpson, Christopher (ed.), *Universities and Empire: Money and Politics in the Social Sciences During the Cold War* (New York: New Press, 1998).

Singer, Merrill, "Nathaniel Baldwin, Utah Inventor and Patron of the Fundamentalist Movement," *Utah Historical Quarterly* 47:1 (Winter 1979), 42–53.

Smith, Bathsheba Wilson Bigler, "Autobiography," typescript, HBLL, BYU.

Smith, Ethan, *View of the Hebrews*, edited by Charles Tate (Provo, UT: BYU Religious Studies Center, 1825).

Smith, George (ed.), *Faithful History: Essays on Writing Mormon History* (Salt Lake City: Signature, 1992).

Smith, James, and Phillip Kunz, "Polygyny and Fertility in Nineteenth-Century America," *Population Studies* 30 (1976), 465–480.

Smith, Joseph, *An American Prophet's Record: The Diaries and Journals of Joseph Smith*, edited by Scott Faulring (Salt Lake City: Signature, 1987).

Smith, Joseph, "Church History: Wentworth Letter," *Times and Seasons* 3 (1 March 1842), 706–710.

Smith, Joseph, *The Papers of Joseph Smith*, Volume 1, edited by Dean Jessee (Salt Lake City: Deseret, 1989).

Smith, Joseph, *The Personal Writings of Joseph Smith*, edited and compiled by Dean Jessee (Salt Lake City: Deseret, 1984).

Smith, Joseph, *The Papers of Joseph Smith*, two volumes, *Volume 1: Autobiographical and Historical Writings, Volume 2: Journal, 1832–1842* (Salt Lake City: Deseret, 1989, 1992).

Smith, Joseph Fielding, *Essentials in Church History: A History of the Church from the Birth of Joseph Smith Until the Present Times with Introductory Chapters on the Antiquity of the Gospel and the "Falling Away"* (Salt Lake City: Deseret News, 1922).

Smith, Mark, *Social Science in the Crucible: The American Debate Over Objectivity and Purpose, 1918–1941* (Durham, NC: Duke University Press, 1994).

Smith, Timothy, "The Book of Mormon in a Biblical Culture," *Journal of Mormon History*, 7 (1980), 3–21.

Smith, Timothy, *Revivalism and Social Reform* (New York: Harper and Row, 1957).

Smith-Rosenberg, Carroll, "The Cross and the Pedestal: Women, Anti-Ritualism, and the Emergence of the American Bourgeoisie," in Carroll Smith-Rosenberg, *Disorderly Conduct: Visions of Gender in Victorian America* (New York: Oxford University Press, 1985), 129–164.

Smith-Rosenberg, Carroll, "Women and Religious Revivals: Anti-Ritualism, Liminality, and the Emergence of the American Bourgeoisie" in Leonard Sweet (ed.), *The Evangelical Tradition in America* (Macon, GA: Mercer University Press, 1984), 199–231.

Smith-Rosenberg Carroll, "Bourgeois Discourse in the Age of Jackson: An Introduction," in Carroll Smith-Rosenberg, *Disorderly Conduct: Visions of Gender in Victorian America* (New York: Oxford University Press, 1985), 79–89.

Smith-Rosenberg Carroll, *Disorderly Conduct: Visions of Gender in Victorian America* (New York: Oxford University Press, 1985).

Snow, Eliza Roxey, *The Personal Writings of Eliza Roxey Snow*, edited by Maureen

Ursenbach Beecher (Salt Lake City: University of Utah Press, 1995).

Sorenson, John, *An Ancient American Setting for the Book of Mormon* (Provo, UT: FARMS, 1985).

Spaulding, Solomon, *The Complete Original Spaulding Manuscript Found*, edited by Kent Jackson (Provo, UT: Religious Studies Center, BYU, 1996).

Spencer, Geoffrey, "Anxious Saints: The Early Mormons, Social Reform, and Status Anxiety," *John Whitmer Historical Association Journal* 1 (1981), 43-53.

Spitz, Lewis, *The Protestant Reformation 1517-1559* (New York: Harper and Row, 1985).

Stack, Peggy Fletcher, "Despite Church Warnings, 1500 Attended Sunstone Symposia," *Salt Lake City Tribune*, 15 August 1992, A-5 and A-7.

Stack, Peggy Fletcher, "LDS Intelligentsia is Grouping to Fight Defamation," *Salt Lake City Tribune*, 27 June 1992, A-7.

Stark, Rodney, "The Rise of a New World Faith" in James T. Duke (ed.), *Latter-Day Saint Social Life: Social Research on the LDS Church and its Members* (Provo, UT: Religious Studies Center, BYU, 1998), 9-27.

Stark, Rodney, and Roger Finke, *Acts of Faith: Explaining the Human Side of Religion* (Berkeley: University of California Press, 2000).

Stark, Rodney, and William Bainbridge, *The Future of Religion: Secularization, Revivals, and Cult Formation* (Berkeley: University of California Press, 1986).

Stayer, James, *The German Peasants War and Anabaptist Community of Goods* (Kingston, Ont.: McGill-Queens University Press, 1991).

Stein, Stephen, *Communities of Dissent: A History of Alternative Religions in America* (New York: Oxford University Press, 2003).

Stein, Stephen, *The Shaker Experience in America: A History of the United Society of Believers* (New Haven, CT: Yale University Press, 1992).

Stocking, George, Jr., *Race, Culture, and Evolution: Essays in the History of Anthropology* (Chicago: University of Chicago Press, 1982).

Stockman, Robert, "The American Baha'i Community in the Nineties" in Timothy Miller (ed.), *America's Alternative Religions* (Albany: State University of New York Press, 1995), 243-248.

Stoeffler, F. Ernest, "Pietism" in Daniel Reid, Robert Linder, Bruce Shelly, and Harry Stout (eds.), *Dictionary of Christianity in America* (Downers Grove, IL: IVP Press, 1990), 902-904.

Stoeffler, F. Ernest, *The Rise of Evangelical Pietism* (Leiden, 1971).

Stoeffler, F. Ernest (ed.), *Continental Pietism and Early American Christianity* (Grand Rapids: Eerdmans, 1976).

Stokes, Melvin, and Stephen Conway (eds.), *The Market Revolution in America: Social, Political, and Religious Expressions, 1800-1880* (Charlottesville: University Press of Virginia, 1996).

Strout, Cushing, *The New Heavens and the New Earth: Political Religion in America* (New York: Harper and Row, 1974).

Sunderland, La Roy, *Mormonism Exposed and Refuted* (New York: Piercy and Reed, 1838).

Sutton, Robert, *Communal Utopias and the American Experience: Religious Communities, 1722-2000* (Westport, CT: Praeger, 2003).

Swenson, Sharon Lee, "'The Godmakers' Examined: Does the Camera Lie: A Structural Analysis of 'The Godmakers,'" *Dialogue* 18:2 (Summer 1985), 16-23.

Tanner, Jerald, and Sandra Tanner, *Did Spalding Write the Book of Mormon?* (Salt Lake City: Modern Microfilms, 1977).

Tanner, Jerald, and Sandra Tanner, *Evolution of the Mormon Temple Ceremony: 1842-1990*, updated edition (Salt Lake City: Utah Lighthouse Ministry 2005).

Tanner, Jerald, and Sandra Tanner, *Joseph Smith and Polygamy* (Salt Lake City: Modern Microfilms, 1967).

Tanner, Jerald, and Sandra Tanner, *Mormonism: Shadow or Reality?* (Salt Lake City: Utah Lighthouse Ministry, 1987).

Tanner, Jerald, and Sandra Tanner, *Problems in The Godmakers II* (Salt Lake City: Utah Lighthouse Ministry, 1993).

Taves, Ann, *Fits, Trances, and Visions: Experiencing Religion and Explaining Experience from Wesley to James* (Princeton, NJ: Princeton University Press, 1999).

Taylor, Eugene, "Swedenborgianism" in Timothy Miller (ed.), *America's Alternative Religions* (Albany: State University of New York Press, 1995), 77-86.

"The Testimony of the Three Witnesses, and The Testimony of the Eight Witnesses" in the Book of Mormon.

Thomas, George, *Revivalism and Cultural Change: Christianity, Nation Building, and the Market in the Nineteenth-Century United States* (Chicago: University of Chicago Press, 1989).

Thomas, Robert David, *The Man Who Would Be Perfect: John Humphrey Noyes and the Utopian Impulse* (Philadelphia: University of Pennsylvania Press, 1977).

Thrupp, Sylvia L. (ed.), *Millennial Dreams in Action* (New York: Schocken, 1962).

Tönnies, Ferdinand, *Community and Society* (New York: Harper Torchbooks, 1935).

Toon, Peter (ed.), *Puritans, the Millennium and the Future of Israel: Puritan Eschatology 1600 to 1660*, new edition (Cambridge, UK: James Clarke, 2002).

Topping, Gary, "One Hundred Years at the Utah State Historical Society," *Utah Historical Quarterly* 65 (Summer 1997), 223–232.

Toscano, Paul, and Margaret Toscano, *Strangers in Paradox: Explorations in Mormon Theology* (Salt Lake City: Signature, 1990).

Trimble, Shawn Michael, "Spiritualism and Channeling" in Timothy Miller (ed.) *America's Alternative Religions* (Albany: State University of New York Press, 1995), 331–338.

Troeltsch, Ernest, *The Social Teachings of the Christian Churches*, two volumes (Louisville, KY: Westminster, 1931).

Tucker, Pomeroy, *Origin, Rise, and Progress of Mormonism: Biography of Its Funders and History of Its Church* (Salt Lake City: Utah Lighthouse Ministry, 1867).

Turner, Frederick, *The Significance of the Frontier in American History* (New York: Penguin, 1893).

Turner, Victor, "Betwixt and Between: The Liminal Period in Rites of Passage" in Victor Turner, *The Forest of Symbols* (Ithaca, NY: Cornell University Press, 1967), 93–111.

Turner, Victor, "Liminal to Liminoid, in Play, Flow, and Ritual: An Essay in Comparative Symbology," *Rice University Studies* 60 (Summer 1974), 53–92.

Turner, Victor, "Symbols in African Ritual," *Science* Vol. 179, no. 4078, 16 March 1973, 1100–1101.

Tuveson, Ernest Lee, *Redeemer Nation: The Idea of America's Millennial Role* (Chicago: University of Chicago Press, 1968).

Twain, Mark, *Roughing It* (Hartford, CT: American Publishing Company, 1872).

Tyacke, Nicholas, "Puritanism, Arminianism, and Counter-Revolution" in Richard Cust and Ann Hughes (eds.), *The English Civil War* (London: Arnold, 1997), 136–159.

Tyler, Alice Felt, *Freedom's Ferment: Phases of American Social History from the Colonial Period to the Outbreak of the Civil War* (New York: Harper and Row, 1944).

Underwood, Grant, "The Meaning and Attraction of Mormonism Reexamined" *Thetan* (March 1977), 1–15.

Underwood, Grant, *The Millenarian World of Early Mormonism* (Urbana: University of Illinois Press, 1993).

Vann, Richard, *The Social Development of English Quakerism: 1655–1755* (Cambridge, MA: Harvard University Press, 1969).

Van Wagenen, Lola, "In Their Own Behalf: The Politicization of Mormon Women and the 1870 Franchise," *Dialogue* 24 (Winter 1991), 31–43.

Van Wagoner, Richard, *Mormon Polygamy: A History* (Salt Lake City: Signature, 1986).

Vernon, Glenn, "Background Factors Related to Church Orthodoxy," *Social Forces* 34 (March 1956), 252–254.

Vernon, Glenn, "An Inquiry Into the Scalability of Church Orthodoxy," *Sociology and Social Research* 39 (May/June 1955), 324–327.

Veysey, Laurence, *The Emergence of the American University* (Chicago: University of Chicago Press, 1965).

Vidich, Arthur, and Stanford Lyman, *American Sociology: Worldly Rejections of Religion and Their Directions* (New Haven, CT: Yale University Press, 1985).

Vogel, Dan, "Anti-Universalist Rhetoric in the Book of Mormon" in Brent Lee Metcalfe (ed.), *New Approaches to the Book of Mormon: Explorations in Critical Methodology* (Salt Lake City: Signature, 1993), 21–52.

Vogel, Dan, "Echoes of Anti-Masonry: A Rejoinder to the Critics of the Anti-Masonic Thesis" in Dan Vogel and Brent Lee Metcalfe (eds.), *American Apocrypha: Essays on the Book of*

Mormon (Salt Lake City: Signature, 2002), 275-320.

Vogel, Dan, *Indian Origins and the Book of Mormon: Religious Solutions from Columbus to Joseph Smith* (Salt Lake City: Signature, 1986).

Vogel, Dan, "Mormonism's 'Anti-Masonick Bible,'" *John Whitmer Historical Society Journal* 9 (1989), 17-30.

Vogel, Dan, *Religious Seekers and the Advent of Mormonism* (Salt Lake City: Signature, 1988).

Vogel, Dan, and Brent Lee Metcalfe (eds.), *American Apocrypha: Essays on the Book of Mormon* (Salt Lake City: Signature, 2002).

Vogel, Dan (ed.), *The Word of God: Essays on Mormon Scriptures* (Salt Lake City: Signature, 1990).

Vogt, Evon, and Ethel Albert (eds.), *People of Rimrock; A Study of Values in Five Cultures* (Cambridge, MA: Harvard University Press, 1966).

Walker, Ronald, *Wayward Saints: The Godbeites and Brigham Young* (Urbana: University of Illinois Press, 1999).

Walker, Ronald, Richard Turley, and Glen Leonard, *Massacre at Mountain Meadows* (New York: Oxford University Press, 2008).

Walker, Ronald W., David K. Whittaker, and James B. Allen, *Mormon History* (Urbana: University of Illinois Press, 2000).

Wallace, Anthony, *Culture and Personality* (New York: Random House, 1961).

Wallace, Anthony, "Revitalization Movements" *American Anthropologist* 58 (1956), 264-281.

Wallis, Roy, "The Cult and Its Transformation" in Roy Wallis (ed.), *Sectarianism: Analysis of Religious and Non-Religious Sects* (New York: Wiley), 35-49.

Wallis, Roy, "Three Types of New Religious Movement" in Lorne Dawson (ed.), *Cults and New Religious Movements* (Oxford, UK: Blackwell, 2003), 36-58.

Walters, Ronald, *American Reformers 1815-1860* (New York: Hill and Wang, 1978).

Walters, Ronald, *American Reformers 1815-1860*, revised edition (New York: Hill and Wang, 1997).

Ward, Gary L. (ed.), *Mormonism I: Evangelical Christian Anti-Mormonism in the Twentieth- Century* (New York: Garland, 1990).

Ward, John William, *Andrew Jackson: Symbol for an Age* (New York: Oxford University Press, 1955).

Ward, W.R., *The Protestant Evangelical Awakening* (Cambridge, UK: Cambridge University Press, 1992).

Warthen, Lee, "History of *Sunstone*: The Scott Kenney Years, Summer 1974-June 1978," *Sunstone* 22 (June 1999), 48-61.

Waterman, Bryan, and Brian Kagel, *The Lord's University: Freedom and Authority at BYU* (Salt Lake City: Signature, 1998).

Webb, Gisela, "Expressions of Islam in America" in Timothy Miller (ed.), *America's Alternative Religions* (Albany: SUNY Press, 1995), 233-242.

Weber, Max, *Economy and Society: An Outline of Interpretive Sociology* (Berkeley: University of California Press, 1968).

Weber, Max, *The Methodology of the Social Sciences* (New York: Free Press, 1949).

Weber, Max, *Protestant Ethic and the Spirit of Capitalism* (London: Routledge, 1930).

Welch, John, *Chiasmus in Antiquity* (Provo, UT: Utah Research Press, 1999).

Welch, John, "Chiasmus in the Book of Mormon," *BYU Studies* 10: 3 (1969), pp. 69-83.

Wellman, Judith, "Crossing Over Cross: Whitney Cross's Burned-Over District as Social History," *Reviews in American History* 17:1 (March 1989), 159-174.

White, L. Michael, *From Jesus to Christianity: How Four Generations of Visionaries and Storytellers Created the New Testament and the Christian Faith* (San Francisco: Harper San Francisco, 2004).

White, O. Kendall, *Mormon Neo-Orthodoxy: A Crisis Theology* (Salt Lake City: Signature, 1987).

White, O. Kendall, "Mormonism and the Equal Rights Amendment," *Journal of Church and State* 31:2 (1989), 249-267.

Whitney, Elizabeth Ann, "Biography" in Edward Tullidge, *The Women of Mormondom* (New York: Tullidge and Drandell, 1877), 32-35, 41-42.

Wiebe, Robert, *The Opening of American Society from the Adoption of the Constitution to the Eve of Disunion* (New York: Knopf, 1984).

Wiebe, Robert, *The Search for Order 1877-1920* (New York: Hill and Wang, 1967).

Wiebe, Robert, *Who We Are: A History of Popular Nationalism* (Princeton, NJ: Princeton University Press, 2002).

Wigger, John, "Fighting Bees: Methodist Itinerants and the Dynamics of Methodist Growth, 1770–1820" in Nathan Hatch (ed.), *Methodism and the Shaping of American Culture* (Nashville: Kingswood Press, 2001), 88–91.

Wilcox, Linda, "The Mormon Concept of Mother in Heaven" in Maureen Ursenbach Beecher and Lavina Fielding Anderson (eds.), *Sisters in Spirit: Mormon Women in Historical and Cultural Perspective* (Urbana: University of Illinois Press, 1987), 64–77.

Wilentz, Sean, *Chant's Democratic: New York City and the Rise of the American Working Class, 1788–1850* (New York: Oxford University Press, 1984).

Williams, George, *The Radical Reformation*, 3d. ed. (Kirksville, MO: Sixteenth Century Journal Publishers, 1992).

Williams, Peter, *America's Religions: From Their Origins to the Twenty-First Century* (Urbana, IL: University of Illinois Press, 2002).

Wilson, Charles Reagan, *Baptized in Blood: The Religion of the Lost Cause, 1865–1920* (Athens: University of Georgia Press, 1983).

Winn, Kenneth, *Exiles in a Land of Liberty: Mormons in America, 1830–1846* (Chapel Hill: University of North Carolina Press, 1989).

Wolf, Larry, *Inventing Eastern Europe: The Map of Civilization and the Mind of the Enlightenment* (Palo Alto, CA: Stanford University Press, 1994).

Woltjer, J.J., and M.E.H.N. Mout, "Settlements: The Netherlands" in Thomas Brady, Heiko Oberman, and James D. Tracy, *Handbook of European History, 1400–1600: Late Middle Ages, Renaissance, and Reformation, Volume 2: Visions, Programs, and Outcomes* (Grand Rapids: Eerdmans), 385–415.

Wood, Gordon, "Evangelical America and Early Mormonism," *New York History* 41 (October 1980), 359–386.

Wood, Gordon, "Religion and the American Revolution" in Harry Stout and D.G. Hart (eds.), *New Directions in American Religious History* (New York: Oxford University Press, 1997), 173–205.

Woodhead, Linda, *An Introduction to Christianity* (Cambridge, UK: Cambridge University Press, 2004).

Woodruff, Phoebe W. Carter, "Biography" in Edward Tullidge," *The Women of Mormondom* (New York: Tullidge and Crandall, 1877), 399–400, 411–414.

Woodruff, Wilford, Woodruff to Aphek Woodruff, 15 March 1834, copy of original in Aphek Woodruff Collection, LDS Archives.

Worsley, Peter, *The Trumpet Shall Sound* (New York: Schocken, 1957).

Worsley, Peter, *The Trumpet Shall Sound: A Study of Cargo Cults in Melanesia*, 2d. ed. (New York: Schocken, 1968).

Wunderli, Earl M., "Critique of a Limited Geography for Book of Mormon Events," *Dialogue* 35:3 (Fall 2002), pp. 161–197.

Wuthnow, Robert, and Tracy Scott, "Protestants and Economic Behavior" in Harry Stout and D.G. Hart, *New Directions on American Religious History* (New York: Oxford University Press, 1997), 260–295.

Young, Kimball, *Isn't One Wife Enough? The Story of Mormon Polygamy* (New York: Holt, 1954).

Young, Lawrence A., "Confronting Turbulent Environments: Issues in the Organizational Growth and Globalisation of Mormonism" in Marie Cornwall, Tim B. Heaton, and Lawrence A. Young, *Contemporary Mormonism: Social Science Perspectives* (Urbana: University of Illinois Press, 1994), 43–63.

Young, Neil J., "'The ERA Is a Moral Issue': The Mormon Church, LDS Women, and the Defeat of the Equal Rights Amendment," *American Quarterly* 59: 3 (September 2007), 623–644.

Zaitchik, Alexander, "Meet the Man Who Changed Glenn Beck's Life," *Salon*, 16 Sept 2009 (online).

Index

Ahlstrom, Sydney 47
Albrecht, Stan 45
Alexander, Thomas 142, 143, 147
Allen, C. Leonard 78
Allen, James B. 130
Anderson, Lavina Fielding 139
Anderson, Nels 58, 67
Anderson, Robert 47, 77
anti-cultism 23–24
"Anti-Mormon" polemics 24–29
apocalypticism 102, 103, 112–113, 121, 122, 123, 124
apologetics 29–34
Arminianism 115, 122
Arrington, Leonard 63–64, 67, 71, 77, 129–130, 132, 141, 142, 144–145

Bachelor, Origen 25
Bachman, Daniel 67
Backman, Milton 81–82
Bancroft, H.H. 54
Barkun, Michael 77, 80, 94
Becker, Howard 40
Beecher, Maureen Ursenbach 64, 66, 71, 72, 73, 130
Bennett, John 25
Bennion, Lowell "Ben" 70
Benson, Ezra Taft 131, 136, 138
Berthoff, Rowland 76, 77, 79, 90–91, 115
Biblicism 102, 119, 125
Bitton, Davis 69, 130, 144–145
Blomberg, Craig L. 33
Bloom, Harold 37–38, 77, 101
Bringhurst, Newell 77, 79–80, 84
Brodie, Fawn 38–39, 59, 67, 77, 128
Brooke, John 37, 77, 101–102
Brooks, Juanita 59
Brown, Richard 76
Bruce, Dickson 94, 119
Building the City of God 131
Bushman, Claudia 65
Bushman, Richard 135, 142, 143, 147
Butler, Jon 77, 120
BYU Studies 65

Campbell, Alexander 54
Campbell, Eugene E. 62–63, 66, 69
Cannon, Frank Q. 28
Cannon, Gerorge Q. 53
Caswall, Henry 25
Christensen, Harold T. 43, 45
Christianity 36–38
Church History Office 129–130, 132
Clark, John A. 25
Cohn, Norman 75–76, 84–85
Comprehensive History of the Church 55
Conan Doyle, Arthur 26
Conkin, Paul 120
Cooper, Rex 77, 97, 115
Cornwall, Marie 70
Cowdery, Oliver 29, 53
Cross, Whitney 77, 78, 84, 86, 115
cultural approaches and Mormon origins 86, 92–126
culture wars 127–145

Davis, David Brion 77, 97, 115
Decker, Ed 27–28
DePillis, Mario 77, 95 96
Derr, Jill Mulvay 64, 71, 73, 130
Dialogue 64–65, 138
dispensationalism 101, 104–105
Dunfey, Julie 66, 72
Durkheim, Émile 74

Ellsworth, S. George 62–63
Ely, Richard 56–57, 63
Embry, Jessie 66
Emerson, Ralph Waldo 54, 77
Eriksen, Ephraim Edward (E.E.) 57, 128
Essentials in Church History 53
exceptionalism 141
Exponent II 65, 71

FAIR (Foundation for Apologetic Information and Research) 30–31
FARMS (Foundation for Ancient Research and Mormon Studies) 30–31, 32, 134
Farr, Cecilia 140
feminism 139–141

Index

Ferguson, Thomas Stuart 59
Fife, Alta 59
Fife, Austin 59
Flanders, Robert 142
Foster, Lawrence 39, 66, 67, 77–78, 95
Fox, Feramorz 59
fundamentalism 143

Geertz, Clifford 145
Givens, Terryl 33–34, 135, 147
Grandstaff, Mark 81–82
Gunnison, John 25
Gusfield, Joseph 83–84

Hackett, David G. 76
Hall, David 117, 120
Hansen, Klaus 117
Hardy, B. Carmon 72
Harper, Steven 82
Hatch, Nathan 78, 79
Heaton, Tim 45, 49
Heinerman, John 28
Hickman, Bill 26
Higham, John 122
Hill, Marvin 77, 79, 95
historiography 4–6, 56–57, 59–60, 61–62, 74–75, 92–94, 127–128, 133–136, 141–143
history of Mormonism 7–19, 53–54, 74–126, 133–136, 147
History of the Church of Jesus Christ of Latter-day Saints 53
Hofstadter, Richard 76
Houston, Gail 140
Howe, Daniel Walker 94, 122
Howe, Eber D. 24
Hughes, Richard 78, 96
Hullett, J.E. (James) 66, 68, 72
Hurlbut, Doctor Philastus 24

ideology 144–145
Iverson, Joan 66, 71, 72
Ivins, Stanley 67, 68

Jeffrey, Julie Roy 66, 69, 71
Jensen, Richard 64
Jessee, Dean 64, 130
John Whitmer Historical Association (JWHA) 64
John Whitmer Historical Association Journal (JWHAJ) 65
Johnson, Curtis 86, 90, 122
Johnson, Paul 76, 87, 88, 93
Journal of Mormon History (JMH) 65, 71

key symbols 120
Kinney, Bruce 26
Kluckhohn, Clyde 43–44
Knowlton, David 140
Kunz, Phillip 69

Lee, John D. 26
Leonard, Glen 130
Logue, Larry 70

Mackay, Charles 54
Madsen, Carol Cornwall 64, 71, 130
making Mormons 89, 118–126
Marx, Karl 74, 119
Mauss, Armand 132
May, Dean 70
McCarthy, John 76–77, 85
McLoughlin, William 123
Meinig, Donald 77, 97, 115
Metcalfe, Brent 31–32
Midgley, Lou 32, 134, 137
Mooney, James 75
Moore, R. Laurence 98
Morgan, Dale 59
Mormon History Association (MHA) 64
Moser, Carl 33
muckraking 27–28

nationalism 109–111
Nelson, Lowry 57–58, 128
"new" Mormon history 62–74
New World Archaeology Foundation (NWAF) 59
Nibley, Hugh 30
Niebuhr, H. Richard 40
Noah, Mordecai 113–114
Noll, Mark 37, 77, 122

O'Dea, Thomas 37, 44
O'Higgins, Harvey J. 28
"old" Mormon history 51–60
Oneida Community 11, 23, 86, 87, 89, 103, 104, 105, 115, 120, 121, 122, 147
Otherness 21–29
Owen, Paul 33

Packer, Boyd D. 131, 136, 139
Perciaccante, Marianne 77, 86, 97–98, 121
perfectionism 103–104, 115, 116, 121, 122, 123, 124
Peterson, Charles S. 141
Phelps Letters 29, 52
polemics 29–34
polygamy 67–70, 143–145
Pratt, Orson 52
Pratt, Parley P. 29
primitivism 101, 121, 122, 123, 124
professionalization of Mormon studies 60, 78
psychology 38–39, 46–47
Puritanism 115–118

Quinn, D. Michael 64, 72–73, 130, 136–140, 142, 147

religious studies 36–39, 45–46, 47–49
religious typologies 39–41

restorationism 94–97, 105–109
Riley, I. Woodbridge 58–59
Roberts, B.H. 53, 55
Roberts, Tomi-Ann 140
Robinson, Stephen E. 33
Rudé, George 76
Ryan, Mary 76, 93

science 116
sectarianism 121, 124, 143
Sellers, Charles 39, 76, 78–79, 87, 88
Shakers 10–11, 22–23, 86, 87, 89, 103, 104, 105, 107, 115, 120, 121, 122, 125
Shipps, Jan 37, 41, 70, 77, 96–97, 118–119, 135, 142, 143
Shupe, Anson 28
Smith-Rosenberg, Carroll 76, 77, 88–89, 91, 93
Smith, Joseph Fielding 52–53, 133; Wentworth letter 29–30
Smith, Timothy 78, 94–95
Social Movement Theory 74–91, 148
Society for the Sociological Study of Mormon Life (SSSML) 44
sociology 42–45, 47–49, 74–91
spiritualism 10–11
Stark, Rodney 37, 40, 47
Story of the Latter-day Saints 130–131
Strout, Cushing 77
Sunderland, La Roy 25
Sunstone 65, 138

Tanner, Jerald 26–27, 137
Tanner, Sandra 26–27, 137

Thomas, George 88
Toscano, Margaret 139, 140
Toscano, Paul 139, 140
treasure seeking 102–103
Troeltsch, Ernst 39
Tucker, Pomeroy 25
Turner, Victor 119, 123
Twain, Mark 26
Tyler, Alice Felt 39, 77

Ulrich, Laurel Thatcher 65
universalism 117
Utah Historical Quarterly 60

Vernon, Glenn 43, 44
Vogt, Evon 43–44

Walker, Ronald 64
Wallace, Anthony 122–123
Weber, Max 39, 74, 121, 125–126, 145
Welch, John 30
Wiebe, Robert 89
Willson, David 112
Winn, Kenneth 77, 79
women's history 70–72
Wood, Gordon 77
Woodhead, Linda 41, 47–48
Worsley, Peter 75

Young, Kimball 59, 67

Zald, Meyer 76–77, 85
Zionism 111–114

www.ingramcontent.com/pod-product-compliance
Lightning Source LLC
Chambersburg PA
CBHW032039300426
44117CB00009B/1123